A vous la France!

Brian Page

A course on radio and television for beginners in French

Course writer Brian Page
University of Leeds

Language consultant Evelyne Hanquart
Université de Paris-Sorbonne

Researchers Corinne Baudelot
Jane Cottave

Production assistants Morag Hughes
Elizabeth McDowell

Radio producer Alan Wilding

Television producer David Wilson

BBC Books

A vous la France! is a combined BBC Television and Radio course for beginners in French, first broadcast from October 1984

15 Television and 15 Radio programmes running concurrently

One course book covering all the programmes

Two cassettes

One set of Teachers' Notes

Published to accompany a series of programmes in consultation with the BBC Continuing Education Advisory Council

First published 1984. Reprinted 1985 (twice), 1986 (twice), 1987 (twice)
Published by BBC Books, a division of BBC Enterprises Limited
Woodlands, 80 Wood Lane, London W12 0TT
ISBN 0 563 210117

This book is set in 10/11 Sabon Monophoto
by Keyspools Limited, Warrington
Printed in England by Chorley and Pickersgill Ltd, Leeds
Cover printed by Belmont Press, Northampton

Contents

A user's guide

A vous la France! is the sort of phrase you might hear on television or radio meaning 'over to you in France' or 'come in, France'. It also means, 'France is yours – open to you to visit and enjoy'. Either way, it stands for contact with France and the French. This course aims to open up France to you by bringing you the sights and sounds of the country and its people.

A vous la France! is a course for people who speak little or no French and who would like to start speaking the language in a range of ordinary everyday situations, such as getting food, drink and accommodation, using transport, shopping, getting things done and just having friendly chats with French speakers about family and home, work, likes and dislikes, and so on. The course is based on conversations filmed and recorded in France in which French people go about their daily lives using their everyday spoken language.

The course consists of:
15 radio programmes;
15 television programmes;
this book;
2 audio cassettes;
notes for teachers running classes

The radio programmes
The recordings were made in and around Bourg-en-Bresse, in south-east France, where our interviewers were Marie-Pierre Caréra and Jean Fournier, and in Nantes and La Rochelle in western France, where our interviewers were Sara Tomei and Pierrick Picot. In the programmes these recordings will be explained and used as the basis for lots of speaking practice. The programmes cannot show you France, but they will offer an excellent opportunity for you to listen to the sounds of the language and to develop your ability to speak it for yourself and express your own ideas.

Sara Tomei (Radio)

Pierrick Picot (Radio)

Jane Cottave (TV)

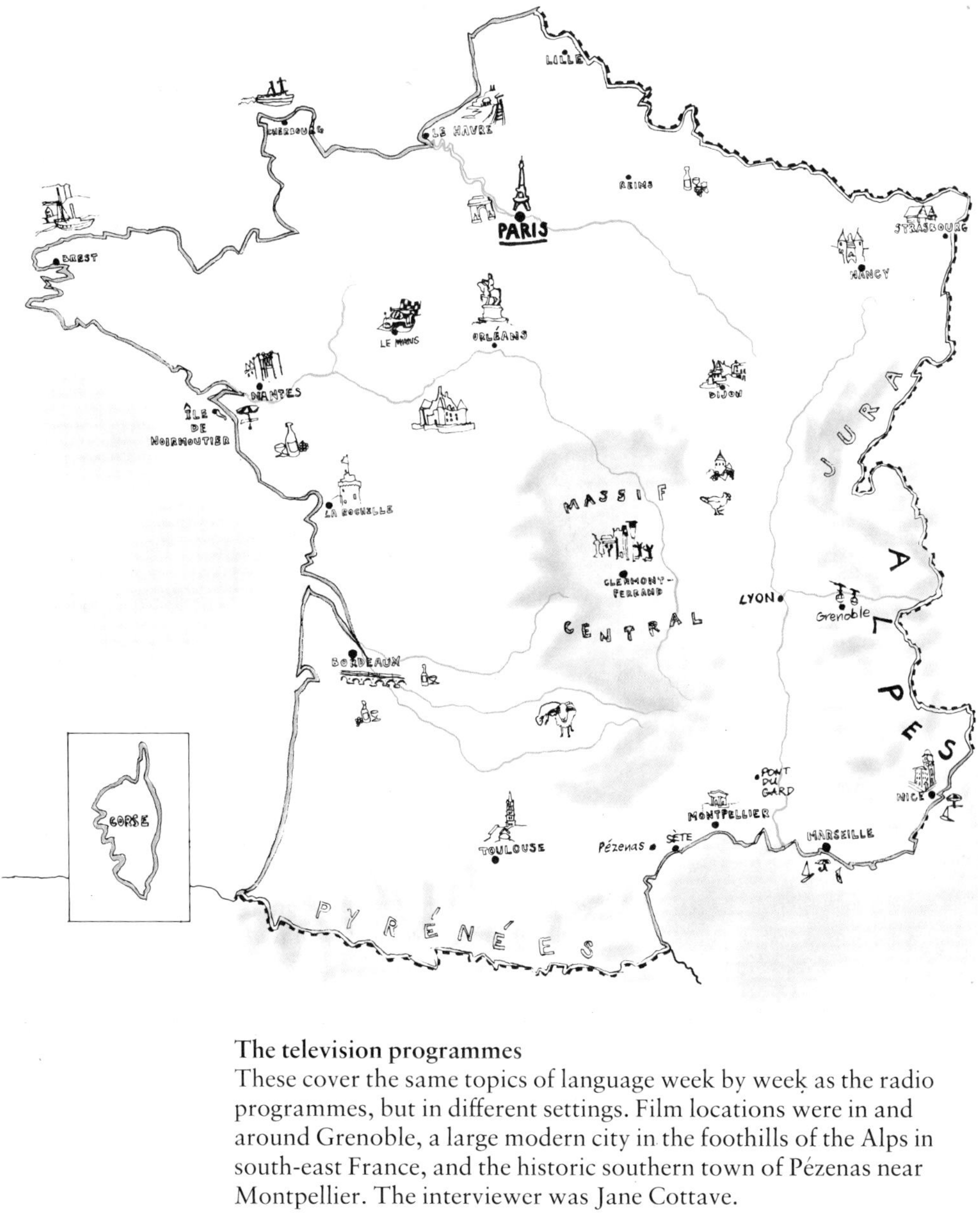

The television programmes

These cover the same topics of language week by week as the radio programmes, but in different settings. Film locations were in and around Grenoble, a large modern city in the foothills of the Alps in south-east France, and the historic southern town of Pézenas near Montpellier. The interviewer was Jane Cottave.

The programmes fall into two main parts. The first consists of simple conversations which illustrate the basic language to be learnt week by week. The second part is a mini-documentary on various aspects of French life. The language used here is rather more complex and the idea is not only to convey the flavour of life in the France of today but also to give you the chance of knowing what it's like to be 'thrown in at the deep end'. You shouldn't expect to understand these documentaries fully straight away, but as time goes by you will discover that you are getting better and better at picking out the bits that really matter.

The book

Each chapter of this book corresponds to the accompanying programme on radio and television and contains:

1 the texts of the basic conversations from the programme. These include *Rencontres:* a series of 'vox pop' interviews in which passers-by in the street speak their minds on a range of subjects. Those texts marked Radio feature in the radio programmes and those marked TV in the television programmes. Unmarked scenes are additional reading material recorded on location but not used in the programmes for reasons of time. Phrases whose meanings are not immediately obvious are translated into English after each conversation.

2 the main French structures to be learnt. These are in boxes placed throughout the conversations.

3 *Quickies:* a series of short questions with which you can check whether you have understood the contents of the conversations and grasped some of the phrases used.

4 *Mots-clés:* a vocabulary list in which we have selected what we consider to be the most useful words to learn by heart.

5 *En bref:* a section which sets out the language to be learnt for each chapter. This is the language on which the exercises (see *Bon courage* below) are based.

6 *En plus:* further, more detailed information about words and usage.

7 *A propos:* a series of short articles in English on aspects of French life.

8 *Bon courage:* a series of exercises which can be used for checking whether you have learnt that chapter's language and also what you have remembered from previous chapters.

9 *Documentaire:* a summary in French of that week's television mini-documentary, with an introduction in English. These can be used to prepare for the TV programmes or as reading practice in their own right. Difficult words and phrases are translated after each summary; other words should be looked up in a dictionary.

Chapters 5, 10 and 15 are revision chapters and also contain tests with which you can check your progress.

At the back there is a general reference section. It contains:
a guide to French pronunciation;
a summary of the French grammar covered in the course;
answers to exercises – both *Quickies* and *Bon courage*;
a French–English vocabulary of the words in this book, except those in the *Documentaire* sections;
two indexes – one of the grammar covered in this book and one of the topics of French life.

The cassettes

Additional material for listening and speaking practice can be found on the two audio cassettes. They last approximately three hours and contain fifteen parts, one for each programme and chapter of the book. Each part contains:

1 a pronunciation section, where words and phrases are presented in isolation so that you can concentrate on the sound. There are pauses for you to copy what you have heard. The text of these pronunciation sections comes with the cassettes.

2 a selection of the basic conversations from the programmes which are also printed in this book.

3 at least two oral exercises per programme which can be used to practise taking part in complete conversation in France in real-life situations. There are pauses for you to speak your side of the conversations, and the printed answers are also given with the cassettes.

The teachers' notes

These are intended for teachers who are using *A vous la France!* as a course book in their classes. They contain suggestions for developing the radio and television broadcasts in class and for presenting more written and oral practice based on the course.

Some hints on using A vous la France!

It is worthwhile bearing a few points in mind when learning a foreign language.

Everyone learns in a different way and at different speeds. So there is no set time to spend with the course each week, but it is suggested that at the very least you watch each television programme and listen to each radio programme and work through the texts of the dialogues in the book.

The boxes between the dialogues represent the minimum language you should become familiar with.

Mots-clés are chosen as the basic words which should be learnt by heart. There is no doubt that the secret of understanding a foreign language and speaking it yourself lies in knowing lots of words and a little grammar – not the other way round.

A propos is intended as relief from actual language learning and introduces you to various aspects of life in France and French customs and how they differ from British ones in a number of respects.

Beyond that, you should spend time learning the contents of *En bref* and, if you have the time and energy, *En plus*, which are designed to help you understand the workings of French in broader terms.

Do the written exercises in the *Bon courage* section, one or two at a time. You can check your answers in the back of the book. You should not treat any mistakes you make as proof of an inability to learn French. To get absolutely everything right would be the exception, not the rule. So remember that there is a positive value in getting things wrong – it demonstrates the gaps in your knowledge and shows what needs to be revised.

If you are really grammar-minded, you might like working through the grammar summary at the back of the book. This is very much an optional section meant for people who feel most at home if they know all the ins and outs of particular aspects of grammar.

Learning vocabulary, as was said above, is vital. The *Mots-clés* sections in this book contain about 750 words. To help in learning them, you could try copying the words on to small cards, English on one side and French on the other, and working through them at odd moments of the day. If your card comes out with the English on it, you say the French and vice versa. (You can even do this on the bus without upsetting the neighbours).

You will find it enormously helpful if you can join an evening class (or even find someone else also working on *A vous la France!*). Broadcast programmes have many advantages in language learning, but they cannot replace the face to face help given by a teacher (and by other learners).

The future
For those who want to take their knowledge of French further, a second level course on BBC Radio, *France Extra!*, has been made to follow *A vous la France!*

Vous désirez?

Buying a drink
Buying bread
Asking for tourist brochures, maps, etc
Telling someone a little about where you live

TV 1 Five friends are in a café in Grenoble. When the waiter comes they order a coffee, a fresh orange juice, two shandies and a white wine with blackcurrant liqueur (*un kir*).

Garçon	Messieurs-dames, bonjour.
Maud et Sophie	Bonjour.
Garçon	Vous désirez?
Fleb	Un express, s'il vous plaît.
Garçon	Un express.
Maud	Une orange pressée.
Garçon	Une orange pressée.
Dan	Qu'est-ce que tu prends, Mimi?
Mimi	Un panaché.
Dan	Ah oui, moi aussi. (*turns to waiter*) Et deux panachés alors.
Sophie	Et moi un kir, s'il vous plaît.
Garçon	Alors, un express, une orange pressée, deux panachés et un kir.
Mimi	Voilà. C'est ça.
Garçon	Merci.
Fleb et Dan	Merci.

vous désirez?	*what would you like?*
qu'est-ce que tu prends?	*what are you having?*
moi aussi	*so will I, me too*
c'est ça	*that's it*

To ask for something, just name it:
une orange pressée, . . .
un panaché, . . .
and add 'please':
. . . s'il vous plaît.

Notice the two words for 'a': **une/un**

How to say 'that's it' or 'that's right':
c'est ça

Quickies REMEMBER whenever you are doing the Quickies COVER UP THE PAGE ABOVE THEM except for the pictures.

1 Name the drinks in the pictures. Don't forget the two words for 'a'.
2 How polite can you be? Can you remember how to greet people, say please, thank someone?

TV 2 Anissa Inoubli is shopping. In a baker's shop (*une boulangerie*) she buys croissants and two different-sized loaves of bread.

Anissa Bonjour, madame.
Boulangère Bonjour, madame, Vous désirez?
Anissa Six croissants, s'il vous plaît.
Boulangère Oui. (*she serves her*) Et avec ceci?
Anissa Un pain et une baguette.
Boulangère Et avec ceci, madame?
Anissa C'est tout, merci.
Boulangère (*ringing up prices on the till*) Alors, six croissants, une baguette et un pain, seize francs quatre-vingts.
Anissa (*paying*) Là. Voilà.
Boulangère Merci, madame.
Anissa Au revoir, madame.
Boulangère Au revoir, madame. Merci.

et avec ceci?	*is there anything else?*
c'est tout	*that's all*

To refer to more than one thing, an 's' is added in writing to most words:
deux panachés
six croissants
In speaking the 's' is not pronounced.

When saying 'hello', 'goodbye', 'thank you', etc *madame/mademoiselle/monsieur* are usually added:
bonjour, madame
merci, monsieur
au revoir, mademoiselle

Quickies

1. The smaller size loaf of bread is the commonest sort bought. What is its name?
2. Can you now say 'Goodbye' to the woman serving in the shop?

Radio 3 Jean Fournier goes to his local café in Bourg with a friend and orders two coffees: *un café* is black and *un crème* is white.

Patronne Bonjour, monsieur.
Jean Bonjour, madame.
Patronne Qu'est-ce que vous désirez?
Jean Un café et un crème, s'il vous plaît.
Patronne Un café et un crème, d'accord. (*she brings the coffees*) Voilà, messieurs. Le crème pour qui?
Jean C'est pour moi, madame.
Patronne (*putting the cups down*) Voilà, messieurs.

Later Jean asks for the bill.

Jean C'est combien, s'il vous plaît?
Patronne Quatre francs cinquante. (*Jean pays*)
Jean Tenez
Patronne Merci beaucoup, monsieur.
Jean Au revoir, madame. Merci.
Patronne Au revoir, messieurs. Bonne journée!

d'accord	*certainly, right*
le crème pour qui?	*who's the white coffee for?*
pour moi	*for me*
bonne journée!	*have a good day!*

To ask how much it comes to, the key word is **combien:**
je vous dois combien? ça fait combien? c'est combien?

Quickies

1. How would you ask for a white coffee?
2. What's the word for 'how much?'?

Radio 4 In a baker's shop in Bourg, Marie-Pierre wants a different kind of loaf. She asks the young girl serving for *une flûte* and some croissants.

Vendeuse Bonjour, madame.
Marie-Pierre Bonjour. Une flûte, s'il vous plaît.
Vendeuse Oui. (*fetching it*) Voici. Avec ça?
Marie-Pierre Quatre croissants.
Vendeuse Oui. Voici. Ce sera tout?
Marie-Pierre Oui. Combien?
Vendeuse Alors, (*adding up*) six quarante et trois francs, neuf quarante, madame.
Marie-Pierre Voilà.
Vendeuse Merci. Au revoir, madame.
Marie-Pierre Au revoir.

avec ça? (*like* avec ceci?)	*anything else?*
ce sera tout? (*like* c'est tout?)	*will that be all?*
combien?	*how much? (rather abrupt)*

Radio **5** In another café Jean wants a fruit juice and there are a lot to choose from: pineapple, apricot, orange, pear, grapefruit . . .

Serveuse Bonjour, monsieur.
Jean Bonjour, madame.
Serveuse Vous désirez, monsieur?
Jean Un jus de fruit, s'il vous plaît.
Serveuse Oui. Ananas, abricot, orange, poire, pamplemousse?
Jean Pamplemousse, s'il vous plaît.
Serveuse Oui. Tout de suite.

She returns.

Jean Merci, madame. C'est combien?
Serveuse Six francs.
Jean (*counting out coins*) Cinq et six. Merci, madame.
Serveuse Merci, monsieur.

tout de suite *right away*

Quickie Can you remember the French for the sorts of juice available?

Radio **6** More choices in yet another café – this time draught beer or bottled beer. Jean is with his friend Alan.

Jean Bonjour, madame.
Serveuse Bonjour, messieurs. Vous désirez?
Jean Deux bières, s'il vous plaît.
Serveuse Oui. Pression ou bouteille, messieurs?
Jean (*to Alan*) Pression?
Alan Oui, oui. Ça va.
Jean Bon, alors deux pressions, s'il vous plaît.
Serveuse Oui, d'accord, messieurs.

Later Jean calls the waitress back to pay.

Jean	Pardon, madame.
Serveuse	Oui, monsieur?
Jean	Combien je vous dois?
Serveuse	Alors, huit francs quatre-vingts, s'il vous plaît.
Jean	(*counting out coins*) Six, sept, huit francs, huit francs cinquante, huit quatre-vingts.
Serveuse	Merci, messieurs.
Jean	Au revoir, madame.
Serveuse	Au revoir, messieurs. Bonne journée!
Alan	Merci. Au revoir, madame.

ça va	*OK, alright*
combien je vous dois?	*how much do I owe you?*

> How to enquire if someone or something's OK:
> **ça va?**
> and to answer 'alright', 'OK' or 'fine':
> **ça va**

Quickies

1 What was the word for 'a beer'?
2 What two sorts were offered?

TV 7 Claude Paccard, a visitor to Grenoble, arrives in the Tourist Office (*le Syndicat d'Initiative*). He asks for a street map and a brochure and gets a list of the hotels and restaurants as well.

Claude	Bonjour, madame.
Hôtesse	Bonjour, monsieur.
Claude	Vous avez un plan de Grenoble, s'il vous plaît?
Hôtesse	Un plan de Grenoble. Voilà.
Claude	Merci beaucoup. Et une brochure aussi?
Hôtesse	Oui, voilà, la brochure . . .
Claude	Merci bien.
Hôtesse	. . . et la liste des hôtels/restaurants.
Claude	Merci.
Hôtesse	Je vous en prie.
Claude	Au revoir, madame.
Hôtesse	Au revoir, monsieur.

merci bien	*thank you very much*
je vous en prie	*don't mention it, you're welcome*

> To ask someone 'have you got . . .?':
> **vouz avez** un plan de Grenoble, s'il vous plaît?

Quickies

1 What two things did he ask for? Make sure you can pronounce them properly.
2 How do you ask if someone has got something you want?

Radio 8 In the *Syndicat d'Initiative* in Bourg, Marie-Pierre asks for a street map and a map of the Ain area.

Hôtesse Bonjour, mademoiselle.
Marie-Pierre Bonjour. Vous avez un plan de Bourg, s'il vous plaît?
Hôtesse Oui. Voici un plan de Bourg avec une liste des hôtels.
Marie-Pierre Et vous avez une carte de l'Ain?
Hôtesse Oui. Voilà une carte de l'Ain et également une brochure sur la ville de Bourg.
Marie-Pierre Bon, je vous remercie.
Hôtesse Je vous en prie. Au revoir, mademoiselle.
Marie-Pierre Au revoir.
Hôtesse Bon séjour à Bourg!

je vous remercie (*like* merci)	*thank you*
bon séjour à Bourg!	*have a pleasant stay in Bourg!*

Quickie A brochure is easy but what are the words for the two different sorts of map?

Radio 9 Pierrick is in the *Syndicat d'Initiative* on the island of Noirmoutier near Nantes and he wants a map.

Pierrick Bonjour, madame.
Hôtesse Bonjour, monsieur.
Pierrick Vous avez une carte de l'île, s'il vous plaît?
Hôtesse Oui. Voilà une carte de l'île.
Pierrick Merci, madame.
Hôtesse Je vous en prie.
Pierrick Au revoir, madame.
Hôtesse Au revoir, monsieur.

Quickie What does Pierrick ask for?

10 Madame Trabut has a pleasant surprise when she finds she doesn't have to pay to go into the Musée Dauphinois in Grenoble.

Mme Trabut Bonjour, madame.
Réceptionniste Bonjour, madame.
Mme Trabut Un ticket, s'il vous plaît.
Réceptionniste Non, non, c'est gratuit, madame.
Mme Trabut C'est gratuit? Ah, mais c'est bien, ça! Vous avez une brochure, un catalogue?
Réceptionniste (*pointing*) Une brochure, ici; un catalogue, ici.

Mme Trabut	(*looking through the catalogue*) Et c'est combien, ça?
Réceptionniste	Vingt-cinq francs, madame.
Mme Trabut	(*giving her the money*) Merci.
Réceptionniste	Merci. Je vous en prie, madame.

c'est bien, ça! *that's good/nice*

Rencontres

TV

What is there to do and see in Grenoble? Our French interviewer, Jane Cottave, asked a number of people in the street and got a whole variety of answers.

Jane	Madame, qu'est-ce qu'il y a à faire ou à voir pour un Grenoblois à Grenoble?
1 ère Passante	Il y a beaucoup de choses, beaucoup d'activités, par exemple, bon, tous les sports d'hiver, le ski, la luge et puis l'été la montagne est très, très belle.
Jane	Monsieur, qu'est-ce qu'il y a à voir ou à faire pour un Grenoblois à Grenoble?
1 er Passant	Eh bien, il y a les spectacles, les musées, cinémas . . .
2 ème Passant	Il y a, disons, il y a beaucoup de théâtres.
2 ème Passante	Il y a le Musée Dauphinois.
2 ème Passant	Il y a de la musique.
2 ème Passante	Il y a la place Saint André, l'église Saint Laurent.
1 ère Passante	Des promenades en ville aussi. Il y a beaucoup de rues piétonnes.
2 ème Passante	Puis il y a des cafés.
Jane	Et vivre à Grenoble, c'est bien?
3 ème Passante	Ah oui, c'est bien, oui, oui, bien sûr.

par exemple	*for example*
en ville	*in the town*
bien sûr	*of course*

To say what there is/are:

il y a	la place Saint André le Musée Dauphinois l'église Saint Laurent les sports d'hiver

Notice the four words for 'the': **le/la/l'/les**

Quickies

1 What is the three-word expression that means both 'there is' and 'there are'?

2 If you like the town (or come to that, the film, the café, etc), how do you say 'It's nice'?

Mots-clés

(f) = *feminine* (m) = *masculine*

la baguette	bread
le croissant	croissant
le pain	bread
la brochure	brochure
la carte	map
le catalogue	catalogue
la liste	list
le plan	plan
le ticket	ticket
le cinéma	cinema
l'église (f)	church
l'hôtel (m)	hotel
le musée	museum
le restaurant	restaurant
le théâtre	theatre
la ville	town
voici	here is/are*
voilà	there is/are*
la bière	beer
la bière pression	draught beer
la bouteille	bottle
le café	(black) coffee
le crème	white coffee
le jus de fruit	fruit juice
l'orange pressée (f)	freshly-squeezed orange
le panaché	shandy
l'abricot (m)	apricot
l'ananas (m)	pineapple
le pamplemousse	grapefruit
la poire	pear
au revoir	goodbye*
beaucoup	a lot
bonjour	good morning/afternoon*
merci	thank you
non	no
oui	yes

* see *En plus*

En bref

1 First and last words

Greeting	**bonjour**
Saying goodbye	**au revoir**
Saying please	**s'il vous plaît**

Thanking

thank you	**merci** **je vous remercie**
thank you very much	**merci bien** **merci beaucoup**

To all these *monsieur/madame/mademoiselle* are usually added.

2 To ask for something in a shop/café etc, name it and add 'please':
un express, s'il vous plaît
une baguette, s'il vous plaît

> There are two French words for the English 'a'/'an':
> **un** panaché — **une** baguette
> **un** plan — **une** brochure

3 To ask if someone has something you want:
vous avez un plan de Bourg?
vous avez la liste des hôtels?

> There are two corresponding French words for the English 'the' (singular):
> **le** panaché — **la** baguette
> **le** plan — **la** brochure
> Both *la* and *le* become *l'* if the following word starts with a vowel:
> l'express — l'orange pressée
> *la* words are technically called feminine nouns and *le* words masculine nouns (see *En plus*).

4 To say 'it is . . .':

c'est	gratuit tout pour moi

or ask 'is it . . .?':

c'est	gratuit? tout? pour moi?

5 To ask how much something costs:
c'est combien?
c'est combien, le plan?
le plan, **c'est combien?**

6 To say what there is/there are:

à Grenoble **il y a**	le Musée Dauphinois un Syndicat d'Initiative beaucoup de cinémas

> When you are talking about more than one thing, the French word for 'the' changes:
>
> *le/la/l'* all become *les*
>
> **le** musée — **les** musées
> **la** bouteille — **les** bouteilles
> **l'**orange — **les** oranges
>
> As in English, 's' is added to the noun but, unlike English, it is not pronounced.

En plus

1 **Feminine/Masculine**
Nouns are the words that, in English, can have 'the' or 'a' in front of them like 'a cat', 'the tree'. English is unique among European languages in not having a gender system for nouns; that is, English nouns are not divided into types which use different words for 'the' and correspondingly different words for 'a' according to the gender of the noun. French has two types: feminine which uses *la* and *une* for 'the' and 'a' and masculine which uses *le* and *un*. It is quite important to learn *le* and *la* along with any new words as the difference can have an effect on other words in the sentence and in some cases can change the meaning.

One thing to remember: while it is true that most nouns denoting females are feminine and most denoting males are masculine, the gender of nouns has really nothing to do with sex. There is nothing particularly female about an orange (*une orange*) or male about a lemon (*un citron*); and *une bière* plus *une limonade* make *un panaché*.

2 **It's not only what you say, it's the way that you say it.**
As you have discovered, French sounds are very different from English ones. It will take you some time to hear and absorb all the differences. A few simple rules may help.

1 All French words sound different from English ones even when they look the same. Listen for the French pronunciations of words like:
orange, ticket, plan, brochure

2 In speaking English we put a stress on part of the word and other parts can almost disappear: 'restaurant' can become '*rest*'r'nt'. In French roughly equal weight is given to all parts of the word: *res-tau-rant*.

As usual, of course, this is not always so. The letter 'e' often gets swallowed as in *au r'voir*. This particularly happens to small words like *je* and *de*; *je vous en prie* becomes *j'vous en prie* and *un plan de Bourg* becomes *un plan d'Bourg*. *Tout de suite* normally sounds as if it were written *toute suite*.

3 In English we usually pronounce the consonant that comes as the last letter of a word: pla**n**, restauran**t**. In French this is the exception; usually the consonant that is the final letter is not pronounced: *croissant, vous désirez, restaurant, gratuit*. (See pronunciation guide p302.)

Remember particularly that the 's' that is added to show the plural generally makes no difference to the pronunciation; the words in these pairs sound exactly the same in French:

orange – oranges
plan – plans
restaurant – restaurants

We will deal with other points as they crop up. So remember:

1 Don't pronounce any French word in the way you would pronounce an English one.
2 Give all the parts of a French word roughly the same stress.
3 Generally speaking, if the last letter of a word is a consonant, don't pronounce it.

3 Set phrases

When you are involved in transactions like buying things in shops, many of the phrases used by shopkeepers are a sort of ritual language that you do not meet in other situations.

Vous désirez? (variations: *que désirez-vous? qu'est-ce que vous désirez?*)
Et avec ceci? (variations: *avec cela? avec ça?*)
are phrases of this type.

In French there are many more words used than is common in English to oil the wheels in these situations. Phrases like *tout de suite/d'accord/oui* to show a request has been understood and *voici/voilà* when things change hands are frequent where, in English, it is more likely that nothing at all would be said.

Monsieur, madame and *messieurs-dames* are also used in this way as a sort of global greeting and leave-taking. You might get the impression, when going into a small shop or café, that everyone knows everyone else. This is because, in these circumstances, the French acknowledge other people's existence even if they don't know them, by a nod of the head or, more likely, by a muttered *Monsieur-dame, Messieurs-dames*, both of which normally sound like ... *sieur-dame*.

4 Have a good day!

In French there are quite a few expressions that you will hear which express a general hope that all will go well with you. Apart from our usual greetings of 'good morning', etc we have very few of these in English. Possibly 'good luck!' is the commonest, we have taken 'bon voyage' from the French and we now have 'have a good day!' imported from America. In French there are the usual greetings:

bonjour means both 'good morning' and 'good afternoon'.
bonsoir good evening
Here are some others:
bon séjour have a good stay
bonne chance good luck
bon travail I hope your work goes well

You will be meeting the phrase *bon courage* very shortly. It is a sort of half-way house between *bonne chance* and *bon travail* and means something like 'I hope you stay cheerful in the face of the coming ordeal'.

An interesting one for which we have no English equivalent – though most European languages have a similar phrase – is said at the beginning of a meal:

bon appétit I hope you enjoy your meal

5 **Here and there**

Voici and *voilà* are words used with things that are within sight and that you can point at. Strictly speaking *voici* means 'here is/are':

voici la carte – here is the map

and *voilà* means 'there is/are':

voilà le musée – there is the museum

Both are also used, however, in a less precise way – as in English we say, when handing something over, 'here you are' or 'there you are'. You will have heard both *voici* and *voilà* used like this in many of the dialogues so far.

A propos

Cafés

Like pubs in Britain, French cafés are a national institution. Unlike pubs (though things in Britain are changing) you can buy almost any sort of drink there and at almost any time. There are no fixed licensing hours and opening times therefore vary a great deal.

Un express is like the Italian espresso coffee – black and freshly made. *Un café* is another way of saying the same thing. *Un crème* (or *un café crème*) is white coffee, though what makes it white will nearly always be milk, not cream. *Un crème*, for some reason, is usually referred to as *un café au lait* when it comes as part of breakfast. If you enjoy drinking coffee at night but it keeps you awake, you can always ask for *un déca* (decaffeinated coffee). *Une orange pressée* means 'a squeezed orange', that is, the juice of a freshly-squeezed orange drunk with water and sugar. You can get *un citron pressé* (lemon) as well. If you order *un jus d'orange*, you will get a small bottle of juice. *Une bière* is beer, usually of the light lager type, though *bière brune* (literally 'brown beer') also exists.

When you buy a drink in a French café the routine is much the same as in a restaurant: you sit at a table, wait to be served and pay when you have finished. You can also stand at the bar and have your drink there, where it is slightly cheaper. What is not done is to buy your drink at the bar and then take it away and sit down at a table, as you might in a British pub.

In most cafés you can get sandwiches and other snacks. Slightly more ambitious is the *café-restaurant* which is what it says – a café that will also provide full set meals at appropriate times.

Daily bread

Anyone who has been to France will have noticed people going around with a loaf (or several) under their arms or in their shopping bag. Bread really seems to be the staff of life. In fact, however, the long

loaf that we always think of as typically French is a 19th century invention. Bread comes in quite a number of shapes but the weights are officially controlled: *un pain* is 500 grams and *une baguette* 300 grams. The *baguette* is probably the commonest size and shape eaten in French towns. *Baguette* also means 'magician's wand', 'conductor's baton', and 'chopstick', so make sure you are in the right shop when you ask for one.

The franc in your pocket

The franc is divided into 100 centimes. Prices are usually written thus: 16F80. There are notes for 20F, 50F, 100F, 200F, 500F and 1000F and coins for 5c, 10c, ½F, 1F, 2F, 5F and 10F.

Tourist offices

These may be called something fairly obvious like *Office du Tourisme* or *Maison du Tourisme* but they usually go under the rather baffling title of *Syndicat d'Initiative*. They exist in all towns and most villages of any size in tourist areas and they are extremely useful places for the traveller. You can get free brochures about all the places of interest in the region, plans of towns, lists of hotels, restaurants, holiday homes, theatres etc, as well as helpful suggestions from the staff. If you are planning a visit to France, it is always worth writing to the *Syndicats d'Initiative* in the towns you expect to visit to ask for information. Don't forget to enclose an International Reply Coupon (available from Post Offices) to pay the postage for your reply.

Départements

For administrative purposes France is divided into ninety-five *départements* (not including its overseas possessions), which are grouped into twenty-two regions. The system of *départements* has existed since 1799 and they are usually named after some geographical feature like mountains or a river. Bourg is in the Ain, Grenoble is in the Isère, Pézenas in the Hérault and Nantes in the Loire-Atlantique. All these *départements* are named after rivers.

The *départements* are numbered in alphabetical order and this number appears as the first two figures in postal codes and at the end of the number plates of cars registered in that *département*. Ain is the first in the alphabet and so it is numbered 01.

Départements

01 Ain
02 Aisne
03 Allier
04 Alpes de Haute-Provence
05 Hautes-Alpes
06 Alpes-Maritimes
07 Ardèche
08 Ardennes
09 Ariège
10 Aube
11 Aude
12 Aveyron
13 Bouches-du-Rhône
14 Calvados
15 Cantal
16 Charente
17 Charente-Maritime
18 Cher
19 Corrèze
20 Corse
21 Côte-d'Or
22 Côtes-du-Nord
23 Creuse
24 Dordogne
25 Doubs
26 Drôme
27 Eure
28 Eure-et-Loir
29 Finistère
30 Gard
31 Haute-Garonne
32 Gers
33 Gironde
34 Hérault
35 Ille-et-Vilaine
36 Indre
37 Indre-et-Loire
38 Isère
39 Jura
40 Landes
41 Loir-et-Cher
42 Loire
43 Haute-Loire
44 Loire-Atlantique
45 Loiret
46 Lot
47 Lot-et-Garonne
48 Lozère
49 Maine-et-Loire
50 Manche
51 Marne
52 Haute-Marne
53 Mayenne
54 Meurthe-et-Moselle
55 Meuse
56 Morbihan
57 Moselle
58 Nièvre
59 Nord
60 Oise
61 Orne
62 Pas-de-Calais
63 Puy-de-Dôme
64 Pyrénées-Atlantiques
65 Hautes-Pyrénées
66 Pyrénées-Orientales
67 Bas-Rhin
68 Haut-Rhin
69 Rhône
70 Haute-Saône
71 Saône-et-Loire
72 Sarthe
73 Savoie
74 Haute-Savoie
75 Ville de Paris
76 Seine-Maritime
77 Seine-et-Marne
78 Yvelines
79 Deux-Sèvres
80 Somme
81 Tarn
82 Tarn-et-Garonne
83 Var
84 Vaucluse
85 Vendée
86 Vienne
87 Haute-Vienne
88 Vosges
89 Yonne
90 Térritoire de Belfort
91 Essonne
92 Hauts-de-Seine
93 Seine-Saint-Denis
94 Val-de-Marne
95 Val-d'Oise

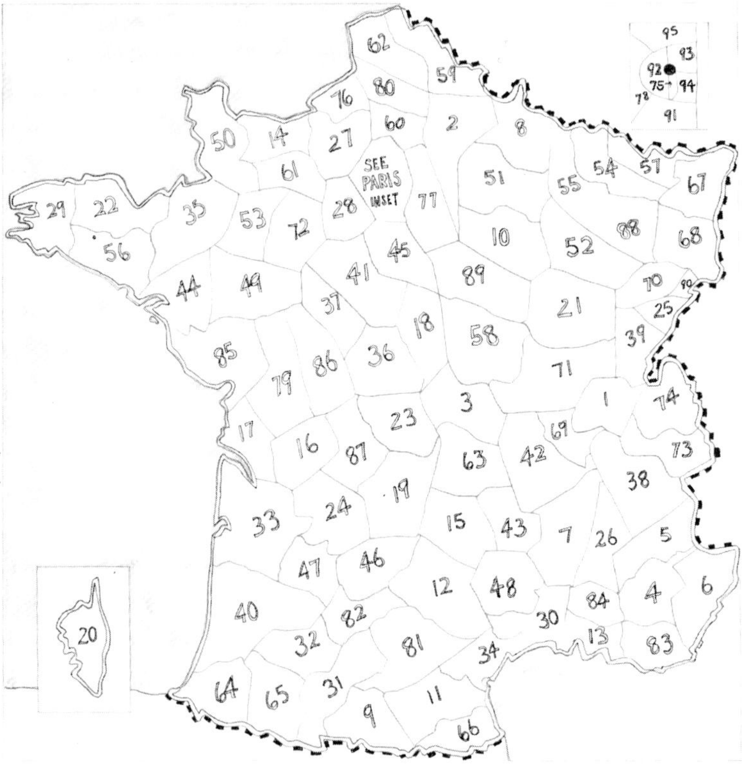

Bon courage

1 Which would you put in front of these – *un* or *une*?
plan, baguette, orange, croissant

2 Which would you put in front of these – *le*, *la*, *l'* or *les*?
panaché, brochure, croissants, orange, pain, bières

3 1 Ask for the drinks made from: coffee and milk; beer and lemonade; white wine and blackcurrant liqueur
2 Ask if these are available:

3 Name these two things:

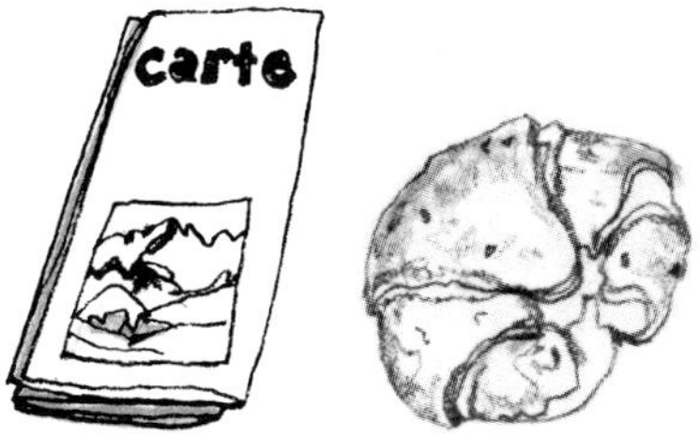

4 1 If you went into a café which of these would you ask for?
un musée dauphinois, un crème, une carte
2 If you went into the *Syndicat d'Initiative* which of these would you ask for?
un plan, une bouteille, un panaché
3 If you went into the *boulangerie* which of these would you ask for?
un jus de fruit, un pamplemousse, une baguette
4 Which of these would you not chop up and put in a fruit salad?
un abricot, un ananas, une boulangère, une poire

5 You are in a café with three friends. Mary wants a freshly-squeezed orange juice, Fred wants a shandy, Carol wants a beer and you want black coffee.
1 What does each of you say when the waiter says: 'Bonjour, messieurs-dames, vous désirez?'
2 How will you ask him how much you owe?

6 You arrive in Grenoble and find the *Maison du Tourisme*. Complete your side of the conversation.

You	*Greet the young woman at the counter.*
Hôtesse	Bonjour, madame.
You	*Ask if she has got a street map of Grenoble.*
Hôtesse	Oui, voilà.
You	*Ask how much it is.*
Hôtesse	C'est gratuit, madame.
You	*Say thank you and goodbye.*
Hôtesse	Je vous en prie, madame. Au revoir et bon séjour à Grenoble.

7 All that effort has taken it out of you so you go into a café.

Garçon	M'sieur-dame, vous désirez?
You	*Ask for two coffees, one white and one black, and two croissants.*
Garçon	Très bien, madame.

The waiter returns.

Garçon	Le crème, c'est pour qui?
You	*Say it is for you.*
Garçon	Voilà, m'sieur-dame.
You	*Say thank you very much.*

8 What vowels do you need to complete the following words?

b – – r –	you can drink it
b – – t – – ll –	you can drink out of it
b – g – – tt –	you can eat it
c – mb – – n	you need this word to find out how much things cost
b – – – c – – p	you need this word to say 'a lot'.

9 Hidden in this square there are at least twelve French words you have met. They read from left to right and from top to bottom.

L	E	P	P	A	I	N	E
L	T	L	A	D	E	U	X
F	R	A	N	C	S	Z	P
N	O	N	A	P	O	U	R
B	R	O	C	H	U	R	E
V	E	U	H	X	I	T	S
D	R	M	E	R	C	I	S

Le Dauphiné

The Dauphiné is a region of the Alps bordering on Italy. Although increasingly popular with tourists, especially for winter sports, its magnificent and varied landscapes remain little-known outside France. Until recently the Dauphiné was an inaccessible rural backwater. Today, the traditional mountain economy is still important – sheep and goats, cereals and forestry.

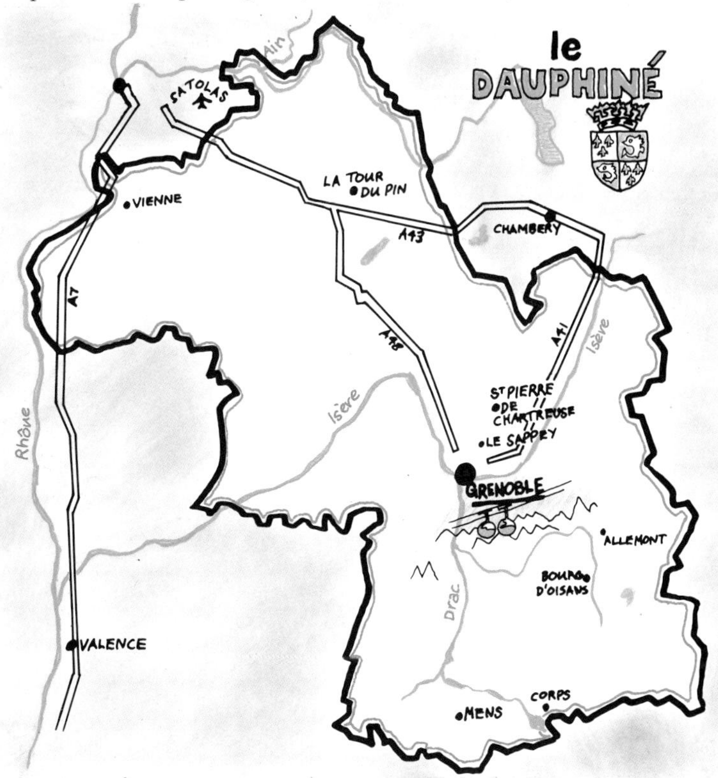

The main town, Grenoble, is in sharp contrast. Squeezed into a mountain valley, it was, until a few years ago, the fastest expanding provincial town in France. Along with the prestige of hosting the Winter Olympics in 1968, Grenoble became known as the most progressive, dynamic city in France outside Paris. Under the energetic guidance of its well-known mayor, Hubert Dubedout, the town began to develop high-technology industries and research, particularly in the field of micro-electronics. Grenoble became a 'ville pilote' where experiments of all kinds – artistic and social, as well as technological, could be made. People from all over France came here to join in the boom and today less than half the inhabitants of Grenoble are native *grenoblois*.

Le Dauphiné est une région de montagnes. C'est une région variée où il y a beaucoup de paysages différents – le plateau du Trièves au sud, le Parc Naturel Régional du Vercors à l'ouest, le massif de la Chartreuse au nord. C'est une région où il y a des activités traditionnelles – l'élevage, l'agriculture et l'exploitation forestière. Des activités de loisirs aussi, comme le ski ou les promenades en montagne.

Au centre du Dauphiné, au milieu des montagnes, il y a la ville de Grenoble, la capitale des Alpes. Grenoble a 400.000 habitants. Ce n'est pas une simple petite ville de province, c'est aussi une ville moderne et très importante en France. C'est une ville en évolution. Il y a beaucoup d'industries, beaucoup de commerces. Grenoble est un centre de recherche et d'industrie microéléctronique, un centre de recherche et d'études nucléaires. C'est une ville où il y a beaucoup d'étudiants, une ville universitaire. C'est aussi une ville où les vieilles industries de la région restent importantes: industrie papetière, industrie hydroéléctrique.

Enfin, Grenoble est un grand centre culturel où il y a des musées particulièrement intéressants, des cinémas, des théâtres et aussi une Maison de la Culture très connue en France. A Grenoble, il y a aussi des festivals: des festivals de musique, de danse, de cinéma et de théâtre.

Hubert Dubedout, maire de Grenoble pendant dix-huit ans, est en partie responsable de l'évolution de la ville. Pour lui, Grenoble est 'une ville vivante et dynamique, une ville jeune, une ville passionnante'.

beaucoup de paysages différents	*many different types of countryside*
très connue	*very well known*
pour lui	*for him*

Grenoble: le quai de l'Isère et le téléphérique

2

Où . . .?

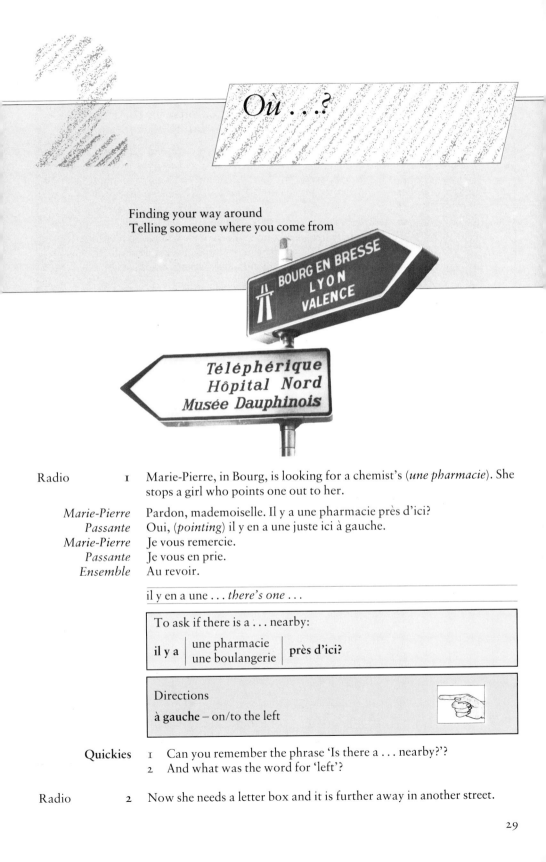

Finding your way around
Telling someone where you come from

Radio 1 Marie-Pierre, in Bourg, is looking for a chemist's (*une pharmacie*). She stops a girl who points one out to her.

Marie-Pierre Pardon, mademoiselle. Il y a une pharmacie près d'ici?
Passante Oui, (*pointing*) il y en a une juste ici à gauche.
Marie-Pierre Je vous remercie.
Passante Je vous en prie.
Ensemble Au revoir.

il y en a une . . . *there's one . . .*

To ask if there is a . . . nearby:

il y a	une pharmacie une boulangerie	**près d'ici?**

Directions

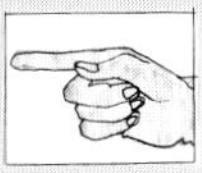

à gauche – on/to the left

Quickies
1 Can you remember the phrase 'Is there a . . . nearby?'?
2 And what was the word for 'left'?

Radio 2 Now she needs a letter box and it is further away in another street.

Marie-Pierre Pardon, mademoiselle. Il y a une boîte à lettres près d'ici?
Passante Oui, il y en a une dans la première rue à droite.
Marie-Pierre Je vous remercie.
Passante De rien. Je vous en prie.

de rien *don't mention it*

Directions

à droite – on/to the right

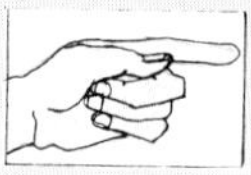

Quickies

1 If you want to post a letter what do you ask for?
2 And what was the word for 'right'?

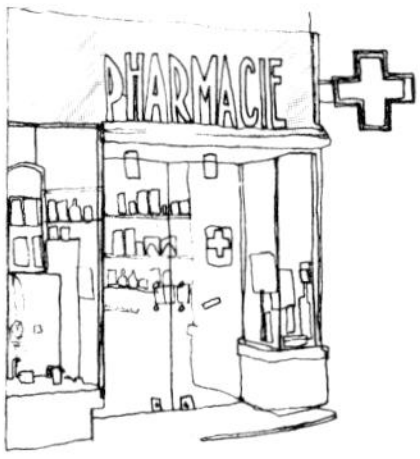

TV 3 In Grenoble, Madame Targes wants to find a chemist's shop. She asks a passer-by.

Mme Targes Pardon, madame. Il y a une pharmacie près d'ici?
Passante Oui, il y en a une rue Barnave. Vous tournez à gauche rue des Clercs (*pointing to it*) . . .
Mme Targes Oui.
Passante Puis à droite . . .

Mme Targes	Oui.
Passante	Et il y a une pharmacie sur votre droite.
Mme Targes	Merci, madame.

vous tournez *you turn*

Quickies

1 If you want a chemist's shop what do you ask for?
2 Are you sure you still know your left from your right? *gauche – droite*: which is which?

Radio 4 Jean, in Bourg, is looking for a tobacconist's (*un bureau de tabac*).

Jean	Pardon, madame.
Passante	Oui?
Jean	Il y a un bureau de tabac près d'ici?
Passante	Vous en avez plusieurs. Il y en a un là (*pointing*) sur la place et vous en avez un autre dans la première rue sur votre gauche.
Jean	Merci, madame.
Passante	Je vous en prie.
Jean	Au revoir, madame.

vous en avez plusieurs *you've got several*
vous en avez un autre *you've got another one*

Three ways of saying something is on/to the left or right:

à **sur la** **sur votre**	gauche droite

Quickies

1 How did Jean attract the attention of the passer-by before asking his question?
2 Where was the first *bureau de tabac* she mentioned?

TV 5 Barbara Michel, looking round the old part of Grenoble, wants to know if there is a bank nearby.

Barbara	Pardon, monsieur. Il y a une banque près d'ici?
Passant	Vous avez trois ou quatre banques Place Victor Hugo.
Barbara	(*getting out a map*) Place Victor Hugo, c'est où sur le plan?

Passant Vous êtes ici Place Saint André (*pointing to the map*) et la Place Victor Hugo est là.
Barbara Ah oui. Merci beaucoup.
Passant Je vous en prie, madame.
Barbara Au revoir, monsieur.

c'est où sur le plan?	*where is it on the map?*
vous êtes ici	*you are here*

Quickies
1 How many banks are there in the Place Victor Hugo?
2 Can you remember the words for 'here' and 'there'?

Radio 6 Marie-Pierre has a real problem. She is at the new station for high-speed trains near Mâcon: it is several kilometres out of town and has no buffet or café nearby.

Marie-Pierre Pardon, monsieur. Il y a un buffet dans la gare?
Employé Non, il n'y a pas de buffet, mais là-bas vous avez un distributeur automatique.
Marie-Pierre Et il y a un café près de la gare?
Employé Non, en ville seulement.
Marie-Pierre Tant pis! Merci.
Employé A votre service.

il n'y a pas de buffet	*there isn't a buffet*
tant pis!	*never mind!*

Quickies
1 Where was the nearest café?
2 Why will Marie-Pierre not die of hunger and thirst?

Radio 7 In the Bourg-en-Bresse *Syndicat d'Initiative*, Marie-Pierre has been given a street map. She asks where the Hôtel de France is on the map, and also the famous church in Brou, a suburb of Bourg.

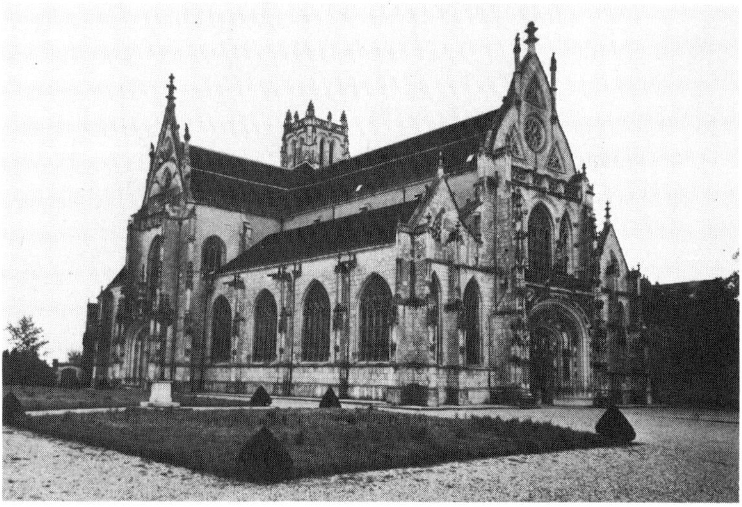

L'église de Brou

Marie-Pierre Pardon, mademoiselle. Où est l'Hôtel de France sur le plan?
Hôtesse Il est ici (*pointing to the map*).
Marie-Pierre Et l'église de Brou?
Hôtesse Elle est là.
Marie-Pierre Je vous remercie.
Hôtesse Je vous en prie. Au revoir, mademoiselle.
Marie-Pierre Au revoir.

To ask where something is:

	la Place Saint André?
où est	le Syndicat d'Initiative?
	l'église de Brou?

Quickie What three-word phrase does Marie-Pierre use to say 'thank you'?

Radio **8** Marie-Pierre has arranged to meet someone in the Café des Sports and asks where it is.

Marie-Pierre Pardon, monsieur. Où est le Café des Sports, s'il vous plaît?
Passant Oui, il est juste ici à gauche.
Marie-Pierre (*seeing it*) Ah oui. Je vous remercie.
Passant De rien. A votre service.

You can avoid repeating nouns already mentioned by using *elle* and *il*:

où est la Place St André?	**la Place** St André **elle**	est là
où est le Café des Sports?	**le Café** des Sports **il**	est là

Quickie Where was the café?

TV **9** Madame Mercant and her friend are driving round Grenoble. They want to get to the *téléphérique* – the cable car that will take them up to la Bastille to see the view. Who better to ask than a policeman?

Un agent de police

Mme Mercant Pardon, monsieur l'agent. Où est le téléphérique, s'il vous plaît?
Agent Vous prenez la deuxième rue à gauche, au bout, là (*pointing*). Ensuite la quatrième rue à droite.
Mme Mercant Oui.
Agent Vous avez le téléphérique sur la droite.
Mme Mercant Merci beaucoup, monsieur l'agent.
Agent A votre service, madame, monsieur (*he salutes them*).
Mme Mercant Au revoir.

Grenoble: le téléphérique

monsieur l'agent	*form of address when talking to a policeman*
vous prenez	*you take*
à votre service	*glad to be of service*

To say 'the first/second/etc on the left or right':

la	**première** **deuxième** **troisième**	**(rue) à**	gauche droite

Quickies

1. What is the difference between *deux* and *deuxième* and *quatre* and *quatrième*?
2. You won't get to the *téléphérique* if you don't know the meaning of:
   la deuxième rue à gauche
   la quatrième rue à droite

TV 10 Madame Trabut in Grenoble wants to get to the Musée Stendhal.

Mme Trabut Pardon, madame. Où est le Musée Stendhal, s'il vous plaît?
Passante Le Musée Stendhal? (*pointing to the other side of the river*) C'est en face. Vous voyez le téléphérique là-bas? Le Musée Stendhal est juste à côte, dans le Jardin de Ville.
Mme Trabut Ah, d'accord. Merci beaucoup.

Passante Au revoir.
Mme Trabut Au revoir, madame.

vous voyez?	*(can) you see?*
le Jardin de Ville	*name of a park in Grenoble*

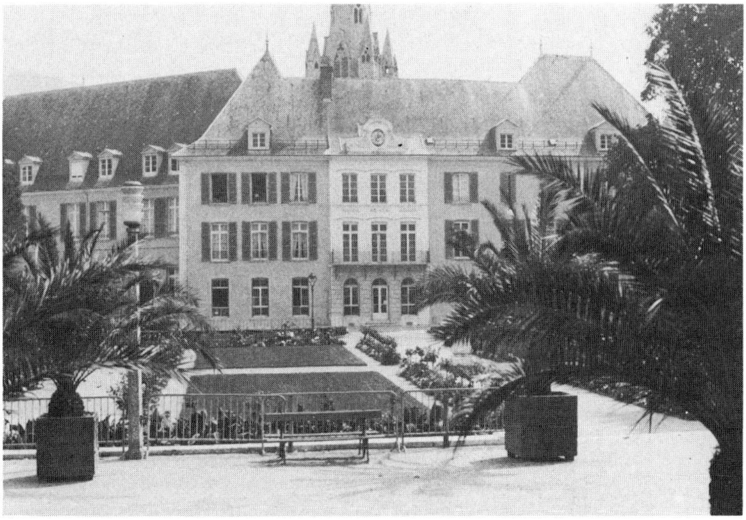

Grenoble: le Jardin de Ville

> Other directions you will hear:
>
> **en face** – opposite
> **à côté** – beside
> **là-bas** – over there
> **au bout** – at the end

Quickies

1 What phrase does Madame Trabut use to show she has understood?
2 What is the difference between *en face* and *à côté*?

TV 11 Patrice Téronne, wanting to get to the *Syndicat d'Initiative* in Grenoble, asks a passer-by. He is told it is in the *Maison du Tourisme*, a large building containing local and regional tourist services.

Patrice Pardon, madame. Où est le Syndicat d'Initiative, s'il vous plaît?
Passante Le Syndicat d'Initiative? C'est à la Maison du Tourisme. Alors, vous prenez la deuxième rue à gauche, puis la première à droite. Vous continuez jusqu'au bout de la rue et c'est en face de vous sur la gauche.
Patrice Donc, par là-bas, la deuxième à gauche, ensuite la première à droite, tout droit et au bout de la rue c'est en face sur la gauche.
Passante Oui, c'est ça.
Patrice C'est loin d'ici?
Passante Non, c'est à cinq minutes.
Patrice Ah bon! Merci. Au revoir, madame.
Passante Au revoir, monsieur.

vous continuez jusqu'au bout	*you carry on to the end*
par là-bas	*over that way*

To ask if it's far (from here):

c'est loin (d'ici)?

You might be told how far away it is in distance or time:

c'est à	**trois cents mètres** **deux kilomètres** **cinq minutes**

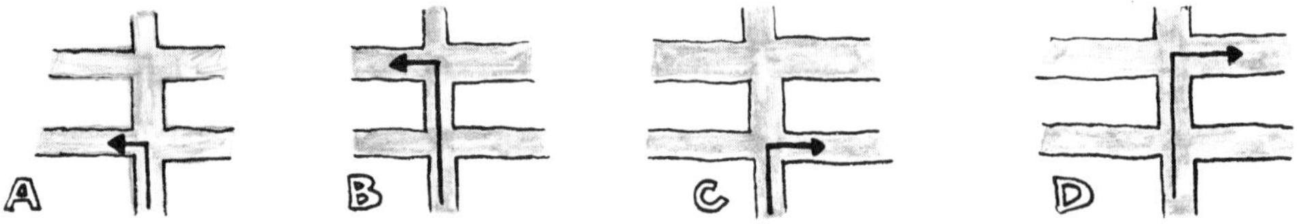

Quickies Which of these pictures represents

1 la deuxième à droite?
2 la première à gauche?
3 la deuxième à gauche?
4 What would you say for the remaining one?

Radio **12** Jean hasn't got a map and wants to get to Bourg-en-Bresse station.

Jean Pardon, madame. Où est la gare, s'il vous plaît?
Passante Vous êtes à pied ou en voiture?
Jean A pied.
Passante Alors tout droit, toujours tout droit.
Jean Bon. C'est loin d'ici?
Passante Dix minutes à pied, environ.
Jean Bon. Merci, madame.
Passante Je vous en prie.

à pied	*on foot*
en voiture	*in a car*

Another direction

tout droit – straight on

Quickies

1 What's the difference between *ici* and *là*?
2 Was Jean *à pied* or *en voiture*?
3 Are you sure you know the difference between *tout droit* and *à droite*?

Rencontres

The church in Brou is one of the most famous in France. We interviewed visitors outside it and asked them where they came from.

Radio 1 This man is just passing through. But where does he come from?

Marie-Pierre Pardon, monsieur. Vous êtes de Bourg?
Visiteur Non, je ne suis pas de Bourg.
Marie-Pierre Et vous êtes d'où?
Visiteur Je suis de Nancy.
Marie-Pierre Vous êtes en vacances?
Visiteur Je suis de passage.
Marie-Pierre Et la région vous plaît?
Visiteur Oui, bien sûr.
Marie-Pierre Je vous remercie.
Visiteur Au revoir.

en vacances	*on holiday*
de passage	*passing through*
la région vous plaît?	*do you like the region?*

To ask where someone is from:

vous êtes de Bourg? / d'où? / d'ici?

To say where you are from:

je suis de Pontypridd / de Nancy / d'ici

To say where you are not from:

je ne suis pas de Bognor Regis / de Bourg / d'ici

Quickies

1 Can you ask where someone comes from?
2 Do you come from Bourg? If not, say so.

Radio 2 The second man comes from much further afield. Which country and which town?

Marie-Pierre Pardon, monsieur. Vous êtes de Bourg?
Visiteur Non, je ne suis pas de Bourg.
Marie-Pierre Vous êtes d'où?
Visiteur Je suis brésilien.
Marie-Pierre Brésilien? Et vous êtes de quelle ville?

Eglise de Brou: le cloître

Visiteur Je suis de São Paulo.
Marie-Pierre Vous êtes ici en vacances?
Visiteur Oui, je suis en vacances.
Marie-Pierre La région vous plaît?
Visiteur Beaucoup.
Marie-Pierre Je vous remercie.
Visiteur Je vous en prie.

de quelle ville? *from which town?*

Radio 3 And finally a woman from another part of France.

Marie-Pierre Pardon, madame. Vous êtes de Bourg?
Visiteur Non, pas du tout.
Marie-Pierre Et vous êtes d'où?
Visiteur Je suis du Havre.
Marie-Pierre Et vous êtes ici de passage ou en vacances?
Visiteur De passage, oui, pour deux jours.
Marie-Pierre Merci, madame.

> When *de* is followed by *le* the two combine to give *du*:
> je suis de + Le Havre *gives* je suis **du** Havre

TV 4 The university at Grenoble attracts students from all over the world. We asked some of them where they came from and what nationality they were.

Jane Mademoiselle, vous êtes française?
1ère étudiante Oui, je suis française.
Jane Vous êtes d'où?
1ère étudiante Je suis de Paris.
Jane Vous êtes de Grenoble?

1er étudiant	Non, je ne suis pas de Grenoble.
Jane	Vous êtes d'où?
1er étudiant	Je viens de Bretagne.
Jane	Mademoiselle, vous êtes française?
2ème étudiante	Non, je suis pas française.
Jane	Vous êtes d'où?
2ème étudiante	Je viens de Taiwan.
Jane	Vous êtes de Grenoble?
2ème étudiant	Non, je ne suis pas de Grenoble.
Jane	Vous êtes d'où?
2ème étudiant	Je suis du sud de la France, de Nice.
Jane	Monsieur, vous êtes français?
3ème étudiant	Non, je suis de nationalité togolaise.
Jane	Vous êtes de Grenoble?
4ème étudiant	Non, je ne suis pas de Grenoble.
Jane	Vous êtes d'où?
4ème étudiant	Je suis des Hautes-Alpes.

je suis pas *I'm not* (see *En plus*)
je viens de *I come from*

To say what nationality you are:

je suis	française (female) français (male)

(There is a difference in pronunciation: see *En plus*)

Other nationalities:

je suis	anglais(e)	English
	écossais(e)	Scottish
	gallois(e)	Welsh
	irlandais(e)	Irish
	antillais(e)	French West Indian
	allemand(e)	German

Quickies

1 Tell someone you're not French.
2 Can you say 'I'm . . .' whatever nationality you are?

Mots-clés

la banque	bank	à côté	beside
la boîte à lettres	letter box	au bout	at the end
le bureau de tabac	tobacconist's	dans	in
la gare	station	la droite	right
la pharmacie	chemist's	en face	opposite
la place	square	la gauche	left
la rue	street	ici	here
		là	there
allemand	German	là-bas	over there
anglais	English	loin	far
antillais	West Indian	près	near
britannique	British	sur	on
écossais	Scottish	tout droit	straight on
français	French	à pied	on foot
gallois	Welsh	en vacances	on holiday
irlandais	Irish	en voiture	in a/by car

En bref

1 To call someone's attention:
Pardon, monsieur/madame!

2 To ask if something is nearby:
il y a un/une ... près d'ici?

3 To ask where something is:
où est le/la ..., s'il vous plaît?

4 Phrases you may hear in reply:

1 variations on 'to/on the left/right':

à / **sur votre** / **sur la**	gauche/droite

2 phrases indicating position:
en face/à côté/au bout
ici/là/là-bas

the first three can be followed by *de* + a noun:
en face de l'église
au bout de la rue
à côté de la gare

3 phrases telling you routes to be followed:
tout droit
la deuxième (rue) **à gauche**
la première (rue) **à droite**

5 To avoid repetition people may use *elle* or *il* in place of a noun:

où est **la gare**?	**elle** est là
où est **le musée**?	**il** est là

6 To ask if it's near (here):
c'est **près** (d'ici)?

or far (from here):
c'est **loin** (d'ici)?

7 Replies might include time or distance:

c'est	**à cinq minutes**
	à cinq cents mètres

8 1 To ask where someone is from:
vous êtes d'où?

2 To say where you are from:
je suis de ...

3 To say what nationality you are:
je suis écossaise (if you are female)
je suis écossais (if you are male)

Any sentence can be made negative by adding *ne* (or *n'*) ... *pas* round the verb:

je **ne** suis **pas** français
je **ne** suis **pas** de Grenoble
le musée **n'**est **pas** à côté de l'hôtel
il **n'**est **pas** loin

de + le → **du**
je suis de + le Havre → je suis **du** Havre
l'église est en face de + le musée → l'église est en face **du** musée

Learn a verb

être – to be

je suis	I am
vous êtes	you are
il est	he is, it is
elle est	she is, it is
c'est	it is, he is, she is

En plus

1 **It's not only what you say it's how you say it**
1 How to ask questions

The simplest way is to turn an ordinary statement into a question keeping all the words in the same order:
c'est loin d'ici
c'est loin d'ici?

In writing we put a question mark to indicate that a sentence is a question. In speaking you have to do the same thing with your voice. This is done in any language, English included. Compare the way you'd say the colours in these sentences:

What colour's your new car? Red?
No, blue.

In French, if you want to make a statement into a question, your voice goes up quite sharply on the last two or three syllables:

c'est loin ↘ d'ici
↗ d'ici?
c'est loin

Listen carefully to the dialogues so that you get the 'tune' of questions and statements into your head.

2 In Chapter 1 we said:
'Generally speaking, if the last letter of a word is a consonant, don't pronounce it.'
In this chapter there are two sets of words where remembering this can be very important. Many nationality words end in *-ais* for a male and *-aise* for a female:
anglais – anglaise

In the first word of this pair the final 's' is not pronounced. In the second, the 's' is pronounced because it is no longer the last letter; in this case it sounds like 'z'. If you say the wrong one you'll have changed sex and then everyone will be confused.

When the man in Grenoble said: *Je suis de nationalité togolaise*, he was not uncertain about his gender; the word *nationalité* is feminine and *togolaise* agrees with it.

The other set of words is:
droit: 't' not pronounced
droite: 't' pronounced

Get these wrong and you may be going straight on (*tout droit*) when you should be going to the right (*à droite*).

2 **Saying something is not so**

To say something is not so in French you put the two words *ne* (or *n'*) ... *pas* round the verb:

je ne suis pas de Newcastle, je suis de Leeds

Notice where the *ne* ... *pas* go when using *il y a*:

il n'y a pas de pharmacie Place Saint André

Often in speech, as you may have noticed, the *ne* is not strongly pronounced and sometimes disappears altogether. One of the people interviewed said:

je suis pas française

Il n'y a pas, in particular, can get concertinaed into a sound rather like *yappa* which can be puzzling if you are not prepared for it. The word to listen for, then, is *pas*; it will always tell you whether the sentence is negative.

3 **Responding to 'thank you'**

In English we have 'don't mention it', 'that's alright', even sometimes 'any time'. You have met several of the equivalent French phrases:

je vous en prie
à votre service
de rien

Other quite common ones are:

il n'y a pas de quoi
avec plaisir

Je vous en prie is probably the commonest.

4 **The numbers game**

Alongside the numbers one, two, three, four, etc, there is also first, second, third, fourth, etc.

one, two, three	first, second, third
un/une	premier/première
deux	deuxième
trois	troisième
quatre	quatrième

As you see, except for *premier/première*, it is a simple matter of adding *-ième* to the numbers in the first group to get the second group.

A couple of small adjustments have to be made: numbers already ending in an 'e' lose it (*quatre – quatrième*) and the 'f' on *neuf* (nine) becomes a 'v' (*neuvième*).

The standard abbreviations for these are:

premier – 1er; première – 1ère; deuxième – 2ème, troisième – 3ème, etc.

5 ***Places* and 'places'**

A French *place* is not an English 'place'. For a start, the pronunciation is quite different. And then, the Place Saint André is a square, like those much more famous ones in Paris, the Place de la Concorde and the Place de la Bastille. The word *square* also exists, having been borrowed from English. Strictly speaking it means the square of garden, often railed off, in the middle of a *place*. Anything called a

square will usually have a garden in the middle though it will not necessarily be square. *Rue* is much the same as 'street'. *Avenue*, before meaning a street, meant a driveway lined with trees; the name *boulevard* for a long wide street also implied it was lined with trees. *Cours* is another word used for much the same sort of thing. Sadly, nowadays, the trees are not always there. When the word *quai* appears in an address, it means a street on a river bank. The French Foreign Office is often referred to by its address, the Quai d'Orsay, one of the roads running alongside the Seine in Paris.

The abbreviations for all these are:
av, bd, crs, r, sq, qu, pl

In English we sometimes use a French phrase *cul de sac* to mean a short road with no exit. You will still hear the phrase used in French but the official word for it is *impasse* and this is what you see on street signs in the same way as *rue*, *place* etc. So if you drive into an *impasse* the only way out is to turn round and come back again.

A propos

The arm of the law
Most Britons believe a French policeman is a *gendarme*. This is not always so.

There are several sets of people carrying out police duties whom the foreign traveller is likely to come into contact with. In the towns there are *agents de police*. They wear dark blue uniforms with silver-coloured buttons and badges. In hot weather they will be in light blue shirts. If you want a police station then that is the *poste* (*de police*) or the *commissariat* where the *commissaire* (the local police chief) can be found. In the country there are *gendarmes*. You will often see their barracks carrying the sign *Gendarmerie Nationale* in or near small towns. They wear navy blue jackets, blue trousers and have gold-coloured buttons and badges. In hot weather they wear light blue shirts. As well as carrying out police duties, specialised corps act as coastguards, mountain rescue teams, etc. They are actually part of the army, being responsible to the Ministry of Defence. In holiday times you will also come across members of the CRS (*Compagnie Républicaine de Sécurité*). They act as life-guards on beaches and help the *gendarmerie* to patrol roads. Otherwise one of their main duties is to deal with riots or civil disturbances and they have acquired an unenviable reputation for toughness.

Others you may meet are the people responsible for parking meters – *les contractuels* (male) or *les contractuelles* (female). The women, in Paris at any rate, wear a blue uniform that has earned them the nickname of *pervenches* (periwinkles).

The regions

Up to the time of the Revolution, France was divided into provinces. Many of their names have remained in common use, eg Provence, Normandie, and some were given new official life in 1972 when the French decided to group *départements* into larger units called *régions*. La Bretagne is one of these. It occupies that finger-like peninsula pointing out into the Atlantic on France's north-west corner. The

name of one of the old provinces, le Dauphiné, has not been revived for one of the new regions but is still widely used to refer to the area round Grenoble covered by the *départements* of Isère, Hautes-Alpes and Drôme. In the days of the French kings, the heir to the throne was called *le dauphin*. In the same way that the Duchy of Cornwall belongs to the heir of the British throne, the Dauphiné was the province that traditionally belonged to the Dauphin – hence its name. Inhabitants of that area are called *les Dauphinois*.

Local loyalties can be very strong. A Frenchman from Grenoble will certainly consider himself *français* but he will also be *grenoblois* or *dauphinois* according to which of his loyalties is engaged. Every community from the smallest village to the largest city has a special word to describe its inhabitants. *Les Parisiens* obviously come from Paris but what about *les Lyonnais* and *les Bordelais*? You will meet *les Bourgeois*, *les Nantais* and *les Piscénois* in this course.

French outside France

French is the official language in those other parts of the world that still belong to France. There are the overseas *départements* – *les départements d'outre-mer* (*les DOM*) – la Guadeloupe, la Guyane, la Martinique, la Réunion and St Pierre-et-Miquelon. These have full departmental status, including a member of parliament, just like the Ain or the Hautes-Alpes. Then there are the overseas territories – *les territoires d'outre-mer* (*les TOM*) – New Caledonia (la Nouvelle Calédonie) and some other Pacific islands, which do not have departmental status but are controlled by France.

French is spoken in many other countries too: Morocco, Algeria, Tunisia, many parts of west and central Africa, Vietnam, Canada, Belgium, Switzerland and even in the former British colonies, Mauritius and the Seychelles. So it is not unusual to find, as at Grenoble University, people from Togo or Senegal or one of the other French-speaking African states living in France.

A little culture

Victor Hugo, who has a square named after him in Grenoble and in practically every other French city, was a nineteenth-century writer. He wrote an enormous amount – poetry, plays and novels, had a huge influence on French literature and lived a long and active life. He was a passionate democrat and yet an admirer of Napoleon. When Louis

Le jeune Victor Hugo

Napoleon seized power in 1850 to become Napoleon III, Hugo, already a national figure, exiled himself in disgust to Guernsey from where, for the next twenty years, he issued vitriolic poems and pamphlets ridiculing the emperor. On the fall of Napoleon III in 1870, Hugo returned to Paris where he died in 1885 aged 83. At his death the whole of France went into mourning and two million people followed his hearse in the funeral procession. He is best known in Britain for his novels *Les Misérables* and *Notre-Dame de Paris* which includes the character Quasimodo, the hunchback of Notre Dame.

Stendhal, the pen-name of Henri Beyle, was also a nineteenth-century writer on a smaller scale in terms of output though not of quality. He was a native of Grenoble and his house there has been made into a museum devoted to him. His two best-known novels *Le Rouge et le Noir* (The Red and the Black) and *La Chartreuse de Parme* (The Charterhouse of Parma) remain justly popular and films have been made of them.

Bon courage

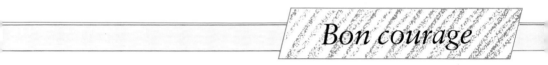

1 Which of these French words and expressions are the equivalents of the English ones?

ici, en ville, beaucoup, à pied, loin, gare, là, en voiture

by car, far, station, here, a lot, on foot, in town, there

2 There is an odd-man-out in each of these groups of words – which is it?

une rue, une place, une avenue, une église

un agent, un hôtel, un musée, un bureau de tabac

un buffet de gare, une pharmacie, une boîte à lettres, un restaurant

3
1 You want to change some money. Ask someone if there is a bank nearby. Don't forget to attract his attention.
2 Now you want a drink. You've heard the Café Hugo is good. Ask where it is.
3 You need a chemist's for some sun-tan cream. Ask if there's one nearby.
4 You'd like to visit the Musée Stendhal. Ask where it is. Find out if it's far away.
5 You'd like to take a trip in the cable car. Go to the *Syndicat d'Initiative*, ask where it is and find out how much it costs.
6 You'd like to post the postcard you've written. Ask if there's a letter box nearby.
7 Now you need to get back to your hotel but can't recognise where you are on your street map. Ask someone where the Hôtel de France is on the map.

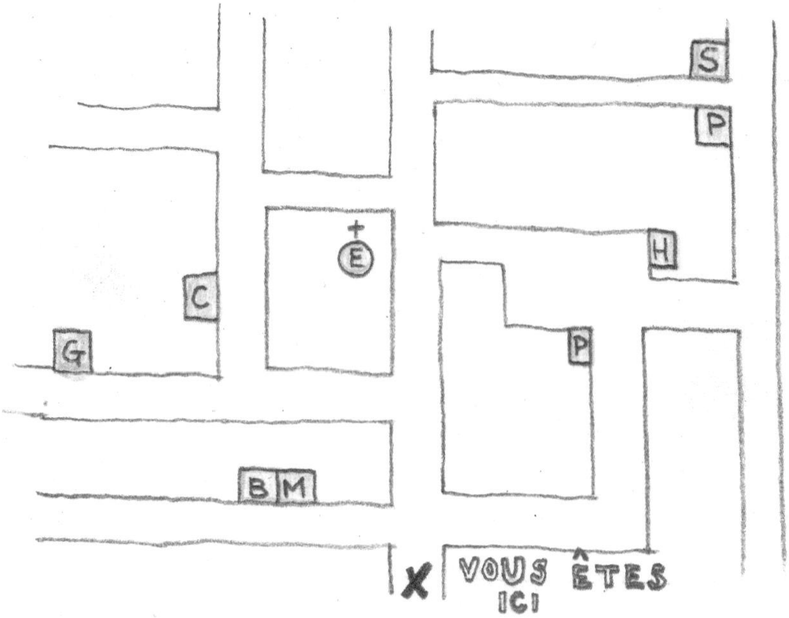

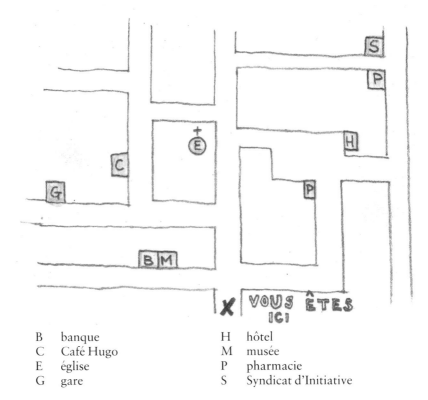

B	banque	H	hôtel
C	Café Hugo	M	musée
E	église	P	pharmacie
G	gare	S	Syndicat d'Initiative

4 You have asked the way to various places on the map above. Here are the answers. Where did you ask to go?

1 Vous prenez la deuxième rue à gauche, puis la première à droite et c'est sur votre gauche.
2 Vous continuez tout droit jusqu'à l'église, puis vous tournez à droite et c'est en face sur la Place St André. C'est à cinq minutes à pied.
3 Vous prenez la troisième à droite, vous continuez jusqu'au bout et c'est sur votre gauche. C'est à trois minutes en voiture.
4 Vous tournez à gauche ici et c'est juste sur votre droite à côté du musée.
5 Vous prenez la deuxième à gauche, vous continuez tout droit et c'est à droite.

5 You are in a café in Bourg. Complete your side of the conversation with the waiter.

You *Ask the waiter if there is a restaurant nearby.*
Garçon Il y en a plusieurs. Vous êtes en voiture?
You *Say no, you're on foot.*
Garçon Bon, alors, le Restaurant de la Gare est très bien et c'est juste à côté.
You *Thank him.*
Garçon Excusez-moi, vous n'êtes pas français. Vous êtes anglais peut-être?
You *Say no, you're Welsh and you're from Pontypridd.*
Garçon Pontypridd. C'est où, ça?
You *Tell him it's near Cardiff.*

Garçon	Ah, Cardiff, le rugby! Et ici, la région vous plaît?
You	*Say yes, a lot.*
Garçon	Très bien, alors, bon séjour à Bourg.
You	*Thank him very much.*

6 How would the following have stated their nationality in French? (Start with *je suis*)

1 Joan of Arc
2 Winston Churchill
3 General De Gaulle
4 Robert Burns
5 Elizabeth I
6 Beethoven
7 Bernard Shaw
8 Mary Queen of Scots
9 Lloyd George
10 Edith Piaf

7 Can you rearrange the letters in these shapes to form French words you have met? Try making a few more shapes of your own.

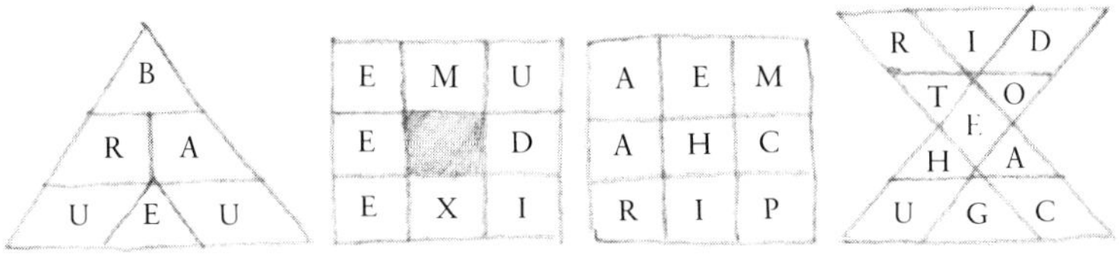

8 Mots croisés – Crossword
Use capital letters because then you don't have to put in accents.

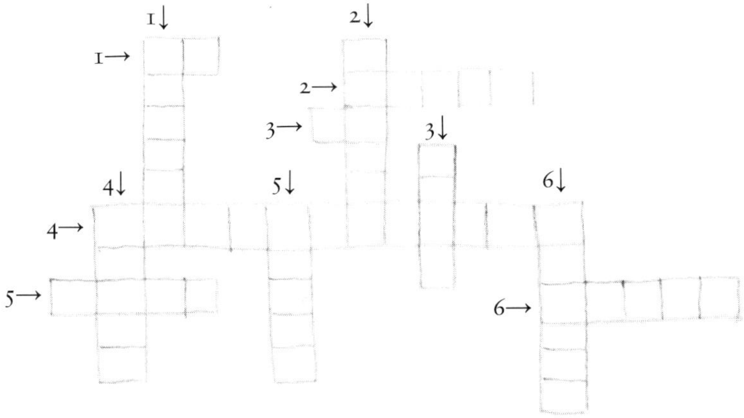

Horizontalement
1 de + le → ?
2 he's not a *gendarme*
3 where?
4 not a common form of transport but you'll find one in Grenoble
5 à .... de (next door)
6 over there

Verticalement
1 c'est à..................
2 c'est à..................
3 vous êtes allemand? non, je .... anglais
4 un, deux, ...
5 its abbreviation is *pl*
6 where the bells may ring

Site du barrage de Grand'Maison

La houille blanche

Grenoble and its surrounding area have some claims to being the birthplace of hydro-electric power. It was here, in 1869, that the energy of mountain streams was first transformed to drive a paper-mill. The engineer responsible coined the term *la houille blanche* – white coal – to describe this energy. Local industries developed rapidly around the twin resources of water and electricity and Grenoble became known as *capitale de la houille blanche*.

Grenoble's industry today owes much to this tradition and in the surrounding mountains dams are an important feature of the landscape. The last major project to be built here, in the beautiful valley of l'Eau d'Olle, was started in the late 1970's. Known as the Grand'Maison project, it consists of two dams. Construction will take 8 years, partly halted each winter by the snows. Apart from its physical impact on the valley, the project has transformed the life of the small agricultural community living here.

L'eau est une ressource naturelle très importante en montagne, surtout en ce qui concerne la production d'énergie hydroélectrique.

Grenoble est la 'capitale de la houille blanche'. Il y a des industries hydromécaniques et hydroélectriques. La SOGREAH (la Société Grenobloise d'Etudes et d'Applications Hydrauliques), par exemple, est un laboratoire où des ingénieurs préparent des projets hydrauliques – des barrages surtout – pour le monde entier.

Il y a beaucoup de barrages dans le Dauphiné. Depuis quatre ans, l'EDF (Electricité de France) est en train de construire le dernier grand barrage de la région. Le projet s'appelle Grand'Maison et consiste en deux barrages: le barrage de Grand'Maison, en haut des montagnes et le barrage du Verney dans la vallée. Entre les deux, il va y avoir une usine souterraine pour transformer l'énergie de l'eau en électricité.

Le travail est souvent dangereux et difficile en haute montagne: des guides sont spécialement employés pour s'en occuper.

Grand'Maison est un grand projet – il y a 2.000 personnes qui y travaillent. Mais il n'y a pas assez de maisons particulières pour les loger dans la vallée. Les ouvriers, qui sont en majorité des immigrés, habitent donc dans des maisons construites spécialement pour eux ou dans des caravannings.

Depuis la construction du barrage, la vie n'est plus la même dans le pays. Jo Ramel, qui est prêtre dans la vallée depuis dix-neuf ans, en parle: selon lui, 'Ça a bien changé la vie du pays. Avant le barrage, la vie du pays était en diminution, en régression'. Depuis, les petites entreprises locales, les habitants, les jeunes ont trouvé du travail sur place. Mais dans quatre ans, une fois le barrage fini, que va-t-il se passer pour les habitants de la vallée?

en ce qui concerne	*with regard to*
depuis quatre ans . . . . . . est en train de construire	*for four years . . .* *. . . has been building*
en haut des montagnes	*up in the mountains*
il va y avoir	*there will be*
pour s'en occuper	*to take care of it*
pour les loger	*to house them*
pour eux	*for them*
la vie n'est plus la même	*life is no longer the same*
ça a bien changé	*it's really changed*
était en diminution	*was on the decline*
ont trouvé	*have found*
une fois le barrage fini	*once the dam is finished*
que va-t-il se passer?	*what will happen?*

3

Combien?

Asking prices
Asking what things are
Saying how many or how much you want
Talking about the family

Radio 1 Marie-Pierre is in the market (*le marché*) checking on the price of eggs.

Marie-Pierre Pardon, monsieur. C'est combien les oeufs, s'il vous plaît?
Marchand Huit francs la douzaine ou quatre francs les six.
Marie-Pierre Je vous remercie.

> *c'est combien?* means 'how much are?' as well as 'how much is?':
>
> **c'est combien** | la bière? / les oeufs?

Quickies
1 How did she say 'how much are the eggs?'?
2 Where does the word 'dozen' come from?

To say 10 francs *a* dozen, *a* bunch, *a* kilo, use *le*, *la*, *les*:	
dix francs	la botte le kilo les six la douzaine

Radio 2 Now she wants to find out how much the leeks are.

Marie-Pierre Pardon, monsieur. C'est combien les poireaux, s'il vous plaît?
Marchand Cinq francs la botte, mademoiselle.
Marie-Pierre Et ils sont bons?
Marchand Mais je pense déjà!
Marie-Pierre Je vous remercie.

mais je pense déjà! *I should think so!*

Radio 3 At the fruit stall there's a special offer.

Marie-Pierre Pardon, monsieur. C'est combien les pommes, s'il vous plaît?
Marchand Deux francs le kilo, neuf francs les cinq kilogrammes.
Marie-Pierre Et les poires?
Marchand Les poires, quatre francs le kilogramme et dix-neuf francs les cinq kilogrammes.
Marie-Pierre Je vous remercie.
Marchand Au revoir, madame.

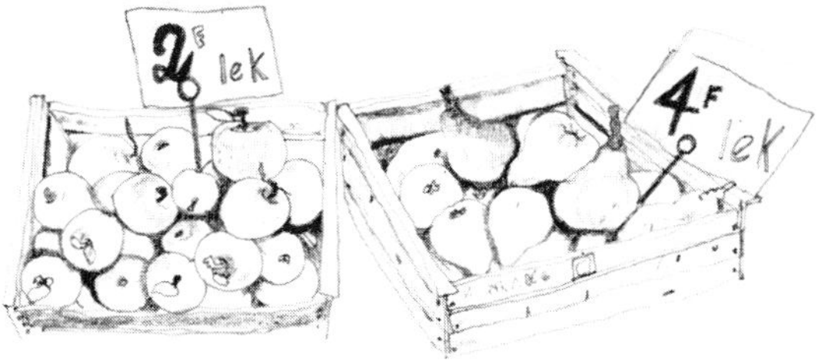

Quickies
1 Name the fruit in the picture above.
2 What was the special offer?

Radio 4 Pierrick finds an unusually-shaped object in a pottery shop and wonders if it is an ashtray.

Pierrick Pardon, madame. C'est un cendrier?
Marchande C'est un cendrier, monsieur.
Pierrick Et ça coûte combien?
Marchande Ça coûte vingt-huit francs, monsieur.
Pierrick Je vous remercie. Au revoir, madame.
Marchande Au revoir, monsieur.

ça coûte combien? *how much does it cost?*

Quickie How much did the ashtray cost?

Radio 5 Marie-Pierre wants to make sure the goat's cheese really is goat's cheese. She asks about it.

Marie-Pierre Pardon, madame. C'est du fromage de chèvre?
Marchande C'est mélangé, madame.
Marie-Pierre Et c'est combien la pièce?
Marchande Deux francs cinquante pièce.
Marie-Pierre Je vous remercie.
Marchande A votre service, m'sieur-dame.

> To ask how much each:
> c'est combien **(la) pièce?**
> *la* is optional

Quickies
1 Was it really goat's cheese?
2 How do you ask how much each?
3 What words suggest that Marie-Pierre is not alone?

Radio 6 This time Marie-Pierre really doesn't know what is being sold and has to ask. She makes a big mistake about the price!

Marie-Pierre Pardon, madame. Qu'est-ce que c'est?
Marchande C'est un canard de Barbarie.
Marie-Pierre Et c'est combien?
Marchande C'est cinquante-trois francs.
Marie-Pierre Le kilo?
Marchande Non! Mais non! La pièce!
Marie-Pierre La pièce?
Marchande Oui, la pièce.
Marie-Pierre Merci bien.

> To ask what something is:
> **qu'est-ce que c'est?**

Quickies
1 What was the mistake she made about the price?
2 What's brown and goes 'Couin! Couin!'?

Michel Bouyssié au marché

TV 7

Michel Bouyssié, at the fruit and vegetable stall, knows exactly what he wants: cherries, asparagus, peaches, a cucumber and also a box to put them all in.

Michel Bonjour, madame.
Marchande Bonjour, monsieur. Vous désirez?
Michel Un kilo de cerises, s'il vous plaît.
Marchande Oui. (*serves him*) Et avec ceci, monsieur?
Michel Une livre d'asperges, s'il vous plaît.
Marchande Oui. Voilà. Vous désirez autre chose, monsieur?
Michel Un concombre, s'il vous plaît.
Marchande Oui. Et avec ça?
Michel Un kilo de pêches, s'il vous plaît.
Marchande Oui. Ce sera tout, monsieur?
Michel Oui, très bien. Je vous remercie. Je vous dois combien?
Marchande Quinze francs, monsieur. (*he hands her a 100F note*) Merci. Alors, (*counting out the change*) quinze francs, vingt, trente, quarante, cinquante francs, cent francs.
Michel Merci beaucoup, madame.
Marchande Merci beaucoup, monsieur.
Michel Vous avez un sac ou une boîte, s'il vous plaît?
Marchande Oui. Voilà, monsieur.
Michel Merci, madame.
Marchande Merci. Au revoir, monsieur.
Michel Au revoir.

Quickies

1 Name as many of the objects in the picture as you can.
2 How many *livres* are there in a *kilo*?

Radio	8	Sara is in a fruit shop in Nantes. She wants cherries, peaches and strawberries. She can see the cherries but has to find out if the shopkeeper has the others.

Sara	Bonjour, madame.
Marchande	Bonjour, madame.
Sara	Je voudrais une livre de cerises, s'il vous plaît.
Marchande	Une livre de cerises. Comme ceci?
Sara	Oui, ça va.
Marchande	Alors, ça fait neuf francs, madame.
Sara	Bon. Vous avez des pêches, s'il vous plaît?
Marchande	Oui, bien sûr. Combien en voulez-vous?
Sara	Quatre.
Marchande	Quatre. Voici (*weighing them*). Alors, vous avez quatre cents grammes. Huit francs.
Sara	Est-ce que vous avez des fraises?
Marchande	Oui, bien sûr.
Sara	C'est combien?
Marchande	Deux cent soixante-dix les cent grammes.
Sara	Bon. Alors, donnez-m'en trois cents grammes, s'il vous plaît.
Marchande	Trois cents grammes, oui. (*weighs them*) Alors, ça fait huit francs. Il vous faut autre chose, madame?
Sara	Non, merci. Ça va comme ça. C'est combien, s'il vous plaît?
Marchande	Alors, (*adding up*) il y a huit francs, neuf francs et huit francs. Vingt-cinq francs, madame.
Sara	Bon. Voilà.
Marchande	Je vous remercie.
Sara	Bon. Au revoir, madame.
Marchande	Au revoir, madame. Merci.

deux cent soixante-dix *270 old francs (ie 2F70)*

To ask for something, *je voudrais* (I'd like) is optional:

(**je voudrais**)	une livre de cerises, s'il vous plaît un kilo de pêches, s'il vous plaît

---

En is the equivalent of 'of it', 'of them'; in English we usually omit these.

combien **en** voulez-vous? – how many (of them) do you want?
donnez-m'**en** 300 grammes – give me 300 grams (of them)

TV	9	Virginie Reitzer at the grocer's (*l'épicerie*) wants some butter, milk, wine and eggs.

Virginie	Bonjour, madame.
Epicière	Bonjour, madame. Vous désirez?
Virginie	Une plaquette de beurre, s'il vous plaît.
Epicière	Vous voulez une plaquette de cent vingt-cinq grammes ou de deux cent cinquante grammes?

Virginie	De deux cent cinquante grammes, s'il vous plaît.
Epicière	(*she brings the butter*) Et avec ceci?
Virginie	Merci. Vous avez du lait?
Epicière	Oui. Combien en voulez-vous?
Virginie	Un litre, s'il vous plaît. (*the milk is brought*) Merci.
Epicière	Il vous faut autre chose?
Virginie	Oui, deux bouteilles de vin rouge.
Epicière	Du vin ordinaire?
Virginie	Oui. (*the wine is brought*) Merci. Vous avez des oeufs?
Epicière	Oui. Vous en voulez combien?
Virginie	Une douzaine, s'il vous plaît.
Epicière	Et avec ceci?
Virginie	Ce sera tout, merci. Je vous dois combien?
Epicière	Vingt-cinq francs, s'il vous plaît, madame. (*taking the money*) Merci beaucoup, madame.
Virginie	Au revoir, madame.

vous voulez . . .?	*do you want . . .?*
il vous faut autre chose?	*do you need anything else?*

With quantities, French uses *de* where English has 'of':

un kilo **de** cerises
une livre **d'**asperges
un litre **de** lait

And French also uses *de* where English doesn't necessarily have 'of':

une douzaine d'oeufs	a dozen eggs
un peu de beurre	a little butter
combien de kilos?	how many kilos?

the	le	la	l'	les
some/any	**du**	**de la**	**de l'**	**des**

the . . .	*some/any . . .*
le lait	du lait
la crème	de la crème
l'eau	de l'eau
les oeufs	des oeufs

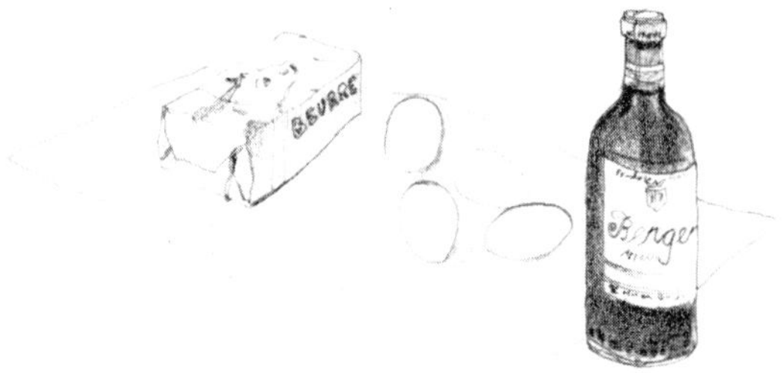

Quickies
1. Name the things in the picture above.
2. How would you ask if the shopkeeper had any milk?

Radio 10 Marie-Pierre is at the market buying wine but she wants something better than *vin ordinaire*.

Marie-Pierre Bonjour, madame.
Commerçante Bonjour, madame.
Marie-Pierre Je voudrais une bouteille de vin rouge, s'il vous plaît.
Commerçante Oui. Qu'est-ce que vous voulez? Du Beaujolais-Villages ou du Morgon?
Marie-Pierre C'est combien?
Commerçante Le Beaujolais-Villages seize francs et le Morgon à vingt-deux.
Marie-Pierre Une bouteille de Morgon.
Commerçante Oui, c'est supérieur. (*handing over the wine*) Voilà.
Marie-Pierre Vingt-deux francs?
Commerçante Oui, c'est ça.

Marie-Pierre	(*paying*) Voilà.
Commerçante	Merci, madame.
Marie-Pierre	Au revoir, madame.

qu'est-ce que vous voulez?	*what do you want?*

Quickies

1 How much wine did she want?
2 Morgon was the better wine; how much did it cost?

Rencontres

TV

1 In a shopping centre in Grenoble, Jane asked shoppers what they thought was the size of the ideal family and how many children they had themselves.

Jane	Madame, selon vous, il y a combien d'enfants dans une famille idéale?
1ère passante	Je pense trois.
Jane	Garçons ou filles?
1ère passante	Les deux.
Jane	Vous avez des enfants?
1ère passante	J'ai trois enfants.
Jane	Des garçons ou des filles?
1ère passante	J'ai un garçon et deux filles.

selon vous	*according to you, in your opinion*
je pense trois	*three I think*
les deux	*both*

1er passant	Dans une famille idéale?
Jane	Oui.
1er passant	Ha ha ha (*he laughs*) . . . Disons un à deux.
Jane	Garçons ou filles?

1er passant	Aucune importance.
Jane	Vous avez des enfants?
1er passant	Oui.
Jane	Combien?
1er passant	Deux.
Jane	Des garçons ou des filles?
1er passant	Deux filles.

aucune importance *it's of no importance, it doesn't matter*

2ème passante	Moi, j'en ai trois. Je pense que c'est la famille idéale.
Jane	Et vous avez des garçons ou des filles?
2ème passante	J'ai deux filles et un garçon.
Jane	Selon vous, il y a combien d'enfants dans une famille idéale?
3ème passante	Oh, je pense trois. Mais la moyenne nationale est de deux virgule un ou un truc comme ça.
Jane	Des garçons ou des filles?
3ème passante	Mélangés!

j'en ai trois	*I have three (of them)*
deux virgule un	*two point one*
un truc comme ça	*something like that*

Quickie What's the French for 'three girls'; 'two boys'?

2 Then we asked if marriage was important for having a family. Attitudes are now much more relaxed; three out of five said marriage was not absolutely necessary.

Jane	Et vous avez des enfants?
3ème passante	Non, non! Moi, je suis étudiante. Je suis ...
Jane	Est-ce que le mariage est important pour avoir une famille?
3ème passante	Oui, je pense, effectivement, que c'est important.
Jane	Est-ce que le mariage est important pour avoir une famille?
2ème passante	Non, je pense pas.
3ème passant	Oh oui, indispensable.
1er passant	Non, pas du tout.
1ère passante	Non. Je ne pense pas.

je (ne) pense pas *I don't think so*

Quickie Apart from the pronunciation, what's the difference between the French and English words for 'marriage'?

TV 3 And, finally, what sort of a place does a family need to live in? Most French city-dwellers live in flats.

Jane Et l'habitation idéale pour une famille, c'est quoi?

1ère passante	C'est une grande maison.
1er passant	C'est certainement un appartement.
3ème passante	Peut-être un grand appartement, mais une maison, c'est agréable également.
3ème passant	Oh, je penserais comme beaucoup de Français que c'est une maison individuelle. Oui, bien sûr.

c'est quoi?	*what is it?*
peut-être	*perhaps*
je penserais	*I should think*

Quickies

1 What are the French words for 'a house' and 'a flat'?
2 What did the last man say was the wish of most French people?

Mots-clés

l'épicerie (f)	grocer's
le marché	market
le gramme	gram
le kilo	kilogram
le litre	litre
la livre	pound
le beurre	butter
le fromage	cheese
le lait	milk
le vin	wine
la cerise	cherry
le concombre	cucumber
la fraise	strawberry
le fruit	fruit
la pêche	peach
la pomme	apple
la boîte	box
le paquet	packet
le sac	bag
certainement	certainly
peut-être	perhaps
l'enfant (m/f)	child
la fille	girl/daughter
le garçon	boy
l'appartement (m)	flat
la maison	house

Other useful words:

l'ami(e) (m/f)	friend
la femme	wife/woman
le fils	son
le frère	brother
habiter	to live in
le mari	husband
marié(e)	married
la soeur	sister

En bref

1 To ask 'how much is/are . . .?':

c'est combien	les oeufs? la crème? le vin?

2 10F *a* kilo, *a* box, *a* bottle, etc:

deux francs **le** kilo	2 francs a kilo
huit francs **la** douzaine	8 francs a dozen
quatre francs **les** six	4 francs for six
c'est combien, **la** bouteille?	how much is it a bottle?

3 For things bought as individual items:

c'est combien (**la**) **pièce**?	how much are they each?
cinq francs (**la**) **pièce**	five francs each

4 Quantities

cinq pommes

but

un kilo une livre une bouteille une douzaine un peu beaucoup	**de . . .**

To ask for 'a piece':

un morceau de	fromage tarte beurre

5 The words *du, de la, de l'* and *des* are used in front of nouns where English has 'some . . .', 'any . . .' or nothing at all.

Singular:

vous avez	**du** lait? **de la** crème?		have you got *any*	milk? cream?	
je voudrais	**du** lait **de la** crème		I'd like *some*	milk cream	
il y a	**du** lait **de la** crème	sur la table	there's	milk cream	on the table

Plural:

je voudrais **des** cerises	I'd like *some* cherries
vous avez **des** oeufs?	have you got *any* eggs?
il y a **des** cendriers sur la table	there are ashtrays on the table

de +	le = **du**	
	la = **de la**	
	l' = **de l'**	
	les = **des**	

6 Nouns introduced by *du*, *des* etc can be replaced by *en*:

vous **en** avez?	have you got any?
vous **en** voulez?	do you want some?
combien **en** voulez-vous?	how many do you want?

7 To ask what something is:
qu'est-ce que c'est?
c'est du fromage?
c'est un cendrier?

Learn a verb (or part of one)

avoir	to have
j'ai	I have
vous avez	you have

En plus

1 **'Some', 'any'**
This is an example of a case where English is much more complicated than French.

Sometimes we use 'some':
I'd like some butter, please.
Sometimes we use 'any':
have you got any milk?
Sometimes we can use either:
do you want some/any cream?
Sometimes we use nothing at all:
in a fruit salad there are peaches, apples and pears
I have friends in Grenoble

In all these cases the French use simply *du*, *de la*, *de l'* or *des*.

So the English sentences above are, in French:
je voudrais **du** beurre, s'il vous plaît
vous avez **du** lait?
vous voulez **de la** crème?
dans une salade de fruits il y a **des** pêches, **des** pommes et **des** poires
j'ai **des** amis à Grenoble

Here are some more examples:

is that cheese over there?	c'est **du** fromage là-bas?
I think it's cheese	je pense que c'est **du** fromage
have you any cheese?	avez-vous **du** fromage?
cheese, please	**du** fromage, s'il vous plait
I'd like some cheese	je voudrais **du** fromage

A point to keep an eye on is that *du, de la, des* are also the equivalent of 'of the':

the price	of the wine	le prix	du vin
	of the cream		de la crème
	of the apples		des pommes

2 There are some *faux amis* or 'false friends' in this chapter – that is, French words that look like English ones but don't mean the same thing. Most of the time you can assume that a French word that looks like an English one does in fact mean what it looks like:
national, plan, brochure, avenue, tomate, concombre

But every now and then this is not so, and it is worth learning the exceptions as they crop up. Here's one to start with:
une pièce has several meanings but rarely means 'piece' in the sense of 'bit'.

une pièce (de théâtre)	a play
l'appartement a trois pièces	the flat has three rooms
une pièce de 5F	a 5F coin
ananas, 10F pièce	pineapples, 10F each

The important thing in the last one is to realise that it is not 10F for a piece of pineapple! A piece (of cheese, pineapple, cake etc) is *un morceau*.

3 **More pronunciation points**

1 The letter 'c' when followed by a vowel is pronounced the same two ways in French as it is in English: cat, cow, cup (hard c); cellar, circus (soft c); *carte, concombre*; *cerise, citron*. Occasionally, a 'c' that needs to be soft appears in front of 'a', 'o' or 'u'. In this case, a small mark (called a cedilla) is attached to the bottom of the 'c' to show that it is still to be pronounced as 's'. Hence *garçon, français*. This also accounts for the cedilla on *ça* (which is short for *cela*).

2 *-ill* in a French word is not pronounced 'ill'. It is pronounced like the 'ee' in 'tree' with a soft 'y' on the end. Words like *fille* and *famille* are not pronounced 'feel' and 'fameel', but 'fee-y' and 'famee-y'. Just to make life difficult, the commonest exception is the word *ville* which is pronounced 'veel'.

4 *Une épicerie* was originally a place that sold *épices* – spices; then it became the general grocery shop we know today. The word illustrates something that can be useful to learners. Words that begin with *é* in French sometimes have an equivalent or near equivalent in English

beginning with 's': *épice* gives 'spice'. You can easily guess *éponge* and perhaps *étudiant* and *école*, but can you get *écureil* and *épagueul*?

5 **Numbers 0–69**

Learning the French numbers up to a million is not as difficult as it may seem; there are only twenty-four different words, and many of them are related to each other. You will find a complete list on p311–312. Here are the first sixty-nine.

The words for the first sixteen numbers are the main problem as they are all different:

zéro	nought	neuf	nine
un/une	one	dix	ten
deux	two	onze	eleven
trois	three	douze	twelve
quatre	four	treize	thirteen
cinq	five	quatorze	fourteen
six	six	quinze	fifteen
sept	seven	seize	sixteen
huit	eight		

The next three are compounds of ten + seven, etc:

dix-sept	seventeen
dix-huit	eighteen
dix-neuf	nineteen

The words for twenty, thirty, etc up to sixty are:

vingt	twenty	cinquante	fifty
trente	thirty	soixante	sixty
quarante	forty		

Twenty-one, thirty-one, forty-one, etc are:
vingt et un/une, trente et un/une, quarante et un/une, etc.

The other numbers are organised in the same way as the English ones:

vingt-deux	twenty-two	quarante-cinq	forty-five
trente-six	thirty-six	soixante-sept	sixty-seven

6 While *garçon* means 'boy' and *fille* means 'girl', both words have extra meanings. *Fille* also means 'daughter'. The word for 'son', however, is *fils* – pronounced 'feece'.

Garçon is also the word for 'waiter' and one would say: *Je suis garçon de café*. In the 1890s cafés might have rung with the sound of customers shouting *Garçon!* but today you'd usually say *Monsieur* to attract his attention. For a waitress you say *Madame* or *Mademoiselle* as you think fit. Or just look expectant and say *S'il vous plaît*.

A propos

In vino veritas

France, with Italy, is the world's largest producer of wine. It makes *vin rouge, vin blanc* and *vin rosé* and some regional wines with less obvious titles like *vin jaune* and *vin gris*. Most of them are still wines, except some called *vins mousseux* and, of course, the most famous wine of them all, *champagne*.

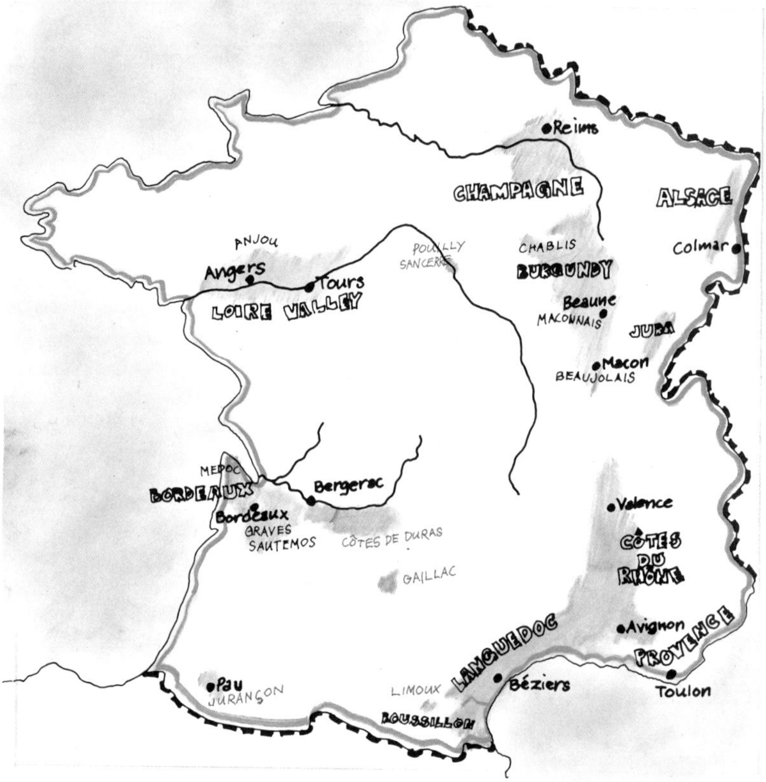

The great wines are all either red or white and can be enormously expensive. At the other end of the price and quality range is *vin ordinaire*. It is a blend of wines that can come from anywhere in France but often from the big wine-growing areas of the south round Montpellier. Above *vin ordinaire* come three main categories that are controlled by government regulations.

Vin de Pays

These have a minimum alcohol content of 8.5% though, in fact, you will find few, if any, below 9% (indicated on the bottle by 9°). They are supposed to be minor local wines but can be blended to a maximum of one third with wines from anywhere so their local character can sometimes be rather obscured.

VDQS – Vins Délimités de Qualitité Supérieure
These are better quality wines of which the area of origin and methods of production are controlled.

AC – Appellation d'Origine Contrôlée
These are subject to a government order which defines the area in which they are grown, the type of grapes used, the maximum permitted production, the minimum alcohol content and the methods of cultivation and production. Among these there are, of course, the very great (and very expensive) wines but there are also plenty to be found at reasonable prices (much less than what you pay for a *vin ordinaire* in Britain) so it is worth experimenting. You will find them in *épiceries* and many other food shops. Big supermarkets often have a good range. There are wine shops, of course, but off-licences, in the British sense, do not exist, so remember to buy your wine before the shops close.

Markets
Markets of all sorts – open air and covered – are very common in France. Big towns may have several permanent markets, small towns and villages will have one on at least one day a week. It is always worth finding out from the *Syndicat d'Initiative* when they are held as they can be vast and colourful affairs. They are mainly for the sale of food of all sorts, including local vegetables, fruit and cheese brought in by farmers and smallholders from the surrounding countryside. Sometimes this can amount to one person selling a few cheeses or a couple of chickens. Often there are also stalls of clothes, pottery, household utensils, etc. Markets have the advantage for foreigners that all goods on sale must, by law, be marked with the price. If you go early in the day you may well see the local *agent* or *gendarme* looking round to check that this is being done. On the other hand, French handwritten prices are not always easy to decipher so you will still need to be able to ask.

Food glorious food
Asperges – asparagus. In Britain this is a rather expensive dish but it is more commonly eaten in France. Piles of *bottes d'asperges* – bundles of asparagus – will be found in the markets from early summer. The best are said to come from the islands off France's west coast, the île d'Oléron and the île de Ré.
Fromage de chèvre – goat's cheese – is common in France, though it has been slow to catch on in Britain. It has a delicious flavour, quite distinct from other types of cheese. It is at its best in the summer when the grass is lush. Making goat's cheese incidentally, has become one of

the most popular forms of alternative lifestyle for city-dwellers who want to take up the rural life in the French countryside. It's becoming quite common to see signs pointing down tracks and saying *fromage de chèvre*.

The great decimal trap

This can be highly dangerous. The woman quoting the statistic about average family size says: 'Deux virgule un'. *Virgule* means 'comma' and therefore this figure is written: 2,1. If you have a figure that includes three decimals then it will be written: 2,135. This looks like two thousand one hundred and thirty-five when it is in fact only two point one three five!

To make matters worse, until quite recently, the way of indicating thousands in French was to use a full stop so that two thousand one hundred and thirty-five was written 2.135. Most people still write it that way. The official method now used internationally is to leave a gap: 2 135. To recapitulate: in written French figures a comma indicates a decimal point and a full stop or a gap indicates thousands.

Bon courage

1 Fill in the gaps in this conversation in a shop with *du*, *de la*, *de l'*, *des* or just plain *de*.

Cliente Bonjour, monsieur.
Epicier Bonjour, madame. Qu'est-ce que vous désirez?
Cliente Je voudrais .... oeufs, ... vin ordinaire et un litre .... lait, s'il vous plaît.
Epicier Bon, vous voulez combien .... oeufs, madame?
Cliente Une douzaine et aussi .... crème, oui, un petit pot .... crème.
Epicier Et avec ça, madame?
Cliente Vous avez .... fromage .... chèvre?
Epicier Oui. Vous en voulez combien?
Cliente Oh, 200 grammes et un peu .... gruyère aussi.
Epicier Voilà.
Cliente Vous avez .... fruits?

Epicier	Oui, ... pêches, ... pommes, ... poires?
Cliente	Donnez-moi un kilo .... poires, s'il vous plaît.
Epicier	Très bien, madame. Ça fait trente-cinq francs.

2 Below is a list of the things you want. List them under the places you'd go to get them: *épicerie*, *café*, *marchand de fruits et légumes*, *boulangerie*. Add *du*, *de la*, *des* or *un*, *une*, etc as appropriate. Some items can come under more than one heading.

pêches	cerises	panaché	beurre
poireaux	croissants	crème (f)	sandwichs
lait	fromage	petit kir	bananes
flûte	crème (m)	oeufs	baguette

3 What is the French for:
5, 11, 13, 15
38, 55, 63
2F45, 16F25, 44F

4 You are stocking up for a party; here is your shopping list. Ask the *épicier* for all these items:

fifteen bottles of beer
10 bottles of red wine
3 kilos of peaches
2 packets of butter
some cheese – a piece of gruyère
And you'll have to ask the *boulanger* for:
10 baguettes

5 The quantities have got mixed up; can you sort them out? Some quantities will fit with more than one item.

un litre		cerises
une plaquette	de	poireaux
une botte	*or*	beurre
une bouteille	d'	oeufs
une livre		lait
une douzaine		vin rouge

6 Ask the shopkeeper if he has got:
any milk, an ashtray, some bread, some apples, any coffee, some cream, some lemonade

7 You want to buy a few things for a picnic. A market is a good place to see what is available. On the dairy stall there is a pile of odd-looking objects.

You	*Point at them and ask the stallholder if that's cheese.*
Marchand	Mais oui, monsieur. C'est du fromage de chèvre. C'est très bon.

You *Say you'd like one goat's cheese and a litre of milk, please.*
Marchand Très bien, et avec ça?
You *A packet of butter, please.*
Marchand Voilà. C'est tout?
You *Yes, that's all, thanks. How much does it come to?*
Marchand Trois et trois, six . . . et huit. Quatorze francs, monsieur.

Now you want some fruit at the next stall.

You *Ask if he has any apples.*
Marchand Oui, monsieur. Vous en voulez combien?
You *Ask for a kilo, please.*
Marchand Et avec ça, monsieur?
You *You'd like a pound of cherries.*
Marchand Comme ceci, monsieur?
You *Say yes, that's fine.*
Marchand Ça sera tout?
You *Say yes, thank you, that's all.*
Marchand Voilà. Ça fait treize francs cinquante.
You *Here's fifteen francs.*
Marchand Quatorze et quinze. Merci et bonne journée!
You *Good bye.*

8 You are exchanging information with the next family on your campsite. Answer your neighbour's questions.

Voisine Vous avez des enfants?
You *Say either no* or *you are not married* or *say what children you have. Ask if she has any children.*
Voisine Oui, deux filles et un garçon.
You *Ask where she is from.*
Voisine De Quimper, en Bretagne. Et vous?
You *Say where you come from.*

9 Like *épicerie*, many shop names end in *-erie*. What do you suppose are the most obvious things to be made or sold in:
une fromagerie, une laiterie, une croissanterie, une crêperie, une poissonnerie, une friterie, une bijouterie?
And what is sold in *une boucherie? Des bouchers?*

Documentaire

La Villeneuve – une ville dans la ville
With the rapid expansion of Grenoble in the 1960s, housing became a major problem. The Council decided to build a huge estate on a disused airfield to the south of the town. La Villeneuve was to be an estate with a difference – a self-contained community with all the necessary facilities, and more besides: the first health centre in France, experimental schools, plentiful leisure facilities, decentralised local administration of social and other services.

The project was a bold one in its size, conception and design. The first inhabitants shared in the optimism of the scheme: all social classes lived side by side and used the same facilities. In some ways a social and architectural experiment, how successful is la Villeneuve today?

La Villeneuve

La Villeneuve est un quartier moderne au sud de Grenoble. C'est une expérience, du point de vue de l'architecture et du point de vue social. A l'origine, la Villeneuve, c'est une nouvelle formule, une nouvelle façon de vivre pour une communauté très mixte. En effet, les 9.000 personnes qui habitent dans ce grand ensemble d'appartements viennent de toutes les couches sociales: immigrés, ouvriers, classes moyennes et professions libérales.

Il y a beaucoup d'équipements à la Villeneuve qui sont là pour animer la vie du quartier: un parc, une piscine, des gymnases, un centre médical, un marché, des magasins et une Maison de Quartier. Les personnes âgées ont aussi leurs équipements – des résidences et des clubs. Pour les enfants, il y a des écoles. Il y en a dix. Ce sont des écoles expérimentales. Beaucoup de projets y sont organisés qui n'existent pas dans les écoles traditionnelles françaises.

La Villeneuve – un succès ou un échec? Les opinions sont différentes. Pour Monsieur et Madame Roume, l'expérience est positive. Pour Martine Perrichon, qui ne travaille pas, la Villeneuve, 'c'est très sale' et 'il y a une trop grosse concentration de personnes'. Marcel, son mari, n'est pas d'accord. Pour lui, 'c'est un quartier sans voitures', sans danger pour les enfants, où 'il y a beaucoup de facilités pour la vie quotidienne qu'on ne connaît pas ailleurs'.

La Villeneuve est un peu une ville dans la ville. C'est une expérience qui reste unique en France.

ce grand ensemble d'appartements	*this big housing development*
les couches sociales	*social classes*
beaucoup d'équipements	*a lot of facilities*
il y en a dix	*there are ten of them*
qu'on ne connaît pas ailleurs	*which don't exist elsewhere*
est un peu	*is a little like*

Qu'est-ce que vous avez comme . . . ?

Saying precisely what you want: flavours, sizes, prices, hotel rooms
Talking about jobs
Saying if you speak other languages and how well

TV 1 Two customers are giving their order in Le Glacier Belle Hélène, a *café-restaurant* which specialises in ice creams.

Claude (*signalling to waitress*) Madame, s'il vous plaît.
Serveuse Bonjour, monsieur-dame. Vous désirez?
Claude Vous faites des sandwichs?
Serveuse Oui, monsieur.
Claude Qu'est-ce que vous avez comme sandwichs?
Serveuse Jambon, fromage, pâté, saucisson . . .
Claude Un sandwich au jambon, s'il vous plaît.
Serveuse Oui.
Claude Et puis, un thé au citron.
Serveuse Oui. Avec du beurre, le sandwich?
Claude S'il vous plaît.
Serveuse Oui. Et pour madame?
Josette Une glace, s'il vous plaît. Qu'est-ce que vous avez comme parfums?
Serveuse Vanille, fraise, chocolat, café, pistache.
Josette Une glace à la fraise, s'il vous plaît.
Serveuse Oui, madame. Et comme boisson?
Josette De l'eau . . . une carafe d'eau.
Serveuse Oui, bien sûr.

vous faites des sandwichs?	*do you do sandwiches?*
et comme boisson?	*and anything to drink?*

To ask what *sorts* of things are available:

qu'est-ce que vous avez comme	glaces? sandwichs? boisson?

To describe by flavour, fillings, ingredients, etc:

un sandwich	**au**	jambon/fromage/pâté/saucisson
un thé	**au**	citron
une glace	**au**	chocolat/café
	à la	vanille/fraise/pistache

à combines with *le* and *les* (but not with *la* and *l'*):

à + le → **au**
à + les → **aux**

Quickies 1 Which of these are sandwich fillings and which are ice cream flavours?
jambon, fraise, pistache, saucisson, fromage

2 If the waiter said *Et comme boisson?*, would you reply:
Un sandwich, s'il vous plaît or *Un thé, s'il vous plaît?*

3 Can you remember the phrase: 'What sort of . . . have you got?'?

Radio 2 Marie-Pierre is at the grocer's and has to choose between two sorts of milk and various flavours of yoghurt.

Epicière Bonjour, madame.
Marie-Pierre Bonjour. Je voudrais six oeufs, s'il vous plaît.
Epicière Oui (*she fetches the eggs*). Voilà. Avec ça?
Marie-Pierre Un litre de lait.
Epicière Entier ou demi-écrémé?
Marie-Pierre Demi-écrémé.
Epicière Voilà.
Marie-Pierre Et quatre yaourts.
Epicière Des yaourts à la fraise, au chocolat, nature?
Marie-Pierre Nature.
Epicière Oui, voilà. Avec ça, madame?
Marie-Pierre Ce sera tout. C'est combien?
Epicière Oui, je vais vous faire la note, madame (*she totals it up on the till*). Alors, quinze francs quatre-vingt-dix, s'il vous plaît.

Marie-Pierre Voilà (*giving her 16F*).

Epicière Je vous remercie. (*counting out the change*) Alors, quinze quatre-vingt-dix et voilà seize. Merci, madame.

Marie-Pierre Merci. Au revoir, madame.

Epicière Au revoir, madame. Merci.

---

je vais vous faire la note *I'll just add it up for you*

Quickies

1 How much milk did Marie-Pierre buy?
2 What sort of yoghurts were available?

Radio 3 In Guérande in Brittany, Pierrick is buying stamps. He gets them from the *bureau de tabac* inside a café.

Pierrick Bonjour, madame.

Buraliste Bonjour, monsieur.

Pierrick Je voudrais quatre timbres à deux francs, s'il vous plaît.

Buraliste Quatre à deux francs, oui. Voilà, monsieur.

Pierrick Et puis, trois timbres à zéro franc cinquante.

Dans un café-tabac

Buraliste Oui, très bien. Voilà, monsieur, trois timbres à zéro franc cinquante.
Pierrick C'est combien, s'il vous plaît?
Buraliste Neuf francs cinquante, s'il vous plaît, monsieur. (*giving change*) Voilà, monsieur.
Pierrick Merci. Au revoir, madame.
Buraliste Au revoir, monsieur.

> To describe things by price:
>
> un timbre à deux francs

Quickie Ask for two 2f and two 0.50f stamps as in the picture above.

TV **4** Every tourist ends up needing postcards. Barbara Michel also needs stamps for Switzerland and some matches.

Buraliste Bonjour, madame.
Barbara Bonjour, monsieur. (*puts cards on counter*) Voilà. Six cartes postales. Vous avez des timbres pour la Suisse, s'il vous plaît?
Buraliste Des timbres à deux francs. Combien en voulez-vous, madame?
Barbara Quatre. Et deux timbres à un soixante, s'il vous plaît.
Buraliste Oui, voici.
Barbara Merci. Ah oui . . . Vous avez une boîte d'allumettes?
Buraliste Une grande ou une petite?
Barbara Une grande boîte.
Buraliste Voici. (*counting up*) Un franc, quatre timbres à deux francs, huit

francs, deux timbres à un soixante, onze francs vingt, douze francs vingt, vingt-deux francs quarante.

Barbara Voilà, monsieur.
Buraliste Merci, madame.
Barbara Merci. Au revoir.
Buraliste Au revoir, madame. Merci.

Words such as *grand* and *petit* are affected by the gender of what they are describing:

masculine	feminine
petit grand	petite grande
un petit déjeuner un grand sac	**une** petite boîte **une** grande glace

Listen for the changes in pronunciation.

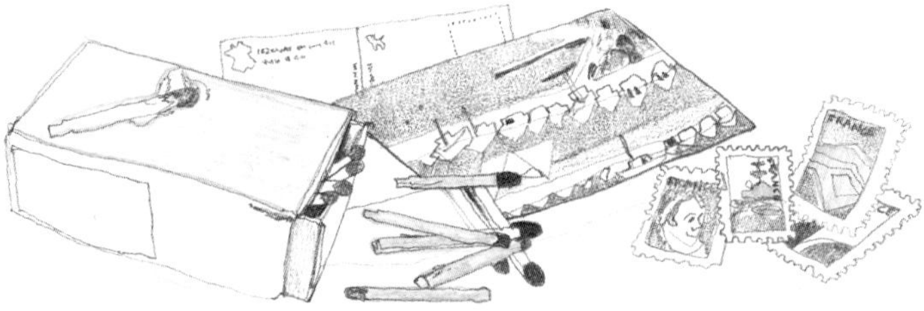

Quickies

1 Name the things in the picture.
2 What is the French name for the country Barbara wanted the stamps for?

TV

5 A couple arrive at the Hôtel Porte de France in Grenoble needing a room for the night.

Bernard Bonjour, monsieur.
Michèle Bonjour, monsieur.
Hôtelier M'sieur-dame, bonjour.
Bernard Vous avez une chambre pour deux personnes?
Hôtelier Oui. Pour combien de nuits?
Bernard C'est pour une nuit. Il y a une salle de bains?
Hôtelier Oui, monsieur. Bain et WC.
Michèle Et c'est combien pour la nuit?
Hôtelier Cent cinquante-cinq francs plus quinze francs le petit déjeuner.

Michèle Bon. C'est d'accord.
Hôtelier Oui. C'est à quel nom?
Michèle Dubost. D.U.B.O.S.T.
Hôtelier Oui. Voici la clef. Avez-vous des bagages?
Bernard Oui, ils sont dans la voiture. Il y a un parking?
Hôtelier Oui, juste derrière l'hôtel.
Bernard Merci.
Hôtelier Je vous en prie, monsieur.

c'est à quel nom	*what name is it?*
ils sont	*they are*

Quickies

1 Where is the car park?
2 What does *ils* stand for in *ils sont dans la voiture*?

Radio 6 Jean is in a hotel in Bourg-en-Bresse wanting a room for the night just for himself.

Patronne Bonjour, monsieur.
Jean Bonjour, madame. Est-ce que vous avez une chambre, s'il vous plaît?
Patronne Oui, monsieur. Pour combien de personnes?
Jean Pour une seule personne.
Patronne (*checking in register*) Oui, c'est possible, monsieur. Pour une seule nuit?
Jean Oui, madame. Pour ce soir.
Patronne Oui, monsieur. Nous avons des chambres avec salle de bains et WC privés.
Jean Vous n'avez pas de chambres avec cabinet de toilette?
Patronne Non, nos chambres sont toutes identiques avec salle de bains et WC privés.
Jean C'est à quel prix, s'il vous plaît?
Patronne Cent vingt francs pour une personne.
Jean Est-ce que le petit déjeuner est compris?
Patronne Non, le petit déjeuner est à part. Il fait quinze francs.
Jean Bon. Je vais prendre la chambre à cent vingt francs.
Patronne Oui. C'est à quel nom, monsieur?
Jean Fournier.
Patronne (*making a note*) Oui.
Jean Jean.
Patronne Merci. Voici votre clef.
Jean Merci, madame.
Patronne C'est au rez-de-chaussée, au fond du couloir, à droite.
Jean Merci, madame.

est-ce que	*used to introduce a question (see En plus)*
c'est à quel prix?	*what's the price?*
à part	*separate*

To ask for a hotel room:
vous avez une chambre?

To describe your requirements:

for how many people	**pour une personne/deux personnes**
for how long	**pour une nuit/deux nuits**
with what amenities	**avec salle de bains/douche**

To ask if breakfast/service is included:

le petit déjeuner le service	**est compris?**

Quickies 1 Did his room have a bathroom as well?
2 Was breakfast included in the price of the room?

Radio 7 In a small village, Jean pulls up at a *boulangerie-pâtisserie*. He asks what tarts they've got.

Boulangère Bonjour, monsieur.
Jean Bonjour, madame.
Boulangère Monsieur?
Jean Qu'est-ce que vous avez comme tartes?
Boulangère Alors, j'ai des tartes aux fruits, donc à la pomme, tartes panachées abricot-poire, ou alors à la crème. C'est pour combien de personnes?
Jean C'est pour quatre personnes.
Boulangère Quatre personnes.
Jean Elles font combien, s'il vous plaît?
Boulangère Onze francs cinquante, la tarte à la crème. La tarte aux pommes à vingt francs.
Jean Je vais prendre la tarte à la crème à onze francs cinquante.
Boulangère Oui. (*taking it out of window display*) C'est pour tout de suite, monsieur?
Jean C'est pour tout de suite, madame.
Boulangère Voilà. Onze francs cinquante, monsieur.
Jean Voici. Dix, onze, onze cinquante.
Boulangère Merci, monsieur.
Jean Au revoir, madame.
Boulangère Au revoir, monsieur. Bonne route!

elles font combien?	*how much do they cost?*
je vais prendre ...	*I'll take ...*
bonne route!	*have a good journey!*

'They' is *elles* or *ils* depending on the gender of the noun being replaced:

elles (= les tartes) font combien?
ils (= les bagages) sont dans la voiture.

Quickies 1 What sorts of tarts are there?
2 How much does the custard tart cost?

Radio 8 Jean now goes to the *boucherie-charcuterie* in the same village.

Charcutier Bonjour, monsieur.
Jean Bonjour, monsieur.

Charcutier Monsieur, vous désirez?
Jean Vous avez du pâté?
Charcutier Oui, j'ai du pâté de campagne et du pâté croûte.
Jean Ils font combien, s'il vous plaît?
Charcutier Le pâté de campagne est à quarante francs le kilo et le pâté croûte cinquante.
Jean Bon, donnez-moi du pâté croûte.
Charcutier Oui. Combien de tranches, monsieur?
Jean Deux tranches, s'il vous plaît.
Charcutier Oui. Les tranches, vous les voulez épaisses ou fines?
Jean Moyennes, s'il vous plaît.
Charcutier (*suggesting a portion*) Comme ceci?
Jean Ça va.
Charcutier (*weighing them*) Douze francs. Ce sera tout, monsieur?
Jean Les saucisses là, ce sont des chipolatas?
Charcutier Oui, des chipolatas. Vous en voulez combien?
Jean Donnez-m'en six, s'il vous plaît.
Charcutier Oui. (*weighing them*) Cinq francs.
Jean Combien le tout?
Charcutier Dix-sept francs, s'il vous plaît, monsieur.
Jean Dix, quinze, et dix-sept.
Charcutier Merci beaucoup, monsieur.
Jean Au revoir, monsieur.
Charcutier Au revoir, monsieur. Merci. Bonne journée!

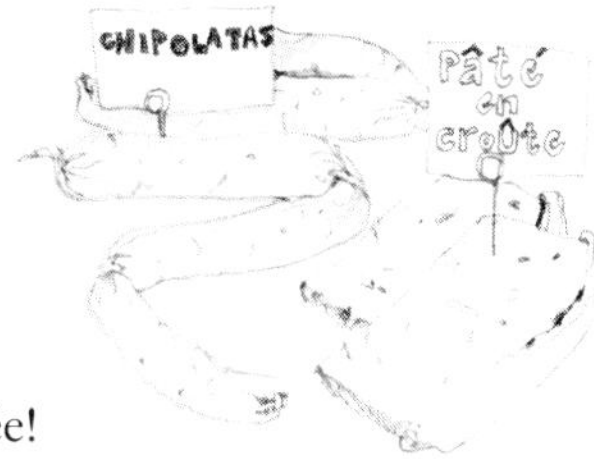

pâté croûte	*pâté in a pastry case, loaf-shaped.*
ce sont . . .	*they're . . .*
combien le tout?	*how much altogether?*

Words describing nouns in the plural add 's' to the singular:

singular	plural
petit fine	petits fines
un petit garçon une tranche fine	**deux** petits garçons **des** tranches fines

Quickies 1 What two types of pâté was Jean offered?
2 What else did he buy?

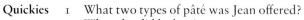

Rencontres

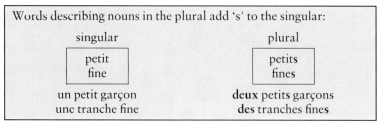

TV 1 Jane asked people in Grenoble what their job was and whether they spoke a language other than French.

Jane Monsieur, quel est votre métier?
1er passant Je suis représentant.
Jane Et est-ce que vous parlez d'autres langues?
1er passant Je parle l'italien et un peu d'anglais, enfin, très, très peu d'anglais.
Jane Et l'italien, vous le parlez comment?
1er passant Assez couramment.

To ask someone what their job is:
Quel est votre métier?

To say what you do:

	réprésentant(e)
je suis	étudiant(e)
	astronaute

Jane Quel est votre métier, mademoiselle?
1ère passante Etudiante.
Jane Et vous parlez d'autres langues que le français?
1ère passante Italien.
Jane L'italien? Vous le parlez bien?
1ère passante Quand je suis en Italie, oui. Quand je suis en France, non.
2ème passante Moi, je suis gemmologiste.
Jane Et vous parlez d'autres langues, mis à part le français?
2ème passante Français, anglais.
Jane Et vous parlez l'angl . . .
2ème passante L'espagnol, l'espagnol!
Jane L'espagnol aussi. Et vous parlez l'anglais comment?
2ème passante Do you want to know?

vous le parlez comment?	*how well do you speak it?*
d'autres langues que . . .	*languages other than . . .*
vous le parlez bien?	*do you speak it well?*
mis à part	*apart from*

> To ask if someone speaks a language:
>
> **vous parlez** | (l') anglais? / (le) français? / (l') espagnol?
>
> To say you speak a language:
> **je parle** (le) français, etc.

Quickies

1 Which of the people interviewed speaks very little English?
2 Translate the following: *couramment, un peu, très peu, pas du tout*
3 What's the French for the following languages: English, French, Spanish, Italian?

TV 2 The next two people Jane asked were another student and a salesman.

3ème passante Etudiante.
Jane Et vous parlez d'autres langues, mis à part le français?
3ème passante Oui, l'anglais, l'allemand.
Jane Vous les parlez comment? Couramment?
3ème passante Non, pas couramment.
Jane Monsieur, quel est votre métier?
2ème passant Ah, commercial dans une société.
Jane Et est-ce que vous parlez d'autres langues?
2ème passant Oui, l'anglais.
Jane Vous le parlez comment?
2ème passant Comme on peut le parler à l'école.

vous les parlez comment?	*how well do you speak them?*
comme on peut le parler	*as one speaks it*
commercial (= agent commercial)	*sales rep*

TV 3 Finally, Jane asked people how important they thought it was to speak another language.

Jane Monsieur, vous parlez d'autres langues?
Agent de police Non, hélas!
Jane Et vous pensez que c'est important de parler d'autres langues?
Agent de police Oui, je pense, oui, que c'est pratiquement indispensable.
Jane Et vous pensez que c'est important de parler d'autres langues?
3ème passante Oui, bien sûr . . .
2ème passant Oui, bien sûr. Et puis de plus en plus, d'ailleurs.
1er passant Disons que ça facilite, oui, quand on part en vacances c'est très, très avantageux de pouvoir parler plusieurs langues.

de plus en plus	*more and more*
quand on part en vacances	*when one goes on holiday*

Quickie 'On holiday' – what's that in French?

Mots-clés

la boisson	drink	le parking	car park
le chocolat	chocolate	le petit déjeuner	breakfast
le citron	lemon	privé	private
l'eau (f)	water	la salle de bains	bathroom
la fraise	strawberry	les WC (m)	lavatory
la glace	ice cream	l'école (f)	school
le jambon	ham	le métier	job
le parfum	flavour	l'espagnol (m)	Spanish
la saucisse	sausage	l'italien (m)	Italian
le saucisson	salami	parler	to speak
la tarte	tart	le pays	country
le thé	tea	l'allumette (f)	match
le yaourt	yoghurt	la carte postale	postcard
les bagages (m)	luggage	le timbre	stamp
la chambre	(bed)room	au fond	at the end
la clé (*or* clef)	key	ce (m)	this/that
la douche	shower	cette (f)	this/that
le lavabo	washbasin	compris	included
le lit	bed	derrière	behind
le nom	name		
la nuit	night		

En bref

1 Adjectives

Words used for describing nouns (called 'adjectives') change at the end according to:

1 whether the noun is masculine or feminine:

un petit village   **une petite** ville

Adding an 'e' changes the pronunciation

NB if the masculine form already ends in *-e*, don't add another.

un vin rouge   une tomate rouge

2 whether the noun is singular or plural:

un petit garçon   **deux petits** garçons

une petite fille   **trois petites** filles

Adding an 's' does not change the pronunciation.

NB if the masculine form already ends in *-s*, don't add another.

un vin français — des vins français

Some adjectives change in other ways (see p309–310). Here's an important example to get your teeth into.

	Masc	Fem
this/that	**ce** saucisson	**cette** saucisse
these/those	**ces** saucissons	**ces** saucisses

NB There is a special masculine singular form if the noun starts with a vowel or silent h:
cet ananas, **cet** hôtel.

2 Position of adjectives

Most go after the noun:
une tranche **épaisse**
du vin **ordinaire**
des timbres **français**

A few common ones go in front of the noun
une **grande** boîte
un **petit** déjeuner

A small number change meaning depending on whether they are before or after:
NB un **grand** homme – a *great* man
un homme **grand** – a *tall* man

3 To describe things by price:
une chambre **à** 250F
une glace **à** 3F
un timbre **à** 1F60

4 To describe things by particular feature (flavour, filling, ingredients, etc) use *à*:
un sandwich **au** fromage
un canard **à l'**orange
une tarte **à la** crème
une tarte **aux** fruits

à + le → **au**
à + les → **aux**

5 For saying 'he/she/it/they', French does not distinguish between people and things

où est	Pierre? l'Hôtel de France?	**il** est là
où est	Elisabeth? la Tour Eiffel?	**elle** est à Paris
où sont	les enfants? les grands magasins?	**ils** sont en ville

où sont	Anne Marie et Brigitte? les clefs?	**elles** sont dans la chambre

6 To ask what sort of things are available:

qu'est-ce que vous avez comme	sandwichs? glaces?

7 To ask for a hotel room . . .:
vous avez une chambre . . .

. . . for one person/two people:
. . . pour une personne/deux personnes?
. . . for one/two nights:
. . . pour une nuit/deux nuits?
. . . with bath/shower:
. . . avec salle de bains/douche?

8 To ask if breakfast/service is included:

le petit déjeuner le service	**est compris?**

9 1 To ask someone if they speak a language:
vous parlez (l')anglais?
2 To say you speak a language:
je parle (le) français

Names of languages are preceded by *le* (or *l'*):
Le français n'est pas difficile
Gilles étudie l'italien à l'école
With *parler*, though, *le* is optional.

10 1 To ask someone what their job is:
quel est votre métier?
2 To say what your job is:

je suis	représentant étudiant boulanger	représentante étudiante boulangère

Learn a verb

faire – to do, make, amount to
le pâté **fait** combien?
vous **faites** des sandwichs?
les tartes **font** combien?

1 **Misleading sounds**

Certain things can make words sound different from what you might expect.

You will have noticed that in French, as in English, words can run into one another as they are spoken. In French this can mean that final letters in words are pronounced when they are usually silent.

In these sentences – vous avez des oranges?
– je voudrais deux oeufs

vous runs into *avez* and *des* into *oranges* and *deux* into *oeufs*. The 's' and the 'x' are pronounced as 'z'.

Similarly in *un oeuf* the 'n', usually nasal, is fully pronounced as the words run together.

There is an extra point about adjectives ending 't' (like *petit*). Usually there is a difference between *petit* ('t' not pronounced) and *petite* ('t' pronounced). But in a phrase like

un petit oeuf

the last two words run together and the final 't' in *petit* **is** pronounced (just as if it were *petite*).

The same applies if the word following *petit* starts with an 'h' (which is usually not pronounced). So in

un petit hôtel

the last two words run together and the final 't' of *petit* is again pronounced.

It all sounds very complicated and it is; the French themselves are by no means consistent about it, but you can't go wrong if you remember that the following groups of words always run together:

pronouns + verbs	*nous avons, ils arrivent*
articles + following word	*un hôtel, des oranges, aux oeufs*
adjectives + nouns	*un grand hôtel, un petit éléphant*
numbers + nouns	*deux hôtels, trois oranges.*

The French words for 'egg' and 'eggs' have a slightly curious pronunciation. In *oeufs* neither the 'f' nor the 's' is pronounced. In *un oeuf* the final 'f' is pronounced. And that gives us a chance to make the famous old joke.

I say, I say, I say! Why does a Frenchman have only one egg for breakfast?

Because one egg is *un oeuf*!

2 Notice how additional information about a noun usually comes before the noun in English and after it in French.

a red car – une voiture **rouge**

a ham sandwich – un sandwich **au jambon**
a two-franc stamp – un timbre **à deux francs**
a mixed apricot and pear tart – une tarte **panachée abricot-poire**
a bathroom – une salle **de bains**
baby shampoo – du shampooing **pour bébés**

In English 'apple pie' is made of apples but 'baby soap' is not made of babies. French makes this clear by using *à, de, pour*, etc following the noun.

This can lead to some interesting reversals in the initials of international organisations:

the United Nations Organisation – UNO
l'Organisation des Nations Unies – ONU
the North Atlantic Treaty Organisation – NATO
l'Organisation du Traité de l'Atlantique Nord – OTAN

3 Small is practical

'The dog had supper and then the dog went to sleep. Soon the dog was dreaming of when the dog was young.'

No-one speaks or writes like that. As soon as you have established that you are talking about 'the dog' you replace it with 'it' (or 'she' or 'he' if you like). These small words are called *pronouns* because they stand for a noun or noun phrase already mentioned and so avoid tedious and sometimes lengthy repetitions. They can stand for quite long phrases. 'That great smelly ginger tom from next door that's always fouling the sand pit' can be replaced by 'it'. And even 'Elizabeth the Second, by the Grace of God Queen of . . . Defender of the Faith, etc' can become just plain 'she'. 'They' stands for plurals ('the ginger tom and the tabby one from across the road that's just as bad').

The French equivalents of 'she', 'he', 'it' are quite simple, consisting of two words: *elle* standing for all feminine singular nouns (*la pharmacie* and also *Marie-Pierre*) and *il* standing for all masculine singular nouns (*le musée* and also *Jean Fournier*). In the plural ('they') these words add 's' in the usual way: *elles, ils*. If the word 'they' represents a mixed group of masculine and feminine nouns, the masculine *ils* is used (even grammar can be sexist!)

4 And what do you want to drink?

As was said in chapter 1, shopkeepers and waiters use a certain amount of ritual language in transactions which is not used in other situations:

vous désirez?
et pour madame?
et comme boisson?

If a French friend asks you if you would like a drink, he will not say *Et comme boisson?* This is strictly for waiters who have taken your order for food and now want to know what you are going to drink. Your French friend would say *Qu'est-ce que tu prends?*

5 **Esker and kesker**

The simplest way of asking a plain question when speaking, as was said in chapter 2, is to add an 'audible' question mark to your voice:

vous avez des oeufs?

There are two other ways. You can put *est-ce que* (pronounced 'esker') on the front of the statement:

est-ce que vous avez des oeufs?

Or you can reverse the order of the verb and pronoun:

avez-vous des oeufs?

The French, in speech at least, are using more and more the first and simplest way – and that is also the easiest for a foreigner to learn. You will hear the other two ways, however, so you need to be able to understand them.

Qu'est-ce que – an impossibly complicated-looking phrase – is really quite simple to say: 'kesker'. It means 'what . . .?'

qu'est-ce que vous avez comme parfums?
qu'est-ce qu'il y a à Grenoble?
qu'est-ce que c'est?

6 **Ici on parle français**

In French the words for languages need a *le, l'* in front of them:

j'apprends le français/l'allemand

However, when using *parler* this *le, l'* is optional:

je parle français; je parle le français

Notice that the names of languages are not written with a capital letter.

A propos

Stamps and tobacco

Almost as soon as tobacco appeared in France, the king, Louis XIII, tried unsuccessfully to ban it. The next king, Louis XIV, had a minister called Colbert who, recognising a good thing when he saw one, took over the business. It has been a nationalised industry ever since. Because tobacco was sold in state shops or kiosks it was convenient to add, as time went on, another state business – selling stamps. That is why you can now conveniently buy stamps at a tobacconist's – *le bureau de tabac*. You can get them at the post office – *le bureau de poste* or *la poste* – as well, of course, but tobacconists are more numerous.

Many tobacconists are found in cafés, the traditional *café-tabac* or *bar-tabac*. There is usually a small counter separated off from the main bar where you can buy stamps, matches, cigarettes, sweets, newspapers and magazines without any obligation to buy a drink as well. You can always tell a *bureau de tabac* by the red cigar-like sign outside.

Hotels

Quality and service vary in France as in Britain. In France, however, the hotels are strictly controlled by the official tourist bodies and graded into categories. A one-star hotel would usually be small and simple: rooms would usually have washbasins but there would not be many other facilities. At the other end of the scale, in four-star hotels, most rooms would have a private bathroom and a telephone. There would be public rooms of various sorts, lifts, night porters, room service, foreign exchange facilities, etc. Above them is a small group of very expensive and luxurious hotels marked L in the lists.

All *Syndicats d'Initiative* carry local lists where the facilities and the star rating of each hotel are given. Many will make enquiries and book rooms for you. Most French hotel rooms are double ones (*une chambre pour deux personnes*); they can be either twin-bedded (*une chambre à deux lits*) or with a double bed (*une chambre avec un grand lit*). As in Britain, hoteliers will put in an extra third bed if you want one. On the whole, in French hotels the cost of breakfast is not included in the price of the room and is charged quite separately. If you don't eat breakfast you don't have to pay for it. The price of the room and breakfast must, by law, be displayed in the room. In spite of our old joke above, French people do not usually have eggs for breakfast. *Le petit déjeuner* consists of coffee, tea or chocolate with croissants, bread, butter and jam. A cooked breakfast of the traditional British sort is not usually available.

La charcuterie

A *charcuterie* stocks all sorts of sausages, salamis, pâtés and cooked meats, in fact what you would expect to find in a good delicatessen. (The word comes from *chair cuite* which means 'cooked meat').

The charcutier frequently makes much of his own produce. In many areas he will make local specialities that are not found elsewhere. He usually takes considerable pride in the elegant presentation of his wares and so his window is often worth looking at for that reason alone. In supermarkets and other food stores there will almost always be a well-stocked *charcuterie* department.

Bon courage

1 You want each of these; what are you going to ask for? Decide which of *à, au, à la, à l', aux* fits the blank:
un sandwich .... pâté
un thé .... citron
un timbre 1F60
un yaourt .... abricot
un tarte 15F50
une glace .... fraise
une tarte .... fruits
un canard .... l'orange
un coq .... vin
une omelette .... fines herbes

2 Fill in blanks in these sentences with *elle, elles, il* or *ils*:
.... est délicieux, ce pâté.
Où est la voiture, chéri? .... est derrière l'hôtel.
.... font combien, les tartes à la crème?
Pablo est espagnol. .... ne parle pas français.
.... sont tranquilles, ces rues piétonnes.
Des bagages? Oui. .... sont dans la voiture.
Où sont les enfants? .... sont à l'école.
.... est idéale, cette chambre.

3 What are the pronouns *il, elle, ils* and *elles* representing in these sentences? Choose a phrase from the second list to replace them. There might be more than one possibility. For example in:
Ah oui, il est à côté de l'église
the *il* could be representing either *l'Hôtel de la Poste* or *le Glacier Belle Hélène.*

1 elles sont trop épaisses
2 il est excellent avec le fromage
3 elle est derrière l'hôtel
4 elles sont vraiment délicieuses
5 ils ne sont vraiment pas bons
6 il est à côté de l'église

a) les glaces du Glacier Belle Hélène
b) le Beaujolais
c) la voiture
d) les yaourts de Monsieur Martin
e) la carte postale
f) le Glacier Belle Hélène

7 elle est dans le sac de Mme Michel
8 elles sont dans la voiture
9 il est confortable

g) les saucisses de Toulouse
h) les tranches de jambon
i) l'Hôtel de la Poste

4 Which of these adjectives or phrases:
grands, petite, délicieuses, italien, rouges, au saucisson, à la crème,
will go with these nouns?
une chambre, un hôtel, des glaces, les sandwichs, un vin, des cerises, la tarte, les tartes
You will find that some adjectives will go with more than one noun.

5 Which of these can you eat?
des croissants, un sac, des cerises, une baguette, une salle de bains
Which of these can you drink?
un panaché, un express, une carte postale, un timbre, un citron pressé
Which of these would you be surprised to find in your hotel room?
une douche, un lit, une chèvre, des bagages, une église
Which of these are unlikely flavours for a yoghurt?
à la fraise, nature, au canard, à l'ananas, au thé

6 On the right are the contents of Madame Durand's basket at the supermarket checkout. On the left is her shopping list. Which items did she not buy that day?

une petite boîte d'allumettes
une bouteille de vin rouge
un morceau de fromage
un saucisson
250g de beurre
un litre de lait
une livre de tomates
des pêches
quatre tranches de jambon
un pot de crème

Now cover up the words on the left and name the items on the right, starting *du/de la/des*.

7 Ask for these:

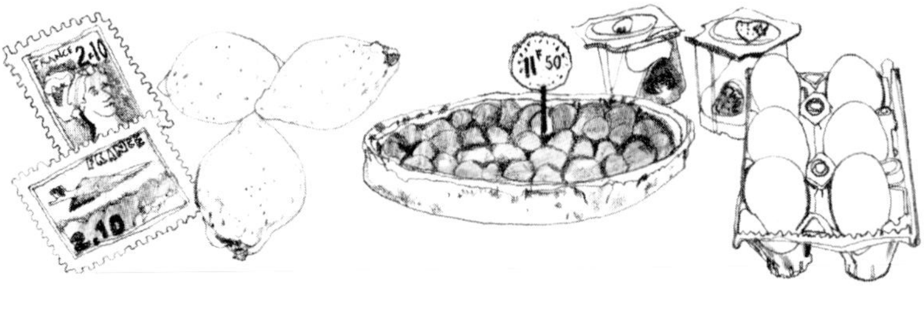

8 Marie-Pierre is just finishing interviewing Fiona McPhee on holiday in Bourg. Fill in each blank in the dialogue with a word from this list:

métier	il	vacances	quel
parlez	peu	région	suis
école	français	beaucoup	grand
êtes	parle	revoir	couramment
prie	bien	vendeuse	est

Marie-Pierre Mais, vous .... très .... le français, madame.
Fiona Oh, un peu.
Marie-Pierre Et votre mari, il parle le ....?
Fiona Non. Mais .... parle un .... l'italien. Mais mon fils, Andrew, parle .... le français et il .... aussi l'allemand à l'........
Marie-Pierre Mais c'est très bien, ça! Et .... est votre ...., madame?
Fiona Je .... dans un .... magasin.
Marie-Pierre Ah oui. Et votre mari?
Fiona Il .... représentant.
Marie-Pierre Et vous .... ici en ....?
Fiona Oui, la .... me plaît ....
Marie-Pierre Alors, merci, madame. Bon séjour à Bourg et au ....
Fiona Je vous en .... Au revoir, madame.

9 You and your family (husband and two children) arrive in a small village. It looks a likely place to stay for a few days so you stop at the café to have a drink and make enquiries. The owner (*le patron*) comes up.

Le patron Bonjour, m'sieur-dame. Vous désirez?
You *Return his greeting and ask for a fresh lemon drink and a beer.*
Le patron Très bien.
You *Ask him what sort of ice-cream he has.*
Le patron Fraise, vanille, chocolat.
You *Order one chocolate and one strawberry ice.*
Le patron Très bien.

He returns with the orders.

You *Ask him if there is a small hotel nearby.*
Le patron Non, pas dans le village, mais nous avons des chambres ici. Qu'est-ce que vous voulez comme chambres?
You *Say one room with a double bed and one twin-bedded room.*
Le patron Très bien, c'est possible. C'est pour combien de nuits?
You *Say it's for three nights and ask if there is a bathroom.*
Le patron Oui, bien sûr. C'est à côté des deux chambres.
You *Ask him if there's a car park.*
Le patron Pas ici mais là, juste derrière la boulangerie. Ce n'est pas loin.
You *Thank him very much.*
Le patron Je vous en prie, madame.

Guy Berland – scieur en Chartreuse

The Chartreuse is a mountain area just north of Grenoble. Today, it is perhaps most famous for the liqueur made there by monks of the monastery of *la Grande Chartreuse*.

Paysage de Chartreuse

On the border between the Dauphiné and Savoie, the Chartreuse has long been a sort of no-man's-land: a hiding place for smugglers, a sanctuary for victims of religious wars (there are quite a few Protestants in the area) and the chosen place of meditation for St. Bruno and his disciples – the founders of the Chartreux order, as well as the home of shepherds and woodcutters.

The villains have disappeared but the shepherds and woodcutters remain, along with increasing numbers of tourists who come to enjoy the ski-slopes in winter, and the unspoilt mountain valleys and forests in summer.

La Chartreuse est un petit pays de traditions avec une longue histoire. Les Cartusiens – les habitants de la Chartreuse – exploitent les forêts du massif depuis de nombreuses générations. Guy Bècle Berland est un de ces Cartusiens attachés aux traditions du pays. Sa famille est originaire de Berland – un petit village de Chartreuse – et travaille le bois depuis longtemps. Guy Berland est scieur. Il habite au Sappey-en-Chartreuse, sur la route de Grenoble, et travaille avec son frère, son neveu et un ami qui s'appelle Nono.

Guy Berland et son frère sont propriétaires d'une centaine d'hectares de forêts. Ils coupent près de quatre cents arbres par an. C'est surtout du sapin et de l'épicéa: du bois blanc, du bois tendre. La Chartreuse est une région où il pleut beaucoup; c'est une bonne chose, car il faut beaucoup d'eau pour faire pousser tous ces arbres. Le bois, une fois transformé en planches et en poutres, est destiné à des artisans pour la construction de maisons.

La scierie de Guy Berland est une entreprise familiale. Guy Berland s'occupe de tout: du travail administratif comme de la coupe du bois.

Les scieries sont en voie de disparition parce que l'économie actuelle favorise la production de masse. Il n'y a plus que deux scieries au Sappey-en-Chartreuse.

Guy Berland aime son métier, il aime son pays. La Chartreuse, c'est le berceau de son enfance, il y aime la vie telle qu'elle est. L'avenir ne l'inquiète pas beaucoup; son neveu, Jean-Paul, est là qui va continuer le travail ancestral.

exploitent les forêts ...	*have been exploiting the forests ....*
... depuis de nombreuses générations	*... for many generations*
travaille le bois	*works with timber*
car il faut	*because it takes*
pour faire pousser tous ces arbres	*to make all these trees grow*
une fois transformé	*once transformed*
en voie de disparition	*disappearing*
telle qu'elle est	*just as it is*

3

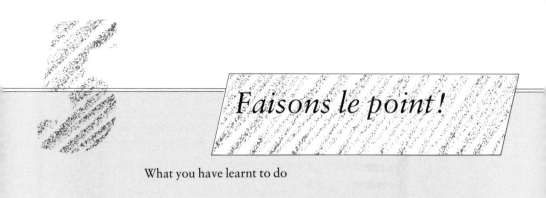

Faisons le point!

What you have learnt to do

You can greet people and say thank you and goodbye. There are examples in almost all the dialogues in this chapter.

You can also ask for things in shops, cafés, etc, ask how much they cost, and what they are if you don't recognise them.

Radio **1** Marie-Pierre is in a café with a friend and asks for two beers.

Serveuse Bonjour messieurs-dames. Que désirez-vous?
Marie-Pierre Deux bières, s'il vous plaît.
Serveuse Bière pression ou bouteille?
Marie-Pierre Deux pressions.
Serveuse Bien.
Marie-Pierre C'est combien?
Serveuse Dix francs, messieurs-dames.
Marie-Pierre Voilà.
Serveuse Merci.

Quickie What sorts of beer were there?

Radio **2** In the market she wants to know whether the chickens are the famous ones from Bresse and how much they cost each.

Marie-Pierre Pardon, madame. C'est du poulet de Bresse?
Marchande C'est du poulet de Bresse.
Marie-Pierre Et c'est combien?
Marchande Le prix de la pièce?
Marie-Pierre Oui.
Marchande La pièce ... Bon, ben, trente-trois et trente-six francs la pièce.
Marie-Pierre Les plus petits trente-trois francs ...?
Marchande Voilà!
Marie-Pierre ... les plus gros trente-six francs.
Marchande Trente-six francs.
Marie-Pierre Je vous remercie.

bon, ben	*well*
les plus petits	*the smaller ones*
voilà!	*that's it!*
les plus gros	*the bigger ones*

Quickie How do you say 'the bigger ones' referring to chickens?

You can ask whether the shopkeeper, waiter, etc has something that you want, and you can describe it by price or by the flavour or filling you prefer.

Radio 3 Marie-Pierre asks in a café if they have any sandwiches.

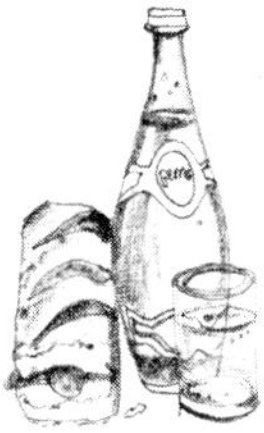

Serveuse Bonjour, madame. Vous désirez?
Marie-Pierre Bonjour. Vous avez des sandwichs?
Serveuse Oui, madame. Jambon, pâté, fromage, saucisson.
Marie-Pierre Quel fromage?
Serveuse Camembert.
Marie-Pierre (*deciding against the cheese*) Un sandwich au saucisson.
Serveuse Très bien, madame. Et comme boisson?
Marie-Pierre Une eau minérale gazeuse, s'il vous plaît.
Serveuse Très bien, madame. Je vais vous servir cela. Merci.

je vais vous servir cela	*I'll get that for you*

Quickies
1 What sorts of sandwiches are there?
2 What does Marie-Pierre have to drink?

Radio 4 On a hot day in Guérande, Pierrick fancies an ice cream. On the pavement outside a café is an ice cream stall.

Pierrick Bonjour, monsieur.
Garçon Bonjour, monsieur.
Pierrick Vous avez des glaces?
Garçon Oui, bien sûr, oui.
Pierrick Quels parfums vous avez?
Garçon Alors, vanille, fraise, Grand Marnier, chocolat, café . . .
Pierrick Je voudrais une . . . un cornet au chocolat, s'il vous plaît.
Garçon Oui. Simple ou double?
Pierrick Simple.
Garçon Oui. (*serves the ice cream*) Et voilà.
Pierrick Merci. C'est combien?
Garçon Alors, quatre francs.

Pierrick	(*counts out money*) Un, deux et quatre.
Garçon	Merci bien.
Pierrick	Au revoir, monsieur.
Garçon	Au revoir.

quels parfums vous avez? = vous avez quels parfums?

Quickies

1 What's the French for 'a chocolate cornet, please'?
2 What sizes of ice cream were there?

You can ask for things either by exact quantity ('a pound of . . .', 'a dozen of . . .') or less precisely ('some . . .', 'any . . .') and describe them with an adjective.

Radio 5 Marie-Pierre wants a kilo of small tomatoes, a cucumber, some green beans and 200 grams of mushrooms.

Marie-Pierre	Bonjour, madame.
Vendeuse	Bonjour, madame. Vous désirez, madame?
Marie-Pierre	Un kilo de tomates, s'il vous plaît.
Vendeuse	Oui, madame. Des grosses, des petites?
Marie-Pierre	Quel est le prix?
Vendeuse	Six francs les petites et sept francs cinquante les grosses.
Marie-Pierre	Un kilo de petites.
Vendeuse	Oui, madame, très bien (*she serves her*). Et avec cela?
Marie-Pierre	Un concombre.
Vendeuse	Oui, madame, un franc cinquante. Vous voulez autre chose?
Marie-Pierre	Vous avez des haricots verts?
Vendeuse	Oui, madame. J'ai des fins et des plus gros. Que voulez-vous, madame?
Marie-Pierre	Une livre de fins.
Vendeuse	Oui, madame. Voilà. Voulez-vous autre chose, madame?
Marie-Pierre	Deux cents grammes de champignons.
Vendeuse	Oui, madame. Ce sera tout, madame?
Marie-Pierre	Oui, ce sera tout.
Vendeuse	Merci, madame. Vingt-deux francs quarante, s'il vous plaît.
Marie-Pierre	(*counting out coins*) Dix, vingt, vingt-cinq francs.
Vendeuse	Alors (*counting out change*) vingt-deux quarante, vingt-trois, et deux, vingt-cinq. Voilà, madame. Merci beaucoup, madame.
Marie-Pierre	Au revoir, madame.
Vendeuse	Au revoir, madame. Merci, madame.

que voulez-vous? *what do you want?*

Quickies

1 How would you say 'a kilo of the small ones' referring to tomatoes?
2 What two words are used to describe the size of the beans?

Chez un charcutier-traiteur

TV 6 In a *charcuterie*, Madame Billat is buying food for a picnic. She asks for a quiche, some ham and then wants to know if they have any grated carrot salad (*salade de carottes râpées*).

Mme Billat	Bonjour, madame.
Vendeuse	Bonjour, madame. Vous désirez?
Mme Billat	Une quiche, s'il vous plaît.
Vendeuse	Une quiche. Une grande ou une petite?
Mme Billat	C'est pour six personnes. Une grande, s'il vous plaît.
Vendeuse	Oui. Voilà. Et avec ceci?
Mme Billat	Quatre tranches de jambon.
Vendeuse	Du jambon cru ou cuit?
Mme Billat	Du jambon cuit, s'il vous plaît.
Vendeuse	Oui. Vous voulez des tranches comment: normales, épaisses ou fines?
Mme Billat	Normales, s'il vous plaît.
Vendeuse	Vous désirez autre chose?
Mme Billat	Vous avez de la salade de carottes râpées?
Vendeuse	Oui. Il vous en faut combien?
Mme Billat	Voyons . . . deux cent cinquante grammes.
Vendeuse	Et avec ceci?
Mme Billat	Ça sera tout, merci. Je vous dois combien?
Vendeuse	Soixante-neuf trente, madame.
Mme Billat	Voilà (*handing over the money*).
Vendeuse	Merci. Voilà, madame, (*giving change*), merci.
Mme Billat	Merci, madame.

il vous en faut combien?	*how much do you want/need?*
voyons	*let's see*

Quickies

1 Which quiche did Madame Billat buy?
2 How much ham did she buy?
3 How did she ask if they had any carrot salad?

Radio **7** In Nantes, Sara asks in a café for a glass of white wine. There are two types produced locally – Muscadet and Gros Plant.

Serveuse Bonjour, madame. Qu'est-ce que vous voulez boire, madame?
Sara Un verre de vin blanc, s'il vous plaît.
Serveuse Muscadet ou Gros Plant?
Sara Du Muscadet, s'il vous plaît.
Serveuse Un petit ou un grand?
Sara Un petit.
Serveuse Un verre comme ça? (*putting a not particularly small glass on the counter*)
Sara Oui, ça va, merci.
Serveuse (*she pours the wine*) Voilà, madame.
Sara C'est combien?
Serveuse Trois francs. (*Sara pays*) Merci. (*she brings the change*) Voilà, madame.
Sara Merci.

Quickies
1 What did Sara say to order a glass of white wine?
2 How would you say 'a glass like that', pointing at one?

Radio **8** Marie-Pierre is in a *charcuterie*. She wants a slice of pâté.

Marie-Pierre Bonjour, madame.
Vendeuse Bonjour, madame.
Marie-Pierre Je voudrais une tranche de pâté, s'il vous plaît.
Vendeuse Du pâté de foie . . . de porc, du pâté de foie de volailles ou du pâté de campagne?
Marie-Pierre Du pâté de foie de porc.
Vendeuse Oui, madame. Une tranche pour combien de personnes?
Marie-Pierre Une tranche pour deux personnes.
Vendeuse Oui, madame. (*suggesting a portion*) Comme ceci, ça vous va?
Marie-Pierre Un peu moins, s'il vous plaît.
Vendeuse Voilà (*she cuts it*). Avec ceci, madame?
Marie-Pierre Ce sera tout.
Vendeuse (*she wraps and weighs it*) Ça vous fait trois francs zéro cinq.
Marie-Pierre Voilà. (*putting down coins*) Trois francs . . . et cinq centimes.
Vendeuse Merci, madame.
Ensemble Au revoir, madame.

ça vous va?	*is that alright for you?*
un peu moins	*a bit less*
ça vous fait . . .	*that comes to . . .*

Quickies
1 How much pâté does Marie-Pierre buy?
2 3F05, what is that in French?

You can ask if something is nearby or where something is and understand the usual directions you get in reply.

Radio **9** Marie-Pierre is looking for a chemist's and she's got a letter to post. So she stops people in the street to ask for directions.

Marie-Pierre Pardon, madame, il y a une pharmacie près d'ici?

1ère Passante Oui, il y en a une juste à droite.
Marie-Pierre Je vous remercie.
1ère Passante Je vous en prie.
Marie-Pierre Pardon, mademoiselle, il y a une boîte à lettres près d'ici?
2ème Passante Oui, la deuxième rue à droite.
Marie-Pierre Je vous remercie.
2ème Passante De rien.

Quickie How did Marie-Pierre ask for the letter box?

TV **10** At the *Maison du Tourisme* in Grenoble, Madame Bloch wants to know how to get to the main art gallery, *Le Musée de Peinture*.

Mme Bloch Pardon, madame. Où est le Musée de Peinture?
Hôtesse Le Musée de Peinture? Oui. Nous sommes ici (*pointing at map*), le Musée de Peinture est ici, Place de Verdun. Vous allez tourner à gauche, puis à droite, prendre la rue Général Marchand et au bout de cette rue, Place de Verdun, vous tournez à votre gauche et le musée est juste en face de vous.
Mme Bloch Donc, à gauche, puis à droite, je marche tout droit et sur la Place de Verdun, c'est en face à gauche.
Hôtesse C'est cela, en face de vous à gauche.
Mme Bloch Et c'est loin d'ici?
Hôtesse Non, c'est à cinq minutes.
Mme Bloch Bien, je vous remercie, madame.
Hôtesse Je vous en prie.
Mme Bloch Je peux? (*picking up map*)
Hôtesse Oui, madame. C'est pour vous.
Mme Bloch Merci.

nous sommes	*we are*
vous allez tourner	*you turn*
(vous allez) prendre	*(you) take*
je marche	*I walk*
je peux?	*may I?*

Quickies
1 Where is the *Musée de Peinture* on the map?
2 How did Madame Bloch ask where the gallery was?
3 How do you say 'it's five minutes away'?

You can understand what *elle/il, elles/ils* stand for in any given phrase.

Radio **11** At a market stall Marie-Pierre is asking about the individual fruit tarts.

Marie-Pierre Pardon, madame, c'est combien les tartelettes?
Patronne Alors, vous en avez à differénts . . . à trois francs et trois francs dix.
Marie-Pierre Elles sont à quoi?
Patronne Alors vous en avez ananas, myrtilles, abricots et poires.
Marie-Pierre Et elles sont bonnes?
Patronne Très bonnes, oui.

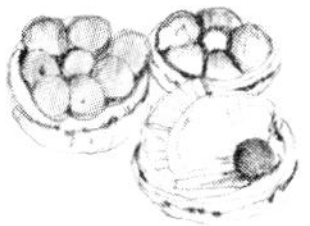

Marie-Pierre Je vous remercie.
Patronne A votre service.

elles sont à quoi? *what sort are they?*

Quickies

1 *Une tartelette* – what would you say that was: *une grande tarte* or *une petite tarte*?

2 What was in the tarts?

3 What is *elles* standing for here?

Radio **12** Sara is in the *Syndicat d'Initiative* in Nantes getting some tourist information.

Sara Bonjour, madame.
Hôtesse Bonjour, madame.
Sara Vous avez un plan de Nantes, s'il vous plaît?
Hôtesse Oui. Voici un plan de la ville. Vous avez la liste des monuments et la liste des musées avec les heures d'ouverture.
Sara Bon. Sur le plan, où est le Château des Ducs de Bretagne?
Hôtesse Il est ici.
Sara Bon. Où sont les grands magasins?
Hôtesse Ils sont dans la rue du Calvaire.
Sara Bon, merci! (*indicating map*) C'est combien?
Hôtesse C'est gratuit.
Sara Ah, merci! Au revoir.
Hôtesse Au revoir, madame.

les heures d'ouverture	*the opening hours*
les grands magasins	*the department stores*

Quickies

1 How did Sara ask for the map of Nantes?
2 What is in the rue du Calvaire?
3 How much was the street map?
4 What are *il* and *ils* standing for?

You can talk to people about yourself and ask them about themselves: where they are from, what nationality they are, what their jobs are, about their families, etc. You have met the pieces marked * before.

Radio 13 Marie-Pierre talked to a woman from Britanny. The Bretons have a strong sense of identity and a language of their own.

Marie-Pierre Pardon, madame. Vous êtes de Bourg?
Bretonne Non. Non, je suis de Saint-Malo.
Marie-Pierre Et vous êtes ici de passage?
Bretonne De passage, seulement, oui, pour quelques jours.
Marie-Pierre Ah, vous êtes bretonne?
Bretonne Oui, je suis bretonne.
Marie-Pierre Vous parlez le breton?
Bretonne Pas du tout.
Marie-Pierre Et c'est bien, Saint-Malo?
Bretonne Très joli, oui.
Marie-Pierre Je vous remercie.

pas du tout	*not at all*

Quickie What was the answer to the question *Vous êtes de Bourg?*?

TV 14* Jane asked people about their jobs and what languages they spoke.

Jane Monsieur, quel est votre métier?
Passant Je suis représentant.
Jane Et est-ce que vous parlez d'autres langues?
Passant Je parle l'italien et un peu d'anglais, enfin, très, très peu d'anglais.
Jane Et l'italien, vous le parlez comment?
Passant Assez couramment.

Quickie Does the man speak Italian better than English?

TV **15*** Jane asked whether people had children.

Jane Vous avez des enfants?
Passante J'ai trois enfants.
Jane Des garçons ou des filles?
Passante J'ai un garçon et deux filles.

TV **16*** She also asked what nationality people were and where they were from.

Jane Mademoiselle, vous êtes française?
Etudiante Oui, je suis française.
Jane Vous êtes d'où?
Etudiante Je suis de Paris.

Quickie How do you say 'I have two children' and 'I am from Leeds'?

And if you want to, you can be negative about things.

TV **17*** Jane asked two other students where they were from.

Jane Vous êtes de Grenoble?
Etudiant Non, je ne suis pas de Grenoble.
Jane Vous êtes d'où?
Etudiant Je viens de Bretagne.
Jane Mademoiselle, vous êtes française?
Etudiante Non, je suis pas française.
Jane Vous êtes d'où?
Etudiante Je viens de Taiwan.

Quickie Can you say you're not French?

You can ask what there is to see and do in a place and reply if someone asks you.

TV **18*** Jane asked people about Grenoble.

Jane Madame, qu'est-ce qu'il y a à voir ou à faire pour un Grenoblois à Grenoble?
1ère Passante Il y a beaucoup de choses, beaucoup d'activités. Par exemple, bon, tous les sports d'hiver, le ski, la luge. Et puis, l'été, la montagne est très, très belle.
Jane Monsieur, qu'est-ce qu'il y a à voir ou à faire pour un Grenoblois à Grenoble?
Passant Eh bien, il y a les spectacles, les musées, cinémas.
2ème Passante Il y a, disons, il y a beaucoup de théâtres.

Quickie How do you say 'What is there to see?'?

Rencontres

TV 1 Jane asked people in a shopping centre to describe their ideal life partner. Remember that some adjectives will change depending on whether they describe men or women, and others won't.

Jane	Monsieur, comment est votre partenaire idéale?
1er passant	Ah, beh, je crois l'avoir trouvée!
Jane	Comment est votre partenaire idéal?
1ère passante	Intelligent, travailleur.
2ème passante	Oh là là! Aucune idée!
2ème passant	Ah, plutôt grande, plus grande que moi.
3ème passante	Le physique, c'est pas trop important.
4ème passante	Grand. Grand. Grand et puis brun.
2ème passant	Très, très calme.
Jane	Très, très calme? Intellectuelle ou manuelle?
2ème passant	Ah! Intellectuelle.
3ème passant	Pas trop intellectuelle quand même.
5ème passante	Gentil.
2ème passante	Sérieux.
5ème passante	Honnête.
1er passant	Excessivement intelligente, excessivement patiente.
5ème passante	Franc.
4ème passante	Calme, pas angoissé, pas mal aussi, quoi!

je crois l'avoir trouvée!	*I think I've found her!*
aucune idée!	*no idea!*
plus grande que moi	*taller than me*
pas mal aussi, quoi!	*not bad-looking either, you know!*

Quickies

1. Two useful words, one of which you have met before: *très, trop*. What do they mean?
2. Here are six words: two can apply to women only, two to men only and two to either. Sort them out.
patiente, honnête, grand, intelligent, calme, intellectuelle

TV 2 Jane asked the same people if they themselves were ideal partners.

Jane	Et vous-mêmê, vous êtes une partenaire idéale?
3ème passante	Je pense pas!
2ème passante	C'est pas à moi qu'il faut poser la question, hein!
4ème passante	Je crois que je m'améliore avec le temps!
Jane	Vous vous considérez comme un partenaire idéal?
2ème passant	Bien sûr!

c'est pas à moi qu'il faut poser la question!	*I'm not the one you should ask!*
je crois que je m'améliore avec le temps	*I think I'm improving with age*

Mots-clés

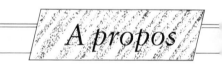

le camembert	camembert	aussi	as well/too
la carotte	carrot	comment	how
le champignon	mushroom	moins	less
l'eau minérale (f)	mineral water	on	one/you/we (see p 148–149)
gazeux	fizzy		
le haricot vert	French bean	(un) peu	(a) little
le porc	pork/pig	calme	even-tempered
la quiche	quiche	cru	raw
le verre	glass	cuit	cooked
la volaille	poultry	double	double
le grand magasin	department store	gentil	kind
		honnête	honest
boire	to drink	important	important
marcher	to walk	intelligent	intelligent
trouver	to find	normal	normal
		sérieux	serious
blond	fair	simple	single (ie not double)
brun	dark		
les yeux (m)	eyes		

A propos

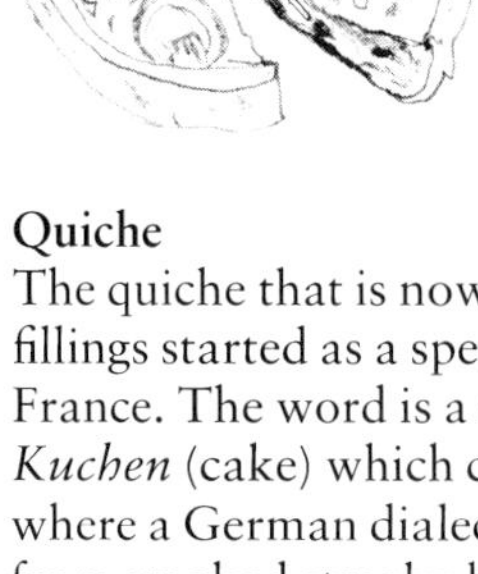

Quiche
The quiche that is now found everywhere in Britain with all sorts of fillings started as a speciality of Lorraine, a province of north-eastern France. The word is a regional one, a corruption of the German *Kuchen* (cake) which came to Lorraine through its neighbour Alsace, where a German dialect is spoken locally. *La quiche lorraine* is made from smoked streaky bacon (*du lard*), ham, eggs and cream and is served hot as a first course.

Eau minérale
Natural spring waters claiming medicinal qualities allegedly good for a variety of ailments have been popular in France since before Roman times; the word *Aix* or *Aigues* that appears as part of many French place names comes from the Latin word for 'water', *aqua*. Over the past twenty years particularly, the producers of mineral waters have been extremely successful in persuading the French to drink bottled water instead of what comes out of a tap. Nowadays piles of big plastic bottles are found in every supermarket and their names (Evian, Vittel, Contrexéville) are better known than ever before. All these are still – *non gazeuses*. If you want fizzy mineral water you must look for the word *gazeuse*. The most famous of the mineral waters, like Perrier and Vichy, usually cost more. Bought by the litre, mineral water is fairly inexpensive, but a small bottle (*un quart Perrier, Vichy*, etc) in a café will cost you as much as a beer.

Camembert
Camembert, one of the best-known French cheeses with its flat, round shape, is made in Normandy. It is a soft cheese with a well-defined taste that is not over-strong when eaten at its best. It soon deteriorates, however, and many a tourist's car has been made uninhabitable by an over-ripe camembert being taken home as a souvenir. France produces a huge number of cheeses, some internationally known, some available only in the region where they are made. It is said that you could eat a different one every day of the year – so there is plenty of room for experiment. Contrary to British custom, cheese is eaten before dessert and not afterwards, and with bread, not biscuits.

Jambon cru
Ham, cured in various ways and sometimes slightly smoked but eaten raw, is found in various regions of France. It is eaten as hors d'oeuvres or in sandwiches in wafer thin slices (*des tranches extra fines*). The most famous is *le jambon de Bayonne*.

Jambons et saucissons dans un supermarché

Le poulet de Bresse

La Bresse is an area of France lying north of Lyon and south of Besançon. It is well known for its local cheese, *le bleu de Bresse*, but above all for its chicken, *le poulet de Bresse*. Experts claim that what champagne is to ordinary wine, *poulet de Bresse* is to a supermarket chicken. Its production is very strictly controlled by the Ministry of Agriculture. For example, an ordinary 'free range' bird spends only the last couple of weeks of its life 'free'. A *poulet de Bresse* runs free in the fields for the whole of its life. Feeding on anything but natural foodstuffs is forbidden. And each bird must have a minimum of ten square metres of land to run about in – more than the average Parisian! Production is limited to about a million birds a year.

In their natural state Bresse chickens are easy to recognise. With their red crests, white plumage and grey-blue legs, they look like miniature French flags turned sideways – a feature which the advertisers make much of. When the bird is cooked the best restaurants will ensure that part of its blue leg is served as proof of authenticity. Gourmets, however, claim that no such proof is needed – the meat, succulent in flavour and firm in texture, is testimony enough on its own.

Naturally such a highly prized and cared for product doesn't come cheaply and *un poulet de Bresse* can cost up to double the price of an ordinary chicken. It is sold with a ring on its claw carrying a number – a guarantee of origin.

Bon courage

Part I

The best person to know what you need to revise is yourself. As you work through this section see what areas you need to look at again.

If you like testing yourself, you can score a maximum of 65 on this first section. Try again next week and see if you can improve your score.

1 Ask how much these are:

Which of these answers fits your question in each case?

a) c'est gratuit
b) ils font 8F le kilo
c) 6F80 la plaquette de 125 grammes
d) elle fait 15F

2 Ask how much these are:
1 a ham sandwich
2 a cheese sandwich
3 the apple tart
4 the custard tart
5 the strawberry yoghurt

3 Ask for these:
1 a kilo of big tomatoes
2 a small chicken
3 three slices of pâté, thick
4 a small glass of wine
5 a big box of matches

4 Ask for these by describing them by price:

5 Ask if the shopkeeper has any of these:
1 French beans
2 beer
3 pâté de campagne
4 cherries
5 goat's cheese

6 At various times you want an ice cream. Ask for:
1 a strawberry ice cream
2 a 3F50 cornet
3 a cornet with two scoops of ice cream
4 a chocolate cornet
5 an ice cream like this (pointing to an advert on the wall)

7 Ask if there is one of these nearby:
1 a bank
2 a chemist's
3 a baker's
4 a tobacconist's
5 a letter box

8 Ask where these things are:
1 the station
2 the Tourist Information Office
3 the cable car
4 the department stores
5 St André's church

9 Ask someone you've just met:
   1 if he's French
   2 if he speaks English
   3 where he comes from
   4 what job he does
   5 what there is to do in Bourg

10 Say:
   1 you are from Newcastle
   2 you are Welsh
   3 you don't speak Italian
   4 you have three children
   5 you are married to a Frenchman

11 Decide which of the following should go in the gaps:
un, un, des; le, la, l', les; du, de la, de, d'
Vous avez .... vin?
Oui, vous en voulez combien?
.... bouteille .... vin ordinaire, s'il vous plaît.
Et avec ça?
Vous avez .... bière?
Mais oui.
Bon, une douzaine .... petites bouteilles. Voux avez .... pêches?
Oui, j'en ai .... grosses à 6F30 et .... moins grosses à 4F80 le kilo.
Très bien, je prends .... kilo .... grosses pêches et donnez-moi .... livre .... abricots et .... petit fromage de chèvre.

Part II

Vingt questions

1 Where would you go if you arrived in a French town and wanted some tourist literature about the area?
épicerie; *Syndicat d'Initiative*; *commissariat*; *boîte à lettres*

2 Why is the *département* Loire-Atlantique so called?

3 Why is it important to distinguish between the words *droit* and *droite* when talking about directions?

4 What are two things you might reply if someone said *Merci* to you?

5 Where would you get to if you drove into a road called *Impasse* ...?

6 What does *VDQS* stand for on a wine label?

7 What's the name of the type of establishment where you could buy stamps, cigarettes, a newspaper and have a coffee?

8 What has a red head, a white body and blue legs?

9 What's the difference between *le crème* and *la crème*?

10 Name two things apart from bread you might be given if you asked for *Une baguette, s'il vous plaît?*

11 What would you find in the Quai d'Orsay in Paris?

12 How would you ask whether breakfast was included in the price of a room?

13 What is *jambon de Bayonne*?

14 If someone asked you *Du Morgon ou du Gros Plant?*, what are you being offered?

15 What is the French word for the type of home most city-dwellers have in France?

16 What dish from north-east France contains the following ingredients: *du jambon, des oeufs, du lard, de la crème*?

17 What are *OTAN* and *ONU*?

18 What's the French name for the drinks you get by:
1 mixing beer and lemonade;
2 putting a slice of lemon into some tea;
3 adding white wine to blackcurrant liqueur?

19 How would a native of the following countries state his nationality? *l'Italie*; *l'Allemagne*; *le Brésil*; *l'Ecosse*; *l'Irlande*

20 Who would you expect to buy cooked meat, pâtés and salamis from? *charcutier*; *pâtissier*; *passante*; *cendrier*

Part III

Some extra practice

1 At a hotel you find yourself interpreting for other people who want rooms. The details of their requirements are below. Ask for rooms for them. You will find *avec* ('with') and *sans* ('without') very useful.

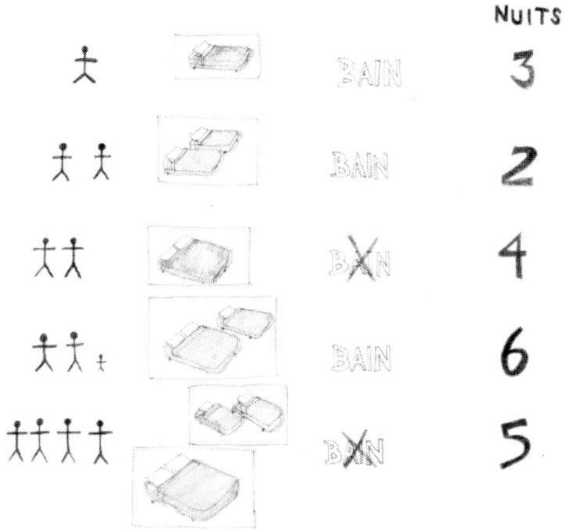

2 You are with three friends in a café. Pierre wants a glass of white wine, Marie a big white coffee, Sara a freshly-squeezed lemon juice and you a beer.

What do you say to the waiter?

Ask him how much it all is. What do you expect his reply to be?

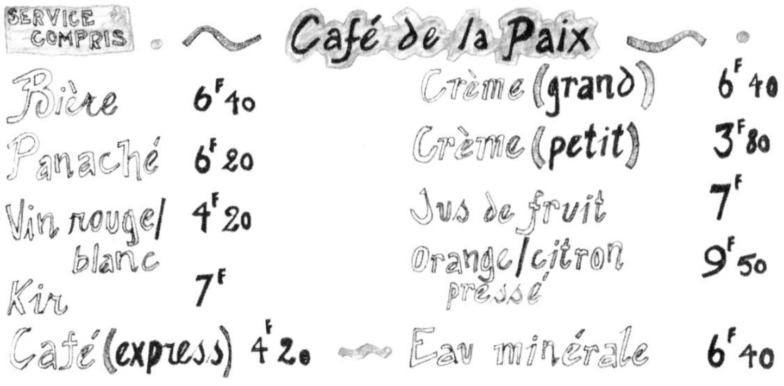

SERVICE COMPRIS
Café de la Paix
Bière 6F40
Panaché 6F20
Vin rouge/blanc 4F20
Kir 7F
Café (express) 4F20
Crème (grand) 6F40
Crème (petit) 3F80
Jus de fruit 7F
Orange/citron pressé 9F50
Eau minérale 6F40

3 The answers in this interview have got jumbled up. Sort them out.

Interviewer Pardon, monsieur. Vous êtes de Grenoble?
Passant Pas trop. C'est à une centaine de kilomètres.
Interviewer Et Grenoble vous plaît?
Passant Non, à Lyon.
Interviewer Quel est votre métier?
Passant Oui, énormément. Il y a beaucoup de choses à faire et les Grenoblois sont sympathiques.
Interviewer Ici à l'Université de Grenoble?
Passant Je suis garçon de café mais je vais être étudiant.
Interviewer C'est loin d'ici?
Passant Non, je suis ici depuis cinq ans mais je viens de Suisse.

4 You arrive at a hotel in a small French town. Complete your side of the conversation.

Hôtelier Bonjour, messieurs-dames.
You *Say good afternoon and ask if he has two double rooms, one with twin beds.*
Hôtelier Avec ou sans salle de bains?
You *Ask what is the price of the room with a bathroom.*
Hôtelier Avec salle de bains c'est 115F, sans salle de bains 85F.
You *Say you want one room with a bathroom, please.*
Hôtelier Très bien. Et l'autre sans salle de bains, alors?
You *That's right.*
Hôtelier D'accord. C'est pour combien de nuits?
You *Say five nights.*
Hôtelier Très bien. C'est à quel nom?
You *England.*
Hôtelier Non, non! Pas la nationalité, le nom!

You	*That's it. It's England like the country.*
Hôtelier	Merci, messieurs-dames, voici les clefs. Les chambres sont au rez-de-chaussée, au fond du couloir.
	There is no restaurant in the hotel so when you come back you enquire.
You	*Ask if there is a good restaurant nearby.*
Hôtelier	Vous avez deux ou trois petits restaurants sur la Place St Etienne. Il y a 'La Chèvre Blanche', 'Les Armes de Bretagne', 'Le Mouton d'Or'.
You	*Ask where St Stephen's square is.*
Hôtelier	Bon, vous prenez l'avenue en face de l'hôtel, vous continuez jusqu'à l'église, vous tournez à gauche et la Place St Etienne est là.
You	*Ask if it's far.*
Hôtelier	Non, c'est à dix minutes, pas plus.
You	*Say thank you and goodbye.*
Hôtelier	Je vous en prie, messieurs-dames. Bon appétit!

5 Où est la charcuterie?

Le musée est dans la rue Victor Hugo à gauche en face de l'église.
La gare est au bout de la rue Victor Hugo à droite près du marché.
La pâtisserie est à gauche du café-tabac.
En face du café-tabac il y a la Maison du Tourisme.
La banque est à droite de la Maison du Tourisme.
De l'autre côté du café-tabac il y a une boulangerie.
Où est la charcuterie?

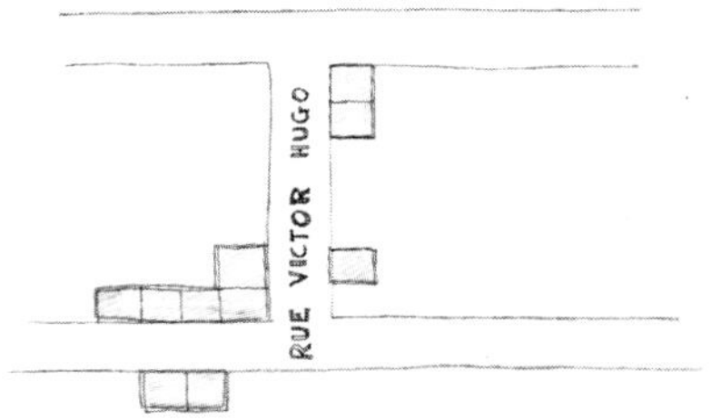

Industrie et tradition

If the future of Grenoble lies in advanced technology, the economy of the surrounding area is linked more closely with tradition. One of the oldest industries is paper-manufacture, which owes its origins here to the once plentiful supply of wood, as well as water and energy. The vast paper factory at Lancey was the first in France to pioneer hydro-electric power; today, technology in the form of automation has considerably reduced the work-force. But for many of those that remain, paper-making is a family tradition.

The concentration of industry around Grenoble is not typical of the Dauphiné as a whole: it is essentially an agricultural region. The Trièves, to the south, is a fertile green plateau surrounded by mountains. Sheep-rearing is an important activity here and each summer the sheep are taken up to the mountain pastures, a journey called *la transhumance*. Most are transported by lorry, but a few farmers continue to take sheep up in the traditional way, on foot. In the mountains, the sheep are left in the care of a professional shepherd, hired each year just for the summer months. The farmers return to the plateau to crop cereals and grass for the winter.

Les moutons traversent la petite ville de Corps

La plus vieille industrie du Dauphiné est l'industrie papetière. L'usine des Papeteries de France à Lancey, une petite ville près de Grenoble, existe depuis 1869: c'est la première usine papetière de la région. Mais pourquoi faire du papier dans le Dauphiné? Michel Bouteille, le directeur de l'usine, explique: 'A l'origine, pour faire du papier, il faut du bois, il faut de l'énergie – l'électricité – et de l'eau . . . et à l'époque, il y avait du bois, de l'eau et de l'énergie.' De nos jours, il n'y a pas assez de bois dans le Dauphiné; il vient d'autres régions de France.

La production de l'usine de Lancey est importante. Elle utilise 60.000 tonnes de bois par an. C'est une usine moderne où les machines sont contrôlées par des ordinateurs. Mais l'industrie du papier reste une tradition familiale à Lancey. Il y a 918 personnes qui travaillent aux Papeteries de France. Souvent, leurs familles sont dans ce métier depuis plusieurs générations. Tradition, technologie de pointe: à Lancey, le mélange est fait.

Pourtant, il y a encore des régions du Dauphiné où les traditions ne changent pas. Au sud de Grenoble, sur le plateau du Trièves, l'agriculture et l'élevage restent les activités principales des habitants. Chaque année, au mois de juin, trois éleveurs de la petite ville de Mens quittent le plateau avec leurs moutons pour aller aux alpages, en haut des montagnes. C'est la transhumance. La transhumance est une vieille tradition. Pour les trois éleveurs de Mens, la montagne n'est pas loin. Ils font donc ce voyage de quarante-cinq kilomètres (et d'un jour et demi) à pied. Sur la route, les 1.700 moutons traversent le plateau du Trièves jusqu'à la petite ville de Corps. Puis, ils prennent des petits sentiers en direction de Notre-Dame de la Salette où se trouvent les alpages.

Le voyage terminé, les moutons vont rester en haut des montagnes pendant la belle saison. René, le berger professionnel qui les accompagne, va rester lui aussi. Il va garder le troupeau pendant quatre mois, tout seul avec ses chiens. Il faut aimer la solitude pour être berger.

la plus vieille	*the oldest*
il faut	*you need*
à l'époque	*at that time*
il y avait	*there was*
de nos jours	*today*
par an	*each year*
leurs familles sont dans ce métier depuis plusieurs générations	*their families have been doing this work for several generations*
technologie de pointe	*advanced technology*
le mélange est fait	*the two are combined*
ils font	*they make*
le voyage terminé	*the journey over*
vont rester	*will stay*
la belle saison	*the warmest months*
qui les accompagne	*who accompanies them*
va rester lui aussi	*will stay as well*
il faut aimer	*you must like*
pour être berger	*to be a shepherd*

Bon voyage!

Using public transport: enquiring about times
buying the ticket
Talking to people about working hours and holidays

TV 1 In Grenoble, Françoise Blanc is at the ticket office in the coach station (*la gare routière*). She wants to know the time of the next coach to Mens, a small town in the region, and also the last coach back to Grenoble.

Françoise Pardon. Le prochain car pour Mens est à quelle heure, s'il vous plaît?
Employé Madame. (*looks at timetable*) Il est à huit heures.
Françoise Il arrive à quelle heure à Mens?
Employé Le car arrive à Mens à neuf heures quarante-cinq, madame.
Françoise Un aller-retour pour Mens alors, s'il vous plaît.
Employé Oui. (*gets ticket*) Vingt-sept francs quatre-vingts. (*giving change*) Vingt-huit, vingt-neuf, trente.
Françoise Merci. Ah, le dernier car pour Grenoble part à quelle heure de Mens?
Employé Il part à quinze heures quinze. (*giving her a timetable*) Tenez, voilà l'horaire.
Françoise Merci.
Employé Je vous remercie.
Françoise Au revoir, monsieur.
Employé Au revoir, madame.

tenez! *here you are!*

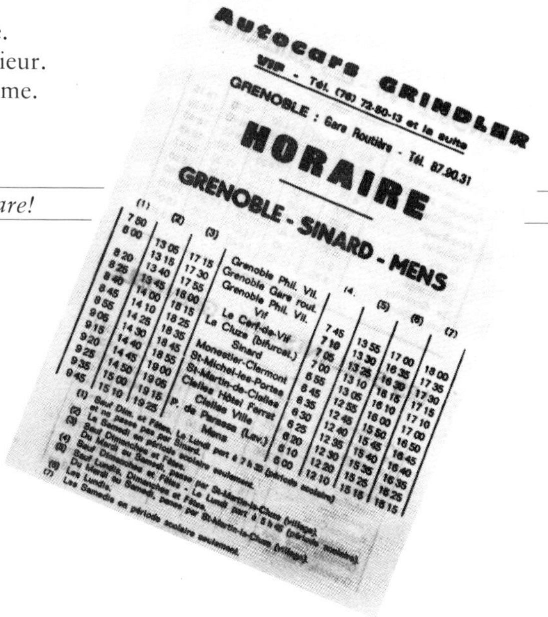

To ask about bus times:

le car pour Mens	arrive part est	**à quelle heure?**

To state the time (24-hour system):

0950	**neuf heures cinquante**
1510	**quinze heures dix**
2230	**vingt-deux heures trente**

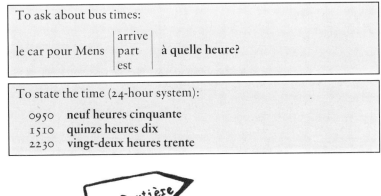

Quickies 1 What's the French for 'the next coach'?
2 Françoise wants a return ticket to Mens. What does she ask for?

TV 2 François Moreau is in the information office (*Renseignements*) at Grenoble station enquiring about trains to Avignon. The one he chooses entails a change at Valence.

M Moreau Bonjour, mademoiselle.
Hôtesse Bonjour, monsieur.
M Moreau Est-ce qu'il y a des trains le matin pour Avignon?
Hôtesse Oui, bien sûr. (*looks up timetable*) Le premier part de Grenoble à six heures quarante et arrive à Avignon à neuf heures vingt-trois. Le suivant est à neuf heures vingt-huit de Grenoble et arrive à Avignon à douze heures cinq. Vous en avez un autre qui part de Grenoble à onze heures vingt-trois et arrive à Avignon à treize heures quarante et une.

To specify a particular train:	
first	le **premier** train
last	le **dernier** train
next	le **prochain** train
the one after that	le train **suivant**
the train to Avignon	le train **pour Avignon**
the 9.28 train	le train **de 9h28**

NB *Le train d'Avignon* is 'the Avignon train', ie going to or coming from Avignon depending on the context

M Moreau Le train de neuf heures vingt-huit est direct?

Hôtesse Non, il n'est pas direct, vous devez changer à Valence.

M Moreau La correspondance à Valence est à quelle heure?

Hôtesse Vous arrivez à Valence à dix heures quarante-neuf et vous en repartez à dix heures cinquante-six.

M Moreau Ah, mais il faut faire vite!

Hôtesse Oui, mais enfin vous avez le temps de changer quand même, hein.

M Moreau Et quel est le prix du billet?

Hôtesse En seconde classe quatre-vingts francs pour l'aller simple et cent soixante francs pour l'aller-retour. Et en première classe cent vingt francs pour l'aller simple et deux cent quarante francs pour l'aller-retour.

M Moreau Merci beaucoup, mademoiselle.

Hôtesse Je vais vous laisser une fiche horaire.

M Moreau Ah! Merci bien. Au revoir, mademoiselle.

Hôtesse Au revoir, monsieur.

vous devez . . .	*you have to . . .*
vous en repartez	*you leave again*
il faut faire vite!	*that's a bit of a rush!*

> To ask if there are trains for . . .:
> (est-ce qu') **il y a des trains pour . . .?**

> To say 'in the morning/afternoon/evening', omit the word for 'in':
> **le** matin
> **l'**après-midi
> **le** soir
> NB After a specific time add *de*:
> sept heures **du** matin
> trois heures **de l'**après-midi
> sept heures **du** soir

Quickies

1 What time of day does Monsieur Moreau want to travel?
2 How does he ask if it's a through train?

TV 3 Next day Monsieur Moreau comes back to the station, buys his ticket and asks which platform the trains goes from.

M Moreau Un billet aller-retour pour Avignon, en seconde classe, s'il vous plaît.
Employée Oui. (*she pushes buttons on ticket machine*) Voilà. Cent soixante francs. (*she takes money and hands over ticket and change*) Merci.
M Moreau Merci. Le train de neuf heures vingt-huit part de quel quai?
Employée Du quai numéro deux, je crois, mais regardez sur les panneaux de départ.
M Moreau Merci, mademoiselle.
Employée Au revoir.

regardez *look*

> To ask for a train ticket:

un	**aller-retour** **aller simple**	pour (Lyon) **en**	**seconde** **première**

> To ask where a train/coach leaves from:

le train le car	de neuf heures part	**de quel quai?** **d'où?**

Radio 4 Marie-Pierre is enquiring about coaches to Lyon in the *Syndicat d'Initiative* in Bourg-en-Bresse.

Marie-Pierre Pardon, mademoiselle. Il y a des cars pour aller à Lyon?
Hôtesse Oui. Au départ de la gare.
Marie-Pierre Vous avez les horaires? Je veux être à Lyon avant midi.
Hôtesse Oui. Vous avez un car qui part de Bourg à sept heures trente et qui arrive à Lyon à neuf heures dix. Et un autre à neuf heures trente qui arrive à Lyon à onze heures dix.
Marie-Pierre Et ils partent d'où?
Hôtesse Ils partent de la gare de Bourg-en-Bresse.
Marie-Pierre Et ils arrivent où exactement?
Hôtesse A la gare de Lyon-Perrache.
Marie-Pierre Et vous vendez les billets?

Hôtesse Non, vous achetez votre billet dans le car.
Marie-Pierre Je vous remercie.
Hôtesse Je vous en prie.

au départ de la gare	*leaving from the railway station*
vous avez les horaires?	*have you got the times?*
je veux être ...	*I want to be ...*

Verb forms:

le car arrive	**il** arrive
le dernier train part	**il** part
les voiture arriv**ent**	**elles** arriv**ent**
les trains part**ent**	**ils** part**ent**

The *-ent* is not pronounced (see *En bref* 7)

Quickies

1 When does Marie-Pierre want to be in Lyon?
2 Where is she told she has to buy the ticket?

Radio 5 Marie-Pierre goes to the station to find out if trains to Lyon are more convenient.

Marie-Pierre Pardon, mademoiselle. Le prochain train pour Lyon part à quelle heure, s'il vous plaît?
Employée Dix heures quarante-quatre.
Marie-Pierre Et il arrive à quelle heure?
Employée Il arrive à Lyon à onze heures trente-six.
Marie-Pierre Et il part de quel quai?
Employée Quai trois.
Marie-Pierre Et pour rentrer à Bourg, il y a un train après neuf heures ce soir?
Employée Eh oui, attendez. Je vais vous donner l'horaire exact. (*consults timetable*) Alors, de Lyon-Perrache vous avez un départ à vingt et une heures trente.
Marie-Pierre Et il arrive à quelle heure à Bourg?
Employée Vous arrivez à Bourg à vingt-deux heures trente.
Marie-Pierre Et c'est combien le billet aller-retour?
Employée Cinquante-six francs aller-retour en seconde.
Marie-Pierre Je vous remercie.
Employée Je vous en prie, madame.

pour rentrer à Bourg	*to get back to Bourg*
je vais vous donner ...	*I'll give you ...*

To say 'before'/'after':

avant midi
après neuf heures

Quickies

1 How do you say 'the next train'?
2 What time did Marie-Pierre want to catch a train back?

Radio **6** She decides to go to Lyon by train. Here she is buying the ticket.

Marie-Pierre Bonjour, monsieur. Un aller-retour pour Lyon-Perrache, s'il vous plaît.
Employé Oui. Vous avez une réduction?
Marie-Pierre Non.
Employé Non. Alors, ça fait cinquante-six francs.
Marie-Pierre Voilà.
Employé (*giving her the change*) Voilà la monnaie.
Marie-Pierre Merci.

---

vous avez une réduction? *are you entitled to a reduction?* (see *A propos*)

Radio **7** In Bourg-en-Bresse, Marie-Pierre is in a travel agency (*une agence de voyages*) finding out the times of flights from Lyon to London.

Employée Bonjour, madame. Vous désirez?
Marie-Pierre Bonjour, madame. Quels sont les horaires des avions pour aller à Londres au départ de Lyon?
Employée Au départ de Lyon. Vous avez une idée du jour de votre départ?
Marie-Pierre La semaine prochaine.
Employée La semaine prochaine. Donc, sur novembre. Je vais vous dire ça. (*she consults timetable*) Alors, du lundi au vendredi vous avez deux vols par jour. Un vol à treize heures vingt pour arriver à treize heures cinquante Heathrow, le deuxième vol dix-huit heures cinquante-cinq départ de Lyon, dix-neuf heures vingt-cinq arrivée Heathrow, heure locale toujours. Mais cet avion n'est pas valable pour le samedi et le dimanche. Alors le samedi et le dimanche vous avez un seul vol à treize heures, arrivée treize heures trente-cinq, heure locale.
Marie-Pierre Je vous remercie.

sur novembre	a colloquial way of saying *en novembre*
je vais vous dire ça	*I'll tell you*

> Days of the week:
> **lundi, mardi, mercredi, jeudi, vendredi, samedi, dimanche**
>
> To say '*on* Saturdays', '*on* Sundays' (or any other day of the week): **le** samedi, **le** dimanche etc

Quickies
1 When does Marie-Pierre want to go to London?
2 There are two flights a day except . . .?

Radio 8 In the information office at Lyon-Perrache station, Marie-Pierre asks where to get the bus to Lyon-Satolas airport.

Marie-Pierre Pardon, mademoiselle. Il y a des cars pour aller à l'aéroport de Satolas?
Employée Oui, à la sortie de la gare, devant la station de taxis, sur votre gauche.
Marie-Pierre Et ils partent quand?
Employée Toutes les vingt minutes.
Marie-Pierre Et le prochain?
Employée Le prochain part à seize heures vingt.
Marie-Pierre Et je l'achète où mon billet?
Employée Vous achetez votre billet dans le car.
Marie-Pierre Je vous remercie.
Employée A votre service.

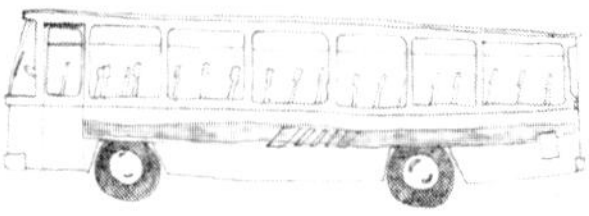

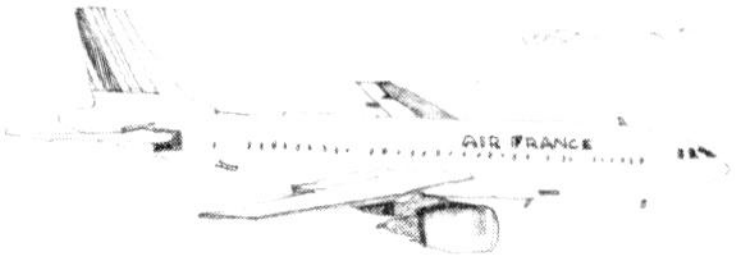

To say 'every twenty minutes/Saturday/three days', etc:

toutes les vingt minutes
tous les samedis
tous les trois jours

Quickies
1 How does Marie-Pierre ask if there are buses to the airport?
2 How would you say 'every ten minutes'?

Radio 9 Marie-Pierre jumps on a bus outside the station and checks that it's the right one.

Marie-Pierre Pardon, monsieur. C'est bien le car pour aller à l'aéroport?
Conducteur A l'aéroport de Satolas, c'est ça.
Marie-Pierre Et il part dans combien de temps?
Conducteur Il part dans cinq minutes.
Marie-Pierre Et il met combien de temps?
Conducteur Trente-cinq minutes à peu près.
Marie-Pierre C'est combien le billet?
Conducteur Vingt-cinq francs.
Marie-Pierre Un billet, alors.
Conducteur D'accord.

il met combien de temps?	*how long does it take?*
à peu près	*about (= approximately)*

To ask if this is the bus/train etc for . . .:

c'est (bien) le car/train etc **pour . . .?**

Quickies
1 How do you ask 'Is this the right train for Calais?'?
2 How long is the journey to the airport?

TV 1 Jane asked people in different jobs about their working hours.

Jane	Monsieur, vous travaillez combien d'heures par jour?
1er ingénieur	Eh bien, nous travaillons un peu plus de huit heures par jour.
Jane	Madame, vous travaillez combien d'heures par jour?
Epicière	Dix heures par jour.
Technicien	Huit heures continues.
2ème ingénieur	Environ huit heures.
Jane	Et vous travaillez combien de jours par semaine?
2ème ingénieur	Cinq jours.
Epicière	Six jours par semaine.
1er ingénieur	Nous travaillons cinq jours par semaine.
Jane	Vous commencez à quelle heure le matin?
1er ingénieur	Entre huit heures et huit heures et demie.
Jane	Vous commencez à quelle heure le matin?
Epicière	Six heures, six heures et quart.
2ème ingénieur	Je peux venir jusqu'à huit heures et demie.
Jane	Et vous terminez à quelle heure le soir?
1er ingénieur	Oh, c'est variable. Entre six heures et six heures et demie.
Jane	Et vous terminez à quelle heure le soir?
Epicière	A huit heures.
2ème ingénieur	Entre cinq heures et sept heures.

un peu plus de . . .	*a little more than . . .*
huit heures continues	*eight hours with only a short break*
je peux venir jusqu'à . . .	*I can come any time up till . . .*

To say 'quarter to/quarter past/half past':

	moins le quart
six heures	**et quart**
	et demie

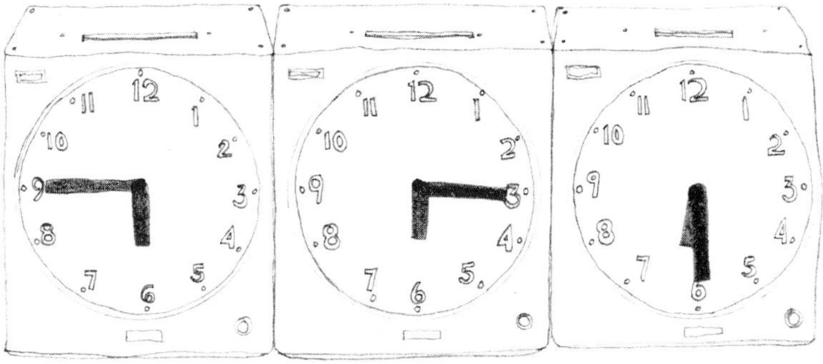

To say 'eight hours *a* day', 'five days *a* week' etc:

huit heures	**par**	jour
cinq jours	**par**	semaine

TV **2** Then Jane asked them about their holidays.

Jane Vous avez combien de congé par an?
Epicière Un mois.
1er ingénieur Nous avons quatre semaines de congé par an.
Technicien Cinq semaines, plus une semaine d'ancienneté.
2ème ingénieur Cinq semaines.
Jane Et quand est-ce que vous prenez vos vacances?
Epicière En principe au mois de septembre.
Technicien Une semaine en mars, et le reste en juillet ou août.
1er ingénieur Oh, je les prends un petit peu en été, un petit peu en hiver.
2ème ingénieur C'est très variable. Une semaine en été et le reste au cours de l'année, au choix.
Jane Et vous allez où en vacances?
2ème ingénieur Je vais au bord de la mer ou bien je visite un pays étranger.

je les prends	*I take them*
ou bien	*or else*

Verb forms
endings with *nous* and *vous*:

nous travaill**ons** **nous** part**ons**
vous travaill**ez** **vous** part**ez**

To say 'in' with a particular month or season:

en / **au mois de** | juillet

en hiver/été/automne *but* **au** printemps

Mots-clés

l'aéroport (m)	airport	l'aller-retour (m)	return ticket
l'avion (m)	plane	l'aller (simple) (m)	single ticket
le car	coach	le billet	ticket
le quai	platform	valable	valid
le taxi	taxi	l'arrivée (f)	arrival
le train	train	arriver	to arrive
changer	to change	le départ	departure
la correspondance	connection	partir	to leave, depart
direct	direct	la sortie	exit
l'horaire (m)	timetable	avant	before
l'heure (f)	hour; time	après	after
la minute	minute	le temps	time, weather
prochain	next	le matin	morning
suivant	following	l'après-midi (m/f)	afternoon
dernier	last		

le soir	evening	regarder	to look (at)
le jour	day	travailler	to work
la semaine	week	à peu près	roughly
le mois	month	environ	approximately
l'an (m)	year	devant	in front of
l'année (f)	year	la mer	sea
acheter	to buy	qui	which, who
commencer	to start	vite	quickly
terminer	to finish		

En bref

Quelle heure est-il? What time is it?

Informal	*Official*
il est huit heures	il est huit heures / vingt heures
il est huit heures dix	il est huit heures dix / vingt heures dix
il est huit heures et quart	il est huit heures quinze / vingt heures quinze
il est huit heures et demie	il est huit heures trente / vingt heures trente
il est neuf heures moins le quart	il est huit heures quarante-cinq / vingt heures quarante-cinq
il est neuf heures moins dix	il est vingt heures cinquante
il est midi	il est douze heures
il est minuit	il est vingt-quatre heures

seven o'clock *in the morning* – sept heures **du matin**
ten past three *in the afternoon* – trois heures dix **de l'après-midi**
half past eight *in the evening* – huit heures et demie **du soir**

1 Using public transport:
  1 To ask if there are trains/coaches for . . .
  (est-ce qu')il y a des trains/cars pour . . .?
  2 To ask for a ticket:
    a) single – un aller (simple)
    return – un aller-retour
    b) first/second class – en première/seconde (classe)
  eg un aller-retour en première pour Avignon, s'il vous plaît

3 To ask about arrival and departure times:

le train le car l'avion	**arrive** **part**	**à quelle heure?** **quand?**

4 To specify a particular train:

first	le **premier** train
last	le **dernier** train
next	le **prochain** train
the one after that	le train **suivant**
the Avignon train	le train **pour Avignon**
the 9.28 train	le train **de 9h28**

NB *Le train d'Avignon* is 'the Avignon train', ie going to or coming from Avignon depending on the context.

5 To ask where something leaves from and arrives:
le train part **de quel quai/d'où?**
le car arrive **où?**

6 To ask if it is the right bus/train for . . .
c'est (bien) le car/train **pour . . .?**

2 To say 'ten hours a day', 'five days a week', etc:

dix heures	**par**	jour
cinq jours	**par**	semaine
six semaines	**par**	an

Les jours de la semaine
lundi mardi mercredi jeudi vendredi samedi dimanche
Les mois

janvier	**avril**	**juillet**	**octobre**
février	**mai**	**août**	**novembre**
mars	**juin**	**septembre**	**décembre**

Les saisons
le printemps **l'été** **l'automne** **l'hiver**

3 1 To say 'on + day of the week':
Jean arrives *on Saturday* – Jean arrive **samedi**
Jean works *on Saturdays* – Jean travaille **le samedi**

2 To say 'in + month or season':

en **au mois de**	février, juin, août

en été, automne, hiver *but* **au** printemps

3 To say 'in + the morning/afternoon/evening':
le matin, l'après-midi, **le** soir
When 'in the morning' means 'tomorrow morning' say *demain matin*
NB nine o'clock *in the morning* – neuf heures **du matin**
six o'clock *in the evening* – six heures **du soir**

4 To say 'every five minutes/Saturday' etc:
toutes les cinq minutes
toutes les heures
tous les samedis
tous les mois

NB Some abbreviations found in timetables, advertisements etc:

tlj – tous les jours
sf – sauf (except)
lun, sam, dim etc – lundi, samedi, dimanche, etc
f – fermé

Verb forms

vous ... ez	**vous** commence**z** **vous** travaille**z** **vous** arrive**z**
nous ... ons	**nous** arriv**ons** **nous** travaill**ons** **nous** part**ons**
elles/ils ... ent	**ils** part**ent** **ils** arriv**ent** **Jean et Sara** travaill**ent**
elle/il ... e	**elle** arriv**e**
elle/il ... t	**il** par**t**

Pronunciation

1 The *-ent* is not pronounced: *arrive* and *arrivent* sound exactly the same.
2 In *part* the 't' is final and is not pronounced. In *partent* the same 't' is no longer final and so *is* pronounced.
3 In *elles/ils arrivent* the two words run together and the 's' is pronounced as 'z'. The only difference in pronunciation between *il arrive* and *ils arrivent* is this 'z' sound.

En plus

1 **Reaching agreement**
In standard English we say 'we *eat*' but 'he *eats*'. We can't say 'we eats' or 'he eat'. In other words, the 'we' and the 'he' affect the form of the verb 'eat'. This system of matching is called 'agreement'; the verb has to agree with 'he', 'we', etc to be correct.

This agreement system exists for French verbs too. The phrases you have met, such as:
vous av**ez**, **vous** désir**ez**, **vous** travaill**ez**, **vous** arriv**ez**
make it obvious that *vous* requires the verb to end in *-ez*.

Similarly *nous* requires – *ons*:
nous av**ons**, **nous** travaill**ons**
and *elles/ils* (or anything that *elles/ils* can stand for) require *-ent*:
elles arriv**ent**, **ils** part**ent**, **Jean et Yves** rentr**ent**

The great majority of verbs follow this pattern, which is convenient because, once you know the pattern, you can predict what a particular part of most verbs will be, even if you have never come across them. So even if you've never used, say **ils/elles** with **travailler**, you can predict that it will be: **ils** travaill**ent**.

The forms of the verb that go with *elle/il* (or anything that *elle/il* stand for) are more varied. To learn them, it is useful to know the 'infinitive'. (The infinitive is the *name* of the verb – in English, to eat, to sing, etc: it's the part given in dictionaries and in our word lists).

There are three types of infinitive:

– er	travaill**er**	to work
– ir	part**ir**	to depart
– re	prend**re**	to take

In the present tense – the only one you are learning for the moment – the endings for *elle/il* are:

– er	**elle/il**	arrive
– ir	**elle/il**	part
–re	**elle/il**	prend

Verbs that follow the pattern above are called 'regular'. But a number of verbs vary slightly, or considerably, from the pattern and are called 'irregular'. For example, some of them follow the pattern only some of the time.

faire	to do, to make	**aller**	to go	**avoir**	to have
je	fais	je	vais	j'	ai
elle/il	fait	elle/il	va	elle/il	a
nous	faisons	nous	allons	nous	avons
vous	faites	vous	allez	vous	avez
elles/ils	font	elles/ils	vont	elles/ils	ont

Others are very eccentric indeed:

être	to be
je	suis
elle/il	est
nous	sommes
vous	êtes
elles/ils	sont

Learning the four irregular verbs above will get you a long way: you can learn others as you come across them. We have marked the most common ones with a † in the vocabulary and the forms are shown on pages 318–319.

2 **Changing times**

The 24-hour system is used in France, both in writing and speech, much more widely than in Britain for all official times: timetables,

times of theatre and cinema performances, in radio and TV announcements, opening and closing times of public buildings, etc. It is written: 9h15, 20h45, etc.
In everyday speech, however, it is usual to hear the 12-hour system. If there is any possibility of confusion, the phrases *du matin* and *du soir* are used to indicate morning and evening. Am and pm are not used at all.

3 **More false friends**
Un car is not 'a car' but 'a coach'. The commonest word for 'car' is *une voiture* but you will hear *une auto* or *une automobile* as well. *Voiture* is also the word for a railway carriage. But *un bus* is always 'a bus'. And on that bus, *le conducteur* is 'the driver'.

La monnaie does not mean 'money' in the everyday sense, but 'change' – the money you get back when you have paid, or the small change in your purse. It also means 'currency'. 'Money' in the everyday sense is *l'argent*, which also, incidentally, means 'silver'.

Like the English word 'station', the French word *station* has many meanings. However, it never means 'railway station' except on the underground.
une station de métro – underground station
une station de taxis – taxi rank
une station service – service station
une station de ski – ski resort

4 **Hein**
This is a very common French noise and its sound is like the word *vin* without the 'v'. It is used in many ways. For example, it can mean 'Will you please say that again?' rather like the English 'Eh?', or it can be the equivalent of the English questions 'isn't it?', 'aren't they?', 'haven't you?' etc in expressions like:
il fait beau, hein? – it's a fine day, isn't it?
vous n'avez pas beacoup de temps, hein! – you haven't got much time, have you!

In this case, it is the casual form of another French phrase: *n'est-ce pas?* but because it feels less like a question, we have not shown a question mark in this book.

5 **Exact, exactement**
This pair of words, illustrates a useful principle. The words mean 'exact' and 'exactly'. So, in order to get the equivalent of an English word ending in '-ly' you add *-ment* to the French feminine adjective:

normal	normale	**normalement**
certain	certaine	**certainement**
rapide	rapide	**rapidement**
premier	première	**premièrement**
heureux	heureuse	**heureusement**

However, it does not always work, so be careful.

Le TGV en gare

French railways

The *Société Nationale des Chemins de Fer Français* or SNCF (pronounced 'ess enn say eff') is justifiably proud of its traditions and service. It provides clean, modern, comfortable trains that run punctually. The *corail* trains introduced over the last few years are indeed very comfortable. The fare structure is almost as complex as that of British Rail. There are reductions for certain classes of persons (pensioners for example), certain periods of time and various excursions. There are also supplements to be paid on some trains – all the Trans Europe Expresses (TEE) and certain others. A word of advice – it is prudent to find out if there is a supplement and to pay it when you buy your ticket since if you pay on the train it costs more.

For short-distance travel (eg from Paris to Versailles), you will probably have to get your ticket from a machine, which can test your understanding of written French quite rigorously. For longer journeys you will probably get your ticket at *le guichet*; look for the sign *Billets*. If you want to make enquiries, look for the sign *Renseignements*.

Tickets are not checked at the barrier but they are likely to be inspected on the train; if yours is not stamped you may well have to pay a fine. You must therefore *composter* your ticket, a reassuringly horticultural-sounding word which means to have it stamped by a machine. The machines (usually red) are at the entrance to the platform and are marked *Compostez votre billet*.

On the platform of many stations there will be a notice labelled *composition des trains*. This shows which carriages are which class, where the restaurants, buffets and guard's van are, which carriages are

going to separate destinations, and where to wait on the platform for the part of the train you want.

The new high speed trains, *les TGV* (*trains à grande vitesse*), the pride of the SNCF, began regular service in 1981 after establishing a new world record of 308km/h (237 mph) in trials earlier that year. They started with the Paris–Lyon route but by 1983 were serving also Besançon, Geneva, Montpellier and Marseille. Apart from being fast – a cruising speed of over 160 mph cuts the Paris–Lyon journey time from just under four hours to two hours – the trains have aeroplane-type seating, air-conditioning, buffets and a shop. All seats have to be reserved but there is no other extra charge except for some trains at particularly popular times. If you have got your ticket in advance but have delayed deciding when to travel, you can reserve your seat right up to the last moment by using special computer terminals at the station. If you want to know more about the many services offered by the SNCF write to French Railways, 179 Piccadilly, London W1V OBA.

Work and play

The working week in France for most people is much the same as in Britain, about forty hours. Some people we interviewed worked *une journée continue*, which shortens the working day by reducing the traditional two-hour lunch break to half an hour or so. A flexi-time system – *les horaires à la carte* – also operates in some firms.

The French are enthusiastic holiday-makers. In 1936 they won the right to a fortnight's holiday with pay. That was increased to three weeks in 1956, four weeks in 1965 and five weeks in 1981. (Incidentally there is a 30% reduction on the return railway ticket for a whole family going on annual holiday – *un billet de congé annuel*).

Bon courage

1 How would you tell someone the times on these clocks using the 12-hour system?

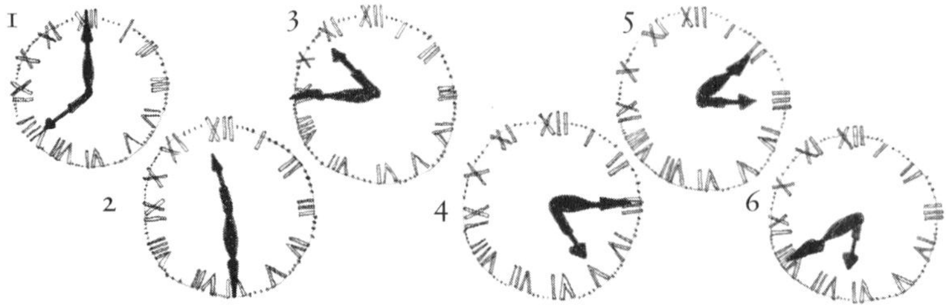

2 In the travel agency you are discussing a journey.

1 You want to arrive before these times. How will you say that using the 24-hour system?
est-ce qu'il y a un train qui arrive . . .?
12.30 pm, 2.30 pm, 10.15 am

2 To get back you want to know if there is a train after these times in the evening. How will you say that?
pour rentrer, est-ce qu'il y a un train qui part . . .?
6.0 pm, 8.15 pm, 9.30 pm

3 Marie-Pierre wants to visit a friend in La Tour du Pin. She asks about trains. Fill in the blanks using words from the list.

Marie-Pierre S'il vous plaît, je voudrais .... à La Tour du Pin. Il y .... des trains à quelle heure l'après-midi?

Hôtesse Oui. Alors, vous .... un train qui .... à 12h39, vous .... à Lyon-Perrache à 13h31. Là vous .... et vous .... l'autorail de 14h21 qui .... à La Tour du Pin à 14h58. Puis, il y .... le train de 16h05 qui .... à La Tour du Pin à 18h11.

Marie-Pierre C'est direct?

Hôtesse Non, vous .... changer également à Lyon-Perrache.

Marie-Pierre Merci bien, madame.

a (twice)
arrive
changez
part
arrivez
aller
devez
avez
arrive
prenez

4 Sara talks to Madame Pinson, a baker's wife who works with her husband Pierre and her sons Albert and Guy. Fill in the blanks using words from the list.

partent
termine
commençons
arrivent
prépare
commencez
prenons
travaillons
déjeunons

Sara Vous .... le travail à quelle heure?

Mme Pinson Alors, mon mari et moi nous .... à cinq heures. Les fils .... à six heures et nous .... jusqu'à midi et demie. Puis nous .... et nous .... un petit moment de repos. Albert et Guy .... à cinq heures et moi je .... le dîner et Pierre .... à six heures environ.

5 After several interviews Jane has these notes in her notebook:
Colette Marchal: hôtesse Syndicat d'Initiative, journée continue 8h30–17h00, sauf dim/lundi.
Michel Dupont: épicier, dix heures par jour, un mois par an, en juin, au bord de la mer.
Yvonne Duglé: technicienne, à 8h, entre 5h30 et 6h du soir, cinq semaines, une semaine au printemps et le reste au mois de septembre.

Which of these questions did she ask each person to get this information? What did the people say in reply?

1 Quel est votre métier?
2 Vous travaillez combien d'heures par jour/de jours par semaine?
3 Vous commencez à quelle heure?
4 Vous terminez à quelle heure?
5 Vous avez combien de congé par an?
6 Quand est-ce que vous prenez vos vacances?
7 Et vous allez où en vacances?

6 In the *Syndicat d'Initiative* you are enquiring about the times and costs of buses and trains to Monlac, a small town nearby. Complete your side of the conversation.

Hôtesse Bonjour, madame.
You *Greet her and ask if there are any trains to Monlac.*
Hôtesse Oui, madame, il y a deux trains par jour.
You *Ask what time they leave.*
Hôtesse Le train du matin part à 10h23 et le train du soir à 19h45.
You *Ask when the 10.23 train arrives.*
Hôtesse A 10h43, madame.
You *Ask how much a return is.*
Hôtesse Bon, alors, l'aller-retour, ça fait vingt francs quatre-vingts.
You *Ask if there are buses.*
Hôtesse Oui, il y a un car toutes les deux heures. Le premier est à 6 heures du matin, le deuxième à 8 heures du matin, le troisième à 10 heures, etc.
You *Ask where they leave from.*
Hôtesse Ils partent de la routière, Place du Marché.
You *Ask how much it is.*
Hôtesse Un aller-retour toujours? Ça fait quinze francs cinquante, madame.
You *Say good, you'd like a return ticket.*
Hôtesse Non, madame, pas ici. Vous achetez votre billet dans le car.

You	*Thank her very much and say goodbye.*
Hôtesse	Je vous en prie. Au revoir, madame, et bonne promenade!

7 You arrive at the coach station. There is a coach waiting and a driver standing by the door.

You	*Say good morning and ask him if it's the bus for Monlac.*
Conducteur	Non, c'est pour Flairon. Le car pour Monlac part à midi. Vous avez encore une demi-heure.
You	*Thank him and ask if there is a buffet in the bus station.*
Conducteur	Non, il n'y a pas de buffet ici mais vous avez le Café du Marché juste là, à la sortie de la gare, sur votre gauche.
You	*Thank him and say goodbye.*
Conducteur	A votre service, madame.

8 I What do you think the 'D's and 'A's stand for in the column on the left? Give the French.

Numéro du train		*5287*	*5705*	*6014*	*5291*	*5707*	*7313*	*1570*	*5709*	*7315*
Notes à consulter		1	2	3	23	5	6	7	2	4
Strasbourg	D							06.27		
Colmar	D							07.04		
Mulhouse	D							07.30		
Belfort	D			05.04				08.02		
Montbéliard	D			05.23				08.16		
Besançon	D	04.50		07.00	07.10			09.07		
Lons-le-Saunier	D	06.00			08.44			10.04		
Bourg en Bresse	D	06.49			09.34			10.44		
Lyon Perrache	A	07.37			10.32			11.36		
Lyon Perrache	D		08.03			11.01	11.18		12.12	12.21
Bourgoin-Jallieu	A		08.30			│	11.46		12.39	13.08
La Tour-du-Pin	A		08.40			│	11.56		│	13.23
Voiron	A		09.15			│	12.39		13.22	14.16
Moirans	A		│			│	12.46		│	14.22
Grenoble	A		09.32			12.26	12.59		13.39	14.36

Tous les trains comportent des places assises en 1re et 2e cl. sauf indication contraire dans les notes

Notes:

1 Circule les lun, sam et lend de fètes de Besançon a Lons-le-Saunier, et tous les jours de Lons-le-Saunier a Lyon-Perrache

2. Circule tous les jours
Turbotrain

3 Circule les lundis et lendemains de fêtes sauf les 1 er novembre. 26 déc. 2 janvier, 4 avril et 23 mai.

4. Circule tous les jours
Autorail

5. Départ de Lyon Brotteaux Turbotrain
Circule tous les jours saul dimanches et fêtes

6. Circule tous les jours sauf les samedis, dimanches et fêtes
Turbotrain

7. Circule tous les jours
Turbotrain

23 Circule les ven et dim jusqu 'au 12 déc et á partir de 22 avr sauf le 22 mai. Du 17 déc, au 17 avr circule les ven, sam et dim sauf fe 3 avr
Circule également les 4 avr et 23 mai Corail

2 If somebody asked you how long the train took from Bourg-en-Bresse to Lyon, would you say *plus d'une heure* or *moins d'une heure*?
3 If Marie-Pierre takes the 9.34 from Bourg-en-Bresse, how long does she have to wait at Lyon for her connection to Grenoble? Answer in French.
4 Marie-Pierre in Bourg-en-Bresse wants to go to Grenoble on Friday. What is the earliest time she can get to Grenoble if she misses the 6 am train?
5 What if she wants to go on a bank holiday?
6 If she wants to visit her friend in La Tour du Pin on a Sunday what choice of trains has she got?

9 Sara and Henri are making plans for a few days in Paris. This is what they have decided so far:
Sunday: morning ice-skating at the *patinoire*; lunch at the Restaurant du Stadium
Monday: visit Les Invalides to see Napoleon's tomb; supper at Le Louis XIV
Tuesday: lunch in Pizza Bruno; afternoon in Pompidou Centre

Look at the small ads and then decide whether they will be disappointed, and why.

Restaurant du Stadium. Tél: 583.11.00. Plat du jour 20F. Fermé dim.

Le Louis XIV. Tél: 208.56.56. Déjeuner, dîner, souper. F lundi et mardi. Fruits de mer, crustacés. Parking.

Pizza Bruno. Tél: 236.98.61. Ouvert t.l.j. Spécial. ital. 14 pizzas feu de bois. Face Musée Grévin.

Stadium. Tél: 583.11.00. Patinoire: 10h à 12h et 14h à 18h. Sam. 21h à 24h. Dim. 14h à 18h. Entrée 12F, jeunes 9F50.

Centre National d'Art et de Culture Georges Pompidou. Tél: 277.12.33. T.l.j. sf. mar. de 12h a 22h. Sam. et dim. 10h a 22h. Musée d'Art Moderne: Entrée 7F, gratuit dim.

Musée de l'Armée, Hôtel des Invalides. Tél: 555.97.30. T.l.j. de 10h à 19h. Entrée 6F. 14h à 17h films sur les deux guerres mondiales. Tombeau de Napoléon t.l.j. sf. mar. de 10h à 18h. Entrée 8F, $\frac{1}{2}$ tarif 4F.

10 The word square contains at least ten words you have met. Can you find them?

T	B	U	S	M	R	H
C	I	N	Q	A	U	E
A	L	L	E	R	E	U
R	L	U	N	D	I	R
S	E	M	A	I	N	E
L	T	R	A	I	N	S

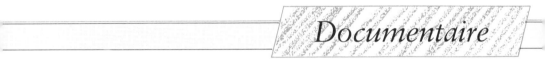

Documentaire

La journée de Michel Destot

Michel Destot is a Parisian. He came to Grenoble to study at the University, where he met his wife Marie, also from Paris. They decided to stay – like so many other people in the early 1970s, partly because of the possibilities offered in this rapidly-expanding city.

Today Michel is a physicist working at the important nuclear research centre: he is responsible for a section which studies the functioning of a small nuclear reactor, and is also involved in the training of engineers who come here to learn how to use reactors.

Marie is a part-time teacher: she fully supports Michel's involvement in political life as a town councillor. It is a busy life but they still find time to enjoy things together.

La famille Destot

Michel Destot habite Grenoble. C'est un homme très occupé. Dans la journée, il travaille comme ingénieur au Centre d'Etudes Nucléaires de Grenoble – le CENG. Mais Michel est aussi conseiller municipal: il va donc à la mairie tous les soirs après son travail.

Le matin, avant de partir travailler, Michel passe un peu de temps avec sa famille: c'est le seul moment où il peut voir ses enfants. Michel arrive au CENG à huit heures et demie. Il est responsable d'une unité qui étudie le fonctionnement d'un petit réacteur nucléaire. Michel organise aussi la formation des étudiants et des ingénieurs qui viennent au centre. Il y a là un ordinateur qui simule le fonctionnement d'un réacteur et qui permet de faire des expériences sans danger.

Vers cinq heures, Michel va à la mairie. Il est le conseiller municipal responsable de l'information et de la communication. Il doit informer les Grenoblois des projets et des actions du Conseil Municipal et écouter leurs réactions. Marier les gens à la mairie fait aussi partie de ses obligations. Pour Michel, son travail et sa passion pour la politique sont deux choses tout à fait compatibles.

Marie, sa femme, est professeur de langues dans un lycée mais elle travaille à mi-temps pour pouvoir s'occuper des enfants. Michel et Marie ont une vie très remplie. Mais, comme le dit Marie, 'on arrive finalement à trouver le temps de faire tout et prendre plaisir à faire des choses ensemble aussi'.

conseiller municipal	*town councillor*
avant de partir travailler	*before going off to work*
il peut voir	*he can see*
qui permet de faire des expériences	*which allows experiments to be made*
il doit	*he must*
marier les gens	*marrying people*
fait aussi partie de	*is also part of*
à mi-temps	*part-time*
pour pouvoir s'occuper de	*in order to be able to look after*
comme le dit Maric	*as Marie says*
on arrive . . . à	*we manage to*
prendre plaisir à faire	*enjoy doing*

7

Bon appétit!

Getting a snack or meal
Talking about likes and dislikes

The vocabulary of food and drink is vast, and eating out in a foreign country can be quite challenging if you don't know the names of the dishes. We can't predict your tastes but in the *Mots-clés* you will find some useful words you're likely to meet in restaurants and, on p145, the other items appearing in this chapter.

Radio

1 To start with, if you fancy a snack, you might want to ask if the café you're in serves food. Sara is in a café in Nantes.

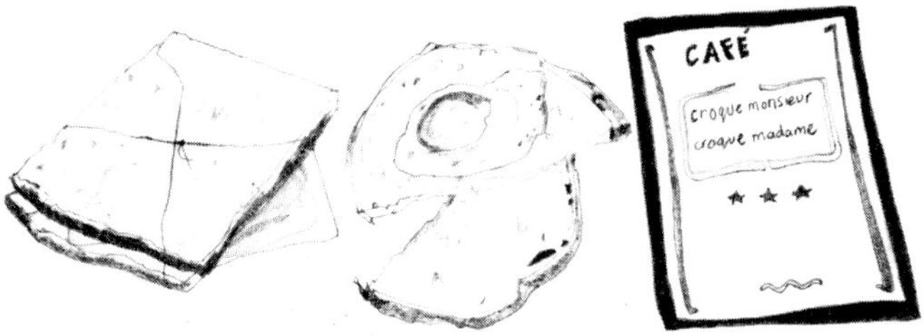

Garçon Bonjour, mademoiselle.
Sara Bonjour, monsieur. Est-ce que vous faites à manger?
Garçon Oui. Que désirez-vous?
Sara Qu'est-ce que vous avez?
Garçon Alors, croque-monsieur, croque-madame, assiette de crudités, assiette de charcuterie et sandwichs.
Sara Un croque-monsieur, s'il vous plaît.
Garçon Bien, mademoiselle. Qu'est-ce que vous voulez boire?
Sara Une eau minérale.
Garçon Très bien. Je vous apporte ça tout de suite.

est-ce que vous faites à manger?	*do you do anything to eat?*
je vous apporte ça	*I'll bring you that*

Quickies

1 What did Sara have to eat?
2 And what to drink?

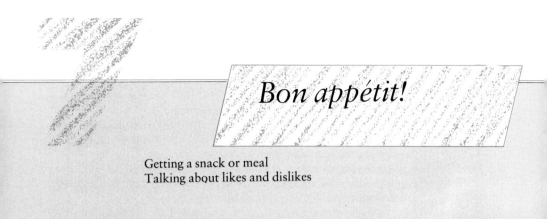

Radio 2 You can't order a *croque-monsieur* with the same confidence as Sara if you don't know what you're going to get. In a pizzeria, Sara wants to know what the *pizza sicilienne* consists of.

Sara Pardon, madame.
Patronne Oui?
Sara La pizza sicilienne, qu'est-ce que c'est, s'il vous plaît?
Patronne Alors la sicilienne, c'est une pizza aux tomates, avec fromage, anchois, oignons, câpres et olives.
Sara Et la pizza fruits de mer, s'il vous plaît?
Patronne Alors, la fruits de mer, c'est une pizza aux tomates avec fromage, moules, coques et crevettes.
Sara Alors, une pizza fruits de mer, s'il vous plaît.
Patronne Très bien, merci.

> To ask what something is:
>
> | | |
> |---|---|
> | la pizza sicilienne,
le croque-madame,
les crudités, | **qu'est-ce que c'est?** |

Quickies
1 What did Sara eat this time?
2 How would you ask what *les fruits de mer* are?

Radio 3 Now, to order a light meal. Pierrick is in *une crêperie*, a restaurant specialising in pancakes, in his home town of St-Philbert-de-Grand-Lieu.

Patronne Bonjour, monsieur.
Pierrick Bonjour, madame.
Patronne Vous désirez des crêpes?
Pierrick Oui. Qu'est-ce que vous avez comme crêpes?
Patronne Alors des crêpes ou des galettes?
Pierrick Je voudrais des galettes, s'il vous plaît.
Patronne Des galettes. Des galettes au beurre, au fromage, au jambon. Aussi, aujourd'hui, nous avons des galettes aux fruits de mer.
Pierrick Je voudrais une galette au jambon, s'il vous plaît.
Patronne Au jambon, oui. Vous désirez une boisson?
Pierrick Je voudrais un verre de cidre, s'il vous plaît.
Patronne Doux ou brut?
Pierrick Brut.
Patronne Brut. Oui, d'accord. Vous désirez une . . . une crêpe après?
Pierrick Oui, qu'est-ce que vous avez comme . . . comme crêpes?
Patronne Alors, crêpe à l'orange, au chocolat, au beurre, à la confiture.
Pierrick J'aimerais une crêpe à la confiture.
Patronne A la confiture. D'accord. Merci.
Pierrick Merci.

j'aimerais = je voudrais

Quickies
1 How does Pierrick ask what sort of pancakes they have got?
2 What two sorts of cider are there (in French)?

Un petit restaurant de quartier

Radio 4 And now, to order a whole meal. We recorded Sara and her friend Alain ordering lunch in a small family restaurant in Nantes. The young woman who owns it took their order.

Patronne Vous avez choisi?
Sara Oui. Alors, une salade de tomates.
Patronne Oui. Et pour monsieur?
Alain Une carottes râpées.
Patronne Oui. Et ensuite?
Sara Pour moi, un steak avec des pommes vapeur.
Patronne Le steak, vous le désirez saignant ou à point?
Sara A point.
Patronne Oui. Et monsieur?
Alain Pour moi un cassoulet maison et puis une salade en supplément.
Patronne Donc, pour madame un steak à point pommes vapeur, un cassoulet maison pour monsieur avec une salade en supplément.
Alain C'est cela.
Patronne Et comme boisson, qu'est-ce que vous désirez? Du rouge, rosé?
Alain Un pichet de rouge.
Patronne Et pour madame?
Sara Une eau minérale.
Patronne Une eau minérale gazeuse?
Sara Oui, gazeuse.
Patronne D'accord. Merci.

She comes back when they have finished the main course.

Patronne Vous avez terminé?
Sara Oui.
Alain Oui, oui.
Patronne Qu'est-ce que vous désirez, fromage ou dessert?
Alain Un fromage.
Patronne Oui. Comme dessert j'ai des crèmes caramel, pistache ou citron, ou alors des glaces.

Sara	Une glace pour moi.
Patronne	Chocolat, vanille ou fraise?
Sara	Chocolat.
Patronne	Merci.
Alain	Tu prends un café, Sara?
Sara	Oui, oui, oui.
Alain	(*to waitress*) Alors, deux cafés et l'addition.
Patronne	D'accord. Merci.

vous avez choisi?	*have you chosen?*
vous avez terminé?	*have you finished?*

> To ask for the bill:
>
> **l'addition**, s'il vous plaît

Quickies

1 What was their answer to the question *Et comme boisson?*?
2 What did Alain ask for along with the coffees?

TV 5 Michel Bouyssié, nicknamed Moustache, has invited his friend Fleb out for a meal. When Moustache arrives with his wife, Michèle, a little late, Fleb is already having a drink at the bar. He has not met Madame Bouyssié, hence the introduction.

Moustache	(*shaking hands*) Bonjour.
Fleb	Bonjour.
Moustache	Tu nous excuses, on est un peu en retard.
Fleb	Non, non, c'est pas grave.
Moustache	(*to his wife*) Je te présente Fleb. (*to Fleb*) Michèle, ma femme.
Michèle	(*shaking hands*) Bonjour.
Fleb	Bonjour. (*turning to Moustache*) Moustache, tu prends un apéritif?
Moustache	Oui, oui, volontiers.
Fleb	Qu'est-ce que tu prends?
Moustache	Un pastis.
Fleb	Et vous, Michèle, que prenez-vous?
Michèle	Un kir.
Fleb	(*to barman*) Monsieur, s'il vous plaît, un pastis et un kir.
Garçon	Le pastis avec des glaçons?
Moustache	Oui, un ou deux, merci.

c'est pas grave *that's alright*

que prenez-vous? = qu'est-ce que vous prenez?

> To introduce people:
>
> **je te/vous présente . . .**

> frequently *on* = *nous*
> on est en retard (see *En plus*) – we're late

Quickies

1 How did Moustache say 'We're a bit late'?
2 A useful phrase to learn: 'What'll you have?'

TV **6** After their *apéritifs*, the three friends sit down and order dinner.

Moustache Vous avez choisi?
Michèle Oui.
Fleb Oui.
Garçon Messieurs-dame?
Moustache Fleb, qu'est-ce que tu prends?
Fleb (*to Michèle*) Après vous.
Michèle On se tutoie, tu es d'accord?
Fleb Oui.
Michèle Tu es notre invité, tu choisis.
Fleb Ben, dans ce cas, (*to waiter*) une salade des moines, s'il vous plaît.
Garçon Oui.
Michèle Et une tranche de jambon cru.
Garçon Oui.
Moustache Pour moi, ce sera une tarte aux épinards.
Garçon Parfait. Et comme viande?
Fleb Les atriaux de Thonon, c'est quoi?
Garçon Les atriaux de Thonon est une charcuterie macérée dans du vin blanc, enveloppée dans une crépine, passée au four et servie chaude.
Fleb (*not convinced*) Oui, oui, je prendrai plutôt la côte et le filet d'agneau avec gratin dauphinois.
Garçon Parfait. Madame?
Michèle Une truite au bleu.
Garçon Une truite au bleu. Et monsieur?
Moustache Un filet grillé, saignant, s'il vous plaît.
Garçon Oui. Et comme légumes?

Moustache	Est-ce que les plats sont garnis?
Garçon	Alors, les viandes sont garnies gratin dauphinois et la truite pommes vapeur.
Moustache	Dans ce cas, mettez-moi donc des haricots en plus, s'il vous plaît.
Garçon	Et comme boisson?
Moustache	(*to the others*) Qu'est-ce qu'on prend? Une réserve du patron?
Fleb	Oui.
Garçon	La réserve du patron est servie en pichet.
Moustache	Bien, alors un pichet de rouge et une carafe d'eau.
Garçon	Parfait.

c'est quoi?	*informal way of saying* qu'est-ce que c'est?
je prendrai	*I'll have*
mettez-moi	*give me*
en plus	*as well*

Verb forms

verbs with *tu* always end in *-s*:
tu excuses
tu prends
tu es
tu choisis

verbs with *on* end the same as with *il/elle*:
on est
on prend
on arrive

Quickies

1 How did Moustache want his steak?
2 What is the *réserve du patron*?

Radio 7 Jean Fournier, in the rather smart La Tour restaurant at Châtillon, has an *apéritif* while he decides which of the fixed-price menus to choose.

Serveuse Bonjour, monsieur. Voici la carte.
Jean Merci, madame.
Serveuse Est-ce que vous désirez un apéritif?
Jean Oui, volontiers. Un petit kir.
Serveuse Un kir, d'accord. (*later*) Alors, monsieur, vous avez choisi votre menu?
Jean Oui. Un menu à soixante francs.
Serveuse D'accord. Comme entrée qu'est-ce que vous avez choisi?
Jean Une assiette de crudités.
Serveuse D'accord. Ensuite?
Jean Votre volaille, c'est du poulet?
Serveuse C'est du poulet, oui.
Jean Du poulet de Bresse?
Serveuse Pas de Bresse, mais un bon poulet.
Jean Bon. Alors, je prends un poulet au Beaujolais.
Serveuse Oui.
Jean Comme garniture?
Serveuse C'est du riz. Mais si vous désirez un autre légume, on peut vous faire un gratin dauphinois.
Jean Alors, je préfère un gratin dauphinois.
Serveuse D'accord. Et comme boisson? Vous avez choisi?
Jean Vous avez des demi-bouteilles?
Serveuse Oui.
Jean Bon. Alors, donnez-moi une demi-bouteille de Beaujolais-Villages.
Serveuse D'accord. Vous désirez de l'eau?
Jean Une carafe, s'il vous plaît.
Serveuse Une carafe d'eau. Très bien. Voilà. Bon appétit, monsieur.
Jean Merci, madame.

She returns after the main course.

Serveuse C'est terminé, monsieur?
Jean Oui, madame.
Serveuse Comme fromage, vous désirez le plateau de fromages ou fromage blanc à la crème?
Jean Plutôt le plateau de fromages.
Serveuse Plateau de fromages, bon. Et comme dessert? Vous avez glace vanille, sorbets fraise ou poire, mousse au chocolat, ou tarte aux pommes.
Jean Donnez-moi un sorbet à la poire, s'il vous plaît.
Serveuse Sorbet à la poire. Bon, c'est d'accord.
Jean Et ensuite, un café, s'il vous plaît.
Serveuse Vous prenez un café. D'accord.
Jean Et l'addition, s'il vous plaît.
Serveuse Entendu.

on peut vous faire . . . *we can do . . . for you*

Quickies

1 How much of Jean's menu can you reconstruct: *apéritif, entrée, plat principal, fromage, dessert*?
2 And what did he have to drink?
3 How did he say he'd rather have the *gratin dauphinois*?

Dans un fast food

We did a survey in the streets of Grenoble about the French and food.

TV **1** Jane first asked people what they thought the national dish was. No two people seemed to agree.

Jane Monsieur, quel est le plat national français?
1er passant Ah, le mien est le steak-frites.
2ème passant Eh ben, ça dépend de la région où on est. Si vous êtes dans le Midi-Pyrénées c'est le cassoulet. Ici, c'est le gratin dauphinois.
Jane Quel est le plat national français?
1ère passante (*sounding surprised*) Français?
3ème passant C'est le couscous.
2ème passante Oh, les pommes de terre, non?
4ème passant Le gratin dauphinois.

le mien *mine*

Quickie Which of the dishes mentioned above can you remember in French?

TV 2 Then Jane asked them about fast food, which has really caught on in France over the last few years – as have the American names for it.

Jane Et le fast food, vous connaissez?
2ème passant Oui, mais je l'apprécie pas beaucoup.
Jane Vous aimez pas les hamburgers, alors?
2ème passant Ah, pas du tout.
Jane Et le fast food, vous connaissez?
1er passant Le . . . pardon?
Jane Le fast food?
1er passant Ah non, j'ai pas cette chance, non.
5ème passant Ah, c'est la nouvelle conception, oui, du repas rapide, oui.
Jane Vous aimez ça?
5ème passant Ah! Moi, moi, je . . . je trouve pas ça désagréable, oui.
3ème passante Le fast food, yes.
Jane Et vous aimez ça?
3ème passante Not very much!

vous connaissez?	*have you heard of it?*
je l'apprécie pas beaucoup	*I don't think much of it*

Quickie What is the opposite of *agréable*?

Notice that French uses *le, l', la, les* in these sentences where English doesn't have 'the':
le steak, c'est le plat national
j'adore **le** champagne
les fraises coûtent moins cher en été
la bière accompagne très bien **la** choucroute

TV 3 Finally, Jane asked people what their own favourite dish was and what foreign food they liked.

Jane Quel est votre plat préféré?
2ème passante Tous.
2ème passant Eh bien, un plat très simple, ce sont les spaghettis à l'italienne, à la bolognaise.
5ème passant Un veau, un veau à l'ancienne, hein.
3ème passant Ah, le steak-frites.
3ème passante La choucroute, que je fais moi-même.
Jane Et dans un repas, qu'est-ce que vous préférez, l'entrée, le plat principal?
3ème passante Les entrées.
2ème passant Le plat de résistance comme on dit, le plat principal et le . . ., et les desserts aussi.
Jane Vous avez un faible pour les desserts?
2ème passant Ah oui, je suis très gourmand.
1er passant Alors, ce que j'aime bien, ce sont les entrées, le fromage et énormément le dessert.
Jane Et quelle est votre cuisine étrangère préférée?
4ème passant La chinoise.
5ème passant Cuisine étrangère? J'adore la cuisine chinoise.

2ème passante	Italienne.
3ème passante	La chinoise.
1er passant	Ce sont les spaghettis.
2ème passant	Ah ben, la cuisine chinoise.
Jane	Merci.
2ème passant	Voilà.

moi-même	*myself*
comme on dit	*as it's called*
ce que j'aime bien ce sont	*what I really like are*

To say how much you like or dislike:

j'aime j'aime bien j'ai un faible pour j'aime énormément j'adore je préfère je n'aime pas je déteste	le steak-frites la choucroute les spaghettis

Quickies

1 How would you say:
   a) 'I like French cooking';
   b) 'I love steak and chips'?
2 When one of the people interviewed says *Je suis très gourmand*, how do you know it's a man speaking?

Food vocabulary in this chapter

à l'ancienne cooked according to a traditional recipe

à point medium (of steak)

la carte the menu, ie the whole list of what the restaurant has to offer (see also *menu*)

le cassoulet a stew of goose, duck, mutton and pork cooked with haricot beans (see *haricots*); speciality of Toulouse region

charcuterie, assiette de- plate of assorted cold meats

la choucroute sauerkraut; shredded salted cabbage; speciality of Alsace

la choucroute garnie sauerkraut served with a variety of sausages, smoked pork, etc

le couscous a kind of semolina served with vegetables, lamb and chicken stew and a hot chili sauce, originally from North Africa

crudités, assiette de- plate of assorted raw vegetables

la crêpe pancake

la crépine sausage skin

le croque-monsieur toasted sandwich of ham and cheese

le croque-madame as above but with a fried egg on top

le fromage blanc a very soft cream cheese

les fruits de mer sea food

la galette a pancake made from buckwheat (see page 190)

garni served with vegetables

la garniture the vegetables provided with a particular dish

le glaçon ice cube

le gratin dauphinois potatoes with cream cooked in the oven until they have a crisp brown topping

Des fruits de mer

les haricots: haricots verts are French or green beans; *haricots blancs* are haricot beans

macéré left to soak for several hours in a liquid

maison when this word is attached to a dish it means special to that particular establishment and sometimes home-made, often to a personal or traditional recipe

le menu set meal; the 'menu' (*la carte*) can consist of several *menus* at different prices

le pastis an aniseed-based spirit drunk with water as an *apéritif*, extremely popular in the south of France

passé au four finished off by being briefly cooked in the oven

le pichet jug or pitcher

les pommes de terre potatoes, is often shortened to *pommes*. Not to be confused with *pommes* = apples

les pommes vapeur plain boiled potatoes

le repas meal

la réserve du patron normally not a named wine but a cheapish one recommended by the *patron*

le riz rice

saignant rare (of meat)

la salade de tomates tomatoes sliced, dressed with oil and vinegar and sprinkled with parsley and sometimes garlic. It's usually served as a cheap hors d'oeuvre.

le service service charge or tip

le steak-frites steak and chips

le sorbet water ice

en supplément as an extra to a set fixed-price menu

la truite au bleu poached trout

Mots-clés

aimer	to like/love	l'agneau (m)	lamb
choisir	to choose	le boeuf	ox; beef
manger	to eat	le cidre	cider
préférer	to prefer	la confiture	jam
l'apéritif (m)	aperitive	la côte	rib
l'entrée (f)	first course (*also* entrance)	la crème caramel	creme caramel
le plat principal	main course	le filet	fillet
le fromage	cheese	les frites (f)	chips
le dessert	dessert	grillé	grilled
l'addition (f)	bill	le légume	vegetable
l'assiette	plate	la pizza	pizza
la cuisine	cooking; kitchen	le poisson	fish
le patron	owner	la salade	salad; lettuce
		le veau	calf; veal
		la viande	meat
		aujourd'hui	today
		le Midi	south of France

En bref

1 To ask in a café 'do you do anything to eat?':
(**est-ce que**) **vous faites à manger?**

2 1 When you've seen the menu, the waiter will say:

vous avez choisi?	have you chosen?
qu'est-ce que vous prenez?	what will you have?

2 To say what you'll have:
un steak-frites, **s'il vous plaît**
je prends un steak-frites
pour moi, un steak-frites
NB French doesn't use *avoir* (to have) when ordering food and drink. The equivalent of 'I'll have' is *je prends*.

3 To ask what something is (eg a dish on the menu):

qu'est-ce que c'est,	la pizza sicilienne?
	la choucroute garnie?
	le TGV?

4 1 To say you like something/somebody:
j'aime énormément = I really like
j'adore = I love
j'aime = I like
j'aime bien = I quite like
j'apprécie = I like/I think highly of

NB *aimer* on its own to refer to a person can mean more than you may intend:
je t'aime = I love you
je t'aime bien = I like you
so be careful.

2 To say you don't like something:
je n'aime pas = I don't like
je n'aime pas du tout = I don't like . . . at all
je déteste = I hate
je n'apprécie pas = I don't think much of

In French *l', le, la, les* are often used where English does not use 'the':

il aime **la** cuisine française	he likes French cooking
elle aime **les** films italiens	she likes Italian films
je déteste **les** spaghettis	I hate spaghetti

5 To introduce people to each other:
Monsieur Marat, **je vous présente** Madame Corday
Pierre, **je te présente** ma femme Mary

6 **On**
1 a pronoun meaning 'one' or 'you' in the general sense:
en France, **on** mange le fromage avant le dessert
2 frequently used in spoken French to mean *nous*:
on prend la réserve du patron?

Verb forms

tu + -s	*on* takes the same form as *il/elle*
tu manges	**on** mange
tu choisis	**on** choisit
tu pars	**on** part
tu fais	**on** fait
tu es	**on** est

NB Whatever the spelling, the *tu* form and the *il/elle/on* forms are pronounced exactly the same in all verbs.

En plus

1 **You and you**
Modern English is unique among European languages in having only one word for 'you'. In French there is *tu* (with the related words *te* and *toi*) and also *vous*. The important difference is that *tu* is used only to talk to someone with whom you are on close terms – members of your family, friends, often people you work with. Young people readily use *tu* to each other as a sign of informality, and everyone uses *tu* with small children. Paradoxically, outside these circumstances, using *tu* can imply contemptuous superiority on the part of the person using it. Irate motorists frequently use it to each other! The rule for foreigners is simple: use *vous* unless your French friends use *tu* to you. There are even two verbs for referring to which form you are using. Using *tu* to someone is called *tutoyer*, using *vous* is called *vouvoyer*.

2 Another use of 'you' is to mean not the person you are talking to but people in general: 'You can't park there on Saturdays'.

On in French means this generalised 'you', 'one' or 'they': *en France, on ne travaille pas le dimanche*, and so it appears in many proverbs: *on ne fait pas d'omelettes sans casser d'oeufs*.

It is also regularly used in spoken French instead of *nous*. When Moustache says *on est en retard*, he means, and could just as well have said, *nous sommes en retard*.

3 **What's cooking?**
Cuisine is the word for 'kitchen' as well as for the action or process of cooking, so *la cuisine* is the place where *vous faites la cuisine*.

The words for meats in English and French have an interesting history. In English the names of the animals are Anglo-Saxon and the names of the meats are French, brought over with William the Conqueror.

cow	beef	*boeuf*
calf	veal	*veau*
pig	pork	*porc*
sheep	mutton	*mouton*

At some stage the British developed the dish 'beefsteak' ('steak' is an old Norse word for 'roast') and the name was taken up by the French who to this day call it *le bifteck*, though the word *steak* has almost replaced it. You will also come across *le rosbif*. Steak and chips – *le biftek-frites* or *le steak-frites* – has become probably the most popular everyday French dish. So, by one of those ironies of history, the British, whose cooking is scarcely respected by the French, gave them their national dish.

Eating out
By law, restaurants must display their menu (*la carte*) outside so that customers can consult it freely before entering. Many restaurants display two or three fixed-price set meals (*les menus*), possibly with choices within each one. Most places also have the *à la carte* system of listing all their first courses, main dishes, etc and you make up your own menu from that. In some cases, restaurants will advertise *les plats du jour* (that day's special dishes) as a separate item.

Most dishes are *garnis*, that is, they have vegetables with them. You can usually order extra vegetables from those on the menu, but in a fixed-price meal these might be *en supplément*. A green salad is traditionally eaten as a course on its own after the main dish and normally consists of lettuce dressed with oil and vinegar. On some of the cheaper menus, *salade* is not included in the price and the third course will be *fromage ou dessert* (cheese or dessert) and not both. Wine, beer or mineral water is sometimes included in the cheaper menus, in which case the menu will probably say *boisson comprise*. Otherwise it will say *boisson non comprise* and you'll have to pay extra for the drink.

When it comes to paying the bill (*l'addition*) you will find that a service charge of about 15% is usually included in fixed-price menus but may not be if you have chosen *à la carte*. Something about it should be printed on the menu. The phrases to look out for are:

service compris	service included
service non compris	service extra
le service est à l'appréciation de la clientèle	service is at the customer's discretion

If you are not sure, it is perfectly normal to ask: *le service est compris?*

Meals
Eating habits are changing in France as elsewhere and the traditional times and types of meal are by no means observed by everybody. Nevertheless they still remain the general pattern for most people.

le petit déjeuner breakfast

The English and French express the same idea, as *jeûner* means 'to fast' and so *déjeuner* means 'to break one's fast'. And, as the phrase suggests, *le petit déjeuner* is thought of as a little something to get you through to . . .

le déjeuner midday meal

This is traditionally the biggest meal of the day and the French lunch hour can last about two hours. Except in the very biggest towns, life seems to come to a stop between noon and 2 pm and streets, towns and even main roads suddenly become deserted as if by magic just after 12. Sometimes even parking meters are free.

le goûter teatime snack

Eaten usually only by children when they come home from school to keep them going during the long gap between *le déjeuner* and *le dîner*.

le dîner evening meal

Eaten around 7.30 onwards. In private homes this is a family meal but not usually as big as *le déjeuner*. In Switzerland and Canada, *le dîner* is the midday meal. In country districts *le dîner* is often referred to as *le souper*.

More changing customs
Like most other European countries, France has been invaded by foreign dishes and styles of cooking, as the mention of *la cuisine chinoise, les spaghettis à la bolognaise*, etc shows. France's former colonies, Indochina and Algeria, have introduced many dishes of which the North African *couscous* and *merguez* have become particularly popular. *Merguez* is a hot spicy mutton sausage. *Le fast food* is more recent.

Le shake-hand
The British shake hands when they are first introduced and then rarely again. Outside the family circle, the French tend to shake hands whenever they meet for the first time that day and when they leave each other. Moustache shook hands with his friend Fleb when they met in the bar, Fleb and Madame Bouyssié shook hands on being introduced and they would all shake hands again when they parted later that evening.

When you are introduced to a French person, you can simply reply *Bonjour, monsieur/madame/mademoiselle/Pierre*, according to how you have been introduced, or you can use the traditional phrase *Enchanté(e), monsieur/madame/mademoiselle.*

Bon courage

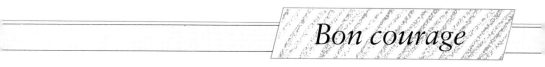

1 Say that you have a weakness for these:
les spaghettis à la bolognaise; le sorbet à la fraise

and that you don't like these at all:
la choucroute; la salade de tomates

2 Say that you love these:
le steak-frites; les hamburgers

and that you hate these:
le gratin dauphinois; le camembert

3 Which of the nouns on the left fit the definitions on the right?

1 le fromage	a) ils sont verts ou blancs
2 le steak-frites	b) du pain, du fromage et du jambon
3 les frites	c) c'est une spécialité italienne
4 les haricots	d) il est rouge ou blanc ou rosé
5 la pizza	e) ce sont des pommes de terre cuites avec de la crème
6 le gratin dauphinois	

7	le vin	f)	les Anglais les aiment beaucoup avec le poisson
8	un croque-monsieur	g)	c'est probablement le plat national français
		h)	les Français le mangent avant le dessert

4 Which of the phrases on the right complete the sentences begun on the left? There is more than one completion for some of the beginnings.

1	tu	a)	préfères le thé?
2	Fleb	b)	sommes de Cleckheaton
3	elle	c)	se tutoient
4	on	d)	prenez quelque chose?
5	nous	e)	aimes ça?
6	vous	f)	adore les hamburgers
7	ils	g)	n'aimons pas le fast food
8	Sara et Alain	h)	est gourmande
9	j'	i)	mange à une heure
		j)	êtes allemand?
		k)	aiment beaucoup les frites
		l)	faites des sandwichs?

5 Can you sort out these words to make sentences?

1 les desserts et adore fromages les j'
2 le c'est fast rapide le food repas
3 j' énormément qu'on dans cassoulet mange Midi le aime le
4 n' hamburgers vous les pas aimez?

6 The two parts of these snippets of conversation have got mixed up. Can you sort them out?

1 Je vous présente Monsieur Moineau.
Oui, fraise, vanille ou chocolat?
2 Qu'est-ce que vous prenez?
Je vous apporte ça tout de suite.
3 Vous avez des glaces?
Un kir, s'il vous plaît.
4 Une glace à la pistache, s'il vous plaît.
Enchanté, monsieur.

7 You and your friend fancy a snack and you sit down on the terrace of a likely-looking café. Here comes the waiter.

You *Ask him if they do food.*
Garçon Mais oui, monsieur. Qu'est-ce que vous désirez?
You *Ask what they have got to eat.*
Garçon Alors, nous avons des pizzas, croque-monsieur, assiettes de crudités, assiettes de charcuterie et des sandwichs.
You *Ask what sort of pizzas they have.*
Garçon Nous avons des pizzas napolitaines, siciliennes et des pizzas quatre saisons.
You *Ask him what a four seasons pizza is.*

Garçon C'est une pizza aux champignons, coeurs d'artichaut et tomates avec saucisse et fromage.
You *Say you'd like a Sicilian pizza.*
Garçon Très bien, monsieur, et pour madame?
You *After consultation say 'madam' prefers a* croque-monsieur.
Garçon Et comme boisson?
You *Say a mineral water for you and a beer for 'madame'.*
Garçon Très bien, monsieur. Je vous apporte ça tout de suite.

8 This time you want a full meal. You've gone to a small restaurant with a friend who speaks only English. The owner gives you the menu (see opposite).

Patron Bonsoir, m'sieur-dame. Voici la carte.

He comes back later.

Patron Vous avez choisi?
You *Yes, you want two fifty-franc menus.*
Patron Parfait. Alors, pour commencer?
You *You've forgotten to translate the first section for your companion. Tell him what's on. He chooses the egg and you the pâté. Tell the owner.)*
Patron Très bien, madame.
You *Ask him what* boeuf à la provençale *is.*
Patron C'est du boeuf cuit au four avec des herbes et du vin rouge.
You *Say no, you prefer the* cassoulet.
Patron Et pour monsieur?
You *A steak.*
Patron Comment le voulez-vous, votre steak?
You *Rare, please. Ask what sort of vegetables there are.*
Patron Avec le steak il y a des pommes frites, ou bien des épinards, des petits pois, des carottes . . .
You *Ask for some chips please, and have they got any green beans?*
Patron Oui, bien sûr, madame. Et qu'est-ce que vous voulez boire?
You *Say a jug of red wine.*
Patron Un grand ou un petit?
You *Say a big jug.*

Later he returns with the first course.

Patron Voilà, bon appétit, m'sieur-dame.
You *Reply appropriately.*

Later he returns again.

Patron Vous avez terminé?
You *Yes, thank you.*
Patron Vous voulez un fromage ou un dessert?
You *Ask him what cheese he has got.*
Patron Cantal, Munster et camembert.
You *You'd like some camembert, please.*
Patron Et pour monsieur?
You *An ice cream.*
Patron Chocolat, fraise, vanille, pistache . . .?
You *A strawberry one and two coffees, please.*

Patron Très bien, madame.
You *Oh, and the bill, please!*

After your cheese and dessert the patron reappears with two coffees and two brandies you haven't ordered.

Patron Voilà vos cafés, m'sieur-dame. Vous parlez très bien le français. Vraiment très, très bien. Permettez-moi de vous offrir un petit cognac.
You *Thank him very much. It's very kind.*

Le restaurant Paul Bocuse

For Paul Bocuse, cooking is a family tradition going back to the eighteenth century, when his ancestors ran a restaurant on the banks of the Saône, just north of Lyon. Bocuse trained with some of the greatest chefs in France and set up on his own in 1959 just a few yards from the restaurant of his ancestors.

Success was rapid. In 1961 he was awarded his first Michelin star, and by 1965 had gained the coveted three stars awarded to only a handful of restaurants in the country. In 1975 he became the first chef in France to be awarded the Légion d'Honneur.

Today, he is probably the most famous chef in France, perhaps the world. He has restaurants in Japan, the United States and South America; he writes books and is often on TV and in the press. He is proud to proclaim the glories of French cooking to the world.

Paul Bocuse dans son restaurant

Le restaurant de Paul Bocuse est un des plus connus en France. Les gens viennent de Paris, de Genève, d'un peu partout pour y manger. Et d'après Luigi Ricci, le maître d'hôtel, ce ne sont pas tous des gens fortunés. Il y a aussi des clients qui ne viennent qu'une fois dans leur vie, pour fêter un anniversaire chez Bocuse.

Cinquante personnes travaillent dans le restaurant pour préparer et servir 160 repas par jour. Paul Bocuse ne passe pas tout son temps dans les cuisines. Il doit s'occuper de toute l'organisation du restaurant. Roger Jaloux, son chef de cuisine, est donc responsable de la qualité des plats. Il a dix-huit personnes sous ses ordres.

Selon Bocuse, 'un bon cuisinier, c'est l'homme qui sait acheter ses produits'. Il attache beaucoup d'importance à la qualité et à la fraîcheur des ingrédients. Tous les matins, Paul Bocuse va au marché de Lyon et achète lui-même ce qu'il faut pour le restaurant. Il pense que la région lyonnaise est un véritable 'garde-manger', avec les vins de Bourgogne, du Beaujolais et des Côtes du Rhône, les poulets de Bresse, le boeuf du Charolais, les fromages et les poissons. C'est pourquoi Lyon est un des grands centres de la gastronomie française.

Au restaurant Paul Bocuse, la cuisine est basée sur des principes traditionnels: la crème et le beurre sont des ingrédients essentiels. Les sauces sont très importantes, mais elles ne doivent pas cacher le goût de la nourriture. Chez lui, Bocuse fait une cuisine beaucoup plus simple – un potage poireaux-pommes de terre, un pot au feu ou des fraises du jardin avec un peu de vin et un peu de sucre. Pour lui, l'art de cuisiner, c'est de savoir acheter de bons produits et faire ressortir les parfums naturels des ingrédients.

un des plus connus	*one of the best-known*
d'un peu partout	*from just about everywhere*
des gens fortunés	*wealthy people*
qui ne viennent qu'une fois	*who only come once*
il doit s'occuper de	*he has to take care of*
sait acheter	*knows how to buy*
lui-même	*himself*
ce qu'il faut	*what's needed*
elles ne doivent pas cacher	*they mustn't hide*
savoir acheter	*knowing how to buy*
faire ressortir	*to bring out*

Faites votre choix

Shops and shopping
Opening and closing times
Making choices from a range of goods
Saying what you like doing in your spare time
Saying what you're going to do

Opening and closing hours of French banks, offices and shops can be very different from those in Britain so it is as well to know how to find out about them.

1 In the *Maison du Tourisme* in Grenoble, Jane Cottave asks about the opening times.

Jane L'Office du Tourisme ouvre à quelle heure le matin?
Hôtesse L'Office du Tourisme ouvre à neuf heures le matin et ferme à dix-huit heures trente le soir, avec une fermeture pour le déjeuner de douze heures trente à treize heures trente.
Jane Et c'est ouvert tous les jours de la semaine?
Hôtesse C'est ouvert tous les jours de la semaine du lundi au samedi inclus.
Jane Et c'est ouvert toute l'année?
Hôtesse C'est ouvert toute l'année sauf les dimanches et les jours de fête.

du lundi au samedi *from Mondays to Saturdays*

Quickies
1 Seven days make ... Answer in French.
2 What are the phrases for 'every day' and 'all the year round'?

2 Now Jane asks about opening hours in a clothes shop (*un magasin de vêtements*).

Jane Madame, vous ouvrez à quelle heure le matin?
Commerçante J'ouvre à neuf heures quinze, je ferme à midi, et l'après-midi de quatorze heures à dix-neuf heures.

Jane Vous êtes ouvert tous les jours de la semaine?
Commerçante Tous les jours de la semaine sauf le lundi matin, et le dimanche, bien entendu.

Radio 3 Bakers tend to stay open much longer. Here's Jean in a small town near Lyon.

Jean Nous sommes chez Madame Archeny, boulangère à Châtillon-sur-Chalaronne. Madame Archeny, quelles sont vos heures d'ouverture?
Mme Archeny Alors, mes heures d'ouverture: de cinq heures du matin à huit heures du soir, et le lundi nous fermons.
Jean Tous les jours donc.
Mme Archeny Oui. Ouvert tous les jours, sauf le lundi.
Jean Vous ne fermez pas à midi?
Mme Archeny Non, monsieur. Nous ne fermons pas. Nous restons ouvert toute la journée.

toute la journée *all day long*

To indicate time from . . . to . . .:

ouvert | **de** six heures (**jusqu'**)**à** midi
du lundi **au** samedi

To say 'the whole day/month/year':

toute la journée
tout le mois
toute l'année

Quickies

1 The shop opens at five o'clock in the morning: what's that time in French?
2 What is the difference between *toute la journée* and *tous les jours*?

Radio 4 Tobacconists stock a range of smokers' accessories including inexpensive throw-away lighters. Marie-Pierre is buying one in Bourg.

Buraliste Bonjour, madame.

Marie-Pierre Bonjour, monsieur.
Buraliste Madame?
Marie-Pierre Vous avez des briquets jetables?
Buraliste Oui, j'en ai à tous prix. Cinq francs, six francs, sept francs et huit francs.
Marie-Pierre (*pointing to one*) Il coûte combien, celui-ci?
Buraliste Alors, celui-ci, six francs.
Marie-Pierre (*pointing to another*) Et celui-là?
Buraliste Alors, ceux-là font sept francs.
Marie-Pierre Et ceux-là avec les messages?
Buraliste Avec les messages, six francs également. Oui, c'est ça, hein. Et j'en ai aussi d'ordinaires à cinq francs. Sans dessin. Normal.

Marie-Pierre Je vais prendre celui-ci.
Buraliste Alors celui-ci. Quel motif vous préférez?
Marie-Pierre La banane.
Buraliste La banane. (*taking it down for her*) Voilà, madame.
Marie-Pierre Il marche?
Buraliste Ah oui, (*trying it*) impeccable.
Marie-Pierre C'est combien?
Buraliste Alors, six francs.
Marie-Pierre Voilà.
Buraliste Merci, madame. Au revoir, madame.
Marie-Pierre Au revoir, monsieur.

à tous prix	*at all prices*
j'en ai d'ordinaires	*I have plain ones*

To say 'this one', 'that one' when referring to masculine nouns:	
celui-ci	this one
celui-là	that one
And in the plural 'these (ones)', 'those (ones)':	
ceux-ci	these (ones)
ceux-là	those (ones)

Quickies

1 If you're buying a lighter how do you say 'How much is that one?'?
2 What did the banana have to do with it?

Radio 5 Marie-Pierre has gone into a rather smart glass and china shop to look for a present.

Marie-Pierre Bonjour, madame.
Vendeuse Bonjour, madame. Vous désirez?
Marie-Pierre Est-ce que je peux regarder, s'il vous plaît?
Vendeuse Bien sûr, je vous en prie. Regardez.
Marie-Pierre C'est combien, cette assiette, s'il vous plaît?
Vendeuse Quatorze francs l'une.
Marie-Pierre Et celle-là?
Vendeuse Vingt-huit francs. Elle est décorée main.
Marie-Pierre C'est joli.
Vendeuse C'est très joli.
Marie-Pierre Et cette tasse, c'est combien?
Vendeuse Cette tasse avec sa soucoupe vaut trente-six francs.
Marie-Pierre Et ça, qu'est-ce que c'est? C'est un cendrier?
Vendeuse C'est un cendrier, madame.
Marie-Pierre C'est combien, s'il vous plaît?
Vendeuse Il vaut cent quarante-cinq francs.
Marie-Pierre Bon. Je vais réfléchir. Je vous remercie, madame.
Vendeuse Mais je vous en prie, madame. A votre service.
Marie-Pierre Au revoir, madame.
Vendeuse Au revoir, madame.

est-ce que je peux . . .?	*may I . . .?*
décorée main	*hand-painted*
il vaut 145F = il fait 145F	

> To escape gracefully if you think something's too expensive:
> **je vais réfléchir** – I'll think about it

> To say 'this one', 'that one' when referring to feminine nouns:
> **celle-ci** this one
> **celle-là** that one
>
> And in the plural 'these (ones)', 'those (ones)':
> **celles-ci** these (ones)
> **celles-là** those (ones)

Quickies

1 If you're buying a cup, how do you say 'How much is this one?'?
2 In a shop how would you say 'May I look round, please?'?
3 And as you leave, how would you say 'I'll think about it'?

TV 6 In Grenoble, Claudine Billiez also wants to buy a present. She goes to a shop that sells the work of local craftsmen.

Claudine Bonjour, madame.
Vendeuse Bonjour, madame.
Claudine Qu'est-ce que vous avez comme vases en terre cuite?
Vendeuse Nous avons beaucoup de choix. Vous cherchez quoi exactement?
Claudine Un vase assez simple.
Vendeuse (*showing her one*) Comme celui-ci par exemple à cent francs?
Claudine Oui. Il est joli. Vous avez d'autres couleurs?
Vendeuse Oui. Celui-ci en blanc ou celui-là en bleu.
Claudine Le bleu est joli mais il est un peu trop grand. Vous en avez un plus petit?
Vendeuse Oui. Comme celui-ci, par exemple?
Claudine Ah, très bien. Il fait combien?
Vendeuse Cent francs, madame.
Claudine Parfait. Je le prends.
Vendeuse Vous voulez un paquet-cadeau?
Claudine Oui, volontiers.

vous voulez un paquet-cadeau? *do you want it gift-wrapped?*

> *Grand* on its own means 'big'. Here are some variations:
>
> | | | | |
> |---|---|---|---|
> | **assez** | grand | quite | big |
> | **très** | | very | |
> | **trop** | | too | |
> | **un peu trop** | | a bit too | |
>
> and
>
> | | |
> |---|---|
> | **plus** grand | bigger |
> | **un peu plus** grand | a bit bigger |
> | **beaucoup plus** grand | much bigger |

Quickies	1	What sort of vase does Claudine want?
	2	What does she say is wrong with the blue one?

TV 7 Maud Cottave and Mireille Lamour go into a clothes shop to buy a dress.

Mireille Bonjour.
Vendeuse Bonjour, mesdames.
Maud Bonjour.
Vendeuse Que désirez-vous?
Maud Je cherche une robe en coton, s'il vous plaît.
Vendeuse Elles sont ici.
Maud Merci. (*holds up a dress*) Elle est jolie.
Mireille Ah oui, très jolie. (*showing Maud another dress*) Et la grise? Regarde.
Maud (*not too sure*) Oui . . .
Mireille Non? (*she puts it back*)
Maud (*pointing to a green dress*) Vous avez la même en bleu?
Vendeuse Non. Je ne l'ai pas en bleu. Je l'ai en vert, en rouge, mais pas en bleu.
Mireille (*taking out another dress*) Et la beige?
Maud Ah oui. Vous l'avez en trente-huit?
Vendeuse Oui, c'est une taille trente-huit. Voulez-vous l'essayer?
Maud Oui, s'il vous plaît. Merci.
Vendeuse (*pointing to changing room*) Allez-y.

Later Maud comes out wearing the dress

Maud Attends, je vais regarder.
Vendeuse Elle vous va très bien, cette petite robe. C'est très joli.
Maud Qu'est-ce que tu en penses?
Mireille Moi, j'aime beaucoup.
Maud Oui?
Vendeuse Ah oui.
Maud Et elle fait combien?
Vendeuse Sept cent quinze francs. Vous la prenez?
Maud Ah oui, je la prends. (*looking in mirror*) Oui, oui, ça va.

voulez-vous l'essayer?	*do you want to try it on?*
allez-y	*go ahead*
elle vous va	*it suits you*

To avoid repeating a noun already mentioned by using pronouns *le/la/les* (see *En plus*):
je prends **la robe** — je **la** prends
j'ai **la même robe** en vert — je **l'**ai en vert

To say 'the big one(s)', 'the red one(s)', etc, don't use the word for 'one':
tu aimes la robe verte? — je préfère **la grise** (ie **la robe grise**)
tu aimes le petit vase? — je préfère **le grand** (ie **le grand vase**)
vous voulez les grandes tasses? — je prends **les petites** (ie **les petites tasses**)

To specify colour/size/material:		
j'ai cette robe	(en)	rouge
vous l'avez	**en**	trente-huit?
une robe	**en**	coton
un vase	**en**	terre cuite

Quickies

1. What sort of dress does Maud want?
2. How many colours can you remember?
3. What size does she want?

Rencontres

Grenoble has plenty of leisure facilities, but which are the most popular?

TV 1 Jane asked people how they liked to spend their spare time (*le temps libre*).

Jane Qu'est-ce que vous aimez faire quand vous avez du temps libre, madame?
1er passant Me promener à pied, je suis collectionneur, je lis, je vais quelquefois au cinéma et la vie de famille est importante pour moi.
1ère passante Moi, ce que j'aime faire, la cuisine.
2ème passant Il y a plein de trucs. Ça manque pas.
2ème passante J'aime bien aller dans les musées voir les tableaux.
3ème passante Tout.
Jane C'est-à-dire?
3ème passante Du sport, tout.
Jane Qu'est-ce que vous aimez faire le soir?
1er passant Le soir, je lis . . . quelquefois la télévision . . . ou chez des amis.
Jane Qu'est-ce que vous aimez faire le soir?
2ème passant Le soir? Surtout lire.
3ème passante Cinéma . . . danser.
2ème passante Je regarde un peu la télé mais pas trop, hein.
Jane Et qu'est-ce que vous aimez faire le soir?
3ème passant Lire . . . le cinéma, la télévision pas trop souvent.
Jane Et vous préférez aller au théâtre, au cinéma ou regarder la télévision?
1ère passante Au théâtre, certainement.
1er passant Le cinéma plutôt.

2ème passant Théâtre, surtout en ce moment il y a pas mal de pièces qui passent.
3ème passante Cinéma.
4ème passante Ah le cinéma et le théâtre, mais certainement pas la télé.

ce que j'aime faire	*what I like doing*
il y a plein de trucs	*there are loads of things*
ça manque pas	*there's no shortage*
c'est-à-dire?	*meaning?*
pas mal de pièces qui passent	*quite a lot of plays on*

To say what you like/prefer doing:

j'aime / **je préfère**	**faire** la cuisine **aller** dans les musées **lire** **regarder** la télé

Quickies

1 How would you ask someone 'What do you like doing in the evening?'?
2 How would you say 'I like going to the cinema'?

TV 2 Then Jane asked them what they were going to do that particular evening.

Jane Et ce soir, qu'est-ce que vous allez faire?
4ème passante Ah, je ne sais pas, je prévois jamais à l'avance.
1er passant Ce soir, lundi, j'ai pas de projets particuliers.
1ère passante Ce soir, oh, ce soir, c'est beaucoup moins drôle que ce qu'on pourrait croire. Je vais faire de la tapisserie, nettoyer, refaire ma maison.
2ème passant Je vais voir ma petite copine.
Jane Et qu'est-ce que vous allez faire ce soir?
3ème passante Ce soir je vais me coucher.

moins drôle que ce qu'on pourrait croire	*less amusing than you might think*

To say what you are going to do:

je vais	**voir** ma petite copine **faire** de la tapisserie **nettoyer** la maison **me coucher**

Mots-clés

fermé	closed
fermer	to close
ouvert	open
ouvrir	to open
le coton	cotton
la robe	dress
la taille	waist; size
la tasse	cup
allez-y	go ahead
chercher	to look for
chez	at the home/shop of
par exemple	for example
sauf	except
danser	to dance
libre	free
lire	to read
le sport	sport
la télévision	television
la vie	life
en ce moment	at the moment
(ne) . . . jamais	never
quelquefois	sometimes
souvent	often

En bref

1 To give time from . . . to . . .:

ouvert | **de** dix heures (**jusqu'**)**à** midi
ouvert | **du** lundi **au** samedi

To say:

	this one	that one
masculine	**celui-ci**	**celui-là**
feminine	**celle-ci**	**celle-là**
	these ones	those ones
masculine	**ceux-ci**	**ceux-là**
feminine	**celles-ci**	**celles-là**

2 To specify what colour/size/material you want:
vous avez cette robe **en** rouge?
je l'ai **en** quarante-quatre
un vase **en** terre cuite

3 To say 'bigger'/'smaller':
ce vase est **plus grand**
cette robe est **plus petite**

4 To say '*too* big', '*very* big', '*quite* big':

trop **très** **assez**	grand

These can be made negative by adding *pas*: *pas trop grand*, etc

To say 'bigg*er*'/'*not so* big':

plus **moins**	grand

And to say '*a bit* bigg*er*'/'*a lot* bigg*er*':

un peu **beaucoup**	**plus** grand

5 To avoid repetition of nouns already mentioned, you can use the pronouns *le/la/l'/les* (see *En plus*):
vous aimez *la robe,* madame? oui, je **la** prends
vous connaissez *Monsieur Martin?* oui, je **le** vois tous les jours
Henri est gentil oui, je **l'**aime bien
vous prenez *des spaghettis?* non, je ne **les** aime pas

6 To say things like 'the green one', 'the big one', etc:
tu aimes *le vase blanc*? non, je préfère **le rouge**
je voudrais *un briquet* alors, nous en avons **des bleus** et **des verts**

7 To say what you like/prefer doing:
aimer/préférer + infinitive

j'aime **je préfère**	lire aller au cinéma

8 To say what you are going to do:
aller + infinitive
qu'est-ce que vous **allez faire** ce soir?
je **vais regarder** 'A vous la France!'

Learn a verb
aller – to go

je	vais
tu	vas
il/elle/on	va
nous	allons
vous	allez
ils/elles	vont

1 I and he or him and me?

Marie-Pierre buys the lighter

Henri drinks the red wine

the wine makes Henri ill

cats sometimes have fleas

In all these cases it is quite easy to see the relationships between, for example, Marie-Pierre and the lighter, and the cat and the fleas. Technically this relationship is referred to as *subject* and *object*. 'Henri' is the subject of the verb 'drinks' and 'the red wine' is the object. In the next sentence, 'the wine' is the subject of 'makes' and 'Henri' is the object.

This subject/object difference is important when it comes to using pronouns. Pronouns, like the nouns they stand for, can be subjects or objects. In chapter 4 we introduced the subject pronouns *elle, il, elles, ils*. In this chapter we have introduced three object pronouns:

la	her/it
le	him/it
les	them

je prends *la robe*	je **la** prends
j'aime *les épinards*	je **les** aime
vous connaissez *Pierre?*	non, je ne **le** connais pas

Two things to notice:

1. The order of words is different from English: the pronoun goes in front of the verb instead of after it.
   je *l'*aime bien   I like *her/him/it*
   je vais *le* faire   I'm going to do *it*
2. The *ne . . . pas* goes round the object pronoun as well as the verb.
   je *ne* le connais *pas*   I don't know him

Don't be confused because these object pronouns are also the words for 'the'. Two completely different jobs are simply being done by the same set of words.

2 Enough is not always enough

Assez is a word that has several uses.

With *de* + a noun it means 'enough':
j'ai assez de fromage, merci   I have enough cheese, thank you

With an adjective it means 'enough' or 'quite' or 'rather':
assez joli   pretty enough, quite pretty, rather pretty
assez grand   big enough, quite big, rather big

But when it has *pas* in front of it, *assez* can only mean 'enough':
pas assez grand   not big enough

3 **Another nearly false friend**

Marcher does not mean 'to march' though it can mean 'to walk'. Another of its common meanings is 'to work (of mechanical things)' – watches, cars, television sets, lighters. It is also used in a more general way to mean things are going well, *ça marche*, and even, on a good day, *ça marche bien*, or those desperate times when *ça ne marche pas*. In this sense it is equivalent to *ça va*, *ça va bien*, *ça ne va pas*.

4 **A bit of 'this' and 'that'**

There are no separate words for 'this' and 'that' in French: *ce/cet/cette/ces* mean both. If it is important to make the distinction, then *-ci* (for 'this') or *-là* (for 'that') is added to the end of the noun.

ce café-*ci*	*this* café
cet hôtel-*là*	*that* hotel
cette voiture-*ci*	*this* car
ces tomates-*là*	*those* tomatoes

In many cases the difference is not felt to be important and so *-ci* and *-là* are not used. But, the words for 'this one', 'that one', 'these (ones)' 'those (ones)' *must* be accompanied by *-ci* or *-là*: *celui-ci/celle-ci, celui-là/ celle-là, ceux-ci/ ceux-là, celles-ci/ celles-là.*

5 **Wotcher, mate!**

French has at least as many slang, near-slang, swear words and other not-so-proper words as English. The ones you meet in this book are reasonably safe to use.

Une copine/un copain are much used among young people instead of *une amie/un ami.*

Un truc: sometimes this just means 'a thing', sometimes it means the thing you can't remember the word for, 'a whatsit'. Another very similar word is *un machin*:
  tu as le truc pour ouvrir le machin?
  have you got the whatsit for opening the thingummy?

Plein de: the standard expression for 'full of', but also commonly used as a colloquial equivalent of *beaucoup de*:
  il y a plein de trucs – there are loads of things

Pas mal: used of a person this means 'good-looking':
  il est pas mal, celui-là he's not bad (looking), that one
pas mal de . . . means 'quite a lot of . . .':

  il (n')y a pas mal de musées à Grenoble
  there are quite a lot of museums in Grenoble

Not too little, not too much, but just right!
Some clothes sizes can be different in France so here's how to get the right fit.

For men and children it is relatively easy. You need to know your measurements in centimetres and, for children, your height.

neck	*tour de cou*
chest	*tour de poitrine*
waist	*tour de taille*
hips	*tour de bassin*
inside leg	*entre-jambes*
height	*hauteur*

Occasionally you may find the old sizes being used. For trousers these are half the waist measurement – waist 80 cms, old style size 40.

For jackets, sweaters etc

chest measurement	88	92	96	100	104	108	112	116
old size	40	42	44	46	48	50	52	54

For women, it is useful, of course, to have your measurements but size numbers are still widely used. They are:

GB	8	10	12	14	16	18	20
France	36	38	40	42	44	46	48

All shoe sizes are different. These equivalents can only be approximate and may be half a size out:

France	36	37	38	39	40	41	42	43	44	45
GB women	4	5	6	7	8	9				
men				5	6	7	8	9	10	11

Gift wrapping
If you buy an item in a shop that may be given as a present the assistant will probably ask you if you want it gift-wrapped. You may be asked:

je vous fais un paquet-cadeau? shall I gift-wrap it for you?

or

c'est pour offrir? are you going to give it as a present?

The item will then be carefully wrapped in coloured paper (sometimes you may be able to choose) and often decorated with coloured ribbons, all at no extra charge.

Public holidays (*les jours fériés* or *les jours de fête*)
Le Jour de l'An – New Year's Day

Le lundi de Pâques – Easter Monday

Le Premier Mai – 1st May, Labour Day. Trade Unions have

celebratory demonstrations and friends give each other bunches of lily of the valley (*le muguet*).

L'Ascension – Ascension Day, the sixth Thursday after Easter

Le lundi de Pentecôte – Whit Monday, the seventh Monday after Easter

Le Quatorze Juillet – 14th July. *La Fête Nationale* commemorating the day the people stormed the Bastille in 1789 and thus started the French Revolution.

L'Assomption – 15th August, the feast of the Assumption

La Toussaint – 1st November, All Saints Day. This is the day when French people visit the family grave, in some cases travelling across the country to do so. Traditionally, potted chrysanthemums are put on the graves, which is why they are never otherwise given as presents.

Le Onze Novembre – 11th November, Armistice Day

Le Jour de Noël – Christmas Day

Girl friends and boy friends

In English, when we say we are going out with a friend, nobody knows whether the friend is male or female. If we say 'girl friend', 'boy friend', 'lady friend' etc, the nature of the relationship seems to have changed and become rather more than platonic. The same doesn't go for French. You can't help mentioning the gender of your friends:

ce soir je dîne avec	un ami une amie

Nothing more than friendship is implied with these words. If you want to stress that it's your boyfriend or girlfriend, adults would probably say:
mon ami/amie
Younger people might well say:
mon petit ami/ma petite amie
mon (petit) copain/ma (petite) copine

The man in *Rencontres* who said *Je vais voir ma petite copine* was making rather a joke of it.

Les Maisons de la Culture

These are the dream of André Malraux, De Gaulle's Minister of Culture in the 1960s, who was himself a world-renowned writer. The idea was to create arts centres in the provinces in order to bring art to the ordinary people, to counteract the centralising cultural effect of Paris and to encourage local artistic development. The buildings were to include theatres, concert halls, book and record libraries, art galleries and meeting rooms. Many of them, like the one in Grenoble, are built in bold and interesting new styles. Fifteen such centres now exist of which Grenoble is the largest with a full-time staff of eighty-four.

1 How would you say 'I like this one' or 'I like these' referring to the following things?

2 How would you say 'I prefer that one' or 'I prefer those' referring to the following things?

3 *Le, la, les* in the following sentences stand for nouns. Which nouns in the list are they most likely to be representing?

1 Jean le mange.
2 Maud la prend en taille 38.
3 L'hôtesse la donne à Madame Trabut.
4 A Grenoble, vous le prenez pour aller à la Bastille.
5 Monsieur et Madame Bouyssié ne les aiment pas.
6 Sara le cherche; elle aime regarder les tableaux.
7 C'est très bien, je le prends.

le musée, le téléphérique, le steak saignant, la robe beige, la liste des hôtels, les crêpes, le vase

4 Put the appropriate part of the verb *aller* in the gaps:

1 Marie-Pierre .... acheter un briquet.
2 Sara et Alain .... déjeuner au restaurant La Tour.
3 Pierrick .... visiter l'île de Noirmoutier.
4 Mireille: 'Maud, qu'est-ce que tu .... faire aujourd'hui?'
5 Maud: 'Je .... chercher une robe en coton. Tu viens avec moi?'
6 On .... rester à la maison ce soir.
7 Monsieur et Madame Bouyssié: 'Nous .... voir notre ami Fleb'.
8 Et vous, qu'est-ce vous .... faire?

5 You are telling a French person about your family and friends. From the description, which present are you going to give each of them when you get home?

1 Mon frère George adore le fromage.
2 Ma soeur Caroline aime beaucoup faire la cuisine.
3 Ma cousine Kay préfère le vin français.
4 Mon cousin Henry aime énormément regarder les tableaux.
5 Mon amie Sandra adore les films de Truffaut.
6 Peter, le mari de Sandra, aime beaucoup le thé.

Cadeaux

un catalogue illustré du Musée de Peinture, un livre sur la Nouvelle Cuisine française, un camembert, une jolie tasse, une 'Histoire du Cinéma Français', une bouteille de Beaujolais-Villages

6 Our interviewer has caught up with you and wants to know what your pet hates are and what you really like.

Interviewer Bonjour, madame. Je voudrais vous poser quelques questions. Vous êtes d'accord?
You *Certainly, go ahead.*
Interviewer Qu'est-ce que vous n'aimez pas, qu'est-ce que vous détestez, qu'est-ce que vous n'aimez pas faire du tout?
You *You don't like cleaning the house.*
Interviewer Oui?
You *You hate rosé wine.*
Interviewer Ah, ça, c'est intéressant.
You *You hate trying on dresses.*
Interviewer Bon.
You *You don't much like going to the cinema, you prefer watching the telly.*
Interviewer Bon, et qu'est-ce que vous aimez?
You *You quite like French bread. You like banana sandwiches a lot and you love big moustaches . . .*
Interviewer Ah, mais c'est formidable! Qu'est-ce que vous aimez faire?
You *You love eating in small restaurants.*
Interviewer Ah bon, alors un sandwich à la banane dans un petit restaurant avec un homme qui a une grande moustache, c'est le paradis pour vous?
You *Yes, exactly.*

7 Your Aunt Mabel always expects a very special present. A vase seems a good idea. You are in a shop trying to find something suitable.

You *Ask what they have in the way of vases.*
Vendeuse Oh, j'en ai beaucoup, madame, de toutes les couleurs et à tous les prix. Celui-là par exemple à cent cinquante francs.
You *It's too big.*
Vendeuse Alors, celui-là, le vert.
You *Yes, it's pretty. Ask how much it is.*
Vendeuse C'est décoré main, très à la mode, n'est-ce pas? Il fait deux cent cinquante francs.
You *That one's too big as well.*
Vendeuse Alors, voici un joli petit vase.
You *No, that one's much too small.*
Vendeuse Qu'est-ce que vous pensez des gris, là-bas, sur la table?
You *Those ones? No, you don't like them in grey. Ask if she has them in blue.*
Vendeuse Oui, un seul, celui-là, à gauche.
You *That's it. Ask how much that one is.*
Vendeuse Quatre-vingt trois francs, madame.
You *Say good, you'll take it.*
Vendeuse C'est pour offrir, madame?
You *Yes, thank you. (You pay and she wraps the vase.)*
Vendeuse Voilà.
You *Say thank you and goodbye.*
Vendeuse Je vous en prie, madame, au revoir.

8 Find your way out of the maze. A sentence begins at the first arrow and ends at the second one. You can move only into the next square but in any direction including diagonally. Spaces between words are not included but hyphens are. The first is done for you.

E	U→	S	+	+
O	L	E	V	+
+	V	L	R	A
+	+	E	T	E
+	S→	B→	I	N

elle vous va très bien.

J	S	I	+	+
E	A	L	N	E
V	A	D	R	+
+	+	P	R	+
+	+	+	+	E

C	L	E	+	+
—	E	A	S	T
I	L	+	+	J
U	+	+	O	L
+	+	+	+	I

J	P	R	T	U
E	E	E	A	H
R	F	R	E	E
+	E	L	A	+
A	L	T	R→	E

Amateurs et professionnels du spectacle

The circus may have originated in England, but it seems to be flourishing in France, where the number of small troupes is increasing. The existence of circus schools might have something to do with this. Although most are not intended specifically as a training ground for circus artists, they offer children of any age and ability a chance to learn the skills of the ring. A small circus school set up recently in Grenoble has proved tremendously popular.

Grenoble has a reputation as being one of the liveliest cultural centres outside Paris. It is particularly well endowed with museums, galleries, concert halls, cinemas and theatres. There are frequent festivals, and Grenoble is well-known as a centre for jazz. But it is the *Maison de la Culture* which has contributed most to the town's cultural life. It presents all types of artistic activity, but is best known as home of the *Centre Dramatique National des Alpes*, a theatre with its own resident acting company which has a nationwide reputation.

'J'ai toujours été passionné de cirque': c'est André, organisateur et responsable de la petite école de cirque de Grenoble, qui parle ainsi. André lui-même n'est pas un professionnel du cirque: il est professeur d'éducation physique. André pense que les techniques du cirque sont des activités sportives très motivantes pour les enfants. Son école a quatre ans. Les 140 enfants qui viennent ont entre trois et quinze ans. Ici, ils peuvent se détendre en apprenant le monocycle, l'acrobatie ou le jonglage. Mais tous ne vont pas devenir des artistes de cirque; sur plusieurs centaines d'enfants, il y en a seulement deux ou trois qui feront peut-être un jour un spectacle dans un vrai cirque. Pour faire du cirque, il faut d'abord des qualités physiques – de la force et de la souplesse. Et il ne suffit pas d'être doué, il faut aussi énormément de travail.

Grenoble: la Maison de la Culture

Après le cirque, le théâtre. A la Maison de la Culture, les acteurs du Centre Dramatique National des Alpes – le CDNA – répètent une pièce de Tchékhov, 'les Trois Soeurs'. Ariel Garcia Valdès, le metteur en scène, adore Tchékhov. Pour lui, c'est l'un des rares auteurs qui permettent aux acteurs de s'exprimer pleinement sur le plan de la psychologie des personnages. Dans 'Les Trois Soeurs' le rôle principal est celui d'Olga. Il est interprété par Annie Perret, une comédienne de la troupe. Presque tous les acteurs du CDNA sont grenoblois. Beaucoup sont amis depuis l'âge de dix-sept ou dix-huit ans. Il y a aussi des comédiens qui viennent de Paris. Grâce à la ville de Grenoble et à sa Maison de la Culture, le CDNA a pris des dimensions nationales et la troupe est connue dans toute la France. Comme le dit Ariel Garcia Valdès, 'c'est un phénomène rare en France'.

son école a quatre ans	*his school is four years old*
ont entre trois et quinze ans	*are between 3 and 15 years old*
ils peuvent se détendre en apprenant	*they can have fun while learning*
sur plusieurs centaines d'enfants	*out of several hundred children*
qui feront peut-être un jour	*who will perhaps one day do*
il ne suffit pas d'être doué	*it's not enough to be gifted*
énormément de travail	*a tremendous lot of work*
s'exprimer pleinement	*to express themselves fully*
sur le plan de . . .	*as far as . . . is concerned*
une comédienne	*an actress*
a pris des dimensions nationales	*has become important at a national level*
comme le dit Ariel	*as Ariel says*

Dites-moi

Asking what to do and how to do it
Talking about sports and games

Radio

1 To reduce motor traffic around the old part and town centre, the municipality of La Rochelle runs a scheme for the free loan of bikes. Sara has taken one and is trying to find her way to the station to meet a friend.

Sara Mademoiselle, s'il vous plaît?
Jeune fille Oui?
Sara Pour aller à la gare?
Jeune fille Oui. Alors, (*pointing to the right*) vous allez descendre là tout droit, cette rue.
Sara Oui.
Jeune fille A l'Hôtel de Ville vous tournez à gauche, tout droit, toujours tout droit, jusqu'au canal. Vous traversez le canal et ensuite vous continuez toujours tout droit. Vous avez le port sur votre droite et la gare est juste devant vous.
Sara D'accord. Alors donc, (*recapping*) je tourne à droite ici, ensuite je vais jusqu'à la mairie.
Jeune fille Oui, c'est ça.
Sara Je traverse le canal et puis c'est toujours tout droit.
Jeune fille C'est ça.
Sara C'est loin?
Jeune fille Eh non. En vélo vous allez y arriver en cinq minutes, hein.
Sara D'accord. Au revoir.
Jeune fille Au revoir.

vous allez y arriver *you'll get there*

To ask the way to somewhere:

pour aller	**à la gare,** **au port,**	s'il vous plaît?

Quickies
1. How is Sara getting around?
2. How long will it take her to get to the station?
3. What two expressions both mean 'town hall'?

TV

2 Bernard and Michèle, in the Hôtel Porte de France in Grenoble, want to know how to get to a village in the Chartreuse. So Bernard asks Monsieur Charvoz, the proprietor of the hotel.

Un village de Chartreuse

Bernard Pardon, monsieur. Comment fait-on pour aller en Chartreuse?
M Charvoz En Chartreuse, oui. Dans quelle direction désirez-vous aller?
Bernard La Brévardière. Je crois que c'est du côté de St-Pierre.
M Charvoz Oui. Vous longez l'Isère, vous prenez le quatrième pont, vous traversez l'Isère. Arrivés au bout, vous tournez à droite. Vous continuez tout droit jusqu'à la première jonction. Vous prenez à gauche la direction du Sappey et arrivés au Sappey, vous demandez. Ils doivent connaître . . . sûrement, hein.
Bernard Oui. Donc, je longe les quais . . .
M Charvoz Oui. Jusqu'au quatrième pont. Vous traversez l'Isère. Arrivés au bout du pont, vous prenez à droite. Vous marchez tout droit jusqu'à la première jonction. A la jonction vous prenez la direction du Sappey. Et arrivés au Sappey, vous demandez à nouveau. Ils connaissent sûrement.
Bernard Très bien. Merci beaucoup.
M Charvoz Voilà. Bonne journée, m'sieur-dame!

comment fait-on pour . . .?	*how do you . . .?*
je crois que	*I think (that)*
du côté de	*in the direction of/towards*
arrivés à	*once you've got to*
ils doivent connaître	*they're bound to know*

Quickies
1. Which bridge did Michèle and Bernard have to cross?
2. Once across the bridge, which way did they have to go?

TV 3 Having got to Le Sappey, Bernard and Michèle pull up to ask the way again.

Michèle Pardon, monsieur. C'est bien la route de St-Pierre?
Passant Oui, madame. Vous continuez tout droit.
Michèle Et pour aller à La Brévardière?
Passant La Brévardière. C'est entre Le Sappey et St-Pierre, ça, non?
Michèle Je ne sais pas. Je ne suis pas d'ici.
Passant Oui, oui. C'est un petit hameau après le Col de Porte. Bon. Vous continuez tout droit. Vous traversez une forêt de sapins. Vous montez le . . . au Col de Porte, et de l'autre côté, je crois que c'est la première ou la deuxième route à droite, mais c'est mal indiqué.
Michèle Bon. Je vous remercie.
Passant Je vous en prie, madame.
Michèle Au revoir.
Passant Au revoir, madame.

---

c'est mal indiqué *it's badly signposted*

Quickies

1 *Vous montez* is the opposite of *vous descendez*. What do they mean?
2 How do you say you're a stranger in the place?

TV 4 Bernard is hiring a car and has asked to be shown how it works. The man from the office holds the car door open for him to get in.

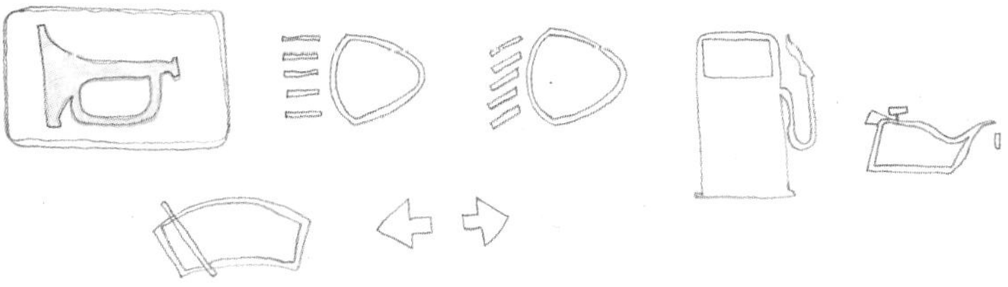

Employé Veuillez prendre place, s'il vous plaît.
Bernard Merci. Pour mettre en route qu'est-ce qu'il faut faire?
Employé Alors, vous tournez le contact. Alors . . .
Bernard Et il y a un starter?
Employé Alors, il n'y a pas de starter. C'est une voiture automatique.
Bernard D'accord. Et qu'est-ce qu'il faut faire pour l'éclairage?
Employé Pour avoir les veilleuses, vous tournez une première fois la commande.
Bernard Oui.
Employé Vous tournez une deuxième fois pour avoir les codes.

Bernard Oui.

Employé Et vous appuyez sur la commande pour avoir les phares.

Bernard D'accord. Et les essuie-glace?

Employé Pour avoir les essuie-glace, vous appuyez une première fois pour avoir les essuie-glace intermittents.

Bernard Oui.

Employé Vous tournez une deuxième fois pour avoir les essuie-glace petite vitesse.

Bernard Oui.

Employé Et vous tournez une troisième fois pour avoir les essuie-glace grande vitesse.

Bernard D'accord.

Employé Pour avoir le klaxon, vous appuyez simplement sur la commande.

Bernard D'accord. Bien. Je pense que ça va.

Employé Très bien.

Bernard Je vous remercie.

Employé Je vous en prie. Au revoir, monsieur. Et bonne route!

Bernard Merci.

veuillez . . .	*would you kindly . . .*
vous tournez le contact =	vous tournez la clé de contact
je pense que ça va	*I think that's alright*

To ask what has to be done:

qu'est-ce qu'il faut faire | pour mettre en route?
pour l'éclairage?

Quickies

1 Apart from how to start the car, what other three things was Bernard told about?

2 If *le starter* is not 'the starter' what is it?

Radio 5 Pierrick has been bitten by insects so he's in the chemist's looking for a cure.

Pharmacien Bonjour, monsieur.

Pierrick Bonjour, monsieur.

Pharmacien Vous désirez quelque chose?

Pierrick Est-ce que vous avez quelque chose pour les piqûres d'insectes?

Pharmacien Oui. C'est-à-dire pour prévenir ou pour guérir?

Pierrick Vous voyez, j'ai des piqûres d'insectes sur le bras et sur le dos également.

Pharmacien (*looking at the bites*) Oui. Alors vous voulez quelque chose de curatif, donc.

Pierrick C'est ça, oui.

Pharmacien Attendez, je vais vous montrer. (*he fetches some cream*) Voici une crème. Vous la mettez trois fois par jour: matin, après-midi et le soir. Ou autrement vous l'appliquez avant d'être exposé aux piqûres de moustiques, hein. Et ça protège pendant quatre à cinq heures, à peu près.

Pierrick D'accord. Merci beaucoup. Et c'est combien?

Pharmacien Alors, le prix est indiqué (*looking for the price*). Dix-sept francs quarante.

Pierrick	Voilà. Dix, quinze et dix-sept quarante.
Pharmacien	Oui. Merci beaucoup.
Pierrick	Merci. Au revoir, monsieur.
Pharmacien	Oui. Bonne journée! Au revoir.

c'est-à-dire	*that's to say*
je vais vous montrer	*I'll show you*
avant d'être exposé à	*before being exposed to*

Quickies

1 What two parts of Pierrick's body are mentioned?
2 When did he have to put the cream on?

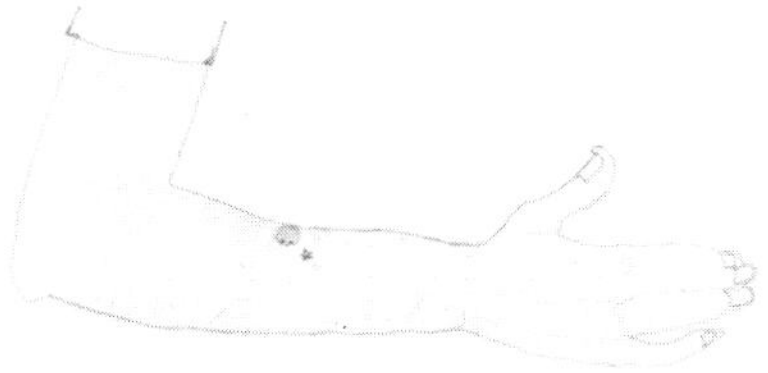

Radio 6 Sara is suffering from sunburn, so she has also gone to the chemist's.

Pharmacienne	Bonjour, madame.
Sara	Bonjour, madame. Je voudrais quelque chose pour les coups de soleil, s'il vous plaît.
Pharmacienne	Oui. Est-ce que je peux voir, s'il vous plaît?
Sara	C'est là, sur les épaules.
Pharmacienne	Oui, en effet, c'est très rouge. Je vais vous donner une crème.
Sara	Oui.
	The chemist returns with the cream.
Pharmacienne	Alors, voici. Voici une crème. Il faut l'appliquer matin et soir, pendant plusieurs jours.
Sara	Merci. Je vous dois combien?
Pharmacienne	Vingt-quatre francs.
Sara	Voilà.
Pharmacienne	Merci.

est-ce que je peux voir? *may I see?*

To ask for something for a particular purpose:

je voudrais **vous avez**	**quelque chose pour**	les coups de soleil(?) les piqûres d'insectes(?)

Quickies

1 What part of Sara's body is mentioned?
2 When did she have to put the cream on?

Radio 7 In Chapter 7 Pierrick ordered a *galette* in his local *crêperie*. He's there again, but this time to ask the owner, Madame Douaud, to make a *galette* and give us a running commentary.

Pierrick Madame Douaud va nous montrer comment on fait une galette à l'oeuf et au jambon. N'est-ce pas, madame?

Mme Douaud Oui, bien sûr. Alors, vous prenez un peu de pâte. Vous étalez sur la galettière. Vous la mettez bien sur la plaque – sur la galettière, quoi. Il faut la laisser cuire environ une minute ... une minute à peu près.

Pierrick De chaque côté une minute?

Mme Douaud Non, non, non, d'un seul côté ... d'un seul côté. Ensuite vous cassez l'oeuf dessus – l'oeuf ou deux oeufs. Vous poivrez ... un peu de sel. Et puis vous préparez votre tranche de jambon ... voilà ... que vous posez sur l'oeuf comme ça. Ensuite avec votre spatule vous pliez votre galette. Moi, je la plie en quatre.

Pierrick Pour faire un carré.

Mme Douaud Pour faire un carré, oui. Et puis voilà, l'opération est terminée. Un peu de beurre dessus et elle est prête à servir. Voilà.

Pierrick Ça a l'air très, très bon!

Mme Douaud Bon appétit!

ça a l'air ... *it looks ...*

To say something has to be done:

il faut	la laisser cuire	you have to let it cook
	l'appliquer	you have to rub it on

Rencontres

Grenoble is a very sports-conscious town. The winter Olympic Games were held there in 1968 and exceptionally good, modern facilities are available for winter and other sports.

TV 1 First, Jane asked people if they thought the French were keen on sport.

Jane D'après vous, est-ce que les Français sont sportifs?

1er passant Oui, un tout petit 'oui'.

Jane Est-ce que les Français sont sportifs, selon vous?

1ère passante Oui.

Jane Oui?

1ère passante Oui.

2ème passant Pas tellement.

2ème passante	En spectateurs plus qu'en acteurs, oui.
3ème passant	C'est plus un supporter qu'un sportif, je crois.
Jane	Selon vous, les Français sont sportifs?
3ème passante	Non. Pas . . . pas tous.

d'après vous/selon vous	*in your opinion*
un tout petit 'oui'	*a very hesitant 'yes'*
pas tellement	*not very much*
en spectateurs plus qu'en acteurs	*more as spectators than as performers*
plus un supporter qu'un sportif	*more a supporter than a player*

TV 2 Then Jane asked what the French national sport was. You'll probably guess that the interviews were filmed during the football season.

Jane	Quel est le sport national français?
3ème passante	Le football.
Jane	Et quel est le sport national français?
1ère passante	Le foot (*laughs*), le football, oui.
1er passant	Je pense que c'est le football.
2ème passant	Le foot . . . le football.
3ème passant	J'hésiterais entre le football et la bicyclette.
2ème passante	Le football.
4ème passante	Pour les hommes ça doit être le football, mais pour les femmes, je sais pas . . . le tennis, la gymnastique, différents sports. Je peux pas vous dire exactement.

j'hésiterais	*I'd hesitate*
ça doit être	*it must be*

Quickie What three sports other than football were mentioned?

TV 3 Next, Jane asked people if they took part in a sport. They seemed to be quite energetic.

Jane	Et vous, vous faites du sport?
4ème passante	Très peu. Du tennis, un petit peu en été . . . de la natation.
Jane	Et vous, vous faites du sport?
1er passant	Oui.
Jane	Qu'est-ce que vous faites comme sports?
1er passant	Du ski, on est bien placé . ., du vélo. Et puis un peu de football entre les deux.
1ère passante	De la natation et puis de la danse.
2ème passant	Du ski, de la natation, un peu de volley-ball.
3ème passant	Ah, j'aime beaucoup la bicyclette, j'aime beaucoup la marche, mais je ne pratique ni sports de groupe ni sports violents.
3ème passante	Natation . . . je fais de la gymnastique et maintenant je danse.
Jane	Et vous, vous faites du sport?
2ème passante	Je fais du tennis, mais je débute depuis dix ans! Voilà (*laughs*).

on est bien placé	*we're in the right place for it*
je débute depuis dix ans!	*I've been a beginner for ten years!*

To say you take part in a sport or activity:	
je fais	**du** tennis **de la** gymnastique **du** ski **de la** natation **du** vélo **de la** danse

Quickie What are the words for: skiing; dancing; swimming?

TV 4 As far as France is concerned, *boules* are as much of a cliché as *baguettes* and *bérets*. So it's perhaps surprising that the people interviewed didn't seem to take the game very seriously.

Jane Et les boules? Est-ce que vous jouez aux boules?
1er passant Pas beaucoup, non.
3ème passante Ah non, je n'aime pas.
1ère passante En été seulement, mais pour rire, enfin.
2ème passant Pas souvent, quelquefois.
Jane Et les boules? Est-ce que vous jouez aux boules?
3ème passant Absolument pas.
Jane Et vous considérez ça comme un sport?
3ème passant Absolument pas non plus, non!
Jane Et selon vous, c'est un sport?
1er passant Oui, oui.
2ème passante Non, non, c'est plutôt un délassement, non.
2ème passant Oui, c'est un sport. Oui, il y a des . . . des Championnats du Monde qui sont organisés et cetera.

pour rire	*just for a laugh*
absolument pas non plus, non!	*likewise absolutely not, no!*

To say you play a game:	
je joue	**aux** boules **au** football **au** tennis

Quickie There are several negative phrases to remember; what is the French for 'not much', 'not often'?

Mots-clés

appuyer	to press	la danse	dance/dancing	le klaxon	car horn
casser	to break	le foot(-ball)	football	le moustique	mosquito
demander	to ask	le jogging	jogging	le pont	bridge
descendre	to go down	la natation	swimming	le sel	salt
jouer	to play	le tennis	tennis	le vélo	bike
montrer	to show	le vélo	bike, cycling	la vitesse	speed
préparer	to prepare	le volley(-ball)	volleyball	chaque	each
traverser	to cross	le coup de soleil	sunburn	entre	between
les boules (f)	bowls	l'homme (m)	man	pendant	during/for
le cricket	cricket			prêt	ready

En bref

1 To ask how to get somewhere:

pour aller	**à la** gare, **au** marché,	s'il vous plaît?

2 To ask for something for a particular purpose:

je voudrais **vous avez**	**quelque chose pour**	les coups de soleil (?) les piqûres d'insectes (?)

3 To ask what has to be done:

qu'est-ce qu'il faut faire	pour mettre en route? pour l'éclairage? pour faire une galette? pour jouer aux boules?

Il faut is used

1 for giving instructions:

il faut	l'appliquer deux fois par jour la laisser cuire pendant une minute traverser le pont tourner la clé de contact appuyer sur la commande

2 to say what is needed:

pour faire une omelette **il faut**	des oeufs du lait du sel du beurre

4 To say you play a game:

	aux boules
je joue	**au** football
	au tennis

5 To say you take part in a sport or activity:

	de la gymnastique
je fais	**du** vélo
	de la natation

En plus

1 **Cars and bikes**
Car vocabulary has some interesting words.

First, a *faux ami*: *le starter* is 'the choke' not 'the starter'. That is *le démarreur*.
Une glace is the usual word for a car window (as well as an ice cream). The connection? The basic meaning of *glace* is 'ice': from its coldness you get 'ice cream' and from its transparency you get 'window'. *Glace* also means 'mirror' but not, unfortunately, 'car mirror'; that's *un rétroviseur*.
And what is the link between an Egyptian island with a Greek name, and car headlights? One of the seven wonders of the ancient world was the lighthouse of the island of Pharos off Alexandria, a white marble tower 135 metres high with a fire burning on top reflected by mirrors. When the French built lighthouses they called them *phares* and the word was transferred to headlights.
Bicyclette is the official word for bicycle but *vélo* is very commonly used. It is short for *vélocipède*, one of the ancestors of the bicycle. One of France's most popular national sports is cycling – *le cyclisme*.

2 **Words that are not altogether what they seem**
Prévenir: the first meaning is 'to do something beforehand in order to prevent something else happening' and is very like the English 'to prevent'. Hence the proverb:
mieux vaut prévenir que guérir
it is better to prevent than cure (ie prevention is better than cure)

From this idea of 'doing something beforehand' came the idea 'to tell someone beforehand', 'to warn' or 'to inform' and this meaning is very common in modern French. So, if there is an accident and someone says: *Il faut prévenir le docteur*, he means the doctor must be informed (not prevented!)

Piqûre: When the doctor gets there, he may well give the victim *une piqûre*, which this time would not be an insect bite or sting: it's also the word for 'an injection'.

Cuire: In English we use the verb 'to cook' in two distinct ways.

where's Henry? he's *cooking*

Henry, where's the chicken? it's *cooking*

The French verb *cuire* is equivalent to the second of these two meanings:

le poulet cuit

If you say *Henri cuit . .*, it means that he is in the pan along with the chicken and browning nicely. So:

the chicken is cooking	*le poulet cuit*
Henry is cooking	*Henri fait la cuisine*
Henry is cooking the chicken	*Henri fait cuire le poulet*

3 **Aches and pains**

Knowing the words for parts of the body is not only useful for buying clothes but also for telling the doctor where it hurts:

docteur, docteur, j'ai mal	au bras à la jambe au dos aux bras

NB avoir mal aux cheveux to have a hangover

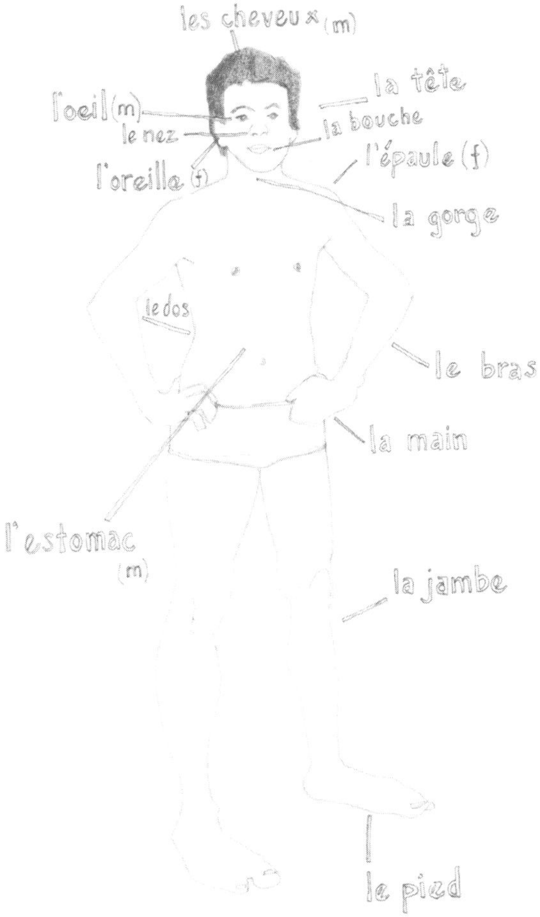

4 **Do's and don't's**

We've met a number of ways in which people can give you directions:

(vous) tournez à gauche

vous devez il faut	tourner à gauche

On public signs and notices you will come across:
Les visiteurs sont priés de ...
Prière de ...

There are equally important phrases telling you what you must *not* do. In speech, people will normally use *ne ... pas*:

vous ne tournez pas à gauche

il ne faut pas tourner à gauche

On public signs you will see:
Défense de ...
Il est défendu de ...
Il est interdit de ...
Interdiction de ...

Driving in France

Most British drivers find driving on the right not as difficult as they'd feared. One of the main problems is *la priorité à droite*, which means that vehicles coming from your right have precedence unless you have been told otherwise. It is particularly important to remember this in towns, though side roads do not normally have priority over main roads.

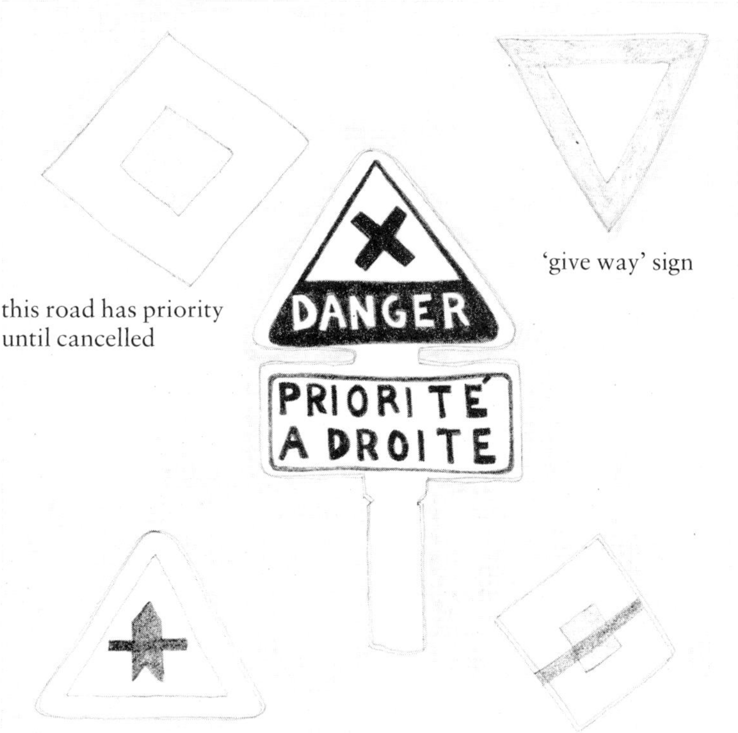

this road has priority until cancelled

'give way' sign

this road has priority at the next junction

the priority is cancelled

The driving licence – *le permis de conduire*

A British driving licence is valid in France, even though the driving test is more rigorous than in Britain. When people pass, they are not allowed to drive at more than 90 km/h for a year and the car must carry a label (90) on the back.

There is an excellent book used by many French learner drivers – *Le Code Rousseau* – which is just as useful for foreign drivers. It is full of colour photographs, diagrams and pictures about all the possible things a driver in France would need to know. You can get it in most French bookshops.

Les boules

There are British 'bowls' and French *boules* and they are not the same thing, though they have obvious similarities. Instead of the carefully constructed 'woods' and the manicured grass of the British bowling green, the French have smaller metal *boules* and play on gravel.

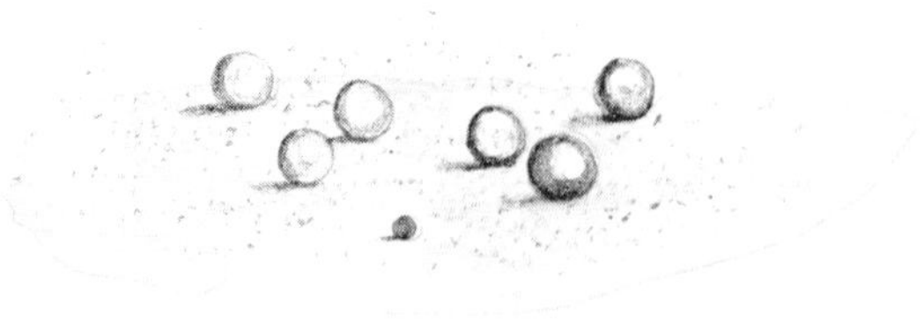

There are two sorts. *Le jeu lyonnais* (the Lyon Game) is governed by an International Federation, organises world championships and has a rule book seventy pages long. It is played in a space defined by a wooden framework of specific shape. *La pétanque* has smaller *boules* and slightly different rules (for example, you don't run up to the spot when throwing your *boule* but stand still, 'feet together' – which is what *pétanque* means). It too has a world championship, but is generally much more relaxed and informal and can be played on any suitable bit of gravel or flat surface – preferably right next to a café. It is particularly popular in the south where the evening *partie de pétanque* in the shade of the lime trees and lubricated with lots of *pastis* is a hallowed tradition.

The aim in both games is similar to 'bowls'. A 'jack' (in *pétanque* it is called *le cochonnet*, 'the piglet', and in the *jeu lyonnais, le but*) is thrown and each player tries to get his *boules* as near to it as possible. The pair who end up with any of their *boules* nearest the jack count a point for each one nearer than the nearest of their opponents'. It sounds simple until you start to play it!

Les crêpes et les galettes

Une crêpe is simply a pancake, and *une crêperie* is a small restaurant specialising in them – usually offering a whole selection of different fillings. A *galette*, on the other hand, can take many forms according to local tradition. In Brittany it can be a savoury pancake made from buckwheat flour, or a biscuit rather like shortbread. One special *galette, la Galette des Rois*, is a kind of cake and is made for celebrations on Twelfth Night. At the start of January the cake shop windows are full of them.

If ever you find yourself staying with a French family around that time, you're bound to find yourself invited to *tirer les rois*. The cake is cut up and distributed by the youngest member of the party (to ensure there's no cheating). In the cake is a small charm (originally a bean, *une fève*, it is nowadays usually a china or plastic figure). The person finding *la fève* is the king (or queen) and chooses a queen (or king).

Both are given paper crowns (these are sold along with the cake) and their health is drunk.

Bon courage

1 Ask how to get to these places:
la gare routière, le restaurant de La Chèvre Blanche, le Musée de la Préhistoire, la Tour Eiffel, Le Havre, les Champs Elysées

2 To do one thing, you usually have to do something else first.
Example: *pour prendre le train, il faut acheter un billet.*
Pair up these phrases in the same way:

1 pour guérir les piqûres d'insectes
2 pour aller à La Brévardière
3 pour passer sur le quai
4 pour faire une omelette
5 pour manger un bon poulet
6 pour bien apprécier le fromage

a) il faut composter son billet
b) il faut boire du vin rouge avec
c) il faut traverser une forêt de sapins
d) il faut mettre de la crème
e) il faut casser des oeufs
f) il faut aller en Bresse

3 And what things do you need to have in order to do the following?
Match up these phrases in the same way:

pour prendre le train	il faut du pain et du jambon
pour louer une voiture	il faut un passeport
pour faire un sandwich au jambon	il faut de la musique
pour danser	il faut un billet
pour aller au Brésil	il faut des boules
pour jouer à la pétanque	il faut un permis de conduire

4

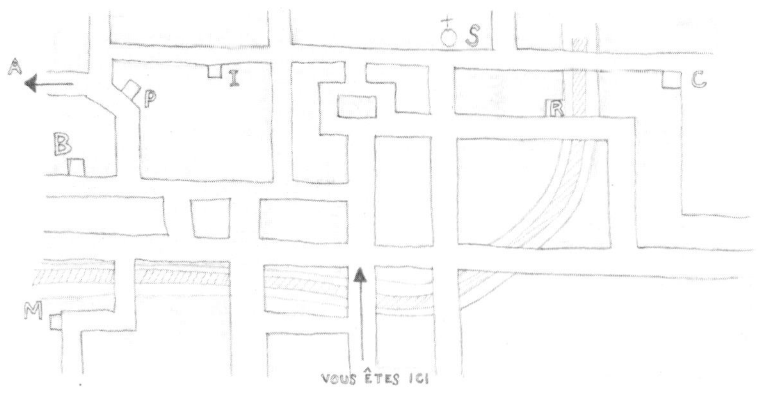

Key:

la route du Havre	A
la Maison de la Culture	B
la gare routière	C
le musée	M
le Syndicat d'Initiative	I
la Pizzeria Tino	P
le restaurant de La Chèvre Blanche	R
l'Eglise St Antoine	S

Asking the question is only half the battle. Understanding the answer is the other half. Using the map, work out where the following instructions would get you:

1 Vous allez tout droit, vous traversez la place et juste après, vous tournez à gauche. Vous continuez tout droit et puis c'est là, à gauche.
2 Oui, vous allez à gauche ici, vous prenez le deuxième pont, vous traversez le canal et vous tournez tout de suite à droite et c'est là, devant vous.
3 Vous allez à gauche ici, vous prenez la deuxième à droite puis la première à gauche. Vous allez tout droit et c'est sur votre droite.
4 Vous allez tout droit jusqu'à la place puis vous tournez à droite. Vous continuez tout droit, vous traversez une rue et puis c'est à gauche, juste avant le pont.

5 Now you've done exercise 4, you must know this place like the back of your hand. So you're well-equipped to deal with these questions from newcomers:

1 Pardon, madame. Pour aller à la gare routière, s'il vous plaît?
2 Excusez-moi, madame. Vous connaissez la Pizzeria Tino, s'il vous plaît?
3 Pardon, madame. L'église St Antoine, s'il vous plaît?
4 Est-ce que le Palais de Justice est par ici?
(*tell him 'I'm not from here. Excuse me. I don't know'*)

6 Here's part of a leaflet from a car hire company.

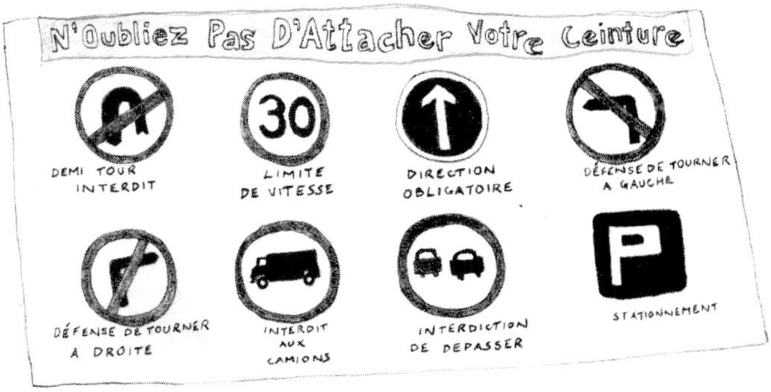

Read the leaflet and find out the French for:

1 seat belt
2 three expressions which show something is not allowed
3 compulsory
4 lorry
5 speed
6 to overtake
7 parking

7 The local reporter knows you are British and ropes you in to help with her survey. She wants to know about sport in Britain. Answer her questions.

Journaliste Est-ce que les Anglais sont très sportifs?
You *There are lots of spectators.*
Journaliste Quel est le sport national anglais?
You *There's football and cricket.*
Journaliste Ah, le cricket. C'est très compliqué, n'est-ce pas?
You *Yes, quite.*
Journaliste Vous jouez au cricket?
You *Yes, a little, but not very often.*
Journaliste On joue au cricket toute l'année?
You *No, in summer. In winter we play football.*
Journaliste Et vous, vous jouez au football?
You *You have several friends who play football every Saturday; your wife plays bowls on Sunday afternoons and your brother goes cycling every evening . . . and your other brother goes jogging at six o'clock every morning. You prefer tennis.*
Journaliste Quelle famille sportive! Vous faites d'autres sports?
You *No, but you like watching sport on television* (à la télévision).
Journaliste Ah, vous avez un sport préféré?
You *You love watching gymnastics and snooker.*
Journaliste Le snooker? Qu'est-ce que c'est que ça?
You *Ah well . . . there's a green table, fifteen little red balls, one black one, one white one, one yellow . . .. Oh, it's very complicated . . .*

Les boules: un sport international

In 1982, *boules* (not to be confused with *pétanque*) was officially declared a sport by the French government. This meant that clubs had to be organised according to national legislation covering all sports – and that includes regular medicals for the players. *Boulistes* tend to specialise in one of two types of play. The *pointeur* rolls the *boules* along the ground in order to get as close as possible to the jack (*le but*); the *tireur* throws the *boules* underarm to knock away opponents' *boules* or to hit the jack itself.

Rhône-Alpes, the region which includes Lyon and Grenoble, has for years claimed the largest number of *boulistes* in France. But France is only one of many countries where the game is popular. There is an International Federation, based in Italy, which publishes the official rules and organises competitions. In 1982, the 27th World Championships were held in Grenoble. France and Italy have always been close rivals, but that year Italy was tipped to win.

L'Equipe de France à l'entraînement

Pour la première fois dans son histoire sportive, Grenoble accueille un Championnat du Monde de Boules. Seize pays participent à ce vingt-septième championnat; il y a des équipes qui viennent d'Afrique, d'Amérique, d'Europe et même d'Australie. Les favoris sont l'Italie et la France. Pour devenir membre de l'Equipe de France il faut être désigné par un comité de sélection et s'entraîner environ deux heures par jour. D'après Jean Védrine, l'entraîneur de l'équipe, pour être un bon bouliste il faut commencer à jouer très jeune et pratiquer beaucoup: la condition physique et la coordination des mouvements sont deux choses très importantes.

Pendant les trois premiers jours du championnat, chaque équipe doit jouer contre toutes les autres: ce sont les matchs de sélection. A la fin du troisième jour, après les demi-finales, la France bat le Maroc. A la surprise de tous, c'est la Yougoslavie qui va recontrer la France en finale: l'Italie a été battue par l'équipe yougoslave.

Le quatrième et dernier jour, les spectateurs sont nombreux. Au bout de quelques parties, l'équipe française contrôle déjà le match et les Yougoslaves semblent avoir abandonné tout espoir. C'est une finale très rapide. En trois quarts d'heure de jeu, les Français ont gagné douze parties: encore une partie et ils sont champions du monde. Dans la partie suivante, les boules françaises sont les plus proches du but. Mais le joueur yougoslave réussit à tirer le but et rend la partie nulle.

Le jeu va donc continuer. Les Yougoslaves ont peut-être une chance de battre les Français après tout. Maintenant, la boule la plus proche du but est celle des Yougoslaves et il ne reste qu'une boule à l'équipe de France. Le joueur français doit tirer la boule yougoslave. S'il y arrive, la France est championne du monde.

a été battue par	*has been beaten by*
semblent avoir abandonné	*seem to have abandoned*
ont gagné	*have won*
encore une partie	*one more game*
les plus proches du but	*closest to the jack*
et rend la partie nulle	*and draws the game*
réussit à tirer le but	*succeeds in hitting the jack*
tirer le but	*hit the jack*
il ne reste qu'une boule	*there's only one boule left*
s'il y arrive	*if he manages it*

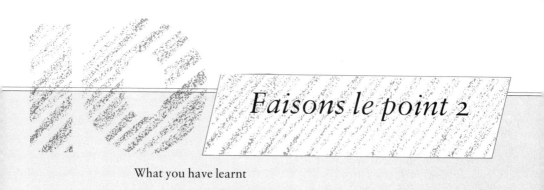

10 Faisons le point 2

What you have learnt

You should now be able to deal with the time, opening hours and days of the week.

Radio **1** Here is Sara in Nantes finding out about the opening hours of a pizzeria.

Sara Quelles sont les heures d'ouverture de la pizzéria, s'il vous plaît ?
Patronne Alors, le matin de midi à quatorze heures et le soir de dix-neuf heures trente à vingt-trois heures.
Sara Tous les jours ?
Patronne Sauf le dimanche et le lundi midi.
Sara Ah bon, merci.

Quickie How do you say 'every day'?

Radio **2** The life of a café proprietor can be hard. Jean spoke to one in Bourg.

Jean Quelles sont vos heures d'ouverture, s'il vous plaît ?
Patronne Eh bien, de six heures et demie le matin jusqu'à une heure ou deux heures suivant la clientèle.
Jean (*surprised*) Une heure ou deux du matin suivant !
Patronne Oui, c'est exact.
Jean Tous les jours ?
Patronne Oui, tous les jours sauf le dimanche.

suivant la clientèle	*depending how busy we are*
le matin suivant	*the following morning*

Quickie How does the *patronne* say 'except on Sundays'?

Knowing the times of the day and the words for the days of the week and the months, you can find out more about what there is to see and do.

TV 3 Madame Bloch wants to know what's on in Grenoble. She asks in the *Maison du Tourisme*.

Mme Bloch Bonjour, madame.
Hôtesse Bonjour, madame.
Mme Bloch Quelles sont les activités culturelles à Grenoble?
Hôtesse (*asking what her special interest is*) Danse, cinéma, théâtre?
Mme Bloch Le théâtre.
Hôtesse Du théâtre, oui. Alors, il y a le théâtre municipal à Grenoble avec deux spectacles, 'Don Pasquale' et 'Les Fourberies de Scapin'. Et à la Maison de la Culture il y a 'Les Trois Soeurs' De Tchekhov.

Mme Bloch 'Les Trois Soeurs' m'intéresse.
Hôtesse Oui. Voici le programme général de la Maison de la Culture.
Mme Bloch Et ça commence quel jour?
Hôtesse Ça commence le treize octobre, jusqu'au vingt-huit octobre.
Mme Bloch Et ça commence à quelle heure?
Hôtesse C'est à vingt heures trente le soir.
Mme Bloch Et vous n'avez pas une matinée?
Hôtesse Oui. Il y a une matinée le dimanche vingt-quatre octobre à quinze heures.
Mme Bloch Est-ce qu'il faut réserver longtemps à l'avance?
Hôtesse Oh, une semaine, c'est suffisant.
Mme Bloch Bien. Merci beaucoup, madame.
Hôtesse Je vous en prie.
Mme Bloch Au revoir, madame.
Hôtesse Au revoir, madame.

Quickies
1 What sort of thing is Madame Bloch interested in?
2 How does she ask 'Do you have to book in advance?'?

You should also be able to use public transport.

Radio 4 Making a train journey from Bourg-en-Bresse to Aix-en-Provence is quite complex and so Marie-Pierre has asked the station information office to prepare a timetable for her.

Marie-Pierre Pardon, mademoiselle, vous avez mon horaire pour aller à Aix-en-Provence?

Employée Oui. Alors, vous avez un train à douze heures trente-neuf qui part de Bourg-en-Bresse. Vous arrivez à Lyon-Perrache à treize heures trente et une. Vous changez. Vous repartez treize heures cinquante. Vous arrivez à Marseille-St Charles dix-sept heures quinze. Vous changez encore une fois. A Marseille-St Charles vous avez la correspondance à dix-sept heures vingt-cinq et vous arrivez à Aix-en-Provence à dix-huit heures six.

Marie-Pierre Les trains partent des mêmes gares?

Employée Des mêmes gares, oui.

Marie-Pierre Et c'est combien le . . .?

Employée Alors, vous avez le . . . l'aller-retour, trois cent quatorze francs.

Marie-Pierre Je vous remercie.

Employée Mais je vous en prie. Au revoir, madame.

encore une fois *again*

Quickies

1 What's the other way you are likely to hear the phrase *douze heures trente-neuf*?

2 If the *hôtesse* in the *Renseignements* tells you *Vous avez la correspondance à dix-neuf heures*, what does she mean?

Radio 5 In La Rochelle, Sara wants to know when there are trains for Nantes.

Sara Bonjour.

Employée Bonjour, madame.

Sara Quand est-ce qu'il y a des trains pour Nantes, s'il vous plaît?

Employée Oui. Quand voulez-vous partir?

Sara Dans l'après-midi.

Employée Oui, vers quelle heure, environ?

Sara Dix-huit, dix-neuf heures.

Employée Oui. Je regarde. (*consults timetable*) Alors, ce soir il y a un train à dix-neuf heures treize au départ de La Rochelle et qui arrive à Nantes à vingt et une heures zéro cinq.

Sara C'est le seul train?

Employée Après, vous avez un train de nuit qui part de La Rochelle à deux heures cinquante-deux et qui arrive à Nantes à cinq heures du matin.

Sara Oh là là! C'est trop tard, là. Celui de dix-neuf heures est direct?

Employée Oui, madame. Toujours pour Nantes.

Sara Et il circule tous les jours?

Employée Je regarde. (*consults timetable*) Alors, le train de dix-neuf heures treize circule tous les jours sauf dimanches et fêtes.

Sara Bon, ben, c'est très bien. Merci.

Employée Oui. Au revoir.

Sara Au revoir.

oh là là! *expression of dismayed surprise*

Quickies 1 What time of day does Sara want to travel?
2 How does she say 'the 7 pm one'?

Radio **6** This time, Sara and a friend want to get the bus from La Rochelle station to the town centre but she has to check first that it is the right bus.

Sara Vous allez en ville, s'il vous plaît?
Conducteur Oui.
Sara Deux tickets, s'il vous plaît.
Conducteur Deux tickets.
Sara C'est combien?
Conducteur Neuf francs, madame. (*Sara pays with 10F*) Alors, neuf et un, dix.
Sara Merci.
Conducteur Merci, madame.

You can explain more precisely what you want in shops, etc by using the French for phrases like 'the green one', 'that one' or 'those'; remember that *le, la, les* don't always mean 'the' – they can also mean 'him/her/it/them'.

7 Maud Cottave is shopping for a skirt (*une jupe*) with her friend, Mireille Lamour.

Mireille Ah, regarde cette blanche. (*takes it from a rack*) Elle est trop longue, non?
Maud Ah oui. Trop longue. (*looks at others*) Oh! Et celle-ci?
Mireille Ah! Très jolie, oui?
Maud Pas mal, hein.
Mireille Très jolie. (*looking through rack*) Mais elle existe en rouge, comme ceci.
Maud (*seeing a black one*) Ah, en noir. Ah, je préfère celle-là.
Mireille Oui, effectivement.
Maud Elle est bien, hein.
Mireille La noire est plus jolie, oui.
Maud OK, bien, je la prends alors.
Mireille D'accord.

Quickies 1 What colours is the skirt available in?
2 What does *la* stand for in *je la prends, alors*?

TV **8** Our friend Moustache (Michel Bouyssié) is buying cheese in the *marché couvert* in Grenoble.

Moustache	Bonjour, monsieur.
Fromager	Bonjour, monsieur.
Moustache	Je voudrais du comté, s'il vous plaît.
Fromager	Oui. Lequel préférez-vous? (*pointing to cheeses*) Doux, demi-sel ou fruité?
Moustache	Le fruité.
Fromager	Voilà. (*suggesting a portion with a knife*) Comme ceci?
Moustache	Un petit peu moins . . .
Fromager	Oui.
Moustache	. . . et puis la moitié de la tranche, s'il vous plaît. (fromager *cuts and wraps cheese. Moustache notices another cheese*) Et ceci, qu'est-ce que c'est?
Fromager	De la tomme de Savoie.
Moustache	Ah! Bien. Est-ce que vous avez du fromage de chèvre frais?
Fromager	Oui. Nous avons la bûche, à la coupe.
Moustache	Et c'est fort?
Fromager	C'est un fromage assez doux et celui-ci est très frais.
Moustache	Vous m'en mettez un petit morceau, s'il vous plaît.
Fromager	(*suggesting a portion again*) Comme ceci?
Moustache	Oh, un peu plus.
Fromager	Un peu plus. Voilà.
Moustache	Très bien.

lequel préférez-vous?	*which one do you prefer?*
la moitié de la tranche	*half of that piece*
à la coupe	*for cutting (the shopkeeper cuts what you want)*
vous m'en mettez un petit morceau	*give me a small piece*

Quickies

1 What's 'a bit less' and 'a bit more'?
2 How do you ask what something is?
3 What is *celui-ci* standing for in *celui-ci est très frais*?

Radio 9 Sara is buying plasters in the chemist's.

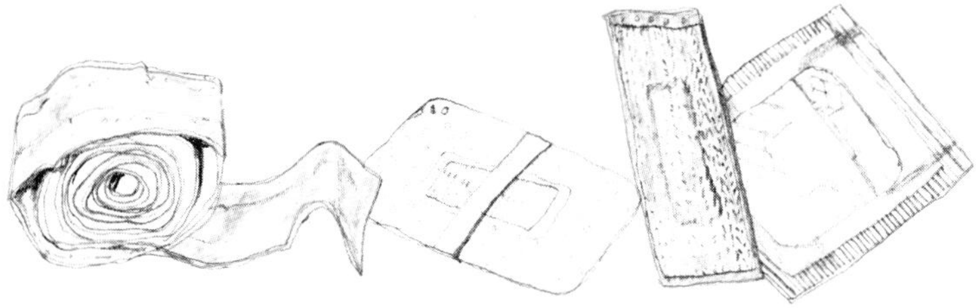

Pharmacienne	A qui le tour?
Sara	C'est à moi, je crois.
Pharmacienne	Oui. Vous désirez?
Sara	Je voudrais une boîte de pansements, s'il vous plaît.
Pharmacienne	Vous avez deux types de pansements: le pansement tout prêt où il y a trois grandeurs de pansement dedans, hein. Des petits, des moyens et des grands. Ensuite, vous avez le pansement au mètre que l'on coupe.
Sara	Il y a combien de pansements?
Pharmacienne	Vous en avez vingt dans la pochette.

Sara Oh, ben, je vais prendre ça, hein. C'est combien?
Pharmacienne Quatorze francs quarante.
Sara Bon. (*she pays*)
Pharmacienne Merci. Voici votre monnaie. Je vais vous donner votre paquet. Voilà.
Sara Merci.
Pharmacienne Au revoir.
Sara Au revoir, madame.
Pharmacienne A qui le tour, s'il vous plaît?

à qui le tour?	*who's next/whose turn is it?*
c'est à moi	*it's me/it's mine*
au mètre	*by the metre*

Quickies
1 What three sizes of plaster were in the box?
2 What other sort of plaster was available?

You know how to order a meal, either a full one or just a snack.

Radio 10 Marie-Pierre orders a snack.

Marie-Pierre Bonjour, monsieur.
Garçon Bonjour, madame. Que désirez-vous?
Marie-Pierre Qu'est-ce que vous avez à manger?
Garçon Alors, des sandwichs, des croque-monsieur et puis des hot-dogs.
Marie-Pierre Ils sont à quoi, les sandwichs?
Garçon Alors, au jambon, au saucisson, au pâté, rillettes et . . . au fromage.
Marie-Pierre Je vais prendre un croque-monsieur, s'il vous plaît.
Garçon Alors, un croque-monsieur. Vous désirez boire quelque chose avec?
Marie-Pierre Une eau minérale gazeuse.
Garçon Une eau minérale gazeuse. Bien. Je vous prépare ça.

Quickie
1 How do you ask 'What have you got to eat?'?
2 What was there for Marie-Pierre to choose from?

Rencontres

TV 1 A very widespread French custom is the famous 'kiss' on the cheek – *la bise*. But who does it to whom?

Jane Lorsqu'on dit bonjour aux gens, à qui fait-on la bise normalement?
1ère passante A ses intimes.
Jane Et lorsque vous dites bonjour à quelqu'un, est-ce que vous leur faites automatiquement la bise?
2ème passante Ah non, absolument pas. C'est pas de ma génération, ça!
3ème passante Oh, à des gens que je connais très bien.
1er passant Ça dépend de la personne à qui je m'adresse. Si c'est les . . ., si c'est une

	personne familière oui, mais sans ça, non.
2ème passant	Ah moi, je suis pas un bisouilleur, alors . . . (*laughs*).
Jane	Lorsqu'on dit bonjour à quelqu'un, à qui fait-on la bise?
3ème passant	(*laughs but doesn't say anything*)
Jane	Et quand vous dites bonjour à quelqu'un, est-ce que vous lui faites la bise?
4ème passante	Ça dépend si je le connais bien.
Jane	Et si vous le connaissez bien?
4ème passante	Oui . . ., oui, oui.

vous leur faites la bise?	*do you give them a* bise?
vous lui faites la bise?	*do you give him/her a* bise?
c'est pas de ma génération	*people of my generation don't do that*
la personne à qui je m'adresse	*the person I'm talking to*
mais sans ça	*but otherwise*
un bisouilleur	*the man's made-up word for someone who gives* bises *to all and sundry*

Quickie What's the word for 'somebody' or 'someone'?

TV 2 And how many *bises* do you give? It seems to depend on regional custom.

Jane	Et vous lui faites combien de bises?
4ème passante	Ça dépend. En France on en fait deux au moins.
Jane	Lorsqu'on fait la bise, on fait combien de bises?
2ème passante	Oh, hélas, on en fait des quantités. Moi, une me suffit.
4ème passant	Deux.
2ème passant	Ah, j'en fais trois.
1ère passante	A Paris on fait quatre bises.
5ème passante	Ici, c'est deux dans la région.
1er passant	On s'embrasse deux fois, et dans certaines régions, c'est trois fois. C'est la coutume.

au moins	*at least*
une me suffit	*one is enough for me*

Quickie In which part of France are you liable to get the most *bises*?

Mots-clés

la matinée	morning; matinée	blanc	white
le programme	programme	certain	certain
réserver	to book, reserve	fort	strong
le spectacle	show, performance	frais	fresh
couper	to cut	général	general
le mètre	metre	long	long
la moitié	half	longtemps	a long time
le paquet	packet	noir	black
la quantité	quantity	normalement	normally
la bise	kiss on the cheeks	tard	late
la bûche	log	circuler	to run, move
les gens (m)	people	exister	to exist
le pansement	dressing, bandage		
les rillettes (f)	type of pâté		

En plus

1 **Tickets** and **billets**
When is a ticket a *billet*? It is largely a matter of convention and not meaning. *Billet* is used for train, plane, theatre and cinema tickets. *Ticket* is commonly used for bus and underground railway tickets but *billets* would not be wrong. If in doubt use *billet*.
The other common meaning of *un billet* is 'a bank note'
un billet de 50F a 50F note

2 **Journée, matinée**
When *-(n)ée* is added to *le jour*, *le matin*, *le soir* to get *la journée*, *la matinée*, *la soirée* the idea of length of time is emphasised:
toute la journée all day long
nous allons passer la soirée avec des amis we're going to spend the evening with friends
You can also add *-née* to *un an* to get *une année*, but in some set phrases *an* and *année* seem to be interchangeable:
l'année dernière = l'an dernier
l'année prochaine = l'an prochain
As far as the theatre is concerned, *matinée* no longer means 'morning' but is an afternoon performance just as it is in Britain. Perhaps actors get up late!

3 **Spectacle**
This has nothing to do with glasses but means any sort of performance for entertainment: films, plays, concerts, etc, whether live or on television.

4 **Flavours**

Some of the words referring to flavours change their meanings according to what is being described. The ones most likely to be met are:

doux	mild, except when used of wine when it means sweet
sucré	sweet (of things other than wine)
salé	salty
demi-sel	slightly salted
fruité	used of wine it means fruity, of olive oil it means very 'olive' tasting. It is hardly ever used of cheese and presumably the *fromager* on p200 means full-flavoured
brut	used of cider and champagne to mean very dry
sec	used of wine to mean dry, ie the opposite of sweet (which, in this case, is not sour!)
demi-sec	medium dry

A propos

Opening hours

These vary – often considerably – from what is usual in Britain. Official buildings and museums will usually close for two hours in the middle of the day; they will often stay open till six or so in the evening, but there's no general rule. Shops, particularly food shops, will frequently be open till seven or eight in the evening. Café opening hours vary enormously. In cities they may be open almost twenty-four hours a day whereas in small towns and villages they can equally well be closed by 9.30 in the evening. Except in the larger towns, restaurant meal times are in fact likely to be no more generous than in Britain. Most restaurants, particularly in smaller places, will have finished taking orders for lunch by about 1.30 pm and for dinner by about 8.30 pm.

More cheese

Comté: a French type of Gruyère from the Franche-Comté region. Yellow in colour and with a firm texture, it is often used in cooking and for *fondues*.
Tomme de Savoie: the word *tomme* is simply an old word for 'cheese' that lives on in the Savoie area. There's a whole family of *tommes* (including a goat's milk version) of which *tomme de Savoie* is probably the best-known. It has a mild, tangy taste.

Les parcs naturels

There are six national parks and twenty-one regional parks in France. The national parks (of which two are in the Alps) are uninhabited areas protected by legislation to conserve flora, fauna and natural beauty. A secondary function of the parks is to encourage tourism and promote a proper appreciation of nature. Within each park, an area is set aside for hotels and services. In the main nature reserve, though, conservation is rigidly enforced: cars and dogs are banned; fishing, hunting, camping and any sort of building are forbidden. Some areas are entirely closed to the public.

Parcs naturels régionaux have a different purpose. They are areas in which people live and work. The function of each park is to develop the local economy, to promote tourism and to preserve the cultural and natural heritage of the area.

The Vercors is one of two regional parks in the Dauphiné. It is famous as *la citadelle de la Résistance*, one of the strongholds of the Resistance during the last war. It is increasingly popular with tourists, mostly French, who come to ski in winter and enjoy the spectacular scenery in summer.

Les randonnées

Hiking or rambling is very popular in France. A *randonnée* can be anything from a day's walk in the country to a thirty-day trek across the Alps. Some long paths of scenic interest are officially designated as *sentiers de grande randonnée* and given numbers – GR1, GR2, etc. These routes are sign-posted and simple overnight shelters are available along the paths for the use of *randonneurs*. The *Comité National des Sentiers de Grande Randonnée* is responsible for their maintenance, and publishes detailed guide-books called *topo-guides*, available in this country in specialist map shops.

Bon courage

Round about this point some people start feeling that learning a language is too much to cope with. If you feel like that, it could be because you've started to lose sight of how much you've actually learned. Why not look back through chapters 1–5, do the test on pages 106–111 again and see if you find it easier than you remember from last time. Here is a new test dealing mainly with what's been covered since chapter 5. In the first section you can score a maximum of 65. Try again in a week's time and see if your score improves.

Part I

1 Say what these times are in the 12-hour system:

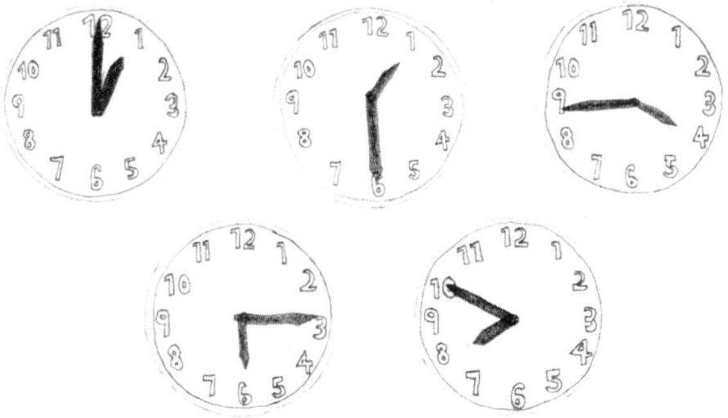

2 Ask for:
 1 that one (pointing to a vase)
 2 this one (indicating a chicken)
 3 those (pointing to some pears)
 4 the blue one (pointing to a skirt)
 5 the little one (pointing to a plate)

3 You're looking at a dress; ask the shopkeeper if she has it:
 1 in size 38
 2 in white
 3 in black
 4 in grey
 5 in cotton

4 In these sentences which nouns in the list are *le*/*la*/*l'*/*les* most likely to be standing for? Which one is left over?

1 on les trouve devant les gares	a) l'apéritif
2 on les mange souvent à la bolognaise	b) le pâté
3 on le prend avant le repas	c) la jupe
4 Maud la préfère en bleu	d) les tasses
5 je l'achète pour l'offrir à ma grand-mère	e) les spaghettis
6 Jean la prend pour une nuit	f) les taxis
7 on l'achète à la charcuterie	g) le vase
	h) la chambre

5 Ask:
1 for a return ticket
2 which platform the train goes from
3 if there are coaches to Bourg
4 if this is the coach for the airport
5 what time the coach leaves

6 Tell someone that you:
1 love *gratin dauphinois*
2 like spaghetti a lot
3 quite like sea food
4 don't like rare steak
5 can't stand *rillettes*

7 Following this example,
il faut plier la galette – you have to fold the *galette*
tell someone they:
1 have to go to the market on Mondays
2 have to cross the square
3 have to buy some plasters
4 have to arrive before 9 pm
5 have to reserve in advance
6 have to change at Lyon

8 Write down all the days of the week, the months and the seasons. If you get them all right give yourself 10 points; $\frac{1}{2}$ point off for each wrong answer.

9 Tell a French friend that you:
1 like reading
2 prefer going to the theatre
3 don't like playing football
4 are going to watch television
5 are not going to buy this bike
6 are not going to play snooker tonight

10 Fit the verbs from this list into the blanks in these sentences:
allons, vais, faites, fait, regarde, allons, part, partent, ai, avez, sommes, est
1 Le soir je .... la télévision.
2 Le samedi nous .... voir un match de football.
3 Je .... acheter un cadeau pour Henri.
4 Nous .... prendre un apéritif.
5 Il .... midi et demie.
6 Ici à Grenoble nous .... près de la montagne.
7 Ça .... combien, s'il vous plaît?
8 Le train .... dans cinq minutes.
9 Les cars .... de la Place St André.
10 Qu'est-ce que vous .... à manger, s'il vous plaît?
11 J'.................. deux filles et un fils.
12 Vous .... du ski?

Part II

Vingt questions

1 Which of the following would you be most likely to have as a dessert? *une tarte aux épinards; une tarte aux fraises; des essuie-glace; des fruits de mer*

2 What is the difference between *un machin* and *un truc*?

3 What is the significance of 14th July for French people?

4 Where are you likely to find signs saying *Compostez votre billet*, and what does it mean?

5 What is *la Galette des Rois*?

6 Can you give the names of two places starting *station* ...?

7 If someone says to you *Voici votre monnaie*, what have you probably just done?

8 Which of the following words fits the gap in this sentence?
Pour arriver à la gare, il faut .... à droite.
tournez; tourner; tourné

9 What are the initials of something that might get you from Paris to Lyon at 260 kilometres an hour?

10 Marie-Pierre is in a restaurant and the waitress asks her *Qu'est-ce que tu prends?* What can you deduce from this?

11 What is the difference between *un car* and *un bus*?

12 If you bought a bottle of champagne described as *brut*, would you expect it to be dry, medium-dry or sweet?

13 In a china shop, you say to the assistant *Oui, je le prends*. Which of the following are you buying?
l'assiette; la soucoupe; le vase; le pansement

14 What is the name of the building where you might find a theatre, art gallery, libraries and concert hall all under one roof?

15 If the menu says *boisson en supplément*, what drink will be included in your meal?

16 What do the letters *SNCF* stand for, and what is the *SNCF*?

17 If a man says that you're going to meet *la petite amie de son frère*, is he implying that:

his brother's not specially fond of her; it's a rather special relationship; she's small; she's a bit thin?

18 Why isn't it advisable to take your French host a bunch of chrysanthemums?

19 Which of these has nothing to do with cooking?
à l'ancienne; le jeu lyonnais; saignant; un croque-madame

20 There is one word for something you might receive from *un médecin* and *un moustique*. What is it?

Part III

1 **National stereotypes**
Answer the following questions along the line of this example:
What sort of cheese does Pierre eat?
du fromage français, (bien sûr!)

1 What sort of beer does Fritz drink?
2 What sort of ice cream does Giuseppe eat?
3 What sort of oranges does Pedro eat?
4 What sort of apples does George eat?
5 What sort of whisky does Jock drink? (whisky = *le whisky*)

2 **Recipes – *des recettes***
Fill in the blanks in these recipes with words taken from the list. One of them has to be used three times:

minutes, quatre, beurre, cassez, four, fromage, manger, cuire, jambon, sel, délicieux, mangez, poivrez, mettez, oeuf, ça, tranche, pliez

Le croque-monsieur (pour une personne)
Vous prenez une .... de pain et du .... Vous .... le beurre sur le pain. Puis, vous mettez du .... râpé sur le pain. Vous mettez une tranche de .... dessus et une autre .... de pain. Vous passez le tout au ...., dix .... environ, et voilà, vous le ...., c'est ....!

La galette de Madame Douaud
Vous mettez votre pâte sur la galettière. Vous la laissez .... environ une minute. Ensuite, vous .... un .... dessus, vous .... et vous mettez un peu de .... Puis vous préparez votre .... de jambon et vous la posez sur l'oeuf comme .... Ensuite vous .... votre galette en .... et c'est prêt à ....

3 Here are three people talking about their lives. Which job descriptions fit what they say?

1 Je travaille huit heures par jour, cinq jours par semaine. Je joue au football le dimanche après-midi. Je ne vais pas beaucoup au cinéma parce que je travaille souvent le soir.

2 Je travaille huit heures par jour mais j'ai seulement une demi-heure pour le déjeuner. Je travaille deux samedis par mois. Quand je ne travaille pas le samedi, en hiver je fais du ski et en été je joue au tennis.

3 Ma fille a un petit magasin; je travaille un peu pour elle. Je travaille le matin. Je prends le train à neuf heures et quart et j'arrive au magasin à dix heures moins le quart. Je déjeune avec ma fille et je rentre chez moi dans l'après-midi vers trois heures et demie. Le soir je regarde la télé.

Job descriptions

a) Sylvie Dupont: hôtesse, Syndicat d'Initiative – journée continue à partir de 9h – cinq jours par semaine – travaille un samedi sur deux

b) Odette Colbert: commence à 9h45 – termine à 13h30 – cinq jours par semaine

c) Michel Cottard: garçon de café – commence à 10h – travaille jusqu'à 14h30 – recommence à 19h30 – termine à 23h – sauf dimanche et lundi

4 How would:
1 the waiter
2 the young woman in the tourist office
3 the lady who helps in her daughter's shop
answer the interviewer's questions:
Quel est votre métier?
Vous commencez à quelle heure?
Vous travaillez combien d'heures par jour?
Qu'est-ce que vous aimez faire quand vous ne travaillez pas?

5 You go into a department store to buy some shoes (*des chaussures*).

Vendeuse	Bonjour, madame.
You	*Greet her and say you would like some shoes.*
Vendeuse	Très bien, madame. Quelle pointure (= *size of shoe*)?
You	*36, you think.*
Vendeuse	Très bien, madame. (*she fetches some shoes*) Vous voulez les essayer?
You	*(you try them on) Say these are too small.*
Vendeuse	Alors, celles-ci, madame?
You	*Say you quite like these but . . .*
Vendeuse	Elles sont très jolies, n'est-ce pas, très à la mode et . . .
You	*Yes, but does she have them in black?*
Vendeuse	Mais oui, madame. Voilà.
You	*Say you like them very much; you'll take them.*
Vendeuse	Très bien, madame. Ça fait 399F
You	*(paying) There you are.*
Vendeuse	Merci, madame. Au revoir.

6 Here are the names of some well-known people and the dates of their birthdays.

1 Can you say what these dates are in English?
2 Which birthday belongs to which person?

le lundi neuf novembre dix-neuf cent vingt-cinq
le mardi premier avril dix-huit cent soixante-treize
le vendredi vingt-huit septembre dix-neuf cent trente-quatre
le samedi premier juillet dix-neuf cent soixante-et-un

Sergei Rachmaninov, la princesse Diana, Richard Burton, Brigitte Bardot

3 Now can you say in French the date of your own birthday?

7 Fit the words in the list to the definitions below:

1 C'est le contraire d'ouvrir.
2 Sept jours
3 Le 14 juillet est ....
4 Entre la tête et les épaules
5 C'est une partie de la journée.
6 On boit du thé dans ....
7 On le prend pour aller de Bourg à Lyon.
8 Le contraire de descendre
9 Il faut .... pour vivre et non pas vivre pour ....
10 On les fait avec des pommes de terre.
11 C'est une boisson qu'on fait avec des pommes.
12 Il n'aime pas .... la télé sauf quand il y a 'A vous la France!', bien sûr!
13 Le contraire de blanc
14 Un poulet de Bresse est ...., blanc et rouge.
15 Sur la galette vous mettez du poivre et du ....
16 Vous allez dans un café pour .... l'apéritif.
17 On le prend pour traverser le canal.
18 Le contraire de rarement
19 Au restaurant, on demande .... à la fin du repas.
20 On en trouve des bons en Bresse.

le train, l'après-midi, manger (twice), *regarder, une semaine, les frites, bleu, le cidre, l'addition, prendre, fermer, une tasse, souvent, un jour de fête, sel, le pont, le cou, des poulets, monter, noir*

Randonnée en Vercors

With magnificent Alpine scenery all round Grenoble, it is not surprising that hiking is a favourite activity for the Grenoblois. But walking in the mountains can be dangerous: inexperienced hikers often hire qualified guides. These will plan a route which takes into account factors like the differences in height to be negotiated (*les dénivelés*), the stamina of the walkers and the weather forecast (*la météo*).

Fleb, a qualified mountain guide, takes a party from Grenoble one Sunday on a walk through the Vercors – a beautiful regional park very popular with *randonneurs*. The route he has planned takes them past one of the most famous landmarks in the park, *le Mont Aiguille*, its strangely-shaped summit reaching over 2000 metres. This peak was once thought to be a place of magic until, in 1489, King Charles VIII, intrigued by its mysteries, commanded some of his soldiers to climb it, thereby sponsoring the first recorded mountain-climb in France.

Le Mont Aiguille

Une randonnée en montagne n'est pas comme une promenade à la campagne, le dimanche après-midi. Il faut donc la préparer avec soin. Fleb est un jeune sociologue de 32 ans et il est aussi accompagnateur de randonnées en montagne. Il nous explique tout d'abord comment il prépare une randonnée: il repère son itinéraire sur la carte; puis il calcule les dénivelés, car on ne peut pas aller aussi loin quand les chemins montent et descendent beaucoup. Le choix de l'itinéraire dépend aussi d'autres paramètres: de la condition physique des randonneurs, de leur résistance et surtout de la météo, car le temps change très vite en montagne et cela peut être dangereux. Sur le plateau du Vercors par exemple, il y a souvent du brouillard et on risque de se perdre ou de tomber dans une fissure; il faut donc toujours rester proche des autres randonneurs pour toujours les voir.

Quand il accompagne une randonnée, Fleb ne marche pas tout le temps. Il s'arrête souvent pour permettre à ses compagnons d'admirer le paysage et pour en parler. Et puis il faut aussi se restaurer en cours de route, manger et boire quelque chose.

Fleb vit en ville, à Grenoble, mais il aime la montagne, peut-être parce qu'il habite une région de montagnes depuis l'âge de six mois. Pour lui, la randonnée, c'est une possibilité d'avoir une autre vision du monde. Il le dit lui-même: 'Quand on est au sommet d'une montagne on a une vision du monde très apaisée, très ouverte.'

tout d'abord	*first of all*
leur résistance	*their stamina*
on risque de se perdre	*one risks getting lost*
pour toujour les voir	*so that you can always see them*
pour en parler	*to talk about it*
en cours de route	*on the way*
il habite . . . depuis	*he has been living in . . . since*
lui-même	*himself*

Possibilités

Asking if you can do something
Asking someone if they can do something for you

Radio

1 The island of Noirmoutier off the Atlantic coast is linked to the French mainland by a toll bridge and, at low tide, by a causeway called *le Gois*. Pierrick is at the tourist office finding out if the causeway is open now.

Le Gois à marée basse

Pierrick Bonjour, madame.
Hôtesse Bonjour, monsieur.
Pierrick Est-ce qu'on peut passer le Gois maintenant?
Hôtesse Maintenant (*checks tide tables*) – non, c'est trop tard.
Pierrick C'est trop tard maintenant. Alors, est-ce qu'on peut passer ce soir?
Hôtesse Ce soir, oui, vous pouvez passer ... (*checks tide tables*) la marée est basse à vingt-deux heures zéro trois ... vous pouvez passer à partir de vingt heures trente jusqu'à onze heures trente, vingt-trois heures trente.
Pierrick Et demain matin?

Hôtesse Demain matin la mer est basse à dix heures vingt-cinq, donc vous pouvez passer entre ... entre neuf heures et midi.
Pierrick Si la mer est haute, comment est-ce qu'on peut retourner sur le continent ?
Hôtesse Alors si la mer est haute vous pouvez prendre le pont qui est ouvert jour et nuit, et c'est huit francs par véhicule.
Pierrick Bon, je vous remercie beaucoup, madame.
Hôtesse Je vous en prie, monsieur.
Pierrick Au revoir, madame.
Hôtesse Au revoir, monsieur.

sur le continent *to the mainland*

To ask/say if it is possible to do something:	
(est-ce qu') on peut ...?	can one ...?
vous pouvez ...	you can ...

Quickies
1 Why can't Pierrick use the causeway now?
2 When he goes over how can he get back at high tide?
3 How much is the toll?

Radio 2 Sara and her boy-friend Patrick are looking for a room, and are trying to find the *château* belonging to Monsieur West, who does bed and breakfast.

Sara (*driving up a bumpy lane she spots a large house*) Tu penses que c'est là ?
Patrick Peut-être. On peut toujours essayer.
Sara Oui, en tout cas c'est joli, hein. Ah! Le gros chien! (*they arrive in front of the house – a dog is barking*) Chien! Viens là! Viens, viens là le chien, viens ici. Voilà. Oh, il est beau, le chien. Oui, oui, oui, il est beau. Viens là. Il n'a pas l'air content, hein.
Patrick Non.
Sara C'est un beau petit château, hein.
Patrick Oui.
Sara On va voir s'il y a quelqu'un. (*rings the doorbell. Monsieur West opens the door*) Bonjour, monsieur.
M West Bonjour, madame. Bonjour, monsieur.
Sara C'est bien ici que vous faites chambre d'hôte ?
M West Ah oui, oui, c'est bien ici.
Sara Ah bon. Vous avez de la place ?
M West Oui, oui, oui. Mais entrez donc, d'abord.
Sara Merci. (*they step inside*) Est-ce qu'on peut voir la chambre, s'il vous plaît ?

M West Oui. Pas de problème. Je vais vous la montrer.
Sara Bon.
M West Bon ben, si vous voulez me suivre. Je passe devant.
Sara Oui, bien sûr.
M West Excusez-moi. (*they follow him along a corridor . . .*) C'est par ici. (*. . . and up some stairs . . .*)
Sara C'est ancien.
M West Oui. Ah oui, c'est une vieille maison.
Sara De quelle époque?
M West Oh, elle a cent cinquante ans à peu près.
Sara Oh, quand même! (*they eventually reach the room*)
M West Oui. Alors, vous avez une petite entrée, puis la salle de bains qui est indépendante, qui est à votre disposition, qui est là. (*opening door of room*) Si vous voulez entrer.
Sara (*stepping in*) Oui. Pardon.
Patrick Pardon.
Sara Oui, mais c'est très bien. C'est parfait. Euh, c'est combien la chambre?
M West Quatre-vingts francs.
Sara Quatre-vingts francs.
M West Pour la nuit, petit déjeuner compris.
Sara Ah bon, le petit déjeuner est compris.
M West Oui.
Sara Et est-ce qu'on peut dîner le soir?
M West Ah oui, oui. Pas de problème. Si vous voulez, nous faisons des repas. Et c'est en supplément et nous demandons trente-trois francs par repas.
Sara Bon, ben c'est très bien.
M West Vous comptez rester ce soir?
Sara Oui, deux nuits, c'est possible?
M West Oui. Pas de problème.
Sara Bon. Alors, on dîne ce soir et demain soir aussi.
M West Bon. Vous êtes donc pour deux, deux personnes.
Patrick C'est ça, merci.
M West Très bien. Merci, madame.
Sara Pour le petit déjeuner, vous avez des heures . . .?
M West Avant neuf heures.
Sara Avant neuf heures.
M West Il n'y a pas de problème. Après c'est un petit peu tard.
Sara D'accord.
Patrick Merci.
M West Voilà. Merci, madame.

chambre d'hôte	*bed and breakfast*
vous avez de la place?	*have you got room/a vacancy?*
entrez donc, d'abord	*do come in first*
si vous voulez bien . . .	*would you like to . . .?*
c'est par ici	*it's this way*
elle a cent cinquante ans	*it is 150 years old*
oh, quand même!	*oh, really?*
vous avez des heures . . .?	*have you got times . . .?*

To ask if there's anyone in: **il y a quelqu'un?**

Quickies

1 What does the accommodation consist of?
2 Is breakfast included in the price of the room or not?
3 By what time do you have to have breakfast?

Radio 3 Some *Syndicats d'Initiative* operate a service called *Accueil de France* and, for a fee, they will book you a hotel room in another town. Sara is in the *Syndicat d'Initiative* in Nantes enquiring about the possibility of booking a room in Saint-Malo.

Nantes : le Syndicat d'Initiative

Sara Bonjour, madame.
Hôtesse Bonjour, madame.
Sara Je peux réserver une chambre à Saint-Malo d'ici?
Hôtesse Oui. Vous êtes combien de personnes?
Sara Nous sommes deux.

Hôtesse	Vous êtes deux. Et pour combien de temps?
Sara	Pour cette nuit seulement.
Hôtesse	Oui. Vous voulez une chambre avec un grand lit ou deux lits simples?
Sara	Deux lits simples.
Hôtesse	Vous avez un prix maximum?
Sara	Cent cinquante francs.
Hôtesse	Oui, cent cinquante francs. Quel est votre nom?
Sara	Tomei. T.O.M.E.I.
Hôtesse	Oui. Vous pouvez patienter quelques instants?
Sara	Oui, bien sûr. Combien de temps à peu près?
Hôtesse	Un quart d'heure.
Sara	Bon. D'accord.
	Sara goes off while the booking is made by telex and returns twenty minutes later.
Hôtesse	Voilà. Vous avez une réservation de chambre à Saint-Malo. C'est l'Hôtel du Centre, et le prix de la chambre est de cent quarante francs.
Sara	Très bien. Merci. Vous me donnez l'adresse?
Hôtesse	Oui. C'est l'Hôtel du Centre, l'adresse est ici (*handing her the booking slip*).
Sara	Très bien. Combien je vous dois?
Hôtesse	Dix-huit francs pour la réservation, et vous payez à l'hôtel pour la chambre.
Sara	Ah bon, très bien.

cette nuit *tonight*

To ask 'Can I . . . ?':

(est-ce que) je peux . . . ?

To say how many people are in your group (eg in a restaurant, booking a room):

	deux
nous sommes	quatre
	douze

Quickies

1 How did Sara say 'there are two of us'?
2 What's the name of the official service that will book a room for you in another town?
3 How much was the room?

TV 4 In Pézenas, Elisabeth Martel takes some clothes to a cleaner's (*un pressing* or *une teinturerie*).

Teinturier	Madame?
Elisabeth	Bonjour, monsieur. J'ai un pantalon et une chemise à faire nettoyer. Vous pouvez le faire?
	He examines the labels in the garments.
Teinturier	Oui, pas de problème. Vous les voulez pour quand?
Elisabeth	Demain matin, c'est possible?
Teinturier	C'est un peu juste. Demain après-midi, ça vous ira?
Elisabeth	Oui. Je peux passer les prendre vers quelle heure?

Teinturier	Passez vers trois heures; ce sera prêt.
Elisabeth	Très bien. Je vous remercie. Au revoir, monsieur.
Teinturier	Au revoir, madame.

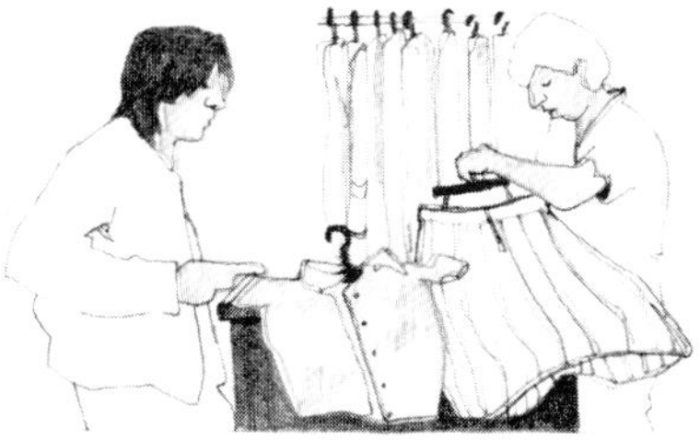

à faire nettoyer	*to be cleaned*
c'est un peu juste	*it's a bit tight*
ça vous ira?	*will that be all right for you?*
je peux passer les prendre?	*can I come and get them?*
ce sera prêt	*it'll be ready*

Quickies

1. What clothes has Elisabeth got for cleaning?
2. How does she say 'tomorrow morning'?
3. What words does the *teinturier* use to tell her when they will in fact be ready?

TV 5 On the road into Pézenas, Jean-Gilbert Iriu drives into a garage to get some petrol and some advice. He speaks to the petrol attendant (*le pompiste*).

Jean-Gilbert	Bonjour, monsieur.
Pompiste	Bonjour.
Jean-Gilbert	Le plein, s'il vous plaît.
Pompiste	Oui.
Jean-Gilbert	J'ai un petit problème avec ma voiture – un problème de démarrage. Vous pourriez regarder?
Pompiste	Allez voir le mécanicien en face. *While the tank is being filled, Jean-Gilbert goes over to the mechanic working on another car.*
Jean-Gilbert	Pardon, monsieur.
Mécanicien	Oui?
Jean-Gilbert	J'ai du mal à démarrer. Vous pourriez regarder?
Mécanicien	Bien sûr. C'est peut-être la batterie, non?
Jean-Gilbert	Non, non, elle est neuve. J'ai l'impression que le moteur chauffe aussi.
Mécanicien	Ah bon. On va regarder ça. *They go over to the car.*
Mécanicien	Vous pourriez ouvrir le capot, s'il vous plaît? *Jean-Gilbert opens the bonnet.*
Mécanicien	Ah, c'est ce que je pensais. La courroie est cassée. (*showing broken fanbelt*) Tenez, regardez. On vous la change tout de suite?
Jean-Gilbert	Oui. Il y en a pour longtemps?
Mécanicien	Une demi-heure environ.
Jean-Gilbert	Bon, je repasserai.
Mécanicien	Oui.

Jean-Gilbert (*showing him the spare wheel under the bonnet*) J'ai un pneu crevé aussi. Vous pourriez le réparer?

Mécanicien Bien sûr. Pas de problème.

Jean-Gilbert Merci bien. A tout à l'heure.

Mécanicien Au revoir, monsieur.

Jean-Gilbert goes to the attendant to settle for the petrol.

Jean-Gilbert Je vous dois combien?

Pompiste Deux cents francs, monsieur. (*Jean-Gilbert gives him the money*) Merci.

Jean-Gilbert Vous pourriez me faire une facture?

Pompiste Oui. Venez avec moi.

le plein	*fill up the tank*
j'ai du mal à ...	*I'm having trouble ...*
c'est ce que je pensais	*it's what I thought/just as I thought*
on vous la change?	*shall we change it for you?*
il y en a pour longtemps?	*will it take long?*

To ask someone if they can do something for you:

vous pouvez ...? can you ...?
vous pourriez ...? could you ...?

Quickies

1 Where does the attendant say the mechanic is?
2 Why is the battery not the problem?
3 You want your tank filled. What do you say?
4 How does the mechanic say 'No trouble'?

TV 6 Paulette Sada has gone to a hotel bar for a coffee, and she needs to make a phone call while she's there.

Paulette Est-ce que je peux téléphoner d'ici?

Serveuse Où voulez-vous téléphoner?

Paulette A Toulouse. C'est possible?

Serveuse Oui. Pas de problème.

Paulette Vous pourriez me donner l'indicatif, s'il vous plaît?

Serveuse Oui, bien sûr. (*looking up dialling code*) Vous faites le seize, puis le soixante et un et ensuite votre numéro. (*pointing to telephone at the end of the bar*) Tenez, vous avez l'appareil là. Je vous laisse faire.

Paulette dials the number and a secretary replies.

Secrétaire Allô, oui. Maison Maurin, bonjour.

Paulette Bonjour, madame. Madame Sada à l'appareil. Est-ce que je pourrais parler à Monsieur Lecomte, s'il vous plaît?

Secrétaire	Ah, il n'est pas là, madame. C'est à quel sujet?
Paulette	Ah, écoutez . . . je suis dans la région pour quelques jours seulement. Est-ce que je peux prendre rendez-vous avec lui?
Secrétaire	Oui. Vous êtes là jusqu'à quand?
Paulette	Après-demain, mercredi. Est-ce que je pourrais le voir demain, par exemple?
Secrétaire	Demain? Demain . . . demain, onze heures trente, ça vous va?
Paulette	Demain onze heures trente. Parfait.
Secrétaire	Vous pouvez me rappeler votre nom?
Paulette	Oui, bien sûr. Sada, S.A.D.A. Paulette.
Secrétaire	Très bien.
Paulette	Merci, madame. Au revoir.
Secrétaire	Au revoir, madame.

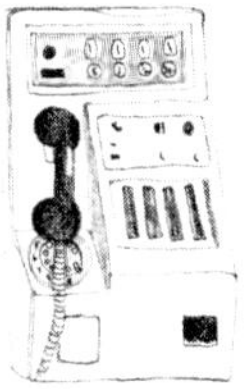

vous faites le seize	*you dial sixteen*
je vous laisse faire	*I'll let you get on with it*
Madame Sada à l'appareil	*Madame Sada speaking*
c'est à quel sujet?	*what's it about?*
ça vous va?	*is that all right for you?*

To ask 'Could I . . .?':

(est-ce que) je pourrais . . .?

Quickies

1 What's the expression for 'to make an appointment'?
2 What's the word for 'the dialling code'?
3 How long is Paulette staying in the area?

Mots-clés

l'adresse (f)	address	la batterie	battery
la chambre d'hôte	bed and breakfast	crevé	punctured
		la facture	bill
le château	castle; country house	le garage	garage
		le moteur	engine
le chien	dog	le plein	full tank
le dîner	dinner	le pneu	tyre
le repas	meal	le problème	problem
la chemise	shirt	bas	low
le pantalon	trousers	content	happy
le slip	pant(ie)s	d'abord	first of all
		haut	high
		par ici	this way
		possible	possible
		vieux	old

après-demain	the day after tomorrow
demain	tomorrow
écouter	to listen (to)
entrer	to go in/come in
payer	to pay
réparer	to repair
retourner	to go back/come back
téléphoner	to telephone

En bref

1 To ask 'Is it possible to . . .?':

(est-ce qu')	**on peut**	passer le Gois maintenant?
	il est possible de	réserver des places pour ce soir?

2 To ask 'Can I . . .?':

(est-ce que) je peux	réserver une chambre?
	téléphoner d'ici?

3 You can also be more tentative when asking favours and say 'Could I . . .?':

est-ce que je pourrais	parler à Monsieur Lecomte, s'il vous plaît?
	voir la chambre, s'il vous plaît?

4 To ask someone to do something for you, start with 'Can you . . .?':
vous pouvez nettoyer cette chemise, s'il vous plaît?

or 'Could you . . .?':
vous pourriez me donner l'indicatif, s'il vous plaît?

5 To invite someone to do something starting 'Will you . . .?':

voulez-vous	me suivre?
	téléphoner demain?
	danser avec moi?

6 If someone asks you a favour, you can use a number of phrases in reply. Here are some common ones:

bien sûr	*of course/certainly*
allez-y	*go ahead*
pas de problème	*no trouble*
je vous en prie	*please do*
or alternatively:	
je suis désolé(e) mais . . .	*I'm terribly sorry, but . . .*

7 When getting things repaired etc, to ask 'Will it be long?':
il y en a pour longtemps?
or 'Will you be long?':
vous en avez pour longtemps?
And to tell someone how long *you'll* be:

j'en ai pour	cinq minutes
	une demi-heure à peu près

Notice the position of the words for 'me' and 'you' in the following:
je **vous** dois combien?
voulez-vous **me** suivre?
They go before the verb like *l'/le/la/les* (see chapter 8, p168)

pouvoir – to be able to	
je	peux
tu	peux
elle/il/on	peut
nous	pouvons
vous	pouvez
elles/ils	peuvent

vouloir – to want (to)	
je	veux
tu	veux
elle/il/on	veut
nous	voulons
vous	voulez
elles/ils	veulent

En plus

1 **Funny business, English**
A normal regular English verb like 'to work' has got four separate parts: *work*, *works*, *working* and *worked*. Some irregular verbs have got more parts than that (eg 'to go' has five – *go*, *goes*, *going*, *went*, *gone*).

The verb 'can', though, has only two parts: *can* and *could* (it doesn't even have an infinitive form 'to can') and very efficient they are too because they cover all the tenses and persons of the verb. *Pouvoir*, on the other hand, exists in all the usual parts that a French verb has. If you're ever in doubt with what tense 'can' and 'could' represent, you can always translate into 'to be able to' and this will lead you towards the correct tense of *pouvoir*.
eg I could tell the time at the age of four = I was able to ...
I could give you a hand tomorrow = I would be able to ...

When you're asking someone a favour, there's a subtle difference between *pouvez-vous ...?* ('can you ...?') and *pourriez-vous ...?* ('could you ...?'), which is more tentative.

2 **Asking questions**
In chapters 2 and 4 there were several ways of asking simple questions (p42/87). The same ways exist if you ask a question using a question

word (the equivalent of 'who?', 'when?', 'where?', 'how?', etc). You can either:

1. put the question word on the end of the ordinary statement: *vous travaillez où?*
2. or put it on the front with *est-ce que*: *où est-ce que vous travaillez?*
3. or put it on the front and reverse the order of the verb and subject pronoun: *où travaillez-vous?*

The first two are probably more frequently used especially in spoken French.

3 **Words**

Appareil means any machine or piece of apparatus. It is commonly used on its own as short for *un appareil photographique* – a camera. *Demander* means simply 'to ask' and not 'to demand'.
A tout à l'heure – there is a whole collection of expressions in French which are loosely equivalent to 'goodbye till . . .'. Even the standard *au revoir* means literally 'until we see each other again'. Some of the others are:

à demain	*see you tomorrow*
à ce soir	*see you this evening*
à mardi	*see you Tuesday*
à tout à l'heure	*see you in a minute*

A tout à l'heure is the origin of 'toodleoo'.

Le pantalon – singular in French, plural in English: one nation sees it as a single garment and the other as a pair of legs. Also singular is what goes under *le pantalon: le slip*. Unlike English, the word is the same whether the wearer is male or female.

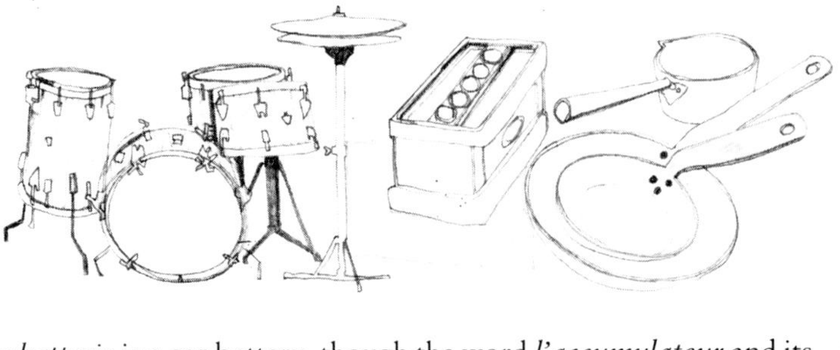

La batterie is a car battery, though the word *l'accumulateur* and its shortened form *l'accu* are also used. *Batterie* has other meanings too. *La batterie de cuisine* means all the pots and pans in your kitchen. And in a band or orchestra the person *à la batterie* is playing not the battery or the saucepans, but the drums. Incidentally, don't ask for *des batteries* for your torch or transistor because you won't get them in. The word for that kind of battery is *une pile*.

L'indicatif is the dialling code when you're talking about telephone numbers. It's also a call-sign, for example of a radio station.

if you're a keen grammarian, you might want to use *l'indicatif* in the sense of 'the indicative'.

4 **Allô! Allô!**
Using the telephone requires some special vocabulary.
Allô is used only on the phone and never otherwise as an equivalent of 'hello'.
A l'appareil literally means 'at the receiver' and is used in phrases like:

qui est à l'appareil?	who's that speaking?
Madame Baudelot à l'appareil	Madame Baudelot speaking

Some other useful phrases are:

c'est de la part de qui?	who's speaking, please?
ne quittez pas	hold the line please
c'est occupé	it's engaged
ça ne répond pas	there's no reply
vous êtes en ligne	you're through
le poste 125, s'il vous plaît	extension 125, please

A propos

Les châteaux
The word *château* may conjure up images of castles and turreted palaces, but it can also be used to describe a vineyard with a humble shed in the middle. The original *château* was a medieval fortified castle (or *château fort*). Gradually the fortifications became less important until, in the sixteenth century, a *château* was a palace or large house for royalty or the aristocracy. Some of the most famous and beautiful *châteaux* of the Loire date from this period.

Chenonceaux: le château

Later, any country house, even a small one, became known as *un château*. In the vineyards around Bordeaux, the wine of a particular estate was named after the country house in which the owners lived. As landed gentry, the early owners could genuinely claim to live in *châteaux*. Today, however, the term is used to identify any estate in the Bordeaux area, even if there's only a glorified shed on it.

Paysage de l'île de Noirmoutier

L'île de Noirmoutier and le Gois
The island of Noirmoutier is situated off the Atlantic coast of France just south of the mouth of the Loire. It is a very popular holiday resort, and its normal indigenous population of 8,500 swells to 120,000 with summer visitors.

It enjoys a very mild winter climate. Frosts are virtually unknown and by February the island is ablaze with mimosa. And its new potatoes (*les pommes de terre nouvelles*) are the first to reach the market in Spring.

Noirmoutier is linked to the French mainland (*le continent*) by a road bridge and also a causeway called *le Gois*. At low tide the sea recedes for more than a kilometre and motorists can drive from the mainland to the island, or vice versa, for a period of about three hours twice a day. A sign at either end tells motorists when it is safe to cross. It is not uncommon, though, for the locals to take risks and try to drive across outside the safe hours, even when the tide is racing in at high speed. For the foolhardy, wooden posts with climbing rungs are placed at intervals along the *Gois*, and you can climb them if caught, and wait until the tide goes out again. Your car will not get off so lightly, so it's best to respect the notice or ask someone *Quand est-ce qu'on peut passer le Gois?*

Les chambres d'hôte
When driving through France you could well come across signs, usually in the countryside, indicating the way to a *chambre d'hôte*. This is simply a private house where you can have bed and breakfast. Some will also do you an evening meal, which might be in the company of the family. Information about *chambres d'hôte* in the vicinity can be obtained from the local *Syndicat d'Initiative*.

Making a phone call
Phoning from a call-box (*une cabine téléphonique*) should be no

problem. Instructions are written up in five languages. You just need the right coins – $\frac{1}{2}$ franc, 1 franc or 5 francs.

Phone calls can usually be made from bars as well, though it costs more. A meter, zeroed at the beginning of a call, tells the person behind the bar how many units to charge.

Unlike in Britain, every *bureau de poste* has public telephones inside. Some are the call-box type which you dial yourself. Others are dialled by a clerk behind the counter, and payment is made at the counter at the end of the call. This can be useful if you need to make a long call or are short of change.

If you are dialling your own call, you'll need to know about dialling codes (*les indicatifs*) and tones (*les tonalités*). For dialling within a *département*, you simply dial the number – six or seven digits. A series of long bleeps means the number is ringing; quick, short bleeps mean it's engaged. If you are dialling to another *département*, you have to dial 16 and wait for a second tone (*la deuxième tonalité*): this means you are connected to inter-departmental lines. You then dial the code for the *département* you want, and then your number.

For international calls, first dial 19 and wait for the *deuxième tonalité*. Then dial the country code (44 for Great Britain), followed by the local code without the 0, and finally the number you require.

During any of these operations, a series of very rapid bleeps indicates that the switching equipment is trying to connect you. Don't hang up. It will, sooner or later, change to the continuous tone, or to a ringing/engaged signal.

Pézenas

Pézenas is a small town on the wine-growing plain of the Languedoc. Fine buildings in the narrow streets of the old quarter indicate the town's former importance. In the Middle Ages it was a major trading centre with annual fairs. It received royal protection and privileges. Later, it became an important political centre, a seat of the regional government, the *Etats du Languedoc*, and residence of its governor. Kings and princes stayed in Pézenas as guests of the governor, entertained by troupes of actors such as that of Molière, France's greatest comic playwright.

But with the centralisation of political power in the eighteenth century, Pézenas gradually declined in importance. At the beginning of this century, its main activities were wine-making and market gardening. Today, the Town Hall is the chief employer, and the population of 8,000 is no bigger than it was two hundred years ago.

Not far from the beaches of the Mediterranean, Pézenas attracts tourists because of its beautiful old streets and its summer crafts fair, the *Mirandola dels Arts*. Visitors can also enjoy a local speciality, the *petits pâtés de Pézenas*: pastry cases filled with sweetened minced mutton, prepared to a recipe left by Lord Clive of India, who happened to be passing through.

Bon courage

1 A word in the first list has some sort of connection with a word in the second list, for example *pantalon* goes with *chemise* because they are both articles of clothing. Find the other pairs:

1	numéro	a)	haut
2	voir	b)	voiture
3	bas	c)	possible
4	pantalon	d)	téléphoner
5	mécanicien	e)	chemise
6	nom	f)	après-demain
7	demain	g)	adresse
8	pouvoir	h)	regarder

2 Match up the English and the French phrases:

1	composer le numéro	a)	the dialling tone
2	l'indicatif	b)	who's speaking?
3	la tonalité	c)	hold the line
4	qui est à l'appareil?	d)	the dialling code
5	ne quittez pas	e)	the number is engaged
6	ça ne répond pas	f)	to dial the number
7	c'est occupé	g)	there is no reply

3 Fill in the blanks in the dialogue with words from this list:
à, vous, voir, aujourd'hui, va, parler, peut, voulez, peux, possible, matin

Client Allô, est-ce que je pourrais .... à Monsieur Reynaud, s'il vous plaît? C'est Monsieur Thouvay à l'appareil.
Secrétaire Il n'est pas là ...., monsieur.
Client Ah, est-ce que je .... prendre rendez-vous avec lui?
Secrétaire Bien sûr. Quand .... -vous venir?
Client Eh bien, jeudi, est-ce que Monsieur Reynaud .... me .... jeudi?
Secrétaire Un moment; jeudi, oui, c'est .... Il .... jouer au golf le .... mais il est libre l'après-midi. Quatorze heures trente, ça .... va?
Client Parfait. Merci bien, madame, ... jeudi.
Secrétaire Oui. Au revoir, monsieur.

4 You find yourself in various situations where you have to ask people to do things for you. Ask the following favours, starting the first three with 'Can you . . .?' and the second three with 'Could you . . .?':
1 You'd like the vase you've bought gift-wrapped.
2 You want the mechanic to look at your car headlights.
3 In the dry cleaner's, you want to have this dress cleaned.
4 Ask someone if they can change (*faire la monnaie de*) ten francs for you.
5 Ask the person sitting opposite to pass you the salt.
6 Ask the hotel receptionist to give you the dialling code for Britain.

5 In these situations you want to ask if you can or may do something. Use 'can I . . .?' for the first three and 'could I . . .?' for the second three. Some phrases are given below to help you.

1. You're leaving your film for developing. You'd like to come back for your photos tomorrow.
2. In the church in Brou you'd like to take some photographs.
3. While in a café you'd like to make a phone call.
4. In the *Syndicat d'Initiative* in Bourg you want to buy a bus ticket for Châtillon.
5. You'd like to see the lighter over there on the left.
6. You'd like to have the recipe for Madame Douaud's *galette*.

regarder le briquet qui est là-bas à gauche
passer prendre mes photos demain
acheter un billet de car pour Châtillon
prendre des photos
téléphoner d'ici
avoir la recette de la galette

6 Tell a French friend that the following things cannot be done:

1. drink in an English pub after 11 o'clock in the evening
2. make an omelette without breaking eggs
3. go skiing in Scotland in summer
4. buy stamps in a tobacconist's in Britain.

7 Unscramble this dialogue:
C'est pas un petit problème, ça, c'est un gros problème.
Disons, dans une demi-heure.
Non? Quand alors?
Bonjour, monsieur. J'ai un petit problème avec ma voiture.
Très bien. Je peux repasser plus tard.
Bonjour, monsieur.
Oui. A tout à l'heure, monsieur.
Ah oui? Qu'est-ce que c'est?
Avec plaisir, monsieur, mais pas tout de suite.
Les phares ne marchent pas.
Oui. Vous pourriez regarder?

8 Your camera has gone wrong and you go into a photo shop to see if they can help. Complete your side of the conversation.

You *Greet the shopkeeper.*
Commerçant Bonjour, monsieur.
You *Tell him you're having a spot of bother with your camera.*
Commerçant Ah oui, qu'est-ce qu'il y a?
You *You don't know but it doesn't work. Can he have a look at it?*
Commerçant Mais oui, bien sûr.
You *(passing over the camera) There you are.*
Commerçant Ah oui! Je vois. Ça arrive souvent avec ce modèle. On va vous réparer ça.
You *Ask him if he could do it for this afternoon.*
Commerçant C'est un peu juste mais, oui, je crois que c'est possible.
You *About what time?*

Commerçant	Disons vers quatre heures.
You	*Ask him what time he closes.*
Commerçant	On ferme à dix-huit heures, monsieur.
You	*Very good, say you can come and collect it about a quarter to six.*
Commerçant	Très bien, monsieur. Ça sera prêt.
You	*Thank him and say goodbye for a little while.*
Commerçant	Au revoir, monsieur.

Documentaire

Pézenas en fête

In France, *Mardi Gras* – Shrove Tuesday – is traditionally a day of celebration before Lent. But in Pézenas, as in many other towns, the local festival on that day has little to do with the Christian calendar. *La fête du Poulain* celebrates a legendary foal.

The story goes that when King Louis VIII passed through Pézenas in 1226, one of his mares was ill. He left it in the care of the townspeople. During his absence the mare recovered its health and gave birth to a foal. The king was so delighted on his return that he gave the foal to the people of Pézenas. It was the first of many royal favours and privileges bestowed on the town.

Le Poulain dans les rues de Pézenas

Since the fifteenth century, the story has been celebrated in *la fête du Poulain*, when a large wooden horse, carried by a number of sturdy men, parades round the streets of Pézenas behind its keeper. Spectators disguise themselves and play practical jokes on each other: anyone not dressed up is liable to get covered in flour.

Recently, another very old tradition, though not exclusive to Pézenas, has been revived and incorporated in the *fête*; that of the Carnival King, *le Roi Carnaval* – an effigy which is paraded through the streets and ceremoniously burnt at the end of the festivities.

Pampille, le gardien du Poulain

Nous sommes en février. Pour la première fois depuis longtemps, la petite ville occitane de Pézenas est dans la neige: ce qui pose un problème, car demain la fête du Poulain va commencer. Il faut, donc, débarrasser les rues encombrées. Non loin du centre, le Poulain et ses amis se préparent à la fête. Le gardien du Poulain, la personne qui s'en occupe toute l'année, s'appelle Pampille. C'est lui qui, chaque année, mène l'animal et le fait danser dans les rues de la ville pour la joie des habitants.

Le Poulain vit à Pézenas depuis 1226. C'est, sans aucun doute, un des plus vieux habitants de la ville! Mais, depuis quelques années, il n'est plus le seul à défiler au moment de la fête. Le soir, il y a une autre effigie qui se promène dans les rues de Pézenas: c'est le Roi Carnaval. Selon la coutume, des habitants et des musiciens en chemise de nuit l'accompagnent. Le Roi Carnaval représente tous les problèmes qu'ont eus les habitants pendant l'année qui vient de passer. Après avoir fait le tour de Pézenas, il va passer en jugement. Cette année, comme chaque année, il est déclaré coupable et condamné à être brûlé sans attendre.

La fête arrive à sa fin; un bal est organisé pour la conclure. Une fois de plus, le Poulain et le Carnaval ont permis aux Piscénois de se retrouver et de bien s'amuser.

ce qui	*which*
la personne qui s'en occupe	*the person who looks after it*
c'est lui qui	*it's he who*
il n'est plus	*he's no longer*
qu'ont eus les habitants	*which the inhabitants have had*
qui vient de passer	*which has just finished*
après avoir fait le tour	*after having gone round*
passer en jugement	*to be tried*
sans attendre	*without delay*
une fois de plus	*once more*
ont permis aux Piscénois de se retrouver	*have enabled the* Piscénois *to get together*

12 Tout sur vous 1

Telling people what you've done
Telling people how long you've been doing something
Telling people what you've decided to do

Radio

1 The French seem to put a lot of time and effort into getting out and having a good time at weekends. We asked our interviewers to do a survey on how some of the people in and around Nantes spent the previous weekend.

To ask someone what they did or have done:

	hier?
qu'est-ce que vous avez fait	aujourd'hui?
	le week-end dernier?

Here's Sara talking to a teenage girl she found strolling with her friends in the small resort of Pornic.

Sara Qu'est-ce que vous avez fait pendant le week-end dernier?
Jeune fille Je suis allée au bord de la mer, et j'ai fait de la planche à voile.
Sara Oui. Toute la journée?
Jeune fille Toute l'après-midi, et le soir nous avons mangé sur la route en revenant.
Sara Vous avez fait un pique-nique?
Jeune fille Oui, c'est ça, un pique-nique. Et ensuite nous sommes revenus à Nantes et nous étions très fatigués. Alors, nous nous sommes couchés tout de suite.
Sara Et dimanche qu'est-ce que vous avez fait?
Jeune fille Dimanche nous avons fait la même chose parce que nous aimons beaucoup la planche à voile.

Sara Vous avez fait de la planche à voile à la mer?

Jeune fille Oui. Mais nous pouvons également faire de la planche à voile à Nantes, sur l'Erdre, qui est la rivière.

Sara Vous avez fait exactement la même chose dimanche? Vous avez pique-niqué sur la route aussi?

Jeune fille Non. Dimanche nous avons pique-niqué à la plage.

Sara Ah bon.

Jeune fille Parce qu'il a fait très beau et nous avons préféré rester sur la plage manger.

en revenant	*coming back*
nous sommes revenus	*we came back*
nous nous sommes couchés	*we went to bed*

To tell someone what you did or have done:

	mangé sur la plage
j'ai	**pique-niqué**
nous avons	**fait** de la planche à voile
	déjeuné au restaurant

For saying what you did or have done, you don't always use *avoir*. Some verbs require you to use *être*:
je suis allée
nous sommes revenus
This is covered in more detail in chapter 13.

Quickies

1 Where did the girl go last weekend?
2 What sporting activity did she get up to?

Radio 2 Pierrick spoke to a neighbour in his home village of St-Philbert-de-Grand-Lieu.

Pierrick Qu'est-ce que vous avez fait, Madame Renaudeau, le week-end dernier?

Mme Renaudeau Le week-end dernier nous sommes allés au bord de la mer, aux Moutiers.

Pierrick Et vous avez passé tout le week-end là-bas?

Mme Renaudeau Non. Nous sommes partis le dimanche matin et rentrés le dimanche soir.

Pierrick Simplement pour la journée, donc.

Mme Renaudeau Simplement la journée.

Pierrick Et vous êtes allée avec votre mari et . . .?

Mme Renaudeau . . . et mon fils, exactement.

Pierrick Oui. Il a fait beau?

Mme Renaudeau Il a fait très beau.

Pierrick Et qu'est-ce que vous avez fait là-bas exactement?

Mme Renaudeau Mon mari a fait de la planche à voile . . .

Pierrick Ah oui.

Mme Renaudeau Mon fils a fait des pâtés dans le sable, et . . .

Pierrick Vous avez déjeuné au restaurant ou vous avez pique-niqué?

Mme Renaudeau Nous avons pique-niqué.

Pierrick Est-ce que c'est un week-end normal pour vous?

Mme Renaudeau	Non. Quand il fait beau, nous allons au bord de la mer parce que ça n'est pas loin. S'il ne fait pas beau, nous restons à la maison. Nous profitons de la maison.
Pierrick	En hiver qu'est-ce que vous faites d'habitude ?
Mme Renaudeau	Nous restons à la maison.
Pierrick	Au coin du feu ?
Mme Renaudeau	C'est ça.
Pierrick	Comme tout bon Français en quelque sorte.
Mme Renaudeau	Comme tout bon Français, exactement.

il a fait beau	*the weather was fine*
nous profitons de la maison	*we enjoy just being at home*
au coin du feu	*by the fireside*

Quickies

1 When did the family go to the seaside?
2 How many of them went?
3 What was the weather like?

TV 3

Pézenas, with a population of only about 8,000 people, has over sixty officially-constituted associations catering mostly for leisure activities. Jane enquired about two of them that have been in existence for some time.
Rugby is a very popular sport in the area around Pézenas. Jane asked Jacques Boularand, the president of the Pézenas club, about its origins.

Le Stade Piscénois 1931

Jane	Le club de rugby existe depuis longtemps à Pézenas ?
M Boularand	Le club, après quelques balbutiements avant la guerre de quatorze, il a vraiment commencé à la suite de la guerre de quatorze-dix-huit, où justement, avec les contacts avec les militaires britanniques, les jeunes Piscénois qui ont commencé à découvrir ce sport, quand ils sont revenus au pays une fois la guerre terminée, ont commencé à jouer, à initier tous les jeunes des villages environnants et à former un club ici à Pézenas.

après quelques balbutiements	*after some false starts*
ils sont revenus au pays	*they came back to the area*
une fois la guerre terminée	*once the war was over*

Quickies

1 Which war did Monsieur Boularand mention?
2 Which soldiers had the young Piscénois met?

TV 4 In the 1920s and 30s *le Stade Piscénois* – the Pézenas club – was one of the top in the region, but then gradually lost its position. How does it rank now?

M Boularand Après un déclin, le Stade Piscénois a réussi à regagner sinon l'élite (puisque l'élite du rugby français c'est la première division groupe A), le Stade Piscénois a regagné la première division groupe B, et donc a acquis de nouveau un certain standing. Mais enfin il n'est pas arrivé aux niveaux très importants comme les clubs voisins, comme Béziers, Narbonne, voire Toulouse, Toulon, Nice.

sinon l'élite	*if not the very best*
aux niveaux très importants	*to the highest levels*

> Notice how French manages with one tense when English needs two, as in these sentences:
>
> | | |
> |---|---|
> | mon fils **a commencé** à jouer au rugby | my son *has started* playing rugby |
> | mon fils **a commencé** à jouer au rugby l'année dernière | my son *started* playing rugby last year |

TV 5 Today the club has a thriving membership – over eighty players and a hundred beginners in the rugby school. Jane asked three members how long they had been in the club.

Jane Jean Rieu, vous jouez au rugby depuis combien de temps?
M Rieu Je joue au rugby depuis seize ans. J'ai commencé dès l'âge de neuf ans en scolaire, donc je vais attaquer ma dix-septième saison cette année.
Jane Vous faites partie de l'équipe depuis longtemps?
M Rieu C'est ma deuxième saison exactement puisque j'ai débuté . . . j'ai fait mon apprentissage à Béziers jusqu'en junior et dès que j'ai été senior j'ai joué dans un village, dans mon village, à Cazouls-lès-Béziers exactement.

> To ask someone how long they've been doing something:
> vous jouez au rugby **depuis combien de temps?**

Jane Daniel Vaylet, vous jouez au rugby depuis combien de temps?
M Vaylet Il y a maintenant sept ans que je joue au rugby. J'ai commencé à l'âge de vingt-deux ans. J'ai actuellement vingt-neuf ans.
Jane Et vous faites partie de l'équipe depuis longtemps?
M Vaylet Il y a cinq ans que je joue à Pézenas.
M Boularand Moi, j'ai commencé assez tard, j'ai commencé à l'âge de dix-sept ans et j'ai joué jusqu'à l'âge de trente et un ans.

en scolaire	*at school*
jusqu'en junior	*up to the end of junior grade*

To say something *has been going on for* a certain period of time:
j'habite Pézenas **depuis** deux mois
je joue au rugby **depuis** sept ans
or
il y a deux mois **que j'habite** Pézenas
il y a sept ans **que je joue** au rugby

Quickies

1 Jane asked Daniel Vaylet 'How long have you been playing rugby?' How did she say that?
2 He replied 'I've been playing rugby for seven years'. He could have said that in two ways. Can you remember one of them?

TV 6 One of the most traditional associations in any French town is the brass band, *la fanfare*. Marius Audibert is the conductor of the Pézenas band, *La Fanfare Piscénoise.*

La Fanfare Piscénoise dans les années 30

Jane Monsieur Audibert, vous dirigez la fanfare depuis combien de temps?
M Audibert Depuis la fin des hostilités, depuis 1944. Et la société elle-même a été créée en 1898. C'est donc une société qui a quatre-vingt-cinq ans, qui est très ancienne, peut-être même une des plus anciennes de Pézenas.
Jane Il y a combien de musiciens?
M Audibert Une vingtaine . . ., vingt, vingt-cinq à l'heure actuelle.
Jane Mais est-ce qu'il y en a eu davantage dans le passé?
M Audibert Davantage, oui . . . Cinquante à soixante peut-être, hein? A ce moment-là on était beaucoup plus nombreux. Mais enfin, ce sont les . . . c'est une période disons en creux de vague, quoi. Mais enfin la société marche quand même.
Jane Et comment expliquez-vous cela?
M Audibert Oh, par l'actualité des choses, hein . . . la mécanisation, la télévision. Automatiquement les jeunes sortent beaucoup plus facilement, tandis qu'à l'époque, on était davantage à maison et on s'intéressait davantage aux sociétés, voilà.

la société . . . a été créée	*the society . . . was founded*
à l'heure actuelle	*at the present time*
on était beaucoup plus nombreux	*there were a lot more of us*
une période en creux de vague	*a bad patch*
on était davantage à la maison	*people stayed at home more*
on s'intéressait davantage aux sociétés	*people took more interest in local societies*

> To say the age of a person or thing:
> j'**ai** 29 ans — I'm 29
> la société **a** 85 ans — the society is 85 years old

Quickies

1 How many players are there now?
2 How many used there to be?

> To say 'I've decided to . . .':
> **j'ai décidé de / d'** aller à La Rochelle
> louer un vélo
> acheter une nouvelle robe

Radio 7

Sara spent one Saturday in La Rochelle, about 150 kilometres down the coast from Nantes. She first of all went to find out about the bicycles that the Town Council make available to locals and visitors, free of charge. She spoke, outside the Town Hall, to Monsieur Molar.

Sara Monsieur Molar, depuis combien de temps cette location de vélos existe-t-elle à La Rochelle?
M Molar Mais environ dix ans, je crois – huit ou dix ans.
Sara Oui. Et pourquoi La Rochelle a-t-elle décidé de mettre ce système à la disposition des gens?
M Molar Eh bien, nous pensions favoriser l'usage de la bicyclette par rapport à l'automobile dans les petites rues du centre-ville, qui sont très étroites et très difficiles à circuler.
Sara C'est donc pour limiter la circulation?
M Molar Pour inciter à une certaine limitation.
Sara Oui, d'accord. Et pour qui c'est? Qui est-ce qui en profite, des vélos?
M Molar Tout le monde, n'importe qui.
Sara Les touristes . . .
M Molar Les touristes, les étrangers, les Rochelais . . .
Sara Tout le monde.
M Molar Tous les volontaires.
Sara C'est presque gratuit mais pas totalement.
M Molar Oui, c'est tout à fait gratuit pendant trois heures et ensuite, si on dépasse, c'est deux francs par heure.
Sara Et qu'est-ce qu'il faut faire pour avoir un vélo?
M Molar Il suffit de présenter au . . . à l'employé une carte d'identité ou un passeport.
Sara Il garde la carte d'identité?
M Molar Non non non, pas du tout. Il note dans un registre le nom et l'adresse de la personne qui vient emprunter.

Sara Combien de vélos est-ce qu'il y a ?

M Molar Nous avons environ cinq cents bicyclettes.

Sara Cinq cents bicyclettes. Et dites-moi, pourquoi est-ce que vous avez choisi le jaune pour les vélos ?

M Molar Eh bien, nous avons cherché au départ une couleur qui soit très voyante, et également nous avons cherché une couleur qui soit peu répandue dans les bicyclettes des particuliers.

Sara Et c'est une belle couleur.

M Molar Couleur du soleil en plus.

Sara Oui, la couleur du soleil. Merci.

M Molar Je vous en prie.

nous pensions . . .	*our intention was to . . .*
qui est-ce qui en profite, des vélos ?	*who makes use of the bikes?*
tous les volontaires	*anyone who wants to*
tout à fait	*completely*
au départ	*at the beginning*
qui soit . . .	*which would be . . .*

La Rochelle : rue piétonne près du vieux port

Radio 8 And here is Sara on the Old Port hiring a bike.

Sara Est-ce que je peux avoir un vélo, s'il vous plaît ?

Employé Oui, bien sûr. Les tarifs sont trois heures gratuit, ensuite deux francs par heure, et il faut le rapporter tous les soirs à dix-huit heures.

Sara D'accord. Qu'est-ce que je dois faire ?

Employé Vous présentez une pièce d'identité, s'il vous plaît.

Sara	Euh, j'ai juste ma carte d'étudiante.
Employé	Oui, ça peut aller.
Sara	Bon ben, d'accord. (*getting it from her bag*) Voilà.
Employé	Merci. Voilà la clé de l'anti-vol, numéro soixante-cinq.
Sara	Merci.

ça peut aller *that will do*

Quickies
1 What sorts of people use the bikes?
2 What's the hire charge once you start paying?
3 What colour are the bikes?

Mots-clés

l'âge (m)	age
la carte d'étudiant	student card
la circulation	traffic
la couleur	colour
l'étranger (m)	foreigner
la fin	end
la guerre	war
la location	hiring; renting
le monde	world; people
le passeport	passport
le pays	country
le pique-nique	picnic
la plage	beach
la planche à voile	wind-surfing
la rivière	river
le rugby	rugby
le tarif	price-list
le/la touriste	tourist
le village	village
le week-end	weekend
parce que	because
pourquoi?	why?
voisin	neighbouring
appeler	to call
avoir besoin de	to need
décider (de)	to decide (to)
garder	to keep
pique-niquer	to picnic
réussir (à)	to succeed (in)
revenir	to come back
sortir	to go out
vivre	to live
vouloir dire	to mean
actuellement	at present
déjà	already
d'habitude	usually
facilement	easily
tout à fait	completely
vraiment	really
faire beau	to be fine (weather)
faire chaud	to be warm/hot (weather)
faire froid	to be cold (weather)
faire mauvais	to be bad (weather)

1 To ask people what they've done or what they did:

qu'est-ce que vous avez fait	hier?
	à Bourg-en-Bresse?
	mardi?
	à Noël?

2 To say what you have done or what anyone else has done or what has happened, use one of these:

j'ai	**nous avons**
tu as	**vous avez**
elle/il/on a	**ils/elles ont**

followed by something like this:

mangé au restaurant	**fait** du ski
réservé une chambre	**loué** un vélo
acheté un pantalon	**perdu** mon passeport

These correspond not only to 'I have eaten', 'they have hired', 'we have done' etc, but also 'I ate', 'they hired', 'we did' etc.
NB Some verbs require *être*, not *avoir*, eg
je **suis** allé
nous **sommes** partis
These verbs are dealt with in the next chapter.

The words for 'eaten', 'done', 'hired', etc are formed as follows:

réserv**er**	réserv**é**
chois**ir**	chois**i**
perd**re**	perd**u**

There are exceptions. Here are some common ones:

avoir	**eu**
être	**été**
faire	**fait**
prendre	**pris**
voir	**vu**

3 To say you *haven't* done something:
je **n'**ai **pas** trouvé mon passeport
il **n'**a **pas** mangé au restaurant
nous **n'**avons **jamais** visité Paris (ie never)

4 To say what you've decided to do:

j'ai décidé de / d'	acheter un vélo
	passer les vacances en Espagne
	apprendre l'allemand

5 To say something has been going on for a certain period of time:

j'étudie le français		une semaine
j'habite à Angers	**depuis**	six mois
nous sommes mariés		trente ans

You can also say:
il y a six mois **que j'habite** à Angers, etc

6 To ask someone how long they've been doing something:

	habitez ici	
vous	venez ici en vacances	**depuis combien de temps?**
	êtes marié	

7 To say how old a person/thing is:
j'**ai** vingt-neuf ans
la société **a** quatre-vingt-cinq ans

8 To talk about the weather:

	beau
il fait	mauvais
	froid
	chaud

En plus

1 **We can't all be perfect**
The so-called Perfect Tense has nothing to do with being perfect. The word comes from the Latin 'perfectus' which means 'complete', 'finished', 'over and done with'. That is precisely what the Perfect Tense tells us – that something happened at some point in the past: you saw, did, said something, something happened and then something else happened next.

One complication in meaning. In English we make this sort of difference about things which happened in the past:
the crocodile ate Mr Smith
the crocodile has eaten Mr Smith
There is no such distinction in French. The equivalent of both English sentences is:
le crocodile a mangé Mr Smith

Another difference is that in English we use a different verb, 'did', for questions and negative sentences:
did the crocodile *eat* Mr Smith?
no, the crocodile *did not eat* Mr Smith
Mr Smith *ate* the crocodile
French is much simpler and uses *avoir* (or *être*) all the time:
est-ce que le crocodile **a mangé** Mr Smith?

non, le crocodile **n'a pas mangé** Mr Smith
Mr Smith **a mangé** le crocodile

2 **For and since**

These two words lead to one of the most common mistakes made by other Europeans speaking English (ie I am living in England since five years). In English, when we say we have been doing something for a period of time, we use two words:

for – to give a length of time, eg
I have been working here *for* seven years (and still am)

since – to say when it started, eg
I have been working here *since* Tuesday (and still am)

Notice that English uses a form of the past ('I have been ...') while French uses the present tense of the verb. Also, one word, *depuis*, does the jobs of 'for' and 'since':
je travaille ici **depuis** sept ans (for seven years)
je travaille ici **depuis** mardi (since Tuesday)

3 **A few things that are not what they seem**

Here are a few more *faux amis* to trap you if they can.
Actuel does not mean 'actual'. It, and the words that come from it, contain the idea of 'present time':
la situation actuelle the present situation
à l'heure actuelle or *actuellement* at the present time
Particulier can mean 'particular', but *un particulier* is a private individual.
Rester does not mean 'to rest', but 'to stay':
en hiver nous restons à la maison
Location does not mean 'place' but the hiring or renting of something. (It's related to the verb *louer*, 'to hire' or 'to rent').

Pièce: one of the other meanings of this word (see also p64) is an official document of some sort; so any document establishing someone's identity is *une pièce d'identité*.

4 **Countries and people**

Un pays means 'a country' – *un pays étranger* is 'a foreign country'. But it can also mean 'a district' or 'an area' as it does when Monsieur Boularand talks of the soldiers coming back home (... *quand ils sont revenus au pays* ...).
'Country' in the sense of 'countryside' is *la campagne*. So if you don't want to go *au bord de la mer* for the weekend, why not go *à la campagne*!

Le monde means 'the world' (and it is the title of one of France's most respected newspapers). But it can also mean 'people' in a number of common phrases:

tout le monde	everybody
beaucoup de monde	lots of people
peu de monde	not many people
trop de monde	too many people

5 **Parisiens and Glaswegians**

Just as the Glaswegian belongs to Glasgow, *le Parisien* (or *la Parisienne*) belongs to Paris. As mentioned in Chapter 2, in France every region, province, *département*, town, village and even the tiniest hamlet has a word to describe its inhabitants and anything else that belongs to it, often ending *-ais*, *-ois*, *-ain* or *-ien*. Here are some fairly obvious ones: Marseillais, Rochelais, Lyonnais, Lillois, Nantais, Niçois, Toulousain, Dieppois

Others are less obvious, and sometimes derive from an older form of the place name:

Pézenas	– Piscénois
Monaco	– Monégasque
Cahors	– Cadurcien
Epinal	– Spinalien
Neufchâtel	– Néocastrain
Béziers	– Bittérois

A propos

Bon week-end!

The French have taken the word from the British, but their weekends can be rather different. In Britain, the Protestant tradition has ensured that nothing 'frivolous' happens on Sundays, or at least that anything noisy or exciting is frowned upon – no theatres, no football matches, no horse racing. Even the pubs were closed in parts of Wales up till a few years ago.

In France the Catholic tradition is that, provided you go to Mass, the rest of Sunday is your own. This, coupled with the fact that the working week lasted six days (even till recent times the five and a half day week was referred to as *la semaine anglaise*), means that Sunday is a day for enjoyment and sport, both amateur and professional. Theatres and other places of entertainment are usually open and the cafés working the *PMU* system (the French equivalent of betting shops) do a brisk trade. Many cafés which have the letters *PMU* written on their windows (standing for *Pari mutuel urbain*) are packed on Sunday mornings with people exchanging money and betting slips. And just so that they can catch people when they have nothing better to do, the Government arranges that all voting takes place on Sundays. With the growing affluence of recent years, this has also led to the phenomenon of 'Sunday motorists' (*les conducteurs du dimanche*) who take to the roads with resultant cost in life and limb. And on summer Sundays, at least, trunk roads into the cities are blocked solid in the evening as people return home after their day or weekend out.

La musique

One of the charming aspects of village life in rural France is the local band called *la musique* or, if it's a brass band, *la fanfare*. Playing at most official functions, it is made up of amateurs: the butcher on saxophone, the chemist's daughter playing the flute and the schoolteacher on drums ... Musical ability is not so important as enthusiasm and the willingness to practise. Nowadays, people want to do other things in their spare time and bands are rapidly disappearing. Those that remain are often invited to play for neighbouring towns as well.

La Rochelle past and present

The town of La Rochelle, in the *département* of Charente-Maritime on France's Atlantic coast and roughly halfway between Nantes and Bordeaux, has many historical associations with Britain. In the Middle Ages the town was part of the Duchy of Aquitaine, which spread over a large area of south-west France. Eleanor of Aquitaine married Louis VII of France and thus became Queen of France. Her second marriage, to Henry Plantagenet, Henry II of England, made her Queen of England, and so Aquitaine passed to the English crown. At the end of the Middle Ages La Rochelle had an English governor and garrisons with English troops.

Trading links were very firmly established over the centuries, with the ships of La Rochelle setting sail for England laden with salt and wine, and returning with copper.

The links became even stronger in the seventeenth century. La Rochelle, as an English colony, was firmly Protestant. The French crown was Catholic. Under the orders of the French king, Louis XIII, and the Prime Minister, Cardinal de Richelieu, a French army laid siege to the town. For fourteen months La Rochelle resisted while an English fleet anchored just off the coast looked more or less helplessly on. 20,000 Rochelais died of starvation before giving in to the French siege.

Today La Rochelle is a thriving town with some 80,000 inhabitants.

Its main source of income is the sea. It is France's fifth largest fishing port and has the largest pleasure craft harbour in the whole of France. In the summer months tourists throng the streets on three sides of *le vieux port*, which are packed with bars, restaurants specialising in fish, boutiques, fishermen selling their catch by the quayside, jazz bands and students playing guitars. It is not a quiet city in summer and, because of its superb climate (it claims to be the second sunniest town in France), anyone who prefers a rather more peaceful time would be best advised to visit La Rochelle outside the months of July and August. Even in winter its position on the Atlantic coast ensures that it has a very mild climate. And the twin towers that stand guarding the entrance to *le vieux port* look even more attractive wrapped in sea-mist.

La Rochelle: le vieux port

With a history stretching back so far, it's clear that the narrow streets around *le vieux port* were never intended for twentieth-century motor traffic, and a partial solution to the traffic problems was worked out in the mid-seventies. The Municipality, under a mayor who later became Minister of the Environment in Monsieur Mitterand's socialist government, brought in a system for the free loan of bicycles. To start with, the bikes were totally free and could be picked up from wherever you found them and left at any point within a boundary marked by a yellow line painted on the ground around the city. The system was altered after a while, when bikes started to be found at the bottom of the harbour, hidden in people's back yards, and as far afield as Belgium and Britain.

Today you must collect your bike from and return it to a depot, and a note is made of your name and address. The loan is free for the first three hours, after which a small charge is made, and a feature of the centre of La Rochelle today is the sight of the bright yellow bikes dashing around the old streets, bells tinkling.

Bon courage

1 Along the lines of *j'ai mangé au restaurant*, say you've done the following things, starting *j'* . . .:
demander une glace; traverser le pont; choisir les crudités; danser avec le Prince de Galles
Now say 'we have . . .':
acheter un nouvel appartement; regarder la télé pendant tout le week-end; dîner avec des amis à la campagne; louer un tandem

2 Part of understanding a language depends on making intelligent guesses. Here are some more words that are used with *avoir* to make the perfect tense:
mis, vu, pris, bu, ouvert, lu, voulu
Which of these verbs do they belong to?
ouvrir, lire, mettre, vouloir, prendre, voir, boire

3 Our indefatigable interviewer is at it again. Jane asks Mariette how she spent yesterday evening. Fill in the blanks with the perfect tense of the appropriate verbs.
faire, boire (three times), *voir* (twice), *danser* (twice)

Jane Qu'est-ce que vous .... hier soir?
Mariette Je suis allée au cinéma avec des amis.
Jane Et qu'est-ce que vous ....?
Mariette Nous .... un vieux film de James Bond.
Jane Ah, intéressant?
Mariette Oui, on a beaucoup aimé ça.
Jane Et c'est tout?
Mariette Non, après nous sommes allés dans un café boire quelque chose.
Jane Et qu'est-ce que vous ....?
Mariette Moi, j'.......... un thé au citron et mes amis . . . euh . . . ils .... de la bière, je crois.
Jane Et puis après?
Mariette Alors, après, on ....; moi, j'.......... jusqu'à deux heures du matin!

4 Jane is interviewing again. This time it's about how people go to work in the morning. Here she is interviewing a commuter, but the questions and answers are all jumbled up. Put the numbers in the correct order.

1 *Jane* Et ce matin, en autobus, c'était bien, ou vous préférez la voiture?
2 *Passant* Oui, oui. Pas de problème. J'ai attendu deux ou trois minutes seulement et j'ai mis vingt-cinq minutes. Oui, c'était bien.
3 *Jane* D'abord vous quittez la maison à quelle heure le matin?
4 *Passant* Normalement, en voiture mais ce matin j'ai pris l'autobus.
5 *Jane* Et comment allez-vous à votre travail?
6 *Passant* Mais oui, mademoiselle. Allez-y!
7 *Jane* Ah bon, et il vous faut combien de temps?
8 *Passant* D'habitude je pars à huit heures moins le quart mais ce matin j'ai quitté la maison à sept heures et demie.
9 *Jane* Excusez-moi, monsieur, est-ce que je peux vous poser quelques questions?
10 *Passant* En voiture une vingtaine de minutes, ça dépend de la circulation.

5 Nathalie has a busy life and so she makes lists of what she has to do. Here is her list for one day; ticks show the things she managed to do and crosses the ones she didn't. Say in French what she did and didn't do.
eg elle a déjeuné avec Charlotte

Mardi
déjeuner avec Charlotte √
porter chemise au pressing √
téléphoner à Jacques ×
réserver places au théâtre √
finir article pour 'Le Monde' ×
nettoyer chambre √
réparer petite lampe ×

And here are some things that she did and that she hadn't foreseen. How would she say she had done all these things?
eg j'ai parlé des vacances avec Pierre

parler des vacances avec Pierre
rencontrer Madame Vidal devant le pressing
casser une tasse
prendre le thé avec Edmée
acheter une jolie petite robe et payer 450F
dîner avec Guy
voir un petit accident au centre-ville
mettre une heure à rentrer à cause de la circulation

6 Now it's your turn to be interviewed about your weekend's activities. You've been to the seaside. Answer Jane's questions.

Jane Qu'est-ce que vous avez fait?
You *You swam* (nager) *for half an hour.*
Jane Et c'est tout?
You *You read a newspaper* (un journal) . . .

Jane Oui?
You *... and you bought a chocolate ice cream.*
Jane Et votre ami(e)?
You *Your friend did some wind-surfing.*
Jane Et vous avez déjeuné au restaurant?
You *No, you picnicked on the beach.*
Jane Et le temps?
You *The weather was good all day.*

7 Find words to fit in the blanks.

1 Le samedi et le dimanche, c'est le ....
2 Quand vous passez une frontière il faut montrer votre ....
3 L'Erdre est une ....
4 En été il y a beaucoup de touristes sur les ....
5 En été il est très agréable de .... à la campagne au lieu de manger au restaurant.
6 Un .... est plus petit qu'une ville.
7 Tout le / Beaucoup de / 'Le | ....

8 How long has this been going on? Tell your French friend using *depuis*:

1 you've been here for two weeks
2 the weather has been fine since Tuesday
3 the children have been on the beach since breakfast
4 George has been playing boules with some French friends for two hours
5 you have been waiting for them for half an hour
6 you've decided to go out without the children tonight
7 you have been spending your holidays here for ten years
8 you've decided to come back here next year

Documentaire

Sète: ville méditerranéenne

Tourism has only recently become an economic resource of the Languedoc coast, developed after the coastal lagoons were cleared of mosquitoes and new tourist resorts had been built.

The traditional economy of the coast is based on fishing, and Sète is the largest French fishing port on the Mediterranean. There are three types of fishing at Sète: tunny fishing in large *thoniers*; fishing with trawlers (*les chalutiers*); and there are the *pêcheurs de petit métier*, fishermen working from small boats just off the shore. Most of the larger boats are owned by families of Italian origin. It's tough work with very long hours and extra manpower (*la main d'oeuvre*) is hard to find.

Behind Sète is a large coastal lagoon, *le Bassin de Thau*. Fishing of a different kind is the main activity here – its technical term is *la conchyliculture*, the cultivation of edible shellfish, chiefly mussels and oysters. Although not as famous as oysters from the Atlantic coast, those in the *Bassin* grow quicker and now supply most of Mediterranean France.

Sète : le port de pêche

La ville de Sète est un des ports de pêche les plus importants en Méditerranée. Il y a environ mille pêcheurs à Sète : six cents, à peu près, travaillent sur des chalutiers ou des thoniers et quatre cents sont des pêcheurs de petit métier. Souvent ils sont d'origine italienne et travaillent en famille depuis plusieurs générations. Mais actuellement il est difficile de trouver de la main d'oeuvre – les jeunes ne veulent pas être pêcheurs parce qu'il faut travailler beaucoup d'heures pour un salaire peu élevé. La main d'oeuvre est donc souvent étrangère – marocaine, portugaise, espagnole.

On peut pêcher plusieurs variétés de poissons en Méditerranée : le thon ; les poissons bleus – la sardine, le maquereau, l'anchois ; et puis les poissons blancs comme la sole, le merlan et tous les poissons de fond. Mais la pêche devient de plus en plus dure. Les réserves de poisson blanc sont en train de diminuer – il y a trop de pêcheurs. Et les gens ne veulent pas acheter le poisson bleu qui est plus facile à attraper.

Derrière Sète, dans le Bassin de Thau, il y a une autre forme d'exploitation de la mer. C'est la conchyliculture – l'élevage de coquillages comestibles comme les moules et les huîtres. C'est aussi une activité familiale qui existe depuis longtemps à Sète. Mais le Bassin de Thau est exploité intensivement surtout depuis 1950. Il y a aujourd'hui sept cents conchyliculteurs dans le Bassin. Les moules et les huîtres sont plus faciles à élever ici. Dans l'Océan il faut trois ans pour élever un coquillage. Mais en Méditerranée il n'y a pas de marées: les huîtres consomment vingt-quatre heures sur vingt-quatre, donc elles grandissent plus vite. Elles sont bonnes à manger au bout de quinze mois.

Grâce au tourisme et à la rapidité des transports, les coquillages sont des produits beaucoup plus demandés qu'avant. Le futur des conchyliculteurs déjà installés semble donc assuré. Mais les choses sont plus difficiles pour les jeunes. En effet, il n'y a plus assez de surface à l'intérieur du Bassin. Les nouveaux conchyliculteurs devront donc exploiter la mer.

L'avenir de Sète? C'est la mer, sans aucun doute. Mais les méthodes de travail vont probablement devoir changer.

peu élevé	*not very high*
les poissons de fond	*fish found on the sea-bed*
de plus en plus dure	*increasingly hard*
vingt-quatre heures sur vingt-quatre	*twenty-four hours a day*
beaucoup plus demandés qu'avant	*much more in demand than before*
devront . . . exploiter la mer	*will have to exploit the sea*
vont probablement devoir changer	*will probably have to change*

Tout sur vous 2

Saying where you've been
Saying where you were born

Radio 1 If you make friends abroad, the conversation might well turn to where you've been and what you've done. Here is Pierrick in St-Philbert-de-Grand-Lieu talking to a friend, Marie-Agnès.

Pierrick L'année dernière qu'est-ce que tu as fait aux grandes vacances, Marie-Agnès?
Marie-Agnès Nous sommes allés quinze jours au mois de juin à Aix-en-Provence dans la famille de Dominique.
Pierrick Oui, et vous ... qu'est-ce que vous avez fait exactement là-bas?
Marie-Agnès Nous nous sommes beaucoup baignés, et puis nous sommes allés visiter la Camargue.
Pierrick Vous avez eu beau temps?
Marie-Agnès Bien sûr, toujours sur la Côte d'Azur.
Pierrick Vous n'avez eu que quinze jours de vacances, alors?
Marie-Agnès Non. Nous sommes allés chez mes parents en Berry, dans le centre de la France, quinze jours au mois de septembre.
Pierrick Et qu'est-ce que vous avez fait là?
Marie-Agnès Dominique s'est occupé des moutons de son beau-frère, et moi, je suis restée avec mes parents.
Pierrick Et est-ce que vous allez aux sports d'hiver parfois?
Marie-Agnès Non, non, non. Les enfants sont trop petits encore. Mais nous sommes allés une semaine au mois de février en Auvergne avec les enfants. Voilà.
Pierrick Tu n'es pas de la région de Nantes, alors?
Marie-Agnès Non. J'habite ... mes parents habitent le centre de la France, à Bourges exactement.
Pierrick Et tu es née à Bourges?
Marie-Agnès Je suis née à Bourges.
Pierrick Et pourquoi tu es venue dans la région nantaise?
Marie-Agnès Je me suis mariée. J'ai donc suivi mon mari, qui travaille près de Nantes.
Pierrick Et tu l'as rencontré où, ton mari?
Marie-Agnès Mon mari est l'ami d'une amie de ma mère.

Pierrick Il est d'où ?
Marie-Agnès Il est bourguignon.
Pierrick De quelle ville exactement ?
Marie-Agnès De Montceau-les-Mines.

quinze jours	*a fortnight*
nous nous sommes beaucoup baignés	*we went swimming a lot*
Dominique s'est occupé de	*Dominique looked after*

To tell someone where you've been:

je suis allé(e)	à Paris en Bretagne sur la Côte d'Azur au cinéma

To say where or when you were born:

je suis né(e)	à Sunderland en Irlande en 1950

To talk about the past, remember that a small group of verbs use *être* instead of *avoir*, eg:

je **suis**	allé(e) resté(e) né(e) venu(e)

Quickies

1 How much time did Marie-Agnès and her husband spend in Aix-en-Provence?
2 What sort of weather did they have?
3 While her husband looked after the sheep what did Marie-Agnès do?
4 Why don't they do winter sports?

Radio 2 It can also be very handy to be able to tell friends abroad something about your past life. Pierrick asked Monsieur Séguin, Marie-Agnès's husband, to give us a kind of potted autobiography.

Pierrick Monsieur Séguin, vous êtes né où ?
M Séguin Je suis né à Montceau-les-Mines.
Pierrick En Bourgogne ?
M Séguin C'est cela, oui.
Pierrick Et vous avez fait toutes vos études à Montceau-les-Mines ?
M Séguin Alors, j'ai fait mes études primaires et secondaires à Montceau-les-Mines, et mes études supérieures à Lyon, la ville universitaire la plus proche de Montceau.

Pierrick	Quelles études avez-vous fait?
M Séguin	Alors, des études vétérinaires.
Pierrick	Ensuite?
M Séguin	Donc j'ai fait mon service militaire, comme tout Français, dans le service d'aide aux pays en voie de développement.
Pierrick	Et dans quel pays exactement?
M Séguin	Je suis allé au . . . en Afrique Noire, au Togo.

St-Philbert-de-Grand-Lieu: intérieur de l'église abbatiale

Pierrick	Vous y êtes resté combien de temps?
M Séguin	J'y suis resté deux années, en réalité deux années scolaires.
Pierrick	Et vous avez enseigné, je suppose?
M Séguin	J'ai enseigné dans une école d'agronomie.
Pierrick	Pourquoi le Togo?
M Séguin	Eh bien, j'ai toujours manifesté un certain attrait pour l'Afrique Noire . . . et les places disponibles . . . euh . . . je bafouille, là, hein. Je m'excuse.
Pierrick	Et après ce service militaire, qu'est-ce qui s'est passé?
M Séguin	Alors, je suis revenu en France en '74, et j'ai naturellement cherché du travail dans ma branche professionnelle, et j'ai tout de suite trouvé une place dans l'Ouest de la France.
Pierrick	Et dans quelle région exactement?
M Séguin	Dans la région nantaise, et j'y suis resté.
Pierrick	Et vous vous êtes donc installé dans la région nantaise?
M Séguin	Je me suis installé à St-Philbert-de-Grand-Lieu en 1976. Je m'y suis marié un petit peu plus tard.

Pierrick Et vous avez des enfants également?
M Séguin Deux petits enfants – une petite fille et un petit garçon.

Pierrick Ils ont quel âge?
M Séguin Trois ans et deux ans.
Pierrick Merci, monsieur.
M Séguin Je vous en prie.

j'ai fait mes études primaires et secondaires	*I went to primary and secondary school*
j'ai fait mes études supérieures	*I went to university*
le service d'aide aux pays en voie de développement	*providing aid to developing countries*
je bafouille, là, hein. Je m'excuse	*I'm rambling a bit. Sorry*
qu'est-ce qui s'est passé?	*what happened?*

To say:

my	*his/her*
ma mère	**sa** soeur
mon mari	**son** beau-frère
mes parents	**ses** enfants

Notice what *y* stands for in the following sentences and where it goes:

Marie est allée *à Paris*	Marie **y** est allée
je suis né *en Auvergne*	j'y suis né
je suis restée *dans la région nantaise*	j'y suis restée

A number of verbs have an extra 'reflexive' pronoun:

je **me** suis marié	*I got married*
vous **vous** êtes installé	*you settled down*
nous **nous** sommes baignés	*we went swimming*

Quickies
1 Where did Monsieur Séguin go to university?
2 Where did he do his military service?
3 How long did he stay there?

TV 3 In Pézenas, Jane spoke to a number of people about their past. Traditional local crafts have almost died out in the town. Three hundred people were employed in barrel-making in the early 1900s; today, there's only one person.

Jane Monsieur André, est-ce que vous êtes né à Pézenas?
M André Je suis né à Pézenas.
Jane Vous y êtes toujours resté?
M André J'y suis toujours resté – ma famille est piscénoise de trois ou quatre générations.
Jane Vous avez appris le métier comment?
M André J'ai appris le métier petit à petit avec mon père. Les grandes vacances, je les ai passées à la tonnellerie et automatiquement, à la sortie de l'école, j'ai travaillé avec mon père. Quand mon père a appris le métier en 1907, ils étaient trois cents. Quand moi j'ai appris le métier en 1942 on était une douzaine entre ouvriers, patrons et apprentis.
Jane Qu'est-ce qui s'est passé alors?
M André Ah, c'est la lutte du progrès. On ne peut rien y faire, hein.

les grandes vacances	*the summer holidays*
à la sortie de l'école	*on leaving school*
quand moi j'ai appris	*when* I *learnt*
on ne peut rien y faire	*you can't do anything about it*

Quickies
1 How long has Monsieur André's family been in Pézenas?
2 How many people were working at the *tonnellerie* when he started?

TV 4 The recent increase of tourism in the Languedoc has attracted people from other regions who have brought new crafts to the area. A number of them have recently set themselves up in the courtyard of what was, in the seventeenth century, an inn – *l'Hostellerie du Bât d'Argent*. The first to arrive was Jean-Pierre de Tugny, an ex-nuclear physicist who decided to become a toymaker.

Jane Monsieur de Tugny, est-ce que vous êtes originaire de Pézenas?
M de Tugny Non. Non, je suis breton – breton de la région de Vannes, dans le Morbihan.
Jane Et vous êtes arrivé quand à Pézenas?
M de Tugny Je suis arrivé à Pézenas en juillet '79 pour venir essayer de vendre ce que je fabriquais – les jouets en bois que je fabrique.
Jane Pourquoi êtes-vous venu ici à Pézenas?
M de Tugny Ah, c'est une vieille histoire, ça. Je suis tombé amoureux de Pézenas vingt ans avant. En me promenant dans la région, comme ça, je suis arrivé à Pézenas. Et alors Pézenas, j'ai trouvé ça joli. Et puis alors on parlait de Molière beaucoup – Molière est venu à Pézenas. Et j'aime beaucoup Molière, j'aime beaucoup les vieilles pierres et je cherchais à m'installer un petit peu dans le Midi.

ce que je fabriquais	*what I was making*
en me promenant	*travelling around*
on parlait de Molière	*people talked about Molière*
les vieilles pierres	*old buildings (literally 'old stones')*
je cherchais à ...	*I was hoping to ...*

Quickies
1 From which region of France does Jean-Pierre de Tugny come?
2 What does he make?

TV 5 The person to arrive most recently at the *Bât d'Argent* is Edmond Charlot, who retired to Pézenas to set up a second-hand bookshop.

Jane Monsieur Charlot, est-ce que vous êtes de Pézenas?

M Charlot Non, je ne suis pas de Pézenas. Je suis né en Afrique du Nord, à Alger.

Jane Qu'est-ce que vous avez fait avant de venir à Pézenas?

M Charlot J'ai été libraire d'abord, puis éditeur, et j'ai été également attaché culturel au Maghreb et en Turquie.

Jane Vous êtes donc allé dans beaucoup de pays?

M Charlot Oui. Je connais bien l'ensemble de la Méditerranée, mais je n'ai travaillé qu'en Turquie, en Algérie et au Maroc, où je suis resté les sept dernières années de mon travail.

Jane Et puis, vous vous êtes installé à Pézenas. Pourquoi ce choix?

M Charlot Simplement parce que Pézenas est une très belle petite ville, une petite ville ancienne et qu'on y vit encore normalement, c'est-à-dire qu'on n'est pas écrasé par la civilisation.

l'ensemble de la Méditerranée	*the whole of the Mediterranean area*

To say you know a particular place:

je connais	la Turquie
	Pézenas
	beaucoup de pays

ne . . . que is not a negative:
je **n'**ai travaillé **qu'**en Turquie – I have *only* worked in Turkey

Quickies

1 Where did Monsieur Charlot originally come from?

2 He says that Pézenas is *une très* .... Complete the phrase.

TV 6 Also working in the courtyard are a painter, a sculptor, a potter, a jeweller and a weaver. Like Edmond Charlot, they were attracted by the whole way of life here, as Monsieur de Tugny explains.

M de Tugny Ils sont venus tous d'un peu partout de la France. Il y en a qui sont de Lyon, il y en a qui sont de Paris et tous des gens qui, à un moment donné, en ont eu assez de faire leur travail. Ils ont voulu aussi, eux, devenir artisans parce que . . . pour le plaisir de travailler de ses mains et puis parce que, être artisan à Pézenas dans le Midi . . . il y a une . . . ce qu'on appelle la qualité de vie. Voilà.

d'un peu partout	*from just about everywhere*
il y en a qui sont de Lyon	*some are from Lyon*
à un moment donné	*at a certain point in their lives*
des gens qui . . . en ont eu assez de . . .	*people who . . . had had enough of . . .*
ce qu'on appelle . . .	*what is called . . .*

Quickie What part of France does Monsieur de Tugny say Pézenas is in?

Mots-clés

le beau-frère	brother-in-law
la civilisation	civilisation
les études (f)	studies
l'histoire (f)	story; history
le jouet	toy
la Méditerranée	Mediterranean
le mouton	sheep
l'ouvrier (m)	workman
le centre	centre
l'est (m)	east
le nord	north
l'ouest (m)	west
le sud	south
apprendre	to learn
devenir	to become
enseigner	to teach
fabriquer	to make/manufacture
rencontrer	to meet
vendre	to sell
se baigner	to go swimming
se marier	to get married
se passer	to happen
s'installer	to settle (down)
s'occuper de	to take care of, deal with
amoureux	in love
ensemble	together
naturellement	naturally
ne . . . que	only
ne . . . rien	nothing

En bref

1 To say where you've been:

(if you're a man) **je suis allé** (if you're a woman) **je suis allée**	à Paris en Transylvanie au Maroc au restaurant Le Rallye

2 To say where and when you were born:

je suis né(e)	à Walsall dans la maison des mes parents en 1914

3 To say you know a place:

je connais	Paris la Normandie l'Afrique du Nord le restaurant Le Rallye

The following verbs use *être* in the perfect tense:

aller	naître
venir	mourir
arriver	rester
partir	retourner
entrer	monter
sortir	descendre
	tomber

Verbs derived from these also take *être*, eg:
revenir, repartir, ressortir, retomber

With all these verbs, the past participle agrees with the subject:
Sara est venu**e** nous voir
nous sommes parti**s** au Tchad
Agnès et Martine sont rest**ées** sur la plage

4 The pronoun *y* can replace any noun or phrase (except those referring to human beings) introduced by *à*, *dans*, *sur*, etc:

il est né *à Pézenas* — il **y** est né
elles sont allées *à la célèbre église de Brou* — elles **y** sont allées
elle a perdu ses bijoux *dans un hôtel de la Côte d'Azur* — elle **y** a perdu ses bijoux

5 The words for 'my', 'your' etc agree with the noun in gender and number:

	m sing	f sing	m & f pl
my	**mon**	**ma***	**mes**
your	**ton**	**ta***	**tes**
his/her/its	**son**	**sa***	**ses**
our	**notre**	**notre**	**nos**
your	**votre**	**votre**	**vos**
their	**leur**	**leur**	**leurs**

* These become *mon*, *ton* and *son* before a vowel or silent 'h'.

Notice the extra pronoun in the following verb:
se laver – to wash (oneself)
je **me** lave
tu **te** laves
elle/il/on **se** lave
nous **nous** lavons
vous **vous** lavez
elles/ils **se** lavent

Many verbs can work in this way (see *En plus*).
In the perfect tense, these verbs take *être*, not *avoir*:
je me **suis** marié en 1914
nous nous **sommes** baignés hier
vous vous **êtes** installé dans la région?

1 **Place names**

In English you use 'to', 'in', 'at' or nothing at all in front of the name of a place, depending on the activity you're talking about:
I live *in* Colchester
I'm going *to* Colchester next week
you've got to change *at* Colchester
I'll telephone Colchester tomorrow

In French, the preposition used depends on the kind of place you're talking about.
For towns, villages, etc, the preposition is *à*:

je vais j'habite il faut changer je veux téléphoner	à Nantes

For countries which are feminine, it's *en*:
nous allons **en** France cet été
mes amis habitent **en** Italie
je voudrais téléphoner **en** Grande Bretagne.
For countries which are masculine, it's *au*:
au Brésil, **au** Canada, **au** Portugal, **au** Togo

For old provinces of France, it's *en* if they're feminine:
en Auvergne, **en** Provence, **en** Normandie, **en** Bretagne
And it's *dans* with the article if they're masculine:
dans le Dauphiné, **dans le** Périgord, **dans le** Languedoc, **dans le** Limousin

For British counties, it's *dans*:

j'habite je vais je voudrais téléphoner	**dans**	le Kent le Ross et Cromarty le Yorkshire

Some feminine countries:	Some masculine countries:
la France	le Canada
l'Italie	le Brésil
l'Espagne	le Japon
la Chine	le Portugal
l'Angleterre	le Maroc
l'Ecosse	le Vénézuela
L'Irlande	le Vietnam
la Belgique	le Pays de Galles
la Pologne	le Mexique
l'Union Soviétique	le Danemark
l'Algérie	*and in the plural*:
la Tchécoslovaquie	les Etats-Unis
la Turquie	les Pays-Bas

2 **On reflection**

You use verbs to say, among other things, what you are doing:

je coupe le pain I cut the bread

and if the knife slips:

je **me** coupe I cut myself

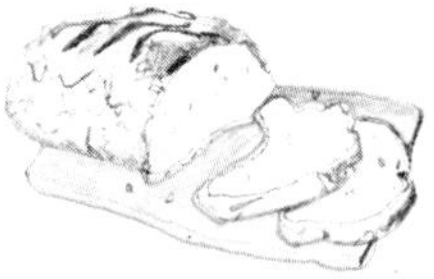

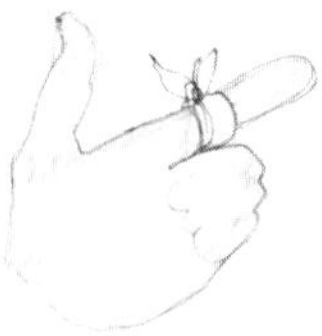

You can look at Henry:

je regarde Henri I'm looking at Henry
je le regarde I'm looking at him

or yourself:

je **me** regarde I'm looking at myself

And, of course, that goes for Henry too:

Henri me regarde Henry's looking at me
Henri **se** regarde Henry's looking at himself

In French, this idea of 'doing something to oneself' is important for two reasons:

1 In the perfect tense these so-called 'reflexive verbs' take *être* not *avoir*:

j'ai coupé le pain I've cut the bread
je **me suis** coupé(e) I've cut myself
j'ai regardé Henri I looked at Henry
je **me suis** regardé(e) I looked at myself

2 They are much more frequent than reflexive verbs in English. Sometimes the idea of doing something to oneself is fairly obvious:

je lave la voiture I'm washing the car
je **me** lave I'm washing (myself)

Sometimes it is less obvious:

nous **nous** sommes couchés we went to bed
je **me** suis marié(e) I got married
je vais **me** promener I'm going to go for a walk

In some cases, the idea of 'oneself' can disappear altogether:

qu'est-ce qui **s'**est passé? what (has) happened?

These so-called 'reflexive' verbs are shown in dictionaries and vocabulary lists with *se* in front of the infinitive:

se promener, **se** coucher, **s'**installer, **s'**occuper

3 **His and hers**

French does not have separate words for 'his', 'her', 'its' and 'one's'. It just has the adjective *son*. Like all adjectives, *son* agrees with its noun.

son château
sa* maison
ses parents
*NB *sa* changes to *son* if the next word starts with a vowel:
son orange

The words in bold type above can all mean 'his' or 'her' or 'its', or 'one's'. The context will tell you which is intended.

4 **Another 'here' and 'there'**

Y usually means 'here', 'there', 'in it', 'on it', eg:

je vais *à Bourg* tous les jours – j'**y** vais tous les jours je joue *dans l'équipe de Pézenas* depuis trois ans – j'**y** joue depuis trois ans

But *y* also appears in a whole range of set phrases where these meanings are not appropriate:

il y a	there is/are
ça y est!	that's it! (said when you've completed a task or when things have gone far enough)
allez-y	go ahead/help yourself
allons-y	let's go/let's get cracking
honni soit qui mal y pense	evil be to him who evil thinks

A propos

Le Midi

The Midi is the southern part of France, and the word itself comes from the fact that at midday – *à midi* – the sun is directly to the south. Precisely where the Midi starts can produce quite a heated debate, but generally speaking, anything south of a line between Bordeaux and Grenoble would qualify as being in *le Midi*.

Of the places mentioned in this chapter, the Côte d'Azur (the Mediterranean coast from Marseille to the Italian border) is certainly in the Midi. So is the Camargue, an area in the Rhône delta west of Marseille now designated as a national park. In the northern part of the Camargue rice is grown, but the southern part is largely a wilderness of salt-marshes famous for wildlife and plants, as well as for the white horses and black bulls which are bred there, and for its flamingoes.

One thing which distinguishes the Midi is the way its inhabitants speak French – quite different from the accent of Paris, the 'received' French accent usually taught abroad. Two features of this accent are particularly noticeable. The first is that the n's are pronounced differently after a vowel. In the middle of a word, the 'n' is pronounced, so *grande* becomes a little closer to English 'grand'. At the end of a word, 'n' preceded by a vowel tends to sound a little more like the English '-ang' or '-ong', so that *fin* sounds a bit like 'fang' and *mon*, a bit like 'mong'. The second feature is that 'e' is often pronounced in the south. So whereas in Paris, *une grande bouteille de bière* has six syllables:

une/grande/bou/teille/de/bière

in Montpellier it has ten syllables:

u/ne/gran/de/bou/tei/lle/de/biè/re

Although the standard accent of the capital has always been dominant in official circles – the government and the media, for example – this is less and less so with the move towards decentralisation. In fact, the southern accent is regarded with some affection, perhaps because it's associated with sun, sea, holidays and comedians like Fernandel.

Paysage d'Auvergne

Between north and south

Two other areas were mentioned in the dialogues. The Auvergne, in the north-east part of the Massif Central, is a rather spectacular mountainous area of extinct volcanoes. It is one of France's three main skiing centres, along with the Alps and the Pyrenees. The area is noted for its mineral waters and has a number of spa-towns, the most important being Vichy. The capital of the Auvergne is Clermont-Ferrand, a big industrial centre. *Le Berry*, just to the north of Auvergne, is the geographical centre of France. Its capital, Bourges, is an interesting old town with a fine cathedral.

Le Maghreb

Maghreb is an Arabic word meaning 'the place where the sun sets'. It is now widely used in French to refer to the area covered by Tunisia, Algeria and Morocco. A person from *le Maghreb* is called *un Maghrébin* or *une Maghrébine*.

Le service militaire

All young Frenchmen do a period of military service – as they have done since the Revolution. The length of time has varied but it is currently twelve months. Students can postpone their service till the end of their studies. Those with professional and technical qualifications can, instead, spend two years using their knowledge working in Third World countries, usually former French colonies. This is what Monsieur Séguin did. This system is known as *la coopération* or, as Monsieur Séguin calls it, *le service d'aide aux pays en voie de développement*.

Molière

Molière (a stage name – his real one was Jean-Baptiste Poquelin) is France's greatest writer of comedies, equal, in his own more limited sphere, to Shakespeare.

His life was theatrical in itself. Son of a well-to-do Parisian family, he completed his law studies and then, in 1643 at the age of 21, gave up a comfortable future to join a group of inexperienced actors. Their attempt to establish themselves in Paris failed and after two years of ups and downs, during which Molière was briefly imprisoned for debt (the theatre candles had not been paid for), they left Paris. For fifteen years Molière and his group toured the French provinces, particularly in the south-west. It was then that he visited Pézenas, staying a number of times at the request of the Governor of the Languedoc, le Prince de Conti, who became his patron. Pézenas still proudly calls

Molière

itself *Ville de Molière* and quotes the words of Marcel Pagnol, a famous twentieth-century writer, to show that it was in Pézenas that Molière learnt his craft as a playwright: *Si Jean-Baptiste Poquelin est né à Paris, Molière, lui, est né à Pézenas.* After touring, he returned to Paris as writer, director and leading actor of his troupe. He became immensely successful and a favourite of the court by writing and staging every sort of comic and musical play from farces like *Les Fourberies de Scapin* to penetrating but still funny studies of contemporary life like *Le Bourgeois Gentilhomme* and *Les Femmes Savantes*. Occasionally his satire provoked official anger and one of his plays, *Le Tartuffe*, was banned for several years.

He made a final and ironic dramatic exit in 1673. When playing the leading part in his latest play, *Le Malade Imaginaire*, he was taken ill on stage and died the same evening.

Bon courage

1 How would you say 'my . . .' for each of the following:

le bateau, les bagages, la tasse, le vélo, la jupe, le passeport, les enfants, l'activité préférée

2 These are Pierrick's. How would you say 'his . . .'?

les boules, le vase, l'amie, la voiture, la mère, l'appartement, le plat préféré, les frères et les soeurs

3 Here are some nouns all of which have a verb connected with them eg *le reste – rester*; the remainder – to remain. Find the others.

l'entrée	la sortie
le choix	la promenade
le jouet	la fabrication
rencontres	une occupation
	une habitation

4 These words are specific to either women or men. What are the words that refer to the opposite sex, eg *le boulanger – la boulangère*:

cette dame	une ouvrière
le père	la vieille patronne
mon mari	une belle-soeur
l'épicière italienne	ma fille
	la petite amie de mon frère

5 For the summer holidays the whole family has split up and gone off in different directions. Here's where they went. Complete the sentences using the right form of the verb in brackets and filling in the blanks.

1. Anne-Marie (aller) .... Turquie avec son nouveau copain.
2. Jérôme (partir) .... Portugal avec Nathalie. Ensuite, Nathalie (aller) .... Espagne avec Vasco; Jérôme (rester) .... Lisbonne.
3. Les parents (aller) passer une semaine avec des amis .... Carnac, ... Bretagne.
4. Sylvie et Isabelle (passer) quelques jours .... St Tropez, ... la Côte d'Azur, puis elles (partir) .... Inde.
5. Oncle Gilbert et Tante Léonie (aller) .... Etats-Unis.
6. Patrick (aller) .... Havre en auto-stop. Puis il (prendre) le bateau pour aller .... Angleterre et il (passer) quinze jours chez une amie anglaise .... Warwickshire. Puis ils (aller) ensemble .... Ecosse.
7. Sophie (passer) ses vacances .... Casablanca, ... Maroc.
8. Jean-Paul et Simone (aller) faire de l'alpinisme .... les Pyrénées.
9. Yves (partir) étudier l'anglais .... Canada.
10. Moi, je (acheter) une nouvelle voiture et je (décider) de rester .... France, ... la maison.

6 You've lost your passport and have to go to the police station. You go over all your movements that morning with the policeman to see if you can remember where you may have left it. Tell him:

you went down for breakfast at 8.45 am – *je suis descendu(e) prendre le petit déjeuner à 8h45*
you went out at 9.45 am
you went to *le Musée de Peinture*
you stayed there until 11.30.
you went to a café and had a beer
then you went to the bank
you got there about 1.00 pm
you returned to the hotel fifteen minutes later

7 You've been on a day trip to France and when you get back to England your French neighbour wants to know all about it. Two words you'll need to know: *rose* – pink, and *cher* – expensive.

Voisine La France! Pour une journée! Vous y êtes allée seule?
You *No. You went there with a friend (female).*
Voisine Ah bon. Et vous avez pris le train?
You *No. You took the car. You went to your friend's house at 6 am, you had a coffee together, then you left at 7 o'clock and got to the port two hours later.*
Voisine Ah. Il y a un très bon service entre Douvres et Calais.
You *Yes. But you went from Folkestone to Boulogne.*
Voisine C'est plus joli quand même! La traversée dure longtemps?
You *An hour and three-quarters.*
Voisine Et qu'est-ce que vous avez fait à Boulogne?
You *Well. When you arrived in Boulogne you found a good little restaurant and you ate there.*
Voisine Ah. La cuisine française! On mange bien en France, n'est-ce pas?
You *Yes. Your friend had a steak and chips ...*
Voisine Mais quand on est au bord de la mer il faut manger du poisson.
You *... and you had seafood.*
Voisine Quelle sorte?
You *You don't know their name in French. In English they're 'prawns'.*
Voisine Pronnes? Qu'est-ce que c'est?
You *No, prawns. They are small and pink and they have very long thingummyjigs in front.*
Voisine Ah! Ce sont des crevettes.
You *Crevettes. Ask her if it's a (masculine) crevette or a (feminine) crevette.*
Voisine C'est *une* crevette. C'est délicieux, non? Moi, j'adore les crevettes.
You *French restaurants aren't very expensive. You had a dessert and two coffees. And you drank a bottle of white wine. And you paid only ninety francs. For two people!*
Voisine Une bouteille de vin! Alors vous n'avez rien fait dans l'après-midi?
You *Yes. You went to the supermarket.*
Voisine A Boulogne?
You *No. It's ten minutes from Boulogne by car. It's in the country. And it's very, very big.*

Voisine	En France, on appelle ça un hypermarché. Vous y avez fait des achats?
You	*Of course.*
Voisine	Et qu'est-ce qui s'est passé . . . qu'est-ce que vous avez acheté?

The story continues in chapter 14, exercise 7.

Documentaire

Le Languedoc, pays de vin

The economy of the Languedoc is dominated by wine. The *département* of l'Hérault has more vineyards than any other in France. But it produces mostly red table wine which is threatened by competition with similar wine from other countries, especially Italy, where it can be produced even more cheaply. Changing public tastes have also swung towards drinking less but drinking better quality wines. The wine-growers (*les viticulteurs*) of the Languedoc are in a state of crisis.

Wine co-operatives are a way of lightening the burden: they have existed for many years in the Languedoc, lending equipment such as harvesting machines (*les machines à vendanger*) and taking care of the wine-making (*la vinification*) and marketing. But many argue that the future lies in keeping up with the changing market. The traditional type of vine in the area is one called Carignan, producing wine in large quantities but of poor quality. The plants (*les vignes* or *les ceps*) must be replaced with vines which will produce a better flavour (*les cépages aromatiques*).

Jean Azéma au moment des vendanges

Le Languedoc est un pays de vignes. Près de la moitié du vin français vient de cette région. C'est surtout du vin de table. Beaucoup de viticulteurs sont membres de coopératives locales. Celle de Montagnac, près de Pézenas, est la plus grosse en France. Créée en 1937, elle produit deux millions cinq cent mille litres de vin par an. Les avantages de ce système sont nombreux. Comme le dit Jean Azéma, le président des caves coopératives de Montagnac: 'Ici, le matériel travaille pour tout le monde. C'est beaucoup plus rentable.' Les mille quatre cents viticulteurs membres n'ont pas besoin de s'occuper de la vinification et de la vente du vin: c'est la coopérative qui s'en charge.

Mais il y a aussi des producteurs indépendants dans la région. A l'Abbaye de Valmagne, par exemple, la tradition viticole continue comme au temps des moines cisterciens. On s'occupe de toute la production, depuis la culture de la vigne jusqu'à la commercialisation du produit fini. Aujourd'hui, l'Abbaye est aussi tournée vers le progrès. Grâce à la machine à vendanger, il faut trois hommes pour faire les vendanges et non plus trente comme autrefois. Des techniques de production modernes sont essentielles pour rendre la viticulture plus rentable.

Mais un des grands problèmes du Languedoc est la qualité du vin. En général, c'est du vin ordinaire, fait avec des cépages traditionnels d'origine méditerranéenne comme le Carignan. Il se trouve donc en concurrence directe avec les vins d'importation les moins chers. Monsieur Clément, le responsable des soixante-dix hectares de vignes de l'Abbaye de Valmagne, est en train de remplacer les vieilles vignes par des cépages aromatiques de meilleure qualité. Il sait que les viticulteurs du Languedoc doivent produire des vins meilleurs pour survivre. Mais les jeunes ceps mettent trois ou quatre ans pour donner de bons raisins. Ce type de projet prend beaucoup de temps et coûte très cher.

Production indépendente ou production coopérative – une chose est sûre: l'avenir du Languedoc dépend de la vigne et du vin. Et les viticulteurs de la région comme Emmanuel Maffre-Baugé, qui est député au parlement européen, le savent bien: 'La vigne, c'est un peu notre chair et le vin, c'est un peu notre sang . . . Nous supprimer la vigne, c'est un peu nous supprimer le sens de notre existence passée, présente et à venir.'

qui s'en charge	*who looks after that*
tournée vers le progrès	*keeping up with new developments*
la machine à vendanger	*grape-harvesting machine*
non plus	*not*
pour rendre la viticulture plus rentable	*to make wine production more profitable*
il se trouve donc	*so it is*
le savent bien	*are well aware of it*
nous supprimer la vigne	*to take away the vine from us*
c'est un peu nous supprimer	*it's a little like taking from us*

14 C'était comme ça

Saying how things were or used to be

Radio 1 Sara Tomei went to the Musée Dobrée in Nantes to talk about the history of the town to her friend, Madame Claude Cossenot, the curator.

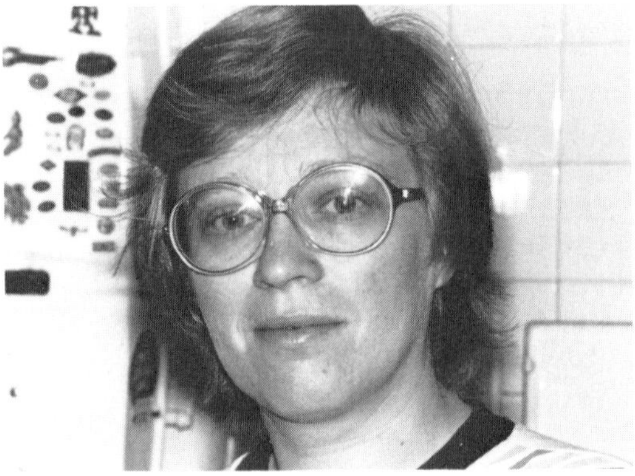

Claude Cossenot

Sara Nous parlons avec Claude Cossenot qui est conservateur au Musée Dobrée de Nantes. Claude, est-ce que tu peux nous parler de l'histoire de Nantes ?

Claude Nantes est une ville française depuis 1532. Avant, elle appartenait à la Bretagne. Elle en était la capitale. Et le Château de Nantes était la résidence des Ducs de Bretagne. Nantes a toujours été une ville extrêmement importante pour le commerce. Elle est en effet située au bord de la Loire et les navires, venant de la mer, ne peuvent pas remonter plus haut que Nantes. La Loire est navigable jusqu'à Nantes. Au seizième siècle le commerce se faisait principalement avec l'Espagne. Au dix-septième siècle le commerce s'est fait avec les pays du nord, en particulier la Hollande et les pays scandinaves. Nantes vendait toujours du sel, du vin et également des toiles et du papier. Elle achetait aux Hollandais des harengs, du bois également. Puis au dix-huitième siècle le commerce s'est étendu vers les pays de l'Extrême-Orient, avec la célèbre Compagnie des Indes.

Nantes: Château des Ducs de Bretagne

venant de la mer	*coming up from the sea*
le commerce se faisait avec	*trade used to be done with*
le commerce s'est fait avec	*trade was done with*
elle achetait aux Hollandais	*it bought from the Dutch*
le commerce s'est étendu vers	*trade was extended to*

To say how things were:
Nantes **appartenait** à la Bretagne

Nantes | *belonged* / *used to belong* | to Brittany

and what used to happen:
Nantes **vendait** du sel

Nantes | *sold* / *used to sell* | salt

Quickies

1 Where does Claude say Nantes is situated?
2 Can you remember two things Nantes used to sell?
3 What countries does she mention?

Radio 2 But Nantes then became the centre of a more profitable but much more sinister business – the slave trade.

Sara Le dix-huitième siècle a également marqué Nantes pour la traite des Noirs, je crois, eh?

Claude En effet, à partir de 1715–1720, la Compagnie des Indes a quitté Nantes, et la ville a dû s'orienter vers un autre commerce, la traite des Noirs.

Sara Comment ça se passait, la traite des noirs?

Claude Il s'agissait d'un commerce triangulaire. C'est-à-dire que de Nantes partaient des navires chargés de pacotille, c'est-à-dire de petits bijoux, de toiles fabriquées spécialement pour la traite. Quand ces bateaux arrivaient dans le Golfe de Guinée, on échangeait la pacotille contre des Noirs, qui avaient été en général capturés dans l'arrière-pays par les Noirs eux-mêmes. Puis on chargeait les bateaux de Noirs, environ 350 par navire, et les navires faisaient voile vers l'ouest. Ils traversaient l'Atlantique, et les esclaves étaient vendus, en particulier à l'île de St-Domingue, où les colons nantais possédaient d'importantes plantations.

Sara Des plantations de sucre?

Claude Des plantations de sucre, mais également de coton. Et lorsque les esclaves étaient vendus, on chargeait à nouveau les bateaux de sucre, de coton et de bois précieux qui servaient à faire des meubles en France. La ville de Nantes a pu ainsi développer une grande industrie de raffinerie de sucre et également fabrication d'étoffes, à partir des produits importés d'Amérique.

Sara Donc ces bateaux revenaient à Nantes chargés de bois et de coton et de sucre, et le cycle triangulaire recommençait.

Claude En effet. Chaque navire pouvait faire plusieurs fois le cycle, mais les voyages étaient très longs, plusieurs mois. Les dangers étaient très grands. En particulier, pendant les voyages les esclaves étaient si mal installés qu'ils étaient souvent malades, que beaucoup mouraient d'épidémies et ces voyages n'étaient pas du tout sûrs pour les capitaines qui dirigeaient les navires.

la ville a dû s'orienter vers	*the town had to turn to*
comment ça se passait?	*how did it work?*
il s'agissait de	*it consisted of*
qui avaient été capturés	*who had been captured*
qui servaient à	*which were used for*

More phrases – plural this time – saying how things were:

les dangers **étaient** très grands – the dangers *were* very great
les esclaves **étaient** mal installés – the slaves *were* badly housed

and what used to happen:

ils **traversaient** l'Atlantique – they *crossed* / *used to cross* the Atlantic

Quickies

1 In what century did the slave trade flourish?
2 What grows in the West Indies and can be put in tea or coffee?
3 Can you remember one of the other things mentioned as being brought back from the West Indies?

Radio 3 The slave trade came to an end but its traces linger on in Nantes.

Sara La traite des Noirs a été abolie à la fin du dix-huitième, je crois.

Claude Effectivement. La Révolution a proclamé l'abolition de la traite des Noirs, mais l'esclavage a continué clandestinement jusqu'au milieu du dix-neuvième siècle.

Nantes: maisons de négriers

Sara Les négociants nantais étaient contre, finalement, cette abolition de la traite?

Claude En effet, malgré leurs idées révolutionnaires, ils ont pris position contre l'abolition de l'esclavage car c'était la seule source importante de revenus pour eux.

Sara Finalement il y avait un paradoxe: ils étaient pour la Révolution et pour la traite des Noirs en même temps.

Claude Exactement.

Sara Il reste des traces de cette époque?

Claude Il reste des traces effectivement dans l'architecture nantaise le long des quais de la Loire et dans une île que l'on appelle l'île Feydeau. Il s'agit de grandes maisons construites par les négriers, qui étaient extrêmement riches et qui avaient fait construire ces demeures par des architectes nantais qui ont décoré les façades de sculptures rappelant la traite des Noirs avec des figures de Noirs ou des figures de l'Amérique ou des vents soufflants dans les voiles des navires. Et ce sont ces demeures qui sont le meilleur témoignage du dix-huitième siècle à Nantes.

Sara C'était une ville très riche à l'époque.

Claude Au dix-huitième siècle, oui. Elle a connu son apogée avec le commerce et la traite des Noirs.

il s'agit de	*it consists of*
qui avaient fait construire ces demeures	*who had had these houses built*
elle a connu son apogée	*it reached its peak*

Quickies

1 Can you remember the French for 'at the end of', 'in the middle of', 'in spite of'?

2 What did the slave traders have built?

TV 4

In the early twentieth century, life in the French countryside was hard but it had its compensations. We spoke to two of the older inhabitants of Pézenas about life in the town before the last war.

Albert Alliès, an amateur local historian and archivist, talks about the main occupation in the town – wine-growing.

Jane Les viticulteurs travaillaient comment à cette époque ?

M Alliès Les viticulteurs travaillaient avec . . . disons manuellement – c'est le mot – avec les chevaux. Il n'y avait pas fatalement les tracteurs, il n'y avait pas ce progrès actuel et donc les journées étaient tout de même assez longues. Et par exemple, en été, lorsqu'il faisait très chaud, la journée chez le viticulteur commençait au lever du jour jusqu'à onze heures ou midi ; et puis l'après-midi le viticulteur allait se reposer et le soir il avait à s'occuper soit de son jardin maraîcher où il cultivait ses légumes ou se distraire en allant jouer aux boules ou à jouer au tambourin, qui était un jeu régional, sur la place publique. Ça se passait pour les périodes de beaux jours, du mois de mai au mois de septembre, le moment des vendanges. Le mois de septembre alors, c'est le gros coup de la vendange, la récolte du vin. Alors là, c'était du travail mais également une fête. Dans les grandes propriétés il y avait le repas et le goûter de la fin des vendanges, il y avait des danses, il y avait des . . . on vivait, disons, c'est le mot, on vivait. On n'était pas sur les nerfs comme maintenant.

étant situé	*being situated*
il avait à s'occuper de	*he had to look after*
ça se passait pour	*that's how it was in*
c'est le gros coup de	*it's the really busy time of*
c'était du travail	*that really was hard work*
on vivait, disons	*let's say we knew how to live*

Quickies

1 What did tractors replace on the farm ?
2 When does *la vendange* begin ?

TV 5 The most important entertainment in Pézenas was provided by the municipal theatre, where touring actors and singers – even the celebrated *Comédie Française* – put on plays and operas. For generations, Madame Arnaud's family were *concierges* and she has childhood memories of the theatre in its heyday.

Le Théâtre de Pézenas

Jane Les gens venaient de loin pour assister aux spectacles?

Mme Arnaud Et bien, c'est-à-dire que tous les villages environnants venaient parce que le théâtre, bon, est . . . on y voit de partout. Alors les gens préféraient venir ici que d'aller dans une autre ville.

Jane Et vous-même, quand vous étiez jeune, vous veniez aux spectacles?

Mme Arnaud Ah oui, on n'en manquait aucun, à part que maman nous défendait de venir quand c'étaient des troupes, disons, un peu osées. Mais autrement, toujours nous avons regardé toutes les opérettes, tous les opéras, tout ce qui passait.

Jane Les acteurs, vous les connaissiez personnellement?

Mme Arnaud Ah oui, madame, oui. On les connaissait parce qu'ils venaient à la maison, ils prenaient les clés, ils venaient prendre le courrier. Puis, étant donné que chaque année à peu près c'étaient les mêmes, euh . . . c'était . . . on connaissait très bien. Maman, d'ailleurs, les appelait par leurs prénoms et nous étions très, très, très bien. L'ambiance était bonne. C'était une très, très, très bonne ambiance en tout et pour tout.

on y voit de partout	*you can see the stage from everywhere in the theatre*
on n'en manquait aucun	*we didn't miss one*
à part que maman nous défendait	*except that mum wouldn't let us*
étant donné que	*given that/since*
en tout et pour tout	*in every way*

> To say how things were, using *nous* and *vous*:
> quand vous **étiez** jeune — when you *were* young
> nous **habitions** Pézenas — we *used to live* in Pézenas

Quickies

1 People came from far and wide to the theatre at Pézenas: what's the word for 'people'?

2 What's the difference between your *nom* and your *prénom*?

Mots-clés

l'acteur (m)	actor
le bateau	boat
le bois	wood
la capitale	capital
le cheval	horse
le commerce	business, trade
le courrier	mail
le danger	danger
l'industrie (f)	industry
le jardin	garden

appeler	to call
mourir	to die
perdre	to lose
quitter	to leave
recommencer	to begin again
se reposer	to have a rest
jeune	young
malade	ill
meilleur	better

le jeu	game
le meuble	piece of furniture
le papier	paper
le prénom	first name
le siècle	century
le sucre	sugar
la vigne	vine; vineyard
le voyage	journey
riche	rich
situé	situated
contre	against
finalement	finally, in the end

En bref

To say how things used to be, what used to happen, or how things were, use the imperfect tense:

Nantes **appartenait** à la Bretagne   Nantes belonged/used to belong to Brittany

nous **étions** amis   we used to be friends
quand vous **étiez** jeune   when you were young
les bateaux **traversaient** l'Atlantique   the boats crossed/used to cross the Atlantic

To form the imperfect tense, take the *nous* form of the present tense:

nous **travers**ons
nous **vend**ons
nous **fais**ons

drop the *-ons* and add the endings of the imperfect:

je	travers	**-ais**
tu	vend	**-ais**
il/elle/on	fais	**-ait**
nous		**-ions**
vous		**-iez**
ils/elles		**-aient**

NB although there are five written forms of the endings, there are only three ways of pronouncing them, because *-ais*, *-ait* and *-aient* all sound the same

There is only one exception: *être* has the present tense form *nous sommes*, but the imperfect tense is:

j'**étais**
tu **étais**
il/elle/on/c'**était**
nous **étions**
vous **étiez**
ils/elles **étaient**

1 **When it's right to be imperfect.**
Since there's a perfect tense it is inevitable that there is an imperfect tense as well.
Consider this event:

A car came round the corner, skidded and narrowly missed a parked van. The car was red and had big, shiny wheels. A man was driving. Finally it hit a lamp post and exploded.

The first thing that happened was that the car came round the corner, then it skidded, then it missed a van. Next it hit a lamp post and then it exploded. But the fact that it was red was not the next thing that happened. It was red before it came round the corner and, presumably, after it exploded. That also applies to its having shiny wheels and the fact that a man was driving (at least till it hit the lamp post).

In French, all the events (the next thing that happened) are expressed in the perfect and all the things that were going on at the same time throughout those events (being red, the man driving) are expressed in the imperfect. For example:
la Révolution **a proclamé** l'abolition de la traite des Noirs – the Revolution proclaimed the abolition of the slave trade
les négociants **étaient** contre cette abolition – the traders were against this abolition
So if you want to tell your French friends about your day out: 'we went to Nantes. It was raining so we bought an ice-cream from a man who had an enormous red nose': 'went' and 'bought' would be in the perfect tense and 'was raining' and 'had' would be in the imperfect.

Another common idea expressed by the imperfect, and the one most used in our interviews in this chapter, is the idea of a state of affairs that used to be so in the past:
quand j'**étais** jeune, on **passait** les vacances à La Rochelle –

when I *was* young we	*used to spend* *would spend* *spent*	our holidays at La Rochelle

Along the same lines:
l'après-midi, le viticulteur **allait** se reposer
les bateaux **revenaient** d'Amérique chargés de bois
Maman les **appelait** par leur prénom

2 **A few more false friends**
Assister can mean 'to assist' but *assister à* means 'to attend' or 'to be present at'. So *l'assistance* can mean 'assistance' or 'help' and also 'everybody present'.
Défendre can mean 'to defend' but also 'to forbid'. Hence all the signs saying: *défense de* . . . it is forbidden to . . .
La figure – not your figure but your face

Un voyage – this can mean any sort of journey and is not restricted to sea voyages.
Les Indes – the old word for India (like the English 'The Indies'); since independence in 1947 the correct title is *l'Inde*. It is feminine, so you talk of going *en Inde*.

A propos

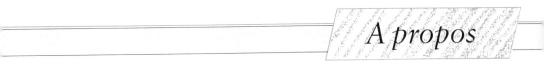

Brittany
Much loved by holiday-makers, both French and foreign, for its combination of superb beaches and dramatic coastline, Brittany has had a turbulent history whose traces are visible everywhere in the province.

Carnac: menhirs

In prehistoric times it was inhabited by people who spent their time putting up large stones (*menhirs*) in ways which still mystify their descendants. At Carnac, over a thousand of them are arranged in long rows stretching a kilometre or so – for what purpose, nobody knows. For 800 years during the Middle Ages, Brittany was an independent country regularly devastated by invaders or internal squabbles over succession to the dukedom. Even after it finally became part of France in 1532, its people retained a fierce local identity supported by their own language, a Celtic one closely allied to Welsh and Cornish. There's even an area of Brittany called *la Cornouaille* and place names often seem to have little to do with what we think of as French eg Trégastel, Penmarch, Plogoff, Roscoff, Kerzerho.

All attempts by central government to suppress the Breton language failed (even up to the First World War, children in schools were forbidden to speak it on pain of punishment) and today it flourishes, having 700,000 speakers. The sea which surrounds Brittany on three sides inevitably dominates its life. Apart from innumerable fishing villages, there are two naval ports (Brest and Lorient) and several commercial ones.

Nantes

Nantes has had as long and eventful a history as Brittany itself. It was the capital for several periods and has the Château des Ducs to show for it. From the sixteenth to the eighteenth centuries its main income came from the related trades of sugar and slaves. The slave trade (euphemistically referred to as 'the ebony trade', *le commerce de bois d'ébène*) showed an average 200% profit – so the enlightened philosophers of the eighteenth century who inveighed against it didn't cut much ice. Even that arch-defender of individual liberty, Voltaire, had a substantial stake in a slave ship. It is not surprising, then, that after the French Revolution, when the new government abolished the slave trade, the traders of Nantes were far from pleased and found ways of getting round the ban for quite some time.

La Loire industrielle à Nantes

Today Nantes is a busy industrial and commercial centre, with a population approaching half a million. Its port still trades with the rest of the world, and some of its industries reflect its past – the importation of sugar from the Americas has given Nantes sugar refineries and a food and biscuit industry.

A number of districts in Nantes are called *îles* – they used to be islands until the channels around them were filled in. The best known of these is *l'île Feydeau*, an elegant eighteenth-century quarter down by the port. Its huge houses were once inhabited by the slave-traders, and wooden carvings of negro heads can still be seen on the façades. It is still inhabited by successful people, though many buildings have been converted into boutiques and elegant (and extremely expensive) restaurants.

Bon courage

1 Each word in the first list has some connection with one in the second. Pair them up:

le courrier, le vin, le papier, le bateau, jeune, le jeu, le nord, travailler, chaud, le prénom

vieux, froid, les boules, le nom, la mer, l'ouest, la vigne, le bois, se reposer, la lettre

2 Find in the list a word or expression to fit in the blanks in each sentence. Rearrange the six words left over to make a French proverb.

Ducs, bien, quitte, aller, tout, qui, Château, voyage, est, malade, bien, riche, Madame, en, finit, perdez, droite, aimais, monde, bateaux, chose, le médecin, tous

1 Si vous êtes .... il faut appeler ....
2 Monsieur Leclerc est très .... Il a deux .... et une grande maison.
3 .... Grasset .... la maison à la même heure .... les matins.
4 .... France, si vous .... quelque .... vous pouvez .... au Bureau des Objets Trouvés.
5 Sur votre .... vous avez le .... des .... de Bretagne.
6 Quand j'étais jeune j'............ beaucoup les romans de Jules Verne, '............ au centre de la Terre' et 'Le tour du .... en 80 jours'.

3 Here is a summary of part of the interview with Monsieur Albert Alliès. Fill in the gaps using the correct form of the words from the list, then look back and read through the original conversation. commencer, être, cultiver, travailler, y avoir, faire, s'occuper, aller (twice), continuer

M Alliès Les viticulteurs .... avec des chevaux. Il n' .... pas de tracteurs à l'époque. Les journées .... assez longues. Lorsqu'il .... très chaud, le viticulteur .... à travailler au lever du jour et .... jusqu'à midi. L'après-midi il ....se reposer et le soir il .... de son jardin où il .... des légumes. Ou bien, il .... jouer aux boules sur la place publique.

4 There has been a jewel robbery and the members of a well-known gang have been interviewed. Here are their replies to the question: Qu'est-ce que vous faisiez jeudi dernier à huit heures et demie du soir? Read their alibis then answer the questions about each person according to their own statements.

Pierrot la Valise
Je regardais la téle avec Fifi la Plume. On passait un film d'horreur. J'adore les films d'horreur. Après, nous sommes allés voir le Gros Jules. Il était environ neuf heures et demie.

Le Petit Gaston
Je n'étais pas chez moi. J'étais chez ma soeur. J'étais malade. J'avais mal à la tête et je me suis couché à huit heures. Je suis rentré chez moi vendredi matin.

Dédé le Gigolo
J'étais au cinéma avec ma petite amie. Après, on est allé au Café de l'Univers. Il était dix heures. Là, nous avons rencontré le Petit Gaston. Il jouait aux dominos avec des amis. Vers dix heures et demie nous sommes allés voir le Gros Jules.

Le Gros Jules
Je buvais avec des amis au Café de l'Univers. Nous jouions aux dominos. Vers dix heures je suis allé voir le Petit Gaston.

Pierrot la Valise
1 Fifi et Pierrot étaient à la maison. Qu'est-ce qu'ils faisaient?
2 C'était quel genre de film?
3 Qu'est-ce qu'ils ont fait à neuf heures et demie?

Le Petit Gaston
4 Est-ce que le petit Gaston était chez lui?
5 Pourquoi est-ce qu'il s'est couché tôt?
6 Est-ce qu'il était toujours chez sa soeur vendredi après-midi?

Dédé le Gigolo
7 Qui est allé au cinéma avec Dédé?
8 Qu'est-ce qu'ils ont fait après le cinéma?
9 Qui est-ce qu'ils ont vu au Café de l'Univers?
10 Ils sont restés au café jusqu'à quelle heure?
11 Qu'est-ce qu'ils ont fait après?

Le Gros Jules
12 Qu'est-ce qu'il faisait au Café de l'Univers?
13 Est-ce qu'il est resté au café jusqu'à minuit?

Why do you think the police found all these stories rather suspicious?

5 Another crime! You've witnessed a bag snatch and the police want you to describe what happened. Here are some words to help you: to wear – *porter*; to get into a car – *monter*; steering wheel – *le volant*; motorway – *l'autoroute* (f); watch – *la montre*

Agent Où étiez-vous?
You *Say you were coming out of the big shop 'Les Anciennes Galeries'.*
Agent Il était quelle heure, à peu près?
You *It was exactly ten past two. You know because you looked at your watch.*
Agent Qu'est-ce que vous avez vu?
You *Tell him that in front of you there was a woman. She was going to cross the street. A young man arrived. He passed behind the lady and took her bag.*
Agent Il était comment?
You *He was tall, he was wearing black trousers and a green shirt.*
Agent Qu'est-ce qu'il a fait ensuite?
You *He crossed the street and got into a red car. There was a woman at the wheel.*

Agent Ils sont partis dans quelle direction?
You *In the direction of the motorway.*
Agent Merci bien, madame.

7 The conversation with your French neighbour about your day trip to Boulogne continues (see chapter 13, exercise 6) You'll need to know: *chanter* – to sing, and *au lit* – in bed.

Voisine Alors, dites-moi. Comment c'était à l'hypermarché?
You *Well, it was a Friday afternoon and it was full of French people. They were buying for the weekend.*
Voisin Ce n'est pas surprenant.
You *And there was a coach full of English people. They were buying dozens and dozens of bottles of beer. And a lot of wine too.*
Voisine Pour Noël, peut-être.
You *In the month of August?*
Voisine Alors, c'est parce que le vin est beaucoup moins cher en France.
You *That's it.*
Voisine Et vous, qu'est-ce que vous avez acheté?
You *Tell her your friend bought lots of cheese, some coffee because it's less expensive in France, and some Swiss chocolate. And six bottles of wine.*
Voisine Six bouteilles! Et vous-même, qu'est-ce que vous avez acheté?
You *A salami, cheese, wine ... lots of things. It was very pleasant. The French people were buying lots of meat and seafood ... and prawns.*
Voisine Ah. Les pronnes, non?
You *No (correcting her English) prawns.*
Voisine Et ensuite?
You *You looked at the trousers, but they were very expensive. And it was 5 o'clock and the boat was leaving at 6.*
Voisine Quelle expédition!
You *You went to the car. The English were singing in the coach. And you went back to the port. But there was a lot of traffic. You arrived in Boulogne at quarter to six.*
Voisine Oh, là, là! Vous avez réussi à prendre le bateau?
You *Luckily, yes. But the English coach arrived too late.*
Voisine Quel dommage. Et la traversée a été bonne?
You *The sea was very calm. And you saw a film.*
Voisine Un film!
You *Well, there was a cinema on the boat.*
Voisine Vous êtes revenues très tard alors.
You *No. You arrived in Folkestone at 7 o'clock – there's a difference of one hour between Britain and France – and you decided to buy some fish and chips.*
Voisine Du poisson et des frites?
You *Yes, it's the British national dish. And you were at the seaside, after all.*
Voisine Bien sûr.
You *You ate it in the car. And you got home at 11. Your friend took the car and you were in bed before midnight.*
Voisine Quelle journée!

Pézenas fait revivre son passé

A walk through the old town of Pézenas is a walk back in time: the narrow cobbled streets have changed little since the eighteenth century. There are still a few medieval houses and a number of magnificent private residences (called *hôtels*) built at a time when Pézenas was an important commercial and political centre. With its declining importance, the old town ceased to develop: the result is that little has changed since that time.

The people of Pézenas are well aware of the value of their heritage. There is a flourishing preservation society, *Les Amis de Pézenas*, which among other things, encourages and helps organise restoration work. But they are careful not to resist change for the sake of it. They do not want to see their town become a museum piece for tourists. In fact, the old town is slowly coming to life again as people take over the neglected buildings.

Not far from Pézenas is one of the most important historic monuments of the Languedoc – l'Abbaye de Valmagne. The present owner's family has lived there for the past 150 years and she is determined to keep the place alive. Since the nineteenth century the towering Gothic church has housed casks of wine made on the estate, and the beautiful cloisters are hired out for concerts and dinners: it all helps towards the massive cost of repairs.

La vieille ville de Pézenas est en cours de restauration. Beaucoup de gens y ont acheté de vieilles demeures alors qu'elles étaient abandonnées ou occupées par des squatters. Monsieur et Madame Lobit sont propriétaires d'un vieil hôtel depuis vingt ans. Au début, ils ne pouvaient même pas habiter leur maison: il n'y avait plus de toit et la façade extérieure tombait en ruines. Ils ont tout reconstruit intérieurement. Comme dans beaucoup de quartiers historiques, la population de la vieille ville a beaucoup changé. Avant, les habitants étaient presque tous très pauvres: il y avait beaucoup de gitans. Aujourd'hui on y trouve des gens plus riches.

Dans le petit hameau de Conas, à l'entrée de Pézenas, l'église aussi est en train de se transformer. Il y a quatre ans, l'association des Amis de Pézenas a entrepris de la restaurer. Tous les ans, pendant le mois de juillet, des bénévoles de dix-huit à quarante ans – souvent des étudiants – viennent s'occuper du chantier. Ils ne sont pas payés mais, en échange du travail, ils sont nourris et logés gratuitement. Les réparations n'ont pas toujours été faciles pour tous ces volontaires. Il a fallu demander conseil à des experts professionnels comme Bruno Mendola, un tailleur de pierre qui habite Pézenas. Beaucoup d'artisans comme Bruno sont venus s'installer dans les environs de Pézenas, car la région est pleine de monuments historiques et de vieilles demeures qui ont besoin de rénovation.

Pézenas: maison médiévale dans la vieille ville

L'Abbaye de Valmagne en est un bel exemple. C'est une abbaye cistercienne fondée en 1138 par des moines bénédictins. Aujourd'hui encore, elle est réputée pour son cloître et ses vins. Elle appartient à la famille de Madame de Gaudart d'Allaines depuis cent cinquante ans. Pour la restauration du cloître et de l'église, Madame de Gaudart d'Allaines reçoit une subvention de l'état qui couvre cinquante pour cent des travaux. Elle doit donc trouver elle-même l'argent pour le reste des réparations et de l'entretien. Heureusement, il y a les visites de touristes et la location du cloître.

Habiter une demeure comme l'Abbaye de Valmagne pose beaucoup de problèmes et demande des sacrifices. Pourtant, Madame de Gaudart d'Allaines continue à le faire car, dit-elle, 'C'est la maison de la famille, j'y suis née ... On s'attache à un monument de cette sorte'.

il n'y avait plus de toit	*there wasn't a roof any more*
alors que	*when*
à l'entrée de	*on the way in to*
est en train de se transformer	*is in the process of being transformed*
viennent s'occuper	*come to work on*
il a fallu demander conseil à	*it was necessary to ask the advice of*
tailleur de pierre	*stone-mason*
sont venus s'installer	*have settled*

Faisons le point 3

What you have learnt

You can now ask if you can do something and ask others if they can do something for you.

Radio **1** Sara is at the cleaners with a pair of trousers.

Employé Bonjour, madame.
Sara Bonjour, monsieur. Est-ce que vous pouvez nettoyer ce pantalon, s'il vous plaît?
Employé Oui, bien sûr.
Sara Il y a une tache là.
Employé Qu'est-ce que c'est comme tache?
Sara C'est une tache de vin, je crois.
Employé (*looking at the stain*) Aucun problème. Vous le voulez pour quand?
Sara Est-ce que je peux l'avoir pour ce soir?
Employé Oui, bien sûr.
Sara Bon.
Employé Alors, ça vous fait douze francs cinquante, s'il vous plaît.
Sara Dix, douze cinquante, voilà.
Employé Merci. Au revoir, madame. A ce soir.
Sara Au revoir, monsieur.
Employé Au revoir, madame.

Quickies
1 How do you say 'these trousers' referring to one pair?
2 How did the man say 'till this evening'?

You can also say where you've been, what you've done, and what happened in the past.

Radio **2** Sara is talking about La Rochelle to a girl from the *Office du Tourisme*, Martine.

Sara Vous aimez vivre à La Rochelle?
Martine Eh oui, mais enfin je ne suis pas née à La Rochelle. J'y suis venue il y a trois ans et j'ai tellement aimé la ville que j'y suis restée.
Sara Qu'est-ce qui vous plaît ici?
Martine Eh bien, tout d'abord la ville en elle-même, très vivante, très agréable,

les gens sont très gentils aussi et puis le climat, certainement beaucoup plus favorable, beaucoup plus agréable que dans d'autres parties de la France.

Sara Oui, en effet, on dit que c'est une ville très ensoleillée en France, La Rochelle.

Martine Oui, nous avons presque autant d'heures d'ensoleillement que sur la Côte d'Azur.

Sara C'est beaucoup, alors.

Martine Eh oui!

il y a trois ans	*three years ago*
la ville en elle-même	*the town in itself*

Quickies
1. When did Martine come to La Rochelle?
2. What does she say was her reason for staying?
3. How does she say 'I stayed here'?

TV 3 The region of the Languedoc takes its name from the language that was spoken here – the *langue d'oc* (see *A propos* p294). It was once politically and culturally quite distinct from the north of France, and today there is a revival of interest in its regional identity. Occitan, almost a dead language twenty years ago, is now a popular subject at secondary schools in the area. André Nos, a teacher at the Lycée Jean Moulin in Pézenas, explains why.

M Nos D'abord, la langue d'oc, c'est une véritable langue et non pas un dialecte. Des conditions historiques ont fait que cette langue a été supplantée, du moins officiellement, dans le sud de la France par la langue française, par la langue d'oïl. Mais c'est une véritable langue avec une littérature importante, riche – en particulier riche au onzième, douzième, au début du treizième siècle, avec les premiers grands troubadours français, et ensuite une littérature qui a continué à exister et qui continue à exister même aujourd'hui.

des conditions historiques ont fait que . . .	*historical factors have meant that . . .*

Quickies
1. What's the opposite of *le nord*?
2. How do you say 'in the twelfth century'?

TV 4 The Occitan language is used a small amount on local television, but not enough for the *occitanistes*. At one of their rallies in Montpellier calling for more Occitan in the media, we asked a leader of the movement, Yves Rouquette, to explain what they stood for.

M Rouquette Mais le mouvement occitan c'est l'ensemble des forces, des personnes, des associations, des organisations, des gens particuliers et des gens regroupés qui ne veulent pas que la langue d'oc meure, et qui veulent la faire entrer dans le monde contemporain.

Jane Le mouvement occitan a commencé à quelle époque?

M Rouquette Il a commencé avec l'annexion, c'est-à-dire à partir du moment où notre pays a été annexé par la France, il y a des gens qui ont fait tout ce qu'ils ont pu pour maintenir des libertés et, entre autres libertés, la liberté de parler et de faire chanter sa langue.

qui ne veulent pas que la langue d'oc meure	*who don't want Occitan to die*
qui veulent la faire entrer	*who want to bring it into*
à partir du moment où . . .	*from the moment when . . .*
tout ce qu'ils ont pu	*everything they could*
faire chanter sa langue	*make their language sing*

You can say what you used to do and what used to happen.

TV 5 Jane talks to André Nos and Yves Rouquette about the future of *l'occitan*.

Jane Est-ce que vous pensez qu'il y a un renouveau d'intérêt pour l'occitan?

M Nos Oui, ce renouveau d'intérêt existe et c'est un renouveau surtout parmi les jeunes – les jeunes qui sont sensibilisés non seulement par la langue occitane mais qui sont sensibilisés par la chanson occitane, par la littérature occitane, par le théâtre occitan et aussi par les problèmes que l'occitanisme soulève.

M Rouquette C'est qu'il y a vingt ans personne ne savait qu'il y avait une langue qui valait la peine d'être . . . d'être parlée, d'être défendue et d'être illustrée – il y avait très peu de monde. Il y avait très peu de monde qui pensait que ça valait la peine de vivre au pays, et aujourd'hui il y a des tas de gens qui commencent à se dire les deux choses un peu à la fois.

Jane Il est important de préserver les langues régionales, selon vous?

M Nos Les langues régionales ne sont pas simplement des restes folkloriques. Elles expriment souvent l'âme profonde d'un peuple. Il y a des choses que l'on peut dire en occitan et qu'on ne peut pas dire en français.

c'est qu'il y a vingt ans	*the fact is that twenty years ago*
qui valait la peine . . . d'être illustrée	*which was worth being made better known*
les deux choses . . . à la fois	*both things at once*

Quickies

1. Which people are particularly open to accepting *l'occitan*?
2. Monsieur Nos mentions *le théâtre occitan, la littérature occitane* and what is the third thing?
3. What is the phrase Monsieur Rouquette used for 'twenty years ago'?

And now for some more general revision.

Radio 6

Here's Marie-Pierre in a rather refined boutique in Bourg-en-Bresse looking for a scarf to give to a young man for his birthday.

Vendeuse Bonjour, mademoiselle.
Marie-Pierre Bonjour, madame. Je cherche une écharpe pour offrir.
Vendeuse Pour une jeune personne ou une personne plus âgée?
Marie-Pierre Pour un jeune homme.
Vendeuse Vous cherchez une écharpe en laine, en soie, en cachemire . . .?
Marie-Pierre Je peux voir quelques modèles?
Vendeuse Oui, madame. Si vous voulez bien me suivre. (*they walk over to a display*) Voici une écharpe en laine, grise et rouge. Une autre, en cachemire. Maintenant j'ai quelques écharpes en soie. Vous avez une préférence pour . . . la soie, la laine?
Marie-Pierre Peut-être celle-ci, là.
Vendeuse Celle en cachemire?
Marie-Pierre La grise, oui.
Vendeuse Oui. Elle est très belle et c'est très agréable à porter, madame.
Marie-Pierre Et celle-ci?
Vendeuse Celle-ci est en laine également, mais . . .
Marie-Pierre Oui, celle-ci est très douce. Et c'est combien?
Vendeuse Trois cent dix francs, madame.
Marie-Pierre Et celle-là?
Vendeuse Deux cents francs.
Marie-Pierre En laine?
Vendeuse En laine également. Mais je vous conseille celle en cachemire.
Marie-Pierre Oui, elle est douce, elle est chaude. Je vais prendre celle-ci.
Vendeuse Bien, madame. Si vous voulez bien attendre cinq minutes, je vais monter vous faire un paquet-cadeau. Asseyez-vous, madame, je vous en prie.
Marie-Pierre Merci.

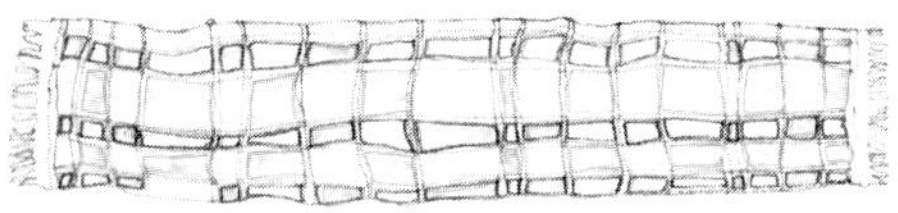

je vais monter vous faire un paquet-cadeau	*I'll just go up and gift-wrap it for you*

Quickies

1. Three choices of materials for the scarf are mentioned. What are they?
2. How did Marie-Pierre say 'the grey one' referring to a scarf?
3. How did she say 'this one' referring to a scarf?

Radio 7 We asked Sara Tomei to give us a radio portrait of a French town and she chose La Rochelle on the Atlantic coast. She spoke first on the edge of the old port (*le vieux port*) to Martine, who works in the *Office du Tourisme*, about some facts and figures.

La Rochelle : vue aérienne du vieux port

Sara Nous sommes sur le vieux port de La Rochelle et nous sommes avec Martine, qui est de l'Office du Tourisme. Martine, combien y a-t-il d'habitants à La Rochelle ?

Martine Environ soixante-dix-huit mille habitants, un petit peu plus avec la banlieue.

Sara Oui. Et de quoi vit La Rochelle ?

Martine Les gens vivent de la pêche – La Rochelle est le cinquième port de pêche de France – du commerce, euh . . . quelques industries et, bien sûr, le tourisme.

Sara Oui. Il semble qu'il y ait un grand port de plaisance à La Rochelle.

Martine Oui. Il est situé un petit peu en dehors de La Rochelle et c'est le plus grand port de plaisance de France, avec ses trois mille postes.

Sara Oui. Euh, je vois des tours derrière nous, là. Qu'est-ce que c'est ?

Martine Bien sûr, ce sont les deux tours. A gauche vous avez la Tour Saint-Nicolas, et à droite la Tour de la Chaîne, qui à l'origine fermaient la ville de La Rochelle.

Sara Est-ce que vous pouvez nous dire combien de touristes visitent La Rochelle, ou passent l'été à La Rochelle ?

Martine La Rochelle n'est pas vraiment une station balnéaire. C'est une ville où les gens passent, donc ils viennent, ils séjournent quelques jours ou une semaine, mais on voit défiler des milliers, des milliers de gens à La Rochelle surtout du mois de juin au mois de septembre.

combien y a-t-il ? = il y a combien	
de quoi vit La Rochelle	*what does La Rochelle live on?*
il semble qu'il y ait . . .	*it appears that there's . . .*

Quickies

1. Martine mentions three ways in which the people of La Rochelle make their living. How many can you remember?
2. What architectural feature of *le vieux port* is mentioned?
3. Most people don't spend all their holidays there. How much time do they spend?

Radio 8

The entrance to the old port, guarded by its two towers, is one of the best-known sights in France. Sara spoke to some of the shopkeepers on the port.

First Madame Leboucher who runs *Les Frégates*, one of the many bars clustered round the old port.

Sara Vous avez beaucoup de soleil en hiver et en été?
Mme Leboucher Ah oui, parce que nous sommes la deuxième ville de France la plus ensoleillée.
Sara Ah oui.
Mme Leboucher Alors, ce qui fait que la région est très belle et le climat est très doux.
Sara Oui. Vous aimez bien le vieux port ici?
Mme Leboucher Ah c'est très agréable. Vraiment, parce que les bateaux vont à la pêche le matin et reviennent l'après-midi. Cela crée une animation.
Sara Madame Leboucher, je crois que vous n'êtes pas du coin.
Mme Leboucher Non, je suis de la région quand même, Poitiers, donc la Vienne . . .
Sara Et vous préférez . . . ?
Mme Leboucher La Rochelle, pour le climat.
Sara Vous préférez La Rochelle pour le climat.
Mme Leboucher Ah oui, ah oui, ah oui! Et c'est très facile à vivre à La Rochelle.
Sara Ah bon.
Mme Leboucher C'est très agréable.
Sara Merci.

la deuxième ville de France la plus ensoleillée	*the second sunniest town in France*
ce qui fait que . . .	*which means that . . .*
cela crée une animation	*it makes it full of life*
vous n'êtes pas du coin	*you're not from round here*

Quickies

1. What two seasons of the year are mentioned?
2. When do the fishing boats go out and come back?
3. Madame Leboucher says that it's very pleasant – how does she say that?

Radio 9

Monsieur Lavigne runs a tobacconist's on the edge of the port.

Sara Monsieur Lavigne, vous tenez un bureau de tabac. Qu'est-ce que vous vendez en plus du tabac, des cigarettes?
M Lavigne Alors, souvenirs, cartes postales, timbres, un petit peu de parfumerie . . .
Sara Oui. Et quelles sont vos heures d'ouverture?
M Lavigne Pendant les vacances, huit heures le matin jusqu'à onze heures le soir.
Sara Oui. Et qu'est-ce que vous appelez 'les vacances'?
M Lavigne Les vacances, nous appelons le mois de juillet et août.
Sara Deux mois, alors?

M Lavigne Deux mois, oui.
Sara D'accord. Et pendant l'hiver?
M Lavigne Pendant l'hiver, de neuf heures trente le matin à dix-neuf heures trente le soir.
Sara Le reste de l'année?
M Lavigne Oui.
Sara D'accord. Eh, je vois que, d'après votre accent, vous n'êtes pas de La Rochelle.
M Lavigne Non. Nous sommes de Villeneuve-sur-Lot.
Sara C'est . . .
M Lavigne En Lot-et-Garonne.
Sara . . . dans le Lot-et-Garonne.
M Lavigne Oui. Dans le sud-ouest.
Sara Est-ce que c'est agréable d'avoir un tabac sur le vieux port?
M Lavigne Oui, c'est très agréable. La clientèle est très bonne . . .
Sara Le site est beau . . .
M Lavigne Le site est très joli, une très belle ville . . .
Sara Vous aimez le climat ici?
M Lavigne Oui, il y a un bon climat. Beaucoup de soleil.
Sara Toute l'année?
M Lavigne Pas de froid. Toute l'année, beaucoup de soleil pendant l'année.
Sara C'est un climat très sain?
M Lavigne Euh, oui et non, parce qu'il y a énormément de vent et brouillard pendant l'hiver. Alors ça fait que, le matin, c'est assez dur.
Sara D'accord. Merci.
M Lavigne Avec plaisir.

d'après votre accent	*from your accent*
il y a énormément de	*there's an awful lot of*
alors ça fait que	*which means that*

Quickies

1 What does Monsieur Lavigne say he sells apart from tobacco and cigarettes?
2 Which two months does he mention?
3 What are his opening hours in the winter?
4 The climate has a couple of drawbacks in winter – what are they?

Radio 10 However wonderful La Rochelle sounds, you might want to get away from it now and again. Here's Sara enquiring about boats to the nearby island, l'île de Ré.

Employé Bonjour, madame.
Sara Bonjour. Est-ce qu'il y a des bateaux pour aller à l'île de Ré?
Employé Oui, bien sûr. Alors, vous en avez de six heures quinze le matin jusqu'à dix-huit heures cinquante. Un toutes les demi-heures.
Sara Ah bon, d'accord. Alors chaque demi-heure de façon regulière à quinze et quarante-cinq.
Employé A quinze et quarante-cinq. Voilà. C'est cela!
Sara D'accord. Euh, et pour revenir?
Employé Pour revenir, vous avez les horaires ici. Je vous donne la fiche.
Sara Merci. C'est combien par personne?
Employé Alors, par personne c'est dix francs si vous passez à pied. Si vous

prenez une voiture c'est cinquante francs, à peu près.

Sara Aller-retour?

Employé Aller-retour, c'est ça.

Sara Bon, d'accord. Merci.

Employé Au revoir, madame.

Sara Au revoir.

de façon regulière	*regularly*
à quinze et quarante-cinq	*at fifteen and forty-five minutes past the hour*

Quickies

1 How many boats an hour are there?
2 If you want a timetable what do you ask for?
3 And a return ticket?

Mots-clés

l'accent (m)	accent
la banlieue	suburb(s)
le brouillard	fog
le climat	climate
le dialecte	dialect
l'écharpe (f)	scarf
l'habitant (m)	inhabitant
l'intérêt (m)	interest
la laine	wool
la littérature	literature
le millier	about a thousand
la pêche	fishing
la soie	silk
le souvenir	souvenir, memory
la tour	tower
le vent	wind
doux	soft; mild
dur	hard
ensoleillé	sunny
facile	easy
favorable	favourable
personne	nobody
la personne	person
du moins	at least
plus de	more than
chanter	to sing
porter	to wear
séjourner	to stay
sembler	to seem

A final few words
le tour – la tour
In modern French the words look the same except for the gender but in fact they come from quite different origins. In chapter 10 the chemist said:
A qui le tour? (Whose turn is it?)
and *un tour* can mean 'a short walk' or 'a tour'.

Le tour de France

But *une tour* is 'a tower'. So compare: *le tour de France* and *la tour Eiffel*.
Alors, on fait un tour autour de la tour?

Paris: la tour Maine-Montparnasse

un souvenir
In English the word 'souvenir' has come to mean the actual thing you buy to remind you of the places you've been to or the people you've met. In French it means that too, but its original meaning is the memories, good or bad, that you have of these places:
j'ai un bon souvenir de La Rochelle – I have happy memories of La Rochelle

personne
Don't be misled by this word, which in different contexts might mean 'person' or 'nobody'. Used with an article or a number (ie as a noun) it means 'person' – plural 'people':
la personne qui a téléphoné n'a pas laissé son nom
je voudrais une chambre pour deux personnes
la traversée coûte cinq francs par personne et vingt francs par véhicule

Used with *ne* . . ., it means 'nobody'. It can be the subject of a verb:
personne ne traverse le parc après minuit – nobody crosses the park after midnight

or it can follow the verb:
il n'y a personne à la maison – there is nobody at home

It can also come on its own:
Qui veut me donner cent francs? Personne!

doux
You have met several meanings:
sweet: un vin doux
mild: en hiver il fait très doux
gentle: c'est une personne très douce
soft: elle est très douce cette écharpe, n'est-ce pas?
You will also often hear the adverb *doucement!* being used to tell you to do something 'gently', 'slowly' or 'quietly' or to 'take it easy'.

chaud
For most purposes this means both 'warm' and 'hot'; the distinction is not made in French.

One thing to note (and this goes for *froid* too): use *faire* for the weather, *avoir* for people and *être* for things.
il **fait** chaud – it (the weather) is warm/hot
Pierre **a** chaud – Pierre is warm/hot
le thé **est** chaud – the tea is warm/hot

À propos

La langue d'oc

Modern French has evolved largely from Latin. In the early days of that process, several related languages grew up. In France, two of these became dominant. One used the word *oc* (from Latin *hoc*) to mean 'yes' and the other *oïl* (from *hoc illi*). *La langue d'oc* (the *oc* language) was spoken south of the Loire and *la langue d'oïl* (the *oïl* language) north of it.

As northern France, centred on the Paris region, became politically more powerful, its language became that of the court and of government and *la langue d'oc* gradually retreated south to cover the area we now call *le Midi*.

After the Middle Ages, the language rapidly lost ground and had almost disappeared when, in the last century, people began to study and revive it. Over the last twenty years in particular, there has been a great renewal of interest and very successful attempts have been made to get the language taught in schools.

The old province known as Languedoc, which has become the new Languedoc-Roussillon region, covers only a small part of the area where the language was originally spoken.

Bon courage

Part I

If you like testing yourself, you can score up to 44 points in this first section.

1 Say that you have:

1. bought a grey shirt
2. asked for the bill
3. lost the street map
4. played boules with your French friends
5. picnicked on the beach

2 Say Henry has:

1. been to the seaside
2. done some windsurfing
3. read *Le Monde*
4. drunk some whisky
5. had five aperitives

3 Say what all these did yesterday:

1 Sara went to Nantes
2 Patrick arrived about midday
3 Daniel and Michel left after lunch
4 Paulette came at four
5 we went out with Marie-Pierre

4 Tell your French friend that when you were about nine or ten years old you used to:

1 go to school by bicycle
2 spend your holidays in the country
3 eat steak and chips every Saturday
4 drink lots of lemonade
5 not like wine at all!

5 Ask:

1 if it's possible to (use *on*);
a) hire a bike in La Rochelle
b) go to the island now

2 if you can (use *je*):
a) see the room
b) try these trousers on
3 and (rather more tentatively) if you could (use *je* again):
a) telephone Great Britain
b) have a glass of water

6 Ask someone

1 if they can (use *vous*):
a open the door please
b pass you the salt
c give you two kilos of peaches

2 and if they could (use *vous* again):
a look at your tyres
b clean this skirt
c reserve you a room for two for Saturday night

7 1 You've taken the car in for repair. Ask if it will be long.
2 Henri has been in the shower for twenty minutes. Ask him if he's going to be long.
3 You've got a bit of work to finish. Tell someone you'll be half an hour.

8 Tell your French friend:

1 your daughter is ten years old
2 your son is six
3 your husband is thirty-five
4 he's been thirty-five for five years now
5 your grandfather (*grand-père*) is 106

9 Tell your French friend that the weather in England is:
1 mild
2 warm
3 fine
4 never very cold!

Part II

Vingt questions

1 Have a guess at where the woman in Bizet's suite *L'Arlésienne* comes from.

2 Which of the following are not items of clothing?
les chemises; *les pantalons*; *les bras*; *les jupes*

3 What is *une chambre d'hôte*?
a kind of menu; a room with hot and cold running water; bed and breakfast

4 What is the difference between *le tour* and *la tour*?

5 A French person says to you *Je vais partir à la pêche*. Is he going to: go fruit-picking; make a fruit salad; go fishing?

6 Can you give two meanings for *l'indicatif*?

7 Fill in the blank: *automne, hiver,* ...., *été*

8 *Vous allez pique-niquer sur la plage*. Which of the following would you not eat?
un pâté de sable; *un pâté de canard*; *des pêches*; *des sandwichs*

9 In what context would you hear the phrase *Qui est à l'appareil?*?

10 If *un tandem* is for two, what is for one?

11 How many different written endings are there in the imperfect tense (*parlais*, etc)? And how many different pronunciations?

12 Where might you see people climbing up poles which are sticking out of the sea?

13 Somebody tells you she is *rochelaise*. What does she mean?

14 Which of these is not normally drunk?
le Morgon; *le port*; *le kir*; *le panaché*

15 What ought to come out of a French tap marked 'C'?

16 What are *oc* and *oïl*?

17 Which of the following is not part of a car?
le phare; *la glace*; *la circulation*; *la veilleuse*

18 Which of these can be high or low twice a day? Which can be calm or rough? Which is for getting married in? And which one is married already?
le mari; *la marée*; *la mairie*; *la mer*

19 Somebody tells you: *J'aime La Rochelle parce que le climat est très sain et que j'y suis née*. What two reasons for liking La Rochelle are given? What else do you know about this person?

20 Who wrote *Le Tartuffe*?
Victor Hugo; Molière; Stendhal; Monsieur West

Part III

1 In each case only one word of the three is correct. Which is it?

		avons		à	
1	Hier nous	sommes	allés	au	bord de la mer.
		sont		à la	

		au		au	
2	Un sandwich	à	fromage et une glace	à la	fraise,
		à la		à	

s'il vous plaît.

		ce		celui-ci
3	Tu aimes	cette	jupe-là? Oui, mais je préfère	celle-ci
		ces		ceux-là

en rouge.

		avoir	
4	Pour	aller	à la gare, s'il vous plaît?
		allons	

		prends		ils	
5	Tu as	parlé	les bagages? Non,	elles	sont toujours dans la
		pris		il	

voiture.

		gros	
6	Une	grande	boîte de sardines, s'il vous plaît, et
		rouge	

	lait.
un litre de	pain.
	fromage.

		a		vas	
7	Attention, le verre	est	cassé, tu	vais	te couper.
		ont		allez	

		allais		fait	
8	Quand j'	était	jeune il	faisait	toujours beau en été.
		étais		était	

		fait		manger	
9	Pour	font	une bonne galette il faut	acheté	de bons oeufs.
		faire		acheter	

		en		là-bas	
10	Sophie va souvent	à	France? Oui, elle	là	va
		à la		y	

tous les ans.

		vers	
11	Henri est toujours	sur	la salle de bains; quand
		dans	

	sortir?
est-ce qu'il va en	entrer?
	sort?

	Avez		soir?
12	Voulez	-vous venir manger avec nous ce	après-midi?
	Aller		semaine?

2 Which of the expressions below:

1 can describe a person's character?
2 is a part of the body?
3 indicates direction?
4 indicates position?
5 indicates someone's origins?
6 is needed for your postcard?
7 will do the same job as *une allumette*?
8 is usually connected with young people?
9 implies it'll take time to get there?
10 might be on a cider label?

un briquet, piscénoise, loin, gentil, l'école, la poitrine, à côté, brut, un timbre, tout droit

3 When you get back home from holiday your French teacher wants to know all about it. Complete your side of the conversation.

Teacher Ah bonjour, quand est-ce que vous êtes revenue?
You *Tell her yesterday evening.*
Teacher Et c'était bien?
You *You all liked it a lot* (*use* on).
Teacher Et vous êtes allés où?
You *First you went to a village near Grenoble and then you spent four days in Paris.*
Teacher Et c'était comment?
You *Tell her it was very very good. And in Paris it was very hot.*
Teacher L'hôtel était confortable?
You *Yes. The owner was very nice and there was a garden. It was very pleasant.*

Teacher Et les enfants, ils ont été contents?
You *Yes, they saw lots of things, did lots of things ... One evening they played in the garden with the owner's dog.*
Teacher Il y avait beaucoup de monde?
You *There were too many tourists in Grenoble but not in the villages. And the countryside was very beautiful.*
Teacher Bravo! Vous parlez très bien le français maintenant.

4 You're in a shop looking for a present.

Vendeuse Bonjour, monsieur. Vous désirez?
You *Say you'd like a tee-shirt for your son.*
Vendeuse Très bien. Nous en avons des petits, des moyens et des grands. Quelle taille?
You *Medium, you think. He's ten years old. Ask her if you can see.*
Vendeuse Mais certainement. Voilà (*showing you a shirt*), c'est le petit.
You *That one is too small.*
Vendeuse Alors, voilà le moyen et le grand.
You *The big one is too big, you think. You'll take the medium one.*
Vendeuse Quelle couleur préférez-vous?
You *What colours have they got them in?*
Vendeuse Nous les avons en noir, jaune, rouge et vert et le moyen, nous l'avons aussi en blanc et en bleu.
You *The white one is pretty, yes, but you prefer the blue one.*
Vendeuse Alors, je crois que j'ai un seul tee-shirt en bleu et blanc. Comme ça vous avez les deux à la fois.
You *Very good. Ask if it's cotton.*
Vendeuse Mais oui, monsieur.
You *How much is it?*
Vendeuse Quarante-cinq francs, monsieur.
You *There's fifty francs.*
Vendeuse Et cinq francs! Merci, monsieur.

Documentaire

L'affaire du Larzac

The Larzac is a high, bleak plateau in the north of the Languedoc – it marks the start of the Massif Central. The traditional activity there is the production of sheep's milk for Roquefort, the famous local cheese. Farmers live mainly in isolated farmhouses; there are one or two small villages and the only town is La Cavalerie, which supports the military camp based there. The military have had a training ground in the Larzac for some years, but problems began when they wanted to extend it.

L'affaire du Larzac a commencé en 1972. Cette année-là, le gouvernement français a décidé d'agrandir le camp militaire de la Cavalerie, une petite ville au milieu du plateau. Le camp devait passer de trois mille à dix-sept mille hectares et devenir ainsi un immense champ de manoeuvres.

Cela faisait des années que le plateau se dépeuplait: les jeunes partaient tous chercher du travail en ville. Mais les habitants qui restaient dans la région s'opposaient à l'extension du camp militaire. Ils ont donc formé un comité pour la défense du Larzac, et ils ont commencé par signer un pacte où ils s'engageaient à ne pas vendre leurs terres à l'état.

Manifestation dans le Larzac

Très vite, l'affaire du Larzac est devenue un événement d'importance nationale; elle a captivé l'opinion publique française et même étrangère pendant plusieurs années. Léon Maillé a participé activement à l'organisation du comité. Il pense que 'le Larzac est devenu très célèbre parce que ce sont des paysans, des gens de la terre qui ont mené eux-mêmes une lutte et une lutte non-violente'. C'était une lutte non-violente mais la vie sur le terrain était mouvementée. Léon Maillé se souvient des grandes manifestations où il y avait cinquante mille ou cent mille personnes. Les écologistes, les antimilitaristes et tous ceux qui défendaient les droits de l'individu contre l'état arrivaient par milliers sur le plateau. Le gouvernement français a alors lancé un ordre d'expropriation pour obliger les paysans à lui vendre leurs terres et à quitter la région. La réaction a été immédiate: les défenseurs du Larzac ont bloqué les routes avec leurs troupeaux ou leurs tracteurs; ils ont saboté des manoeuvres militaires; ils ont marché sur Paris et ont fait du camping sous la Tour Eiffel avec leurs moutons.

Après huit années de résistance, les habitants du plateau ont fini par gagner. En mai 1980, la justice leur a donné raison en déclarant que l'ordre d'expropriation n'était pas valide. Un an plus tard, le gouvernement socialiste est arrivé au pouvoir et a définitivement abandonné le projet du Larzac.

Tous ces événements ont changé la vie du plateau. De jeunes militants qui étaient venus pour aider les habitants au moment des manifestations se sont installés dans des fermes et sont devenus des paysans. C'est le cas de Jean-Claude Roussel. Aujourd'hui il a cent quarante chèvres et une installation moderne dans sa ferme. Il fait et vend son fromage lui-même car il refuse de travailler pour les grandes fromageries de la région. Il pense que la lutte a permis aux paysans du Larzac de retrouver leur indépendance et il veut garder cette indépendance. Comme le dit Léon Maillé 'sur le plateau ici, la vie a été transformée . . . on ne travaille pas toujours dans le même esprit maintenant. Et la vie sociale aussi. Les gens maintenant se tutoient, s'appellent par leurs prénoms, les gens s'embrassent quand on arrive aux réunions. On fait partie d'une grande famille'.

devait passer	*was to be increased*
cela faisait des années que le plateau se dépeuplait	*for years the plateau had been becoming increasingly depopulated*
ils s'engageaient à ne pas vendre	*they resolved not to sell*
eux-mêmes	*themselves*
à lui vendre leurs terres	*to sell it their land*
tous ceux qui	*all those who*
ont fini par gagner	*ended up by winning*
leur a donné raison	*found in their favour*
est arrivé au pouvoir	*came to power*
qui étaient venus pour	*who had come to*

Les moutons du Larzac à Paris

Pronunciation guide

It is notoriously difficult to describe the sounds of one language in terms of another one. The same letter can represent different sounds in different languages. Sometimes a particular sound is very close but not exactly the same in two languages.

The following is intended as a brief guide to the sounds of French. It is no substitute for listening carefully to French speakers, trying to copy the sounds you hear, and asking them to correct your pronunciation.

When reading it, it is worth bearing in mind that:

– very often a single sound is conveyed by a variety of different spellings eg *maison* is pronounced the same as *maisons*, and *parlais*, *parlait* and *parlaient* all sound exactly the same
– accents can vary as much from one region to another as they can in Britain.
– no French word sounds exactly like an English one even if it looks exactly the same. This can mean that words familiar enough when written down may be completely unrecognisable when spoken.
– unlike English words, French words do not bear a heavy stress on one of their syllables. For instance, in the English word 'orange' the stress is quite clearly put on the first syllable. In the French word *orange* equal stress is given to both syllables.

Final consonants

Generally, if the last letter of a word is a consonant it is not pronounced (but see also *Liaisons* below)
grand petit restaurant Bardot Georges franc deux trop

This means that in the vast majority of cases the plural of nouns and adjectives sounds the same as the singular:
un livre deux livres
un restaurant italien deux restaurants italiens

Some exceptions: neuf (f pronounced) un oeuf (f pronounced)
many words ending -l normal total espagnol
many words ending -c Cognac Carnac sac truc
(but *not* tabac)

Other consonants

Many consonants have approximately the same sound as in English. There are, though, a number of variations and exceptions:

c pronounced as in English except for:
ci where this is 'sh' in English it remains 'si' in French
spécialement commercial

ç always like the 's' in 'sit'
garçon français

ch like English 'sh' in 'shop'
château chaud Charles

g Before -a -o-u or a consonant as in English 'good' or 'grand'
garçon golfe Grenoble
before -e or -i like 's' in English 'leisure' or 'measure'
rouge général Brigitte Georges manger

If the first of these two types of 'g' is required before 'e' or 'i', the vowel 'u' is added in writing
guerre naviguer (*but* navigation) Guillaume baguette

gn like the 'ny' sound in the middle of 'onion' or 'opinion'
montagne campagne oignon Avignon

h French people drop their 'h's. In many words it is completely ignored
l'hôtel l'homme
In some others it is sufficient only to cause a break between the words but the 'h' is still not pronounced:
la Hollande le haricot

j is like the 's' in 'measure' and 'leisure'
je Jacques Japon Beaujolais

qu just plain 'k' as in 'quiche' and not 'kw' as in the English 'quick'
qui question quatre musique

r this is pronounced at the back of the throat and not at the front of the mouth. Listen for examples in the programmes
Paris bière frère

s Generally the pronunciation is the same as in English
sud saucisse rose pause
Note however the 's' at the end of a word is not normally pronounced
français les cerises
When liaison occurs the 's' on the end of a word is pronounced (like 'z') and joins the following word
les enfants les grands hôtels

t normally similar to English 't' in 'toast', but in *-tion* . . . the 't' is pronounced 's' and not 'sh'
nation action station

th like 't' in 'total' or 'Thomas' and never like English 'th' in 'thin' or 'this'
thé théâtre thon théorie

w occurs very rarely in French. It is usually like the 'w' in 'water'
whisky week-end
but in some words it is pronounced like English 'v' in 'victory'
le wagon Wagner

Vowels

a is similar to the 'a' in 'cat' or 'bat' as pronounced in the north of England or like the 'u' in southern English 'butter'
bateau Paris café

e 1 often similar to the 'a' in 'above' or the first (and not the second)

'a' in 'attractive'
le petit melon
this sound can almost disappear in fast speech, so that le petit melon might sound like le p'tit m'lon
2 similar to 'e' in 'best' or 'bed'
merci extra veste mer
3 endings -er and -ez are normally pronounced as if they were -é (*parler* and *parlez* both sound the same as *parlé* – see below)
premier prenez nez St Tropez

è/ê as in 2 above
père mère bière honnête

é similar to è above but with the mouth rather more closed
café pâté thé Méditerranée vélo

i not like English 'i' in 'bit' or 'bite': closer to the 'i' in 'police'
ici Paris merci piscine

o 1 as in 'odd'
Ecosse olive Grenoble professeur
2 at the end of a word and with a circumflex accent (ô) the sound is slightly different
vélo auto hôtel allô

u a sound not found in English. First say 'oo', but then keeping the lips in that position try saying 'ee'
du sur Lucerne

eu like the vowel sounds in the words 'spur' or 'sir' in English
heure vapeur peu deux

NB *eu* (past participle of *avoir*) is pronounced as if it were a single 'u'

ou like the 'o' in English 'who' (never like 'loud')
où vous voulez mousse

oi like the 'wa' sound at the start of southern English 'one'
moi trois boîte poisson

au/eau as in type 2 of 'o' above
château beau autoroute originaux

Nasals

These are sounds that don't have exact equivalents in English, and the best thing is to listen to the pronunciation section of the cassettes or records and copy them.

in/im/ain to get a rough idea of the sound required, say southern English 'van' but at the last moment stop the top of your tongue from touching the roof of your mouth. The sound you make should be similar to French 'vin'.
Ain pain prochain train impossible insecte
NB The same applies to 'en' when preceded by an 'i'
chien bien rien

en/an as above, but this time practise with the word 'on' or 'don'
restaurant dans France entrée pense centre

on as for en/an above, but with a larger cavity inside your mouth
bonjour attention bon blond onze question

un most French speakers make no distinction between this and the 'in' nasal above
un aucun commun
NB When coming within a word and before a vowel, *un* is not nasalised – ie 'u' has the sound described in 'vowels' above, and the 'n' is fully pronounced
unique université commune une

NB When 'e's are added the pronunciation changes as follows
ine rather like English 'een'
fine piscine
aine/(i)enne rhyme approximately with English 'hen'
parisienne italienne toulousaine

Liaisons

This describes what happens when the final consonant of a word which is normally silent becomes pronounced because the next word starts with a vowel. There is a great deal of variation between one speaker and the next as to when to make and when not to make the liaison. But the following will be made by all French speakers

1 following the articles *les* and *des* and *aux*, the final 's' or 'x' is pronounced like a 'z'
les oranges des artichauts aux enfants les autres

2 between a pronoun subject and a verb
nous avons vous allez ils achètent elles ont acheté

3 after *très* and *plus* in front of an adjective or adverb
très intelligente plus intéressant très heureux

4 The 'n' in the article *un* is fully pronounced when the next word starts with a vowel
un homme un autre homme

5 In the plural between an adjective and a noun that follows
deux grands hôtels trois petits enfants les petits oiseaux

6 numbers
deux and *trois*. The final consonants are pronounced (as 'z') when a vowel sound starts the following noun or adjective
deux hommes trois amis trois autres amis vingt-trois heures
six and *dix*. These each have three pronunciations
1 when on their own as a number they rhyme with English 'fleece'
vous avez des enfants? Oui, j'en ai six
2 in front of a consonant the final 's' sound is lost and they sound more like 'see' and 'dee'
six femmes dix francs soixante-dix kilomètres
3 in front of a vowel, *six* and *dix* rhyme with 'fleas' or 'knees' (ie ending in 'z' sound)
six enfants dix heures soixante-dix ans

Grammar summary

Introduction

Grammar, in a sense, is not unlike a car user's manual. Just as a car manual explains the workings of transmission, brakes, gears, etc, so a grammar is a description of how the language 'works' and how all the bits function together.

You *can* be a good driver without having an intimate knowledge of the internal combustion engine (though not if you don't know which pedal is the brake) and the same applies to language.

But for those who would like to know what is going on 'under the bonnet' of the French language, here is a more systematic summary of the language appearing in 'A vous la France!'

It helps the understanding of French grammar if two basic principles are kept in mind: *gender* and *agreement*.

Gender: French nouns fall into two categories – masculine and feminine. These are reflected in the articles – ie the words for 'the' and 'a'. The gender of a noun also affects, through the agreement system, many other words associated with it.

Agreement: in English the agreement system is very limited, being confined mainly to verbs: 'eats' agrees with 'he/she/it/Peter/the cat', but not with 'we'; so we can say 'she eats' but we cannot correctly say 'we eats'. Similarly '*this* book', but '*these* books', '*that* man' but '*those* men'. In French this agreement system is much more widespread. For example:

1 verbs agree with subjects:
vous ouvr**ez** à quelle heure?
j'ouvr**e** à neuf heures
2 articles agree with nouns:
la brochure, **les** brochure**s**
3 adjectives agree with nouns in gender and number:
le grand hôtel, **la** grand**e** boîte
les grand**s** hôtel**s**, **les** grand**es** boîte**s**
4 pronouns agree with the noun they represent:
Sara **le** mange (le = **le** sandwich)
Sara **la** mange (la = **la** glace)
Sara **les** mange (les = **les** oranges)

In a lot of cases, making an agreement involves a change in the spelling of a word but not in its pronunciation (eg un *livre*, des *livres*).

Nouns

1 As a general rule, nouns of both genders add 's' when they are plural:
un hôtel, des hôtels
une voiture, des voitures

The main exceptions in this book are:

add 'x'	un bateau	des bateaux
	un château	des châteaux
	un canal	des canaux
no change	un prix	des prix
	un autobus	des autobus
	un croque-monsieur	des croque-monsieur
	un essuie-glace	des essuie-glace
complete change	un oeil	des yeux

Articles

2 Definite article

	masculine	feminine
singular	le	la
plural	les	

le café **la** banque
les cafés **les** banques
le and *la* followed by a word beginning with a vowel change to *l'*:
un oeuf, l'oeuf
une orange, l'orange

3 *le* and *les* preceded by *à* or *de* combine with them to give

à + | le = **au**
| les = **aux**

de + | le = **du**
| les = **des**

je vais **au** cinéma
une tarte **aux** fruits
la femme **du** boucher
le prix **des** oeufs
but
le mari **de la** boulangère
près **de l'**aéroport

4 Indefinite article

	masculine	feminine
singular	un	une
plural	des	

un café **une** banque
des cafés **des** banques

5 *Du, de la, de l', des* are also the equivalent of 'some' or 'any':

je voudrais	**du** lait **de la** crème **de l'**eau minérale **des** oeufs	I'd like *some*	milk cream mineral water eggs
avez-vous	**du** lait? **de la** crème? **de l'**eau minérale? **des** oeufs?	have you got *any*	milk? cream? mineral water? eggs?

6 After a negative, *du, de la, de l'* and *des* (= any) become *de* or *d'*:
I haven't got any milk, cream, etc

je n'ai pas	**de** lait **de** crème **d'**eau minérale **d'**oeufs

7 In some cases French uses a definite article where English doesn't:

1 referring to people and things in general:
Sara aime **les** enfants – Sara likes children
je déteste **le** football – I hate football
le champagne est très cher – champagne is very dear

2 often with names of countries:
la France est un beau pays
Londres est la capitale de **la** Grande Bretagne
je connais bien **la** Normandie

3 with the names of languages:
l'italien est une langue d'origine latine
les langues officielles de l'ONU sont l'anglais, **le** chinois, l'espagnol, **le** français et **le** russe
NB after *parler*, *le* is optional
Sophie parle (l')anglais à la maison et (le) français à l'école

8 In some cases, French uses *du, de la*, etc where English wouldn't normally have 'some' or 'any':
pour faire une quiche il faut du jambon, des oeufs, du sel et du poivre – to make a quiche you need ham, eggs, salt and pepper
vous avez des garçons ou des filles? – have you got boys or girls?

9 The indefinite article is *not* used in French for saying what someone's job is:
je suis boulangère
Sara est étudiante

10 There are a number of other cases where the French and English use of articles differ:

l'année dernière à Marienbad	last year in Marienbad
l'été prochain	next summer
fermé **le** lundi	closed on Mondays
la place du Parlement	Parliament Square
Monsieur **le** Président	Mr President
le Général De Gaulle	General De Gaulle

Demonstratives

11 The demonstrative = this/that/these/those

	masculine	feminine
singular	ce/cet*	cette
plural	ces	

*used with nouns beginning with a vowel or non-pronounced 'h'

ce magasin
cet hôtel
cette dame
ces enfants
Ce magasin, etc above mean either 'this shop' or 'that shop', etc. If it is felt to be necessary to make a distinction between 'this' and 'that', *-ci* or *-là* is added.

ce briquet-**ci** *this* lighter
ce briquet-**là** *that* lighter

Possessives

12 The words for 'my', 'your', 'his', 'her', etc are as follows:

	masc sing	fem sing	plural
my your (tu) his/her/its	mon ton son	ma* ta* sa*	mes tes ses
our your (vous) their	notre votre leur		nos vos leurs

* use *mon, ton, son* if the noun starts with a vowel, eg **mon** amie

ma mère est d'origine russe
le rugby est **mon** sport préféré
mes parents habitent le Berry

Adjectives

13 An adjective agrees in gender and number with the noun it describes.

1 In general with feminine nouns the adjective adds 'e':
un ticket gratuit **une** brochure gratuite
unless it ends in 'e' already:
un vase rouge une voiture rouge

2 Some adjectives double the final consonant in the feminine as well as adding the 'e':
italien italienne

moyen	moyenne
épais	épaisse
gros	grosse
bon	bonne

3 Some adjectives change in other ways in the feminine:

blanc	blanche
gazeux	gazeuse
premier	première
long	longue
beau	belle

4 In general in the plural 's' is added to both masculine and feminine:

des tickets gratuit**s**   **des** brochures gratuite**s**

unless the adjective ends in 's' already:

un hôtel français   des hôtels français

The exceptions are similar to those for nouns (see Para 1):

un accent régional   des accents régionau**x**

un beau château   deux beaux château**x**

14 A few adjectives have an extra form to go in front of masculine singular nouns that start with a vowel:

beau	**bel**
nouveau	**nouvel**
vieux	**vieil**

un beau château *but* un bel homme

un nouveau film *but* un nouvel appartement

15 Adjectives are usually placed after the noun:

la langue française

les vélos jaunes

A small number of common adjectives regularly go before the noun:

un grand hôtel	une petite quiche
un jeune homme	bonne journée!
le premier ministre	la deuxième rue à gauche

16 *Plus* in front of an adjective is equivalent to English 'bigger', 'smaller', 'more expensive', etc:

c'est **plus** grand	it's bigger
les fraises sont **plus** chères cette année	strawberries are dearer this year

'Than' is conveyed by *que*:

Bourg est plus petit que Grenoble

Moins is equivalent to 'not as big', etc:

Grenoble est moins grand que Paris

il fait moins froid aujourd'hui

17 'Biggest', 'most expensive', etc is conveyed as follows:

1 if the adjective follows the noun:

la ville la plus importante de la région

le jour le plus long

2 if the adjective comes first:
le plus grand marché de France
les plus beaux jours de l'été

Numbers

18 The words for the first sixteen numbers are:

un/une	one	neuf	nine
deux	two	dix	ten
trois	three	onze	eleven
quatre	four	douze	twelve
cinq	five	treize	thirteen
six	six	quatorze	fourteen
sept	seven	quinze	fifteen
huit	eight	seize	sixteen

The next three are compounds:

dix-sept	seventeen
dix-huit	eighteen
dix-neuf	nineteen

The words for twenty, thirty, etc, up to sixty are:

vingt	twenty	cinquante	fifty
trente	thirty	soixante	sixty
quarante	forty		

The numbers in between are expressed in the same way as the English ones:

vingt-deux	twenty-two
trente-six	thirty-six
quarante-cinq	forty-five

except for twenty-one, thirty-one, forty-one, which are vingt **et** un, trente **et** un, etc.

After *soixante-neuf* the numbers are compounds of previous ones:

soixante-dix	seventy	soixante et onze, soixante-douze, etc
quatre-vingts	eighty	quatre-vingt-un, quatre-vingt-deux, etc
quatre-vingt-dix	ninety	quatre-vingt-onze, quatre-vingt-douze, etc

NB In Belgium and Switzerland you may hear *septante* (seventy), *octante* (eighty), *nonante* (ninety).

After ninety-nine there are only four extra words:

cent	100	deux cents, trois cents, etc
mille	1,000	deux mille, trois mille, etc
un million	1,000,000	deux millions, etc
un milliard	1,000,000,000	deux milliards, etc

In between, the numbers are made up of existing ones in exactly the same way as in English except that there is no 'and':

245 deux cent quarante-cinq

2,450 deux mille quatre cent cinquante

Dates can be expressed in two ways:

1984 mille neuf cent quatre-vingt-quatre *or*
dix-neuf cent quatre-vingt-quatre

Notes

1 Any number ending *un* becomes *une* if the noun is feminine:
vingt et une maisons, mille et une nuits

2 101 is an exception it's *cent-un* or *cent-une* (without the *et*).

3 *Quatre-vingts, deux cents, cinq cents*, etc only end *-s* when they are round numbers. Otherwise it's:
quatre-vingt-dix
deux cent cinq
cinq cent quatre-vingt-deux

4 Millions and billions as round figures require *de*:
un million de dollars
cinq milliards de francs
but un million cinq cent mille livres sterling

19 Ordinal numbers (first, second, third, etc)
With one exception, *-ième* is added to the above numbers to give the ordinal ones:
deuxième, vingtième, soixante et onzième, etc
The exception is: *un/une – premier/première*
Where a number ends in 'e', this 'e' is omitted:
quatre – quatrième
With *neuf*, 'f' *becomes* 'v': *neuvième, quatre-vingt-neuvième*

20 Approximate numbers
-aine added to certain numbers makes them approximate:
une vingtaine de personnes about twenty people
des centaines et des centaines hundreds and hundreds
Une douzaine is exact when applied to 'eggs' and similar items.
Une quinzaine is frequently used in the expression *une quinzaine de jours* and means 'a fortnight'.
8, 10, 12, 15, 20, 30, 40, 50, 60 and 100 are the only numbers that can take *-aine*.
Un millier means 'about a thousand'.
These approximate numbers are all expressions of quantity just like *un kilo de . . .*:
une dizaine de pêches
des milliers de touristes

Pronouns

21 The forms are:

Subject	je	tu	il	elle	nous	vous	ils	elles
Direct object	me	te	le	la	nous	vous	les	les

NB *Je*, *me*, *te*, *la* and *le* lose their vowel when the following word starts with a vowel:
j'aime le camembert
je **t'**aime

22 *On* is a subject pronoun only, standing mainly for *nous*, but it can also mean 'you' or 'people' in the general sense:
excusez-nous, on est en retard (*we're* late)

au Maroc on parle français et arabe (*people* speak . . .)
on est prié de . . . (*you* are requested to . . .)

23 Position of pronouns

Unlike English, object pronouns come before the verb:

Sara **nous** attend à la gare	Sara is waiting for us at the station
il **m**'a présenté(e) à Pierre	he introduced me to Pierre
vous **le** préférez au rouge?	do you prefer it to the red?

In the negative, the *ne* . . . *pas* go round the whole group of pronoun + verb:

Sara **ne** nous attend **pas** à la gare

24 *Y* can replace whole phrases starting with *à*, *sur*, *derrière* and other expressions of position:

Sara attend son ami	à la gare dans sa chambre près de la banque derrière l'église chez Jean-Claude

can all become
Sara **y** attend son ami

Y is not limited to replacing phrases which indicate position:

je joue	au rugby au tennis	j'**y** joue depuis dix ans

25 *En* can replace whole phrases introduced by *de* or a number:

je voudrais *des oeufs*	j'**en** voudrais
je voudrais une douzaine *d'oeufs*	j'**en** voudrais une douzaine
je voudrais six *oeufs*	j'**en** voudrais six

In the same way:
combien **en** voulez-vous? (combien *de tomates* voulez-vous?)
j'**en** ai en laine et en soie (j'ai *des écharpes* en laine et en soie)
j'**en** ai parlé à Pierre (j'ai parlé *de mes vacances* à Pierre)

Demonstrative pronouns

26

	masculine	feminine
singular	celui	celle
plural	ceux	celles

These are combined with *-ci* to mean 'this one', 'these ones' or *-là* to mean 'that one', 'those ones':

j'aime bien	cet appartement cette jupe ces verres ces chaussures	mais je préfère	celui-ci/celui-là celle-ci/celle-là ceux-ci/ceux-là celles-ci/celles-là

Omission of nouns

27 Expressions like 'the big one', 'the red one', 'the little ones', 'the other ones' are conveyed in French by omitting the noun and leaving the

article and adjective, which must still agree:

tu aimes la robe rouge? oui, mais je préfère **la verte**!
les petites tomates coûtent moins cher que **les grosses**
si vous n'aimez pas ce pantalon, essayez **l'autre**

Verbs

The infinitive

28 This is the form in which verbs are listed in dictionaries, etc. There are three types, which are shown by their final letters:

1 **-er**: commenc**er**, travers**er**, etc. (This is the commonest type).
2 **-ir**: chois**ir**, fin**ir**, etc
-ir: serv**ir**, part**ir**, etc (see p315 for differences between *servir* and *choisir*)
3 **-re**: attend**re**, etc

The infinitive is used:

1 after *à, de, pour, sans*:
il commence à **jouer** au rugby
j'essaie de **parler** français
pour **faire** une omelette il faut des oeufs
2 after other verbs except *avoir* and *être*:
il faut **partir**
j'aime **jouer** au hockey
nous allons **manger** au restaurant
je voudrais **prendre** rendez-vous avec Monsieur Lecomte
vous pouvez me **donner** l'indicatif?

The past participle

29 The past participle is formed as follows:
-er verbs: **-é**
commencer – commenc**é**

-ir verbs: **-i**
choisir – chois**i**
partir – part**i**

-re verbs: **-u**
attendre – attend**u**

Verbs that do not follow the above pattern are given in the vocabulary list thus: mettre (*pp* mis).

30 The past participle is used:
1 as an adjective:
le magasin est **ouvert** jusqu'a midi
2 with *avoir* and *étre* to form the perfect tense:
j'ai **téléphoné** à Sophie hier soir
je suis **arrivé**(**e**) à Pézenas en 1980

When used with *être*, the past participle agrees just as if it were an adjective:

nous sommes arrivées à Pézenas en 1980 (all females)
nous sommes arrives à Pézenas en 1980 (mixed, or all males)

The present tense

31 The forms of the regular types of verbs (see para 28) are as follows:

parler type		*attendre* type	
je	parle	j'	attends
tu	parles	tu	attends
elle/il/on	parle	elle/il/on	attend
nous	parlons	nous	attendons
vous	parlez	vous	attendez
elles/ils	parlent	elles/ils	attendent

choisir type		*servir* type	
je	choisis	je	sers
tu	choisis	tu	sers
elle/il/on	choisit	elle/il/on	sert
nous	choisissons	nous	servons
vous	choisissez	vous	servez
elles/ils	choisissent	elles/ils	servent

NB Verbs ending *-ger* (like *manger, arranger, échanger*) need the addition of an *-e-* in the *nous* form to preserve the soft sound:

nous | mangeons
| arrangeons
| échangeons

This affects the form of the imperfect (see para 37).

32 The present tense is used to refer to something that is happening or is the case in the present:

ils habitent Pézenas
j'ai des tartes aux pommes

As in English, its use can cover:

1 what normally happens:
je travaille tous les jours de 8h à 5h   I work from 8 to 5 every day
2 the future
je pars demain matin   I'm leaving/I leave tomorrow morning

33 To talk about what has been happening for a period of time *and still is*, French uses the present tense where English uses a form of the past.

j'habite Paris depuis trois ans   I've been living in Paris for three years
j'habite Paris depuis Noël   I've been living in Paris since Christmas
je le connais depuis des années   I've known him for years

34 To give orders or make requests (eg wait!, listen!, come on!) the imperative is used. It has two forms, corresponding to *vous* and to *tu*.

For *vous* forms, simply use the *vous* part of the present tense (without *vous*):

écoutez!

attendez, s'il vous plaît!
donnez-moi un kilo de cerises

For *tu* forms, use the *tu* part of the present tense (but drop the final *-s* of the *parler* type only).
attends!
regarde cette robe!
choisis vite!

The perfect tense

35 The perfect tense is formed with the past participle (see para 29) preceded by the present of *avoir* or *être*, depending on the verb:

j'ai		je suis	
tu as		tu es	partie/parti
elle/il a	parlé	elle/il est	
nous avons		nous sommes	partis/parties
bvous avez		vous êtes	parti/partie/ partis/parties
elles/ils ont		elles/ils sont	parties/partis

NB 1 With verbs that form the perfect tense using *être*, the past participle agrees with the subject.
2 There are four possible forms to go with *vous* depending on whether *vous* stands for a singular or plural, masculine or feminine subject.

36 The perfect tense is used to indicate that something happened, or has happened, in the past and is now over.
Madame Trabut **a fait** une quiche
This means either 'Madame Trabut made a quiche' or 'Madame Trabut has made a quiche'.

The imperfect tense

37 To form the imperfect tense, all verbs, with only one exception, follow this rule:
take the *nous* form of the present tense, eg
avons prenons parlons choisissons
remove the *-ons* and add the imperfect endings, eg

je	parlais	j'	avais
tu	parlais	tu	avais
elle/il	parl**ait**	elle/il	av**ait**
nous	parl**ions**	nous	av**ions**
vous	parliez	vous	aviez
elles/ils	parl**aient**	elles/ils	av**aient**

The one exception is *être*: *j'étais, tu étais*, etc.

38 *Daniel jouait au rugby* could be translated into English as:
Daniel played rugby
Daniel was playing rugby
Daniel used to play rugby
according to circumstances. For the differences in use between the imperfect tense and the perfect tense, see p276.

Negative forms

39 The verb is made negative by placing *ne . . . pas* around it:

je **ne** suis **pas** de Lyon
nous **n'**avons **pas** de pain aujourd'hui
à cette époque nous **ne** sortions **pas** beaucoup le soir
ne parlez **pas** si fort!

In the case of the perfect tense, the *ne . . . pas* go around *avoir* or *être*:

je **n'**ai **pas** vu Pierre aujourd'hui
les enfants **ne** sont **pas** revenus avant minuit

40 Other negative words

ne . . . plus	not any more/no longer
ne . . . jamais	never
ne . . . personne	no-one
ne . . . rien	nothing
il ne joue plus au rugby	he doesn't play rugby any more
il ne joue jamais au rugby	he never plays rugby
il n'y avait personne au centre-ville	there was no-one in the town centre
je ne fais rien ce week-end	I'm doing nothing this weekend

Notice the position of *personne* in the perfect tense *after* the past participle:

je n'ai rien fait
je ne suis jamais allé au Maroc

but je n'ai vu personne

41 *Ne . . . que* is equivalent to English 'only':

Sophie **n'**a **qu'**un frère
il **n'**est **que** trois heures
Monsieur Delarue **ne** boit **que** de l'eau

Interrogative forms

42 To ask questions without an interrogative pronoun (ie who?, where?, how?, etc) there are three ways. These questions can normally be answered 'yes' or 'no'.

1 The words remain in the same order as if you were making a statement, but you use a 'questioning' intonation in your voice (rising at the end):

vous avez des sandwichs?
tu veux aller au cinéma?

2 Again leave the words in the same order but start the question with *est-ce que . . .*:

est-ce que vous avez des sandwichs?
est-ce que tu veux aller au cinéma?

3 Reverse the verb and pronoun and link them with a hyphen:

avez-vous des sandwichs?
veux-tu aller au cinéma?

NB If the *elle/il* form ends in a vowel, it is necessary to add a *-t-* to avoid two vowels coming together.

parle-t-elle français?
a-t-il mangé?
va-t-elle téléphoner demain?

43 If the subject is not a pronoun but a noun, make the question according to sections 1 and 2 of para 42.

Sylvie va venir?
est-ce que Sylvie va venir?

The equivalent of 3 is to keep the subject at the beginning and use verb + pronoun:

Sylvie va-t-elle venir?
Pierre a-t-il décidé d'apprendre l'anglais?

44 To form questions with an interrogative pronoun (why?, where?, when?, etc), there are three ways:

1 Leave the words of a statement in the same order but add the interrogative pronoun after the verb.

vous partez quand?
le car part d'où?
vous allez où en vacances cette année?

2 Add the pronoun to the front of an *est-ce que* question:

quand est-ce que vous partez?
d'où est-ce que le car part?
où est-ce que vous allez en vacances cette année?

3 Put the pronoun first and reverse the verb and subject:

quand partez-vous?
d'où part le car?
où allez-vous en vacances cette année?

NB In colloquial French it is common for people not to make the inversion after an interrogative pronoun.

comment tu vas?
d'où tu viens?
pourquoi tu ris?

'Reflexive' verbs

45 So-called 'reflexive' verbs have an extra pronoun:

je	**me**	promène
tu	**te**	promènes
elle/il/on	**se**	promène
nous	**nous**	promenons
vous	**vous**	promenez
elles/ils	**se**	promènent

These verbs always form the perfect tense with *être*:

je me suis promené(e)
nous nous sommes baigné(e)s
elles se sont couchées

Irregular verbs

46 The following eight verbs are constantly required in speech and writing and it is best to give them priority when learning irregular verbs.

aller	*avoir*	*devoir*	*être*
je vais	j'ai	je dois	je suis
tu vas	tu as	tu dois	tu es
elle/il va	elle/il a	elle/il doit	elle/il est
nous allons	nous avons	nous devons	nous sommes
vous allez	vous avez	vous devez	vous êtes
elles/ils vont	elles/ils ont	elles/ils doivent	elles/ils sont

faire	*pouvoir*	*venir*
je fais	je peux	je viens
tu fais	tu peux	tu viens
elle/il fait	elle/il peut	elle/il vient
nous faisons	nous pouvons	nous venons
vous faites	vous pouvez	vous venez
elles/ils font	elles/ils peuvent	elles/ils viennent

vouloir
je veux
tu veux
elle/il veut
nous voulons
vous voulez
elles/ils veulent
Like *venir*: *appartenir, devenir, prévenir, maintenir, revenir, tenir*

47 Here is a selection of other common irregular verbs appearing in this book:

boire	*croire*	*connaître*
je bois	je crois	je connais
tu bois	tu crois	tu connais
elle/il boit	elle/il croit	elle/il connaît
nous buvons	nous croyons	nous connaissons
vous buvez	vous croyez	vous connaissez
elles/ils boivent	elles/ils croient	elles/ils connaissent
dire	*prendre*	*savoir*
je dis	je prends	je sais
tu dis	tu prends	tu sais
elle/il dit	elle/il prend	elle/il sait
nous disons	nous prenons	nous savons
vous dites	vous prenez	vous savez
elles/ils disent	elles/ils prennent	elles/ils savent
suivre	*vivre*	
je suis	je vis	
tu suis	tu vis	
elle/il suit	elle/il vit	
nous suivons	nous vivons	
vous suivez	vous vivez	
elles/ils suivent	elles/ils vivent	

Like *croire*: *voir*, *revoir*
Like *prendre*: *apprendre*, *comprendre*

Key to exercises

Chapter 1

Quickies

1 1 deux panachés; une orange pressée; un express
2 bonjour; s'il vous plaît; merci

2 1 une baguette
2 Au revoir, madame.

3 1 Un crème, s'il vous plaît.
2 combien?

5 ananas; abricot; orange; pamplemousse; poire

6 1 une bière
2 pression; bouteille

7 1 un plan de Grenoble; une brochure
2 Vous avez . . .?

8 la carte; le plan

9 une carte de l'île

Rencontres

1 il y a

2 C'est bien.

Bon courage

1 un; une; une; un

2 le; la; les; l'; le; les

3 1 un crème, s'il vous plaît; un panaché, s'il vous plaît; un kir, s'il vous plaît
2 Vous avez un plan de Grenoble s'il vous plaît?; Vous avez un catalogue, s'il vous plaît?
3 un croissant; une carte

4 1 un crème
2 un plan
3 une baguette
4 une boulangère

5 1 une orange pressée, s'il vous plaît; un panaché, s'il vous plaît; une bière, s'il vous plaît; un express *or* un café, s'il vous plaît.
2 Je vous dois combien *or* combien je vous dois, s'il vous plaît?

6 Bonjour, mademoiselle.
Vous avez un plan de Grenoble, s'il vous plaît?
C'est combien?
Merci. Au revoir, mademoiselle.

7 Un crème, un café et deux croissants, s'il vous plaît.
C'est pour moi.
Merci beaucoup.

8 bière; bouteille; baguette; combien; beaucoup

9 pain; deux; franc(s); pour; non; brochure; merci; et; plan; panaché; express; le; la; de

Chapter 2

Quickies

1 1 Il y a un/une . . . près d'ici?
2 gauche
2 1 une boîte à lettres
2 droite
3 1 une pharmacie
2 gauche – left; droite – right
4 1 Pardon, madame.
2 in the square
5 1 three or four
2 ici; là
6 1 in the town
2 There's a food and drinks machine in the station.
7 Je vous remercie.
8 on the left
9 1 *Deux* means 'two'; *deuxième* means 'second'. *Quatre* means 'four'; *quatrième* means 'fourth'.
2 the second street on the left; the fourth street on the right
10 1 d'accord
2 *En face* means 'opposite'; *à côté* means 'next door'.
11 1 D 2 A 3 B
4 la première à droite
12 1 *Ici* means 'here'; *là* means 'there'.
2 à pied
3 *Tout droit* means 'straight on'; *à droite* means 'to/on the right'.

Rencontres

1 1 Vous êtes d'où?
2 Non. Je ne suis pas de Bourg.
4 1 Je ne suis pas français(e).
2 Je suis . . .

Bon courage

1 ici – here; en ville – in town; beaucoup – a lot; à pied – on foot; loin – far; gare – station; là – there; en voiture – by car
2 une église; un agent; une boîte à lettres
3 1 Pardon, monsieur. Il y a une banque près d'ici?
2 Où est le Café Hugo, s'il vous plaît?
3 Il y a une pharmacie près d'ici?
4 Où est le Musée Stendhal, s'il vous plaît? C'est loin?
5 Où est le téléphérique, s'il vous plaît? C'est combien?
6 Il y a une boîte à lettres près d'ici?
7 Où est l'Hôtel de France sur le plan s'il vous plaît?
4 1 le Café Hugo
2 l'hôtel

3 le Syndicat d'Initiative
4 la banque
5 la gare

5 Il y a un restaurant près d'ici?
Non, je suis à pied.
Merci.
Non, je suis gallois(e) et je suis de Pontypridd.
C'est près de Cardiff.
Oui, beaucoup.
Merci beaucoup, monsieur.

6
1 je suis française
2 je suis anglais
3 je suis français
4 je suis écossais
5 je suis anglaise
6 je suis allemand
7 je suis irlandais
8 je suis écossaise
9 je suis gallois
10 je suis française

7 bureau; pharmacie; droite, gauche

8 Horizontalement
1 du
2 agent
3 où
4 téléphérique
5 côté
6 là-bas

Verticalement
1 droite
2 gauche
3 suis
4 trois
5 place
6 église

Chapter 3

Quickies

1
1 C'est combien les oeufs?
2 douzaine

3
1 des pommes et des poires
2 It works out cheaper buying five kilos.

4 28 francs

5
1 It was a mixture.
2 C'est combien (la) pièce?
3 M'sieur-dame

6
1 She thought the price was per kilo; in fact it was per duck.
2 un canard

7
1 des cerises; des asperges; des pêches; un concombre
2 two

9
1 du beurre; des oeufs; du vin
2 Vous avez du lait?

10
1 one bottle
2 22 francs

Rencontres

1
1 trois filles; deux garçons

2 English has two r's; French has only one.

3
1 une maison; un appartement
2 to live in a detached house

Bon courage

1 des; du; de; d'; de la; de; du; de; de; des; des; des; des; de

2 épicerie: du fromage; de la crème; des oeufs; du beurre; du lait
café: un crème; un panaché; un sandwich; un kir; du lait; des croissants
marchand de fruits et légumes: des cerises; des bananes; des poireaux
boulangerie: des croissants; une baguette; une flûte

3 cinq; onze; treize; quinze
trente-huit; cinquante-cinq; soixante-trois
deux francs quarante-cinq; seize francs vingt-cinq;
quarante-quatre francs

4 quinze bouteilles de bière
dix bouteilles de vin rouge
trois kilos de pêches
deux plaquettes de beurre
du fromage – un morceau de gruyère
dix baguettes

5 un litre de lait/de vin rouge
une plaquette de beurre
une botte de poireaux
une bouteille de vin rouge/de lait
une livre de cerises/de poireaux/de beurre
une douzaine d'oeufs

6 Vous avez du lait; un cendrier; du pain; des pommes; du café; de la crème; de la limonade, s'il vous plaît?

7 Pardon, monsieur. C'est du fromage?
Je voudrais un fromage de chèvre et un litre de lait, s'il vous plaît.
Une plaquette de beurre, s'il vous plaît.
Oui, c'est tout, merci. Je vous dois combien?
Vous avez des pommes?
Un kilo, s'il vous plaît.
Je voudrais une livre de cerises.
Oui, ça va.
Oui, merci. C'est tout.
Voici/voilà quinze francs.
Au revoir.

8 Non./Je ne suis pas marié(e)/J'ai . . . garçon(s) et . . . fille(s). Vous avez des enfants?
Vous êtes d'où?
Je suis de . . .

9 du fromage; du lait; des croissants; des crêpes; du poisson; des frites; des bijoux
de la viande

Chapter 4

Quickies

1 1 sandwich fillings: jambon; saucisson; fromage
ice cream flavours: fraise; pistache

2 Un thé, s'il vous plaît.
3 Qu'est-ce que vous avez comme . . . ?

2 1 un litre
2 strawberry, chocolate, plain

3 deux timbres à deux francs et deux timbres à zéro franc cinquante

4 1 une carte postale; des timbres; des allumettes
2 la Suisse

5 1 behind the hotel
2 les bagages

6 1 yes
2 no

7 1 apple; apricot and pear; custard
2 11F50

8 1 country-style pâté or pâté in a pastry case
2 six chipolatas

Rencontres

1 1 the representative
2 fluently; a little; very little; not at all
3 l'anglais; le français; l'espagnol; l'italien

3 en vacances

Bon courage

1 au; au; à; à l'; à; à la; aux; à; au; aux

2 il; elle; elles; il; elles; ils; ils; elle

3 1 h; 2b; 3c; 4a *or* g *or* h; 5d; 6f *or* i; 7e; 8a *or* g *or* h; 9 i

4 une petite chambre; un hôtel italien; des glaces délicieuses; les sandwichs au saucisson; un vin italien; des cerises délicieuses/rouges; la petite tarte/la tarte à la crème; les tartes délicieuses/à la crème

5 des croissants; des cerises; une baguette
un panaché; un express; un citron pressé
une chèvre; une église
au canard; au thé

6 une petite boîte d'allumettes
quatre tranches de jambon
du lait; du vin; des pêches; du saucisson; du fromage; des tomates; de la crème; du beurre

7 trois citrons; deux timbres à 2F10; une tarte à 11F50; deux yaourts; six oeufs

8 parlez, bien; français; il, peu, couramment, parle, école; quel, métier; suis, vendeuse, grand; est; êtes, vacances, région, beaucoup; revoir; prie

9 Bonjour, monsieur. Un citron pressé et une bière, s'il vous plaît.
Qu'est-ce que vous avez comme glaces?
Une glace au chocolat et une à la fraise.
Il y a un petit hôtel près d'ici?
Une chambre avec un grand lit et une chambre à deux lits.
C'est pour trois nuits. Il y a une salle de bains?
Il y a un parking?
Merci beaucoup.

Chapter 5

Quickies

1 draught or bottled
2 les plus gros
3 1 ham, pâté, cheese and salami
2 sparkling mineral water
4 1 Un cornet au chocolat, s'il vous plaît.
2 single and double
5 1 un kilo des petites
2 fins; gros
6 1 a large one
2 four slices
3 Vous avez de la salade de carottes râpées?
7 1 Un verre de vin blanc, s'il vous plaît.
2 un verre comme ça
8 1 a slice for two people
2 trois francs zéro cinq
9 Il y a une boîte à lettres près d'ici?
10 1 in Place de Verdun
2 Où est le Musée de Peinture?
3 C'est à cinq minutes.
11 1 une petite tarte
2 pineapple, bilberries, apricots and pears
3 les tartelettes
12 1 Vous avez un plan de Nantes, s'il vous plaît?
2 the department stores
3 nothing – it was free
4 il – le Château des Ducs de Bretagne; ils – les grands magasins
13 Non, je suis de Saint-Malo.
14 yes
16 J'ai deux enfants. Je suis de Leeds.
17 Je ne suis pas français(e).
18 1 Qu'est-ce qu'il y a à voir?

Rencontres

1 1 *trés* means 'very'; *trop* means 'too (much/many)'
2 women only: patiente; intellectuelle
men only: grand; intelligent
either: honnête; calme

Bon courage Part 1

1 C'est combien, le plan de Bourg/les haricots verts/la tarte lette aux fraises/la plaquette de beurre?
a) le plan b) les haricots c) le beurre d) la tarte
2 1 C'est combien, un sandwich au jambon?
2 C'est combien, un sandwich au fromage?
3 C'est combien, la tarte aux pommes?
4 C'est combien, la tarte à la crème?
5 C'est combien, le yaourt à la fraise?
3 1 un kilo de grosses tomates

2 un petit poulet.
3 trois tranches de pâté, épaisses
4 un petit verre de vin
5 une grande (*or* grosse) boîte d'allumettes

4 deux timbres à un franc soixante; des pommes à huit francs trente; une bouteille de vin rouge à douze francs vingt; des tartelettes à trois francs

5 Vous avez:
1 des haricots verts?
2 de la bière?
3 du pâté de campagne?
4 des cerises?
5 du fromage de chèvre?

6 1 une glace à la fraise
2 un cornet à trois francs cinquante
3 un cornet double
4 un cornet au chocolat
5 une glace comme ceci

7 1 Il y a une banque près d'ici?
2 Il y a une pharmacie près d'ici?
3 Il y a une boulangerie près d'ici?
4 Il y a un bureau de tabac près d'ici?
5 Il y a une boîte à lettres près d'ici?

8 1 Où est la gare?
2 Où est l'Office du Tourisme (*or* le Syndicat d'Initiative)?
3 Où est le téléphérique?
4 Où sont les grands magasins?
5 Où est l'église St André?

9 1 Vous êtes français?
2 Vous parlez (l')anglais?
3 Vous êtes d'où?
4 Quel est votre métier?
5 Qu'est-ce qu'il y a à faire à Bourg?

10 1 Je suis de Newcastle.
2 Je suis gallois(e).
3 Je ne parle pas (l')italien.
4 J'ai trois enfants.
5 Je suis mariée à un Français.

11 du; une, de; de la; de, des; des, des, un, de, une, d', un

Part 2 Vingt questions

1 Syndicat d'Initiative
2 because it's at the mouth of the Loire
3 because otherwise you might be going straight on when you should be turning right
4 Je vous en prie. De rien.
5 nowhere – it's a cul-de-sac
6 Vin Délimité de Qualité Supérieure
7 un café-tabac
8 un poulet de Bresse
9 *le crème* is a white coffee; *la crème* is cream
10 a chopstick; a conductor's baton; a magic wand
11 the French Foreign Office

12 Le petit déjeuner est compris?
13 raw, cured ham
14 types of wine
15 un appartement
16 la quiche lorraine
17 NATO and UNO
18 1 un panaché
2 un thé au citron
3 un kir
19 je suis italien; allemand; brésilien; écossais; irlandais
20 un charcutier

Part 3

1 une chambre pour une personne avec salle de bains pour trois nuits; une chambre à deux lits avec salle de bains pour deux nuits; une chambre avec un grand lit pour quatre nuits, sans salle de bains; une chambre avec un grand lit et un petit lit avec salle de bains pour six nuits; une chambre avec un grand lit et une chambre à deux lits sans salle de bains pour cinq nuits.

2 Un verre de vin blanc, un grand crème, un citron pressé et une bière, s'il vous plaît.
Je vous dois combien? *or* Ça fait combien?
Vingt-six francs cinquante.

3 Pardon, monsieur. Vous êtes de Grenoble?
Non, je suis ici depuis cinq ans mais je viens de Suisse.
Et Grenoble vous plaît?
Oui, énormément. Il y a beaucoup de choses à faire et les Grenoblois sont sympathiques.
Quel est votre métier?
Je suis garçon de café mais je vais être étudiant.
Ici à l'Université de Grenoble?
Non, à Lyon.
C'est loin d'ici?
Pas trop. C'est à une centaine de kilomètres.

4 Bonjour, monsieur. Vous avez deux chambres pour deux personnes, une à deux lits, s'il vous plaît?
Quel est le prix de la chambre avec salle de bains?
Une chambre avec salle de bains, s'il vous plaît.
C'est ça.
Cinq nuits.
England.
Non, non. C'est England, comme le pays.
Il y a un bon restaurant près d'ici?
Où est la Place St Etienne?
C'est loin?
Merci, monsieur. Au revoir.

5 On the corner of the rue Victor Hugo.

Chapter 6

Quickies

1 1 le prochain car
2 un aller-retour pour Mens
2 1 morning
2 Le train est direct?
4 1 before midday
2 on the coach
5 1 le prochain train
2 after 9 pm

7 1 next week
2 Saturdays and Sundays

8 1 Il y a des cars pour aller à l'aéroport?
2 toutes les dix minutes

9 1 C'est bien le train pour Calais?
2 about 35 minutes

Bon courage

1 1 huit heures
2 onze heures et demie
3 onze heures moins le quart
4 cinq heures et quart
5 trois heures dix
6 sept heures moins vingt

2 1 avant douze heures trente; quatorze heures trente; dix heures quinze?
2 après dix-huit heures; vingt heures quinze; vingt et une heures trente?

3 aller; a; avez; part; arrivez; changez; prenez; arrive; a; arrive; devez

4 commencez; commençons, arrivent, travaillons, déjeunons, prenons, partent, prépare, termine

5 *Colette Marchal*
Q1 A: Je suis hôtesse au Syndicat d'Initiative.
Q2 A: Je travaille huit heures et demie par jour, tous les jours sauf le dimanche et le lundi
Q3 A: Je commence à 8h30.
Q4 A: Je termine à 17h.

Michel Dupont
Q1 A: Je suis épicier.
Q2 A: Je travaille dix heures par jour.
Q5 A: J'ai un mois par an.
Q6 A: En juin
Q7 A: Je vais au bord de la mer.

Yvonne Duglé
Q1 A: Je suis technicienne.
Q3 A: Je commence à huit heures.
Q4 A: Je termine entre cinq heures et demie et six heures du soir.
Q5 A: J'ai cinq semaines par an.
Q6 A: Je prends une semaine au printemps et le reste au mois de septembre.

6 Bonjour, madame. Il y a des trains pour (aller à) Monlac, s'il vous plaît?
Ils partent à quelle heure?
Le train de dix heures vingt-trois arrive à quelle heure?
C'est combien, l'aller-retour?
Il y a des cars?
Ils partent d'où?
C'est combien?
Bon, je voudrais un aller-retour.
Merci beaucoup. Au revoir, madame.

7 Bonjour, monsieur. C'est bien le car pour (aller à) Monlac?
Merci. Il y a un buffet dans la gare routière?
Merci. Au revoir, monsieur.

8
1 *départs* and *arrivées*
2 moins d'une heure
3 vingt-neuf minutes *or* une demi-heure
4 douze heures (*or* midi) vingt-six
5 treize heures trente-neuf
6 le train de six heures quarante-neuf et le train de dix heures quarante-quatre

9 *Patinoire* doesn't open on Sunday mornings; Restaurant du Stadium is closed all day Sunday; Musée de l'Armée is OK; Le Louis XIV is closed on Mondays; Pompidou Centre is closed all day Tuesday.

10 bus; cinq; aller; semaine; lundi; train(s); car(s); billet; un; mardi; rue; heure(s); au; en; le

Chapter 7

Quickies

1
1 un croque-monsieur
2 mineral water

2
1 a seafood pizza
2 Qu'est-ce que c'est, les fruits de mer?

3
1 Qu'est-ce que vous avez comme crêpes?
2 *doux* and *brut*

4
1 un pichet de rouge et une eau minérale gazeuse
2 the bill

5
1 On est un peu en retard.
2 Qu'est-ce que tu prends (*or* vous prenez)?

6
1 rare
2 the house wine

7
1 un kir; une assiette de crudités; un poulet au Beaujolais avec un gratin dauphinois; le plateau de fromages; un sorbet à la poire
2 une demi-bouteille de Beaujolais-Villages et une carafe d'eau
3 Je préfère un gratin dauphinois.

Rencontres

1 le steak-frites; le cassoulet; le couscous; le gratin dauphinois; les pommes de terre

2 désagréable

3
1 a) J'aime la cuisine française.
b) J'adore le steak-frites.
2 because a woman would have said *gourmande*

Bon courage

1 J'ai un faible pour les spaghettis à la bolognaise; le sorbet à la fraise.
Je n'aime pas du tout la choucroute; la salade de tomates.

2 J'adore le steak-frites; les hamburgers.
Je déteste le gratin dauphinois; le camembert.

3 1h; 2g; 3f; 4a; 5c; 6e; 7d; 8b

4 1a *or* e; 2f *or* i; 3f *or* h *or* i; 4f *or* i; 5b *or* g; 6d *or* j *or* l; 7c *or* k; 8c *or* k; 9f

5 1 J'adore les fromages et les desserts.
2 Le fast food, c'est le repas rapide.
3 J'aime énormément le cassoulet qu'on mange dans le Midi.
4 Vous n'aimez pas les hamburgers?

6 1 Enchanté, monsieur.
2 Un kir, s'il vous plaît.
3 Oui, fraise, vanille ou chocolat?
4 Je vous apporte ça tout de suite.

7 Vous faites à manger?
Qu'est-ce que vous avez?
Qu'est-ce que vous avez comme pizzas?
Qu'est-ce que c'est, la pizza quatre saisons?
Je voudrais une pizza sicilienne.
Madame préfère un croque-monsieur.
Une eau minérale pour moi et une bière pour Madame.

8 Oui, deux menus à cinquante francs, s'il vous plaît.
Tomato salad, duck pâté, egg mayonnaise, mixture of raw vegetables.
Un oeuf mayonnaise et un pâté de canard, s'il vous plaît.
Qu'est-ce que c'est, le boeuf à la provençale?
Non, je préfère le cassoulet.
Un steak.
Saignant, s'il vous plaît. Qu'est-ce que vous avez comme légumes?
Des frites, s'il vous plaît, et vous avez des haricots verts?
Un pichet de vin rouge.
Un grand pichet.
Merci.
Oui, merci.
Qu'est-ce que vous avez comme fromages?
Je voudrais du camembert, s'il vous plaît.
Une glace.
Une glace à la fraise et deux cafés. s'il vous plaît.
Oh, et l'addition, s'il vous plaît.
Merci beaucoup. C'est très gentil.

Chapter 8

Quickies

1 1 une semaine
2 tous les jours; toute l'année

3 1 cinq heures du matin
2 *toute la journée* means 'all day long'; *tous les jours* means 'every day'

4 1 Il coûte (or Il fait *or* Il est à) combien, celui-là?
2 It was the design on the lighter.

5 1 Elle coûte (or Elle fait *or* Elle est à) combien, celle-ci?
2 Je peux regarder, s'il vous plaît?
3 Je vais réfléchir.

6 1 earthenware; fairly simple
2 It's a bit too big

7 1 a cotton one
2 gris; bleu; vert; rouge; beige
3 38

Rencontres

1 1 Qu'est-ce que vous aimez faire le soir?
2 J'aime aller au cinéma.

Bon courage

1 j'aime: celui-ci (le vin); celle-ci (l'assiette); celles-ci (les tasses); celles-ci (les soucoupes); celles-ci (les pêches); celui-ci (le briquet)

2 je préfère: celles-là (les truites); celles-là (les bananes); celle-là (la confiture); celle-là (la rose); celle-là (la robe); celui-là (le restaurant)

3 1 le steak saignant
2 la robe beige
3 la liste des hôtels
4 le téléphérique
5 les crêpes
6 le musée
7 le vase

4 1 va 5 vais
2 vont 6 va
3 va 7 allons
4 vas 8 allez

5 George – un camembert
Caroline – un livre sur la Nouvelle Cuisine française
Kay – une bouteille de Beaujolais-Villages
Henry – un catalogue illustré du Musée de Peinture
Sandra – une 'Histoire du Cinéma Français'
Peter – une jolie tasse

6 Bien sûr, allez-y!
Je n'aime pas nettoyer la maison.
Je déteste le vin rosé.
Je déteste essayer des robes.
Je n'aime pas beaucoup aller au cinéma. Je préfère regarder la télé.
J'aime assez le pain français. J'aime beaucoup les sandwichs à la banane et j'adore les grosses moustaches.
J'adore manger dans les petits restaurants.
Oui, exactement!

7 Qu'est-ce que vous avez comme vases?
Il est trop grand.
Oui, il est joli. Il fait combien?
Celui-là est trop grand aussi.
Non, celui-là est beaucoup trop petit.
Ceux-là? Non, je ne les aime pas en gris. Vous les avez en bleu?
C'est ça. C'est combien, celui-là?
Bon. Je le prends.
Oui, merci.
Merci, madame. Au revoir.

8 Elle vous va très bien.
Je vais la prendre.
Celui-là est joli.
Je préfère aller au théâtre.

Chapter 9

Quickies

1 1 by bike
2 five minutes
3 l'Hôtel de Ville; la mairie

2 1 the fourth bridge across the Isère
2 right, then left at the first junction.

3 1 *Vous montez* means 'you go up'; *vous descendez* means 'you go down'.
2 Je ne suis pas d'ici.

4 1 the lights, the windscreen wipers and the horn
2 the choke

5 1 arm and back
2 three times a day: morning, afternoon and evening, or else before he came into contact with mosquitoes

6 1 shoulders
2 every morning and evening for several days

Rencontres

2 cycling, tennis and gymnastics
3 le ski; la danse; la natation
4 pas beaucoup; pas souvent

Bon courage

1 Pour aller: à la gare routière; au restaurant de la Chèvre Blanche; au Musée de la Préhistoire; à la Tour Eiffel; au Havre; aux Champs Elysées, s'il vous plaît
2 1d; 2c; 3a; 4e; 5f; 6b
3 Pour prendre le train il faut un billet.
Pour louer une voiture il faut un permis de conduire.
Pour faire un sandwich au jambon il faut du pain et du jambon.
Pour danser il faut de la musique.
Pour aller au Brésil il faut un passeport.
Pour jouer à la pétanque il faut des boules.
4 1 le Syndicat d'Initiative
2 le musée
3 la Maison de la Culture
4 le restaurant de la Chèvre Blanche
5 1 (NB There's sometimes more than one way to get there. We've given one possibility)
Vous allez à droite ici, vous prenez la première à gauche puis la deuxième à droite. Vous allez tout droit, vous traversez le canal et puis c'est sur votre droite.
2 Vous prenez la deuxième à gauche, puis la deuxième à droite.

Vous continuez tout droit et c'est là, sur votre droite.
3 Vous allez à droite ici, vous prenez la première à gauche. Vous continuez tout droit, vous traversez deux rues et c'est là, devant vous.
4 Je ne suis pas d'ici. Excusez-moi. Je ne sais pas.

6 1 ceinture
2 défense de . . . ; . . . interdit; interdiction de . . .
3 obligatoire
4 camion
5 vitesse
6 dépasser
7 stationnement

7 Il y a beaucoup de spectateurs.
Il y a le football et le cricket.
Oui, assez.
Oui, un peu, mais pas très souvent.
Non, en été. En hiver nous jouons (*or* on joue) au football.
J'ai plusieurs amis qui jouent au football tous les samedis; ma femme joue aux boules le dimanche après-midi et mon frère fait du vélo tous les soirs . . . et mon autre frère fait du jogging tous les matins à six heures. Moi, je préfère le tennis.
Non, mais j'aime regarder le sport à la télévision.
J'adore regarder la gymnastique et le snooker.
Eh bien . . . il y a une table verte, quinze petites boules rouges, une noire, une blanche, une jaune . . . C'est très compliqué . . .

Chapter 10

Quickies

1 tous les jours
2 sauf le dimanche
3 1 theatre
2 Est-ce qu'il faut réserver à l'avance?
4 1 midi trente-neuf
2 You have a connection at 7 o'clock in the evening.
5 1 in the afternoon
2 celui de dix-neuf heures
7 1 white, red and black
2 la jupe
8 1 un peu moins; un peu plus
2 Qu'est-ce que c'est?
3 le fromage
9 1 small, medium and large
2 roll of plaster
10 1 Qu'est-ce que vous avez à manger?
2 sandwiches, croque-monsieur and hotdogs

Rencontres

1 quelqu'un
2 Paris

Bon courage Part 1

1 Il est: une heure/une heure et demie/quatre heures moins le quart/six heures et quart/huit heurcs moins dix

2 1 celui-là
2 celui-ci
3 celles-là
4 la bleue
5 la petite

3 Vous l'avez:
1 en trente-huit?
2 en blanc?
3 en noir?
4 en gris?
5 en coton?

4 1f; 2e; 3a; 4c; 5g; 6h; 7b; les tasses

5 1 Un aller-retour, s'il vous plaît.
2 Le train part de quel quai?
3 Il y a des cars pour (aller à) Bourg?
4 C'est bien le car pour (aller à) l'aéroport?
5 Le car part à quelle heure?

6 1 J'adore le gratin dauphinois.
2 J'aime beaucoup les spaghettis.
3 J'aime assez les fruits de mer.
4 Je n'aime pas le steak saignant.
5 Je déteste les rillettes.

7 1 Il faut aller au marché le lundi.
2 Il faut traverser la place.
3 Il faut acheter des pansements.
4 Il faut arriver avant neuf heures du soir.
5 Il faut réserver à l'avance.
6 Il faut changer à Lyon.

8 lundi; mardi; mercredi; jeudi; vendredi; samedi; dimanche
janvier; février; mars; avril; mai; juin; juillet; août; septembre; octobre; novembre; décembre
le printemps; l'été; l'automne; l'hiver

9 1 J'aime lire.
2 Je préfère aller au théâtre.
3 Je n'aime pas jouer au football.
4 Je vais regarder la télévision.
5 Je ne vais pas acheter ce vélo.
6 Je ne vais pas jouer au snooker ce soir.

10 1 regarde
2 allons
3 vais
4 allons
5 est
6 sommes
7 fait
8 part
9 partent
10 avez
11 ai
12 faites

Part 2 Vingt questions

1 une tarte aux fraises.
2 They both mean 'a thingummyjig'.
3 It's their National Day, Bastille Day.

4 In a station. It means 'date-stamp your ticket'.
5 a special cake made for celebrations on Twelfth Night
6 une station de métro; une station de taxis; une station balnéaire; une station de ski; une station service
7 You've probably paid him – *la monnaie* is the change.
8 tourner
9 TGV
10 The waitress is someone she calls *tu* – a friend or relative.
11 *Un car* is a coach; *un bus* is a bus.
12 dry
13 le vase
14 la Maison de la Culture
15 none – it's extra
16 Societé Nationale des Chemins de Fer Français. It is the French railway company.
17 it's a rather special relationship
18 because they're traditionally put on graves
19 le jeu lyonnais
20 une piqûre

Part 3

1
1 de la bière allemande
2 des glaces italiennes
3 des oranges espagnoles
4 des pommes anglaises
5 du whisky écossais

2 tranche, beurre; mettez; fromage; jambon; tranche; four; minutes, mangez, délicieux
cuire; cassez, oeuf, poivrez, sel; tranche, ça; pliez, quatre, manger

3 1c; 2a; 3b

4
1 Je suis garçon de café.
Je commence à dix heures.
Je travaille huit heures par jour.
J'aime jouer au football.
2 Je suis hôtesse au Syndicat d'Initiative
Je commence à neuf heures.
Je travaille huit heures par jour.
J'aime faire du ski en hiver et jouer au tennis en été.
3 Je travaille dans le magasin de ma fille.
Je commence à dix heures moins le quart.
Je travaille cinq heures trois quarts par jour.
J'aime regarder la télé.

5 Bonjour, madame. Je voudrais des chaussures.
Trente-six, je pense (*or* je crois).
Celles-ci sont trop petites.
J'aime assez celles-ci, mais . . .
Oui, mais vous les avez en noir?
Je les aime beaucoup, je les prends.
Voilà.

6
1 Monday 9th November 1925
Tuesday 1st April 1873
Friday 28th September 1934

2 Richard Burton
Sergei Rachmaninov
Brigitte Bardot

Saturday 1st July 1961

la princesse Diana

7 1 fermer
2 unc semaine
3 un jour de fête
4 le cou
5 l'après-midi
6 une tasse
7 le train
8 monter
9 manger; manger
10 les frites
11 le cidre
12 regarder
13 noir
14 bleu
15 sel
16 prendre
17 le pont
18 souvent
19 l'addition
20 des poulets

Chapter 11

Quickies

1 1 It's too late (because the tide is coming in).
2 over a bridge
3 8 francs per vehicle

2 1 a double room with bathroom (and entrance-hall)
2 yes
3 by 9 o'clock

3 1 Nous sommes deux.
2 l'Accueil de France
3 140 francs

4 1 a pair of trousers and a shirt
2 demain matin
3 demain après-midi

5 1 opposite
2 because it's brand new
3 Le plein, s'il vous plaît.
4 Pas de problème.

6 1 prendre rendez-vous
2 l'indicatif
3 a few days

Bon courage

1 1d; 2h; 3a; 4e; 5b; 6g; 7f; 8c

2 1f; 2d; 3a; 4b; 5c; 6g; 7e

3 parler; aujourd'hui; peux; voulez; peut, voir; possible; va, matin; vous; à

4 1 Vous pouvez me faire un paquet-cadeau?
2 Vous pouvez regarder mes phares?
3 Vous pouvez nettoyer cette robe?
4 Vous pourriez me faire la monnaie de dix francs?
5 Vous pourriez me passer le sel?
6 Vous pourriez me donner l'indicatif pour la Grande Bretagne?

5 1 Je peux passer prendre mes photos demain?
2 Je peux prendre des photos?
3 Je peux téléphoner d'ici?
4 Je pourrais acheter un billet de car pour Châtillon?
5 Je pourrais regarder le briquet qui est là-bas à gauche?

6 Je pourrais avoir la recette de la galette?

6 1 On ne peut pas boire dans un pub anglais après onze heures du soir.

2 On ne peut pas faire une omelette sans casser d'oeufs.

3 En été, on ne peut pas faire de ski en Ecosse.

4 On ne peut pas acheter de timbres dans un (bureau de) tabac en Grande Bretagne.

7 Bonjour, monsieur.
Bonjour, monsieur. J'ai un petit problème avec ma voiture.
Ah oui? Qu'est-ce que c'est?
Les phares ne marchent pas.
C'est pas un petit problème, ça, c'est un gros problème.
Oui. Vous pourriez regarder?
Avec plaisir, monsieur, mais pas tout de suite.
Non? Quand alors?
Disons, dans une demi-heure.
Très bien. Je peux repasser plus tard.
Oui. A tout à l'heure, monsieur.

8 Bonjour, monsieur.
J'ai un petit problème avec mon appareil.
Je ne sais pas, mais il ne marche pas. Vous pouvez le regarder?
Voilà.
Vous pouvez le faire pour cet après-midi?
Vers quelle heure?
Vous fermez à quelle heure?
Très bien, je peux passer (*or* venir) le prendre vers six heures moins le quart.
Merci, monsieur. A tout à l'heure.

Chapter 12

Quickies

1 1 the seaside

2 wind-surfing

2 1 Sunday morning

2 three – Madame Renaudeau, her husband and her son

3 lovely

3 1 the 1914–18 War

2 British soldiers

5 1 Vous jouez au rugby depuis combien de temps?

2 Il y a sept ans que je joue au rugby.
Je joue au rugby depuis sept ans.

6 1 twenty to twenty-five

2 fifty or sixty

8 1 anyone who wants to – tourists, foreigners, people from La Rochelle

2 two francs per hour

3 yellow

Bon courage

1 J'ai demandé une glace. J'ai traversé le pont. J'ai choisi les crudités. J'ai dansé avec le Prince de Galles. Nous avons acheté un nouvel appartement. Nous avons regardé la télé pendant tout le week-end. Nous avons dîné avec des amis à la campagne. Nous avons loué un tandem.

2 mis – mettre; vu – voir; pris – prendre; bu – boire; ouvert – ouvrir; lu – lire; voulu – vouloir

3 avez fait; avez vu; avons vu; avez bu; ai bu, ont bu; a dansé; ai dansé

4 9, 6, 3, 8, 5, 4, 7, 10, 1, 2

5 Elle a déjeuné avec Charlotte.
Elle a porté la chemise au pressing.
Elle n'a pas téléphoné à Jacques.
Elle a réservé des places au théâtre.
Elle n'a pas fini l'article pour 'Le Monde'.
Elle a nettoyé la chambre.
Elle n'a pas réparé la petite lampe.
J'ai parlé des vacances avec Pierre.
J'ai rencontré Madame Vidal devant le pressing.
J'ai cassé une tasse.
J'ai pris le thé avec Edmée.
J'ai acheté une jolie petite robe et j'ai payé 450 francs.
J'ai dîné avec Guy.
J'ai vu un petit accident au centre-ville.
J'ai mis une heure à rentrer à cause de la circulation.

6 J'ai nagé pendant une demi-heure.
J'ai lu un journal . . .
. . . et j'ai acheté une glace au chocolat
Mon ami(e) a fait de la planche à voile.
Non, nous avons pique-niqué sur la plage.
Il a fait beau toute la journée.

7
1 week-end
2 passeport
3 rivière
4 plages (*or* routes)
5 pique-niquer (*or* manger)
6 village
7 monde

8
1 Je suis ici depuis deux semaines.
2 Il fait beau depuis mardi.
3 Les enfants sont sur la plage depuis le petit déjeuner.
4 George joue aux boules avec des amis français depuis deux heures.
5 Je les attends depuis une demi-heure.
6 J'ai décidé de sortir sans les enfants ce soir.
7 Je passe mes vacances ici depuis dix ans.
8 J'ai décidé de revenir ici l'année prochaine.

Chapter 13

Quickies

1 1 a fortnight
2 good
3 She stayed with her parents.
4 The children are too small

2 1 Lyon
2 in Togo
3 two years

3 1 for three or four generations
2 about a dozen

4 1 Brittany
2 wooden toys

5 1 Algeria
2 belle petite ville

6 le Midi – the south

Bon courage

1 mon; mes; ma; mon; ma; mon; mes; mon

2 ses; son; son; sa; sa; son; son; ses; ses

3 l'entrée – entrer; le choix – choisir; le jouet – jouer; rencontres – rencontrer; la sortie – sortir; la promenade – se promener; la fabrication – fabriquer; une occupation – s'occuper; une habitation – habiter

4 cette dame – ce monsieur; le père – la mère; mon mari – ma femme; l'épicière italienne – l'épicier italien; une ouvrière – un ouvrier; la vieille patronne – le vieux patron; une belle-soeur – un beau-frère; ma fille – mon fils; la petite amie de mon frère – le petit ami de ma soeur

5 1 est allée, en
2 est parti, au; est allée, en; est resté à
3 sont allés, à, en
4 ont passé, à, sur, sont parties, en
5 sont allés, aux
6 est allé, au; a pris, en, a passé, dans le; sont allés, en
7 a passé, à, au
8 sont allés, dans
9 est parti, au
10 ai acheté, ai décidé, en, à

6 Je suis descendu(e) prendre le petit déjeuner à 8h45.
Je suis sorti(e) à 9h45.
Je suis allé(e) au Musée de Peinture.
J'y suis resté(e) jusqu'à 11h30.
Je suis allé(e) dans un café et j'ai pris une bière.
Puis je suis allé(e) à la banque.
J'y suis arrivé(e) vers une heure.
Je suis retourné(e) (or rentré(e)) à l'hôtel quinze minutes plus tard.

7 Non. J'y suis allée avec une amie.
Non. J'ai pris la voiture. Je suis allée chez mon amie à six heures du matin, nous avons pris un café ensemble, puis nous somme parties à sept heures et nous sommes arrivées au port deux heures plus tard.

Oui, mais nous sommes allées de Folkestone à Boulogne.
Une heure trois quarts.
Eh bien, quand nous sommes arrivées nous avons trouvé un bon petit restaurant et nous y avons mangé.
Oui. Mon amie a pris un steak-frites . . .
. . . et moi, j'ai pris des fruits de mer.
Je ne sais pas leur nom en français. En anglais, c'est 'prawns'.
Non, prawns. Ils sont petits et roses et ils ont des trucs très longs devant.
Des crevettes! C'est un crevette ou une crevette?
Les restaurants français ne sont pas très chers. Nous avons pris un dessert et deux cafés. Et nous avons bu une bouteille de vin blanc. Et nous n'avons payé que quatre-vingt-dix francs. Pour deux personnes!
Si. Nous sommes allées au supermarché.
Non. Il est à dix minutes de Boulogne en voiture. Il est à la campagne. Et il est énorme.
Bien sûr.

Chapter 14

Quickies

1 1 on the bank of the river Loire
2 salt, wine, cloth and paper
3 Spain, Holland, Scandinavia, the Far East, India

2 1 the eighteenth century
2 sugar
3 cotton, precious wood

3 1 à la fin de; au milieu de; malgré
2 big houses

4 1 horses
2 in September

5 1 les gens
2 Your *nom* is your surname and your *prénom* is your first name.

Bon courage

1 le courrier – la lettre; le vin – la vigne; le papier – le bois; le bateau – la mer; jeune – vieux; le jeu – les boules; le nord – l'ouest; travailler – se reposer; chaud – froid; le prénom – le nom

2 1 malade, le médecin
2 riche; bateaux
3 Madame, quitte, tous
4 en, perdez, chose, aller
5 droite, Château, Ducs
6 aimais, Voyage, monde
Tout est bien qui finit bien.

3 travaillaient; y avait; étaient; faisait, commençait; continuait; allait; s'occupait; cultivait; allait

4 1 Ils regardaient la télé.
2 C'était un film d'horreur.
3 Ils sont allés voir le Gros Jules.
4 non

5 parce qu'il avait mal à la tête
6 Non, il est rentré chez lui vendredi matin.
7 sa petite amie
8 Ils sont allés au Café de l'Univers.
9 Ils ont vu le Petit Gaston.
10 jusqu'à dix heures et demie
11 Ils sont allés voir le Gros Jules.
12 Il buvait avec des amis et il jouait aux dominos.
13 Non, il est parti vers dix heures.

All of them told different stories

5 Je sortais du grand magasin 'Les Anciennes Galeries'.
Il était exactement deux heures dix. Je sais parce que j'ai regardé ma montre.
Devant moi il y avait une femme. Elle allait traverser la rue. Un jeune homme est arrivé. Il est passé derrière la dame et a pris son sac.
Il était grand, il portait un pantalon noir et une chemise verte.
Il a traversé la rue et est monté dans une voiture rouge. Il y avait une femme au volant.
Dans la direction de l'autoroute.

7 Eh bien, c'était un vendredi après-midi et c'était plein de Français. Ils achetaient pour le week-end. Et il y avait un car plein d'Anglais. Ils achetaient des douzaines et des douzaines de bouteilles de bière. Et beaucoup de vin aussi.
Au mois d'août?
C'est ça.
Mon amie a acheté beaucoup de fromage, du café (parce que c'est moins cher en France) et du chocolat suisse. Et six bouteilles de vin.
Un saucisson, du fromage, du vin . . . beaucoup de choses. C'était très agréable. Les Français achetaient beaucoup de viande et de fruits de mer . . . et de crevettes.
Non, 'prawns'.
Nous avons regardé les pantalons, mais ils étaient très chers. Et il était cinq heures et le bateau partait à six heures.
Nous sommes allées à la voiture. Les Anglais chantaient dans le car. Et nous sommes retournées au port, mais il y avait beaucoup de circulation. Nous sommes arrivées à Boulogne à six heures moins le quart.
Heureusement, oui. Mais le car anglais est arrivé trop tard.
La mer était très calme. Et nous avons vu un film.
Eh bien, il y avait un cinéma sur le bateau.
Non. Nous sommes arrivées à Folkestone à sept heures – il y a une différence d'une heure entre la Grande Bretagne et la France – et nous avons décidé d'acheter du poisson et des frites.
Oui, c'est le plat national britannique. Et nous étions au bord de la mer, après tout.
Nous avons mangé dans la voiture. Et nous sommes arrivées à la maison à onze heures. Mon amie a pris la voiture, et moi, j'étais au lit avant minuit.

Chapter 15

Quickies

1
1 ce pantalon
2 à ce soir

2
1 three years ago
2 She liked it so much.
3 J'y suis restée.

3
1 le sud
2 au douzième siècle

5
1 young people
2 la chanson occitane
3 il y a vingt ans

6
1 wool, silk, cashmere
2 la grise
3 celle-ci

7
1 fishing, tourism, some industries
2 the two towers – the Tour Saint-Nicolas and the Tour de la Chaîne
3 a few days or a week

8
1 winter and summer
2 They go out in the morning and come back in the afternoon.
3 C'est très agréable.

9
1 souvenirs, postcards, stamps, perfumes
2 juillet et août
3 9.30 am till 7.30 pm
4 wind and fog

10
1 two
2 une fiche horaire
3 un aller-retour

Bon courage Part 1

1
1 J'ai acheté une chemise grise.
2 J'ai demandé l'addition.
3 J'ai perdu le plan.
4 J'ai joué aux boules avec mes amis français.
5 J'ai pique-niqué sur la plage

2
1 Henri est allé au bord de la mer.
2 Henri a fait de la planche à voile.
3 Henri a lu 'Le Monde'
4 Henri a bu du whisky.
5 Henri a pris cinq apéritifs.

3
1 Sara est allée à Nantes hier.
2 Patrick est arrivé vers midi hier.
3 Daniel et Michel sont partis après le déjeuner hier.
4 Paulette est venue à quatre heures hier.
5 Nous sommes sorti(e)s avec Marie-Pierre hier.

4 Quand j'avais neuf ou dix ans:
1 j'allais à l'école à bicyclette
2 je passais mes vacances à la campagne
3 je mangeais un steak-frites tous les samedis

4 je buvais beaucoup de limonade
5 je n'aimais pas du tout le vin!

5 1 a On peut louer un vélo à La Rochelle?
b On peut aller dans l'île maintenant?
2 a Je peux voir la chambre?
b Je peux essayer ce pantalon?
3 a Je pourrais téléphoner en Grande Bretagne?
b Je pourrais avoir un verre d'eau?

6 1a Vous pouvez ouvrir la porte, s'il vous plaît?
b Vous pouvez me passer le sel?
c Vous pouvez me donner deux kilos de pêches?
2a Vous pourriez regarder mes pneus?
b Vous pourriez nettoyer cette jupe?
c Vous pourriez réserver une chambre pour deux (personnes) pour samedi soir?

7 1 Il y en a pour longtemps?
2 Vous en avez pour longtemps?
3 J'en ai pour une demi-heure.

8 1 Ma fille a dix ans.
2 Mon fils a six ans.
3 Mon mari a trente-cinq ans.
4 Il a trente-cinq ans depuis cinq ans maintenant.
5 Mon grand-père a cent six ans.

9 En Angleterre
1 il fait doux
2 il fait chaud
3 il fait beau
4 il ne fait jamais très froid

Part 2 Vingt questions

1 a woman from Arles
2 les bras
3 bed and breakfast
4 *La tour* is 'the tower'. *Le tour* means 'the turn' or 'the tour'
5 He's going fishing.
6 dialling code; radio call-sign; indicative (grammar)
7 printemps
8 un pâté de sable
9 On the telephone – it means 'Who's speaking?'
10 une bicyclette *or* un vélo
11 five written endings and three pronunciations
12 at the *Gois* leading to Noirmoutier at high tide
13 She is from La Rochelle.
14 le port – the port you drink is *le porto*
15 hot water (eau chaude)
16 languages
17 circulation
18 *La marée* (the tide) can be high or low twice a day. *La mer* (the sea) can be calm or rough. La *mairie*(the town hall) is for getting married in, and *le mari* (the husband) is married already.
19 The climate is healthy and the person was born there. It is a woman.
20 Molière

Part 3

1
1 sommes, au
2 au, à la
3 cette, celle-ci
4 aller
5 pris; ils
6 grande, lait
7 est, vas
8 étais, faisait
9 faire, acheter
10 en; y
11 dans, sortir
12 voulez, soir

2
1 gentil
2 la poitrine
3 tout droit
4 à côté
5 piscénoise
6 un timbre
7 un briquet
8 l'école
9 loin
10 brut

3 Hier soir
On a tous beaucoup aimé.
D'abord nous sommes allés dans un village près de Grenoble et puis nous avons passé quatre jours à Paris.
C'était très, très bien. Et à Paris il faisait très chaud.
Oui. Le propriétaire (*or* le patron) était très gentil et il y avait un jardin. C'était très agréable.
Oui, ils ont vu beaucoup de choses, ils ont fait beaucoup de choses . . .
Un soir ils ont joué dans le jardin avec le chien du patron.
Il y avait trop de touristes à Grenoble mais pas dans les villages. Et la campagne était très belle.

4 Je voudrais un tee-shirt pour mon fils.
Moyen, je pense. Il a dix ans. Je peux voir?
Celui-là est trop petit.
Le grand est trop grand, je pense (*or* je crois). Je prends le moyen.
Vous les avez en quelle couleur?
Le blanc est joli, oui, mais je préfère le bleu.
Très bien. C'est du coton?
Il fait combien; *or* Il coûte combien?
Voilà cinquante francs.

Vocabulary

Notes

Adjectives are listed in their masculine singular form. If the feminine is different and formed other than by adding an *-e*, this is shown as follows: vieux (*f* vieille). If the plural is formed other than by adding an *-s*, this is shown thus: beau (*pl* beaux). Adjectives ending *-s* or *-x* do not have a separate plural form in the masculine.

Adjectives of nationality and origin (eg *anglais*, *grenoblois*) are listed only with small first letters. The same words starting with a capital letter indicate that the word is a noun standing for a person from that place (eg le Français *Frenchman*).

Adverbs closely resembling the adjective from which they are formed (eg automatique *automatic*, automatiquement *automatically*) are not included.

Verbs with an asterisk form the perfect tense with *être*.

Verbs which do not form their past participles like *réserver – réservé*, *choisir – choisi*, *attendre – attendu* are shown thus: vouloir (*pp* voulu).
The present tense of the most common irregular verbs is given on p319. These are shown thus: † vouloir.

In this list the words are given the meanings that fit their use in this book. In most cases they will also have other meanings.

A

à *at; to; in*
abolir *to abolish*
l'abolition *(f)* *abolition*
abord: d'abord *first of all*
absolu *absolute*
l'accent *(m)* *accent*
l'accident *(m)* *accident*
accord: d'accord *agreed, OK*
acheter *to buy*
acquis *acquired*
l'acteur *(m)* *actor*
l'activité *(f)* *activity*
actuel (*f* actuelle) *present*
actuellement *at present*
l'actualité *(f)* *present events*
l'addition *(f)* *bill*
adorable *delightful*
adorer *to love*
l'adresse *(f)* *address*
s'adresser à *to apply to*
l'aéroport *(m)* *airport*
l'Afrique *(f)* *Africa*
l'âge *(m)* *age* quel âge a-t-il? *how old is he?*
âgé *aged; old*
l'agent (de police) *(m)* *policeman*
agit: il s'agit de *it consists of*
l'agneau *(m)* *lamb*
agréable *pleasant*
ailleurs *elsewhere* d'ailleurs *besides*
aimer *to like; to love*
l'air *(m)* *air* avoir l'air *to look, seem*
ainsi *thereby, so*

l'Algérie *(f)* *Algeria*
allemand *German*
†*aller *to go* l'aller (simple) *(m)* *single ticket* l'aller-retour *(m)* *return ticket*
l'allumette *(f)* *match*
alors *then, so*
l'ambiance *(f)* *atmosphere*
l'âme *(f)* *soul*
*s'améliorer *to improve*
l'Amérique *(f)* *America*
l'ami(e) *(m/f)* *friend*
amoureux (*f* amoureuse) *in love*
l'an *(m)* *year*
l'ananas *(m)* *pineapple*
ancien (*f* ancienne) *old, former*
l'ancienneté *(f)* *seniority*
anglais *English*
angoissé *anxious*
l'animation *(f)* *movement*
l'année *(f)* *year*
annexé *annexed*
l'annexion *(f)* *annexation*
annuel (*f* annuelle) *annual*
l'anti-vol *(m)* *anti-theft lock*
antillais *French West Indian*
août *August*
l'apéritif *(m)* *aperitive*
l'apogée *(m)* *peak*
l'appareil *(m)* *machine, device* 'Pierre à l'appareil' *'Pierre speaking' (on telephone)*
l'appartement *(m)* *flat*
appartenir (à) (*pp* appartenu) *to belong (to)*
appeler *to call*
*s'appeler *to be called*
l'appétit *(m)* *appetite* 'bon appétit!' *'enjoy your meal!'*
appliquer *to apply*
apporter *to bring*
apprécier *to appreciate, think highly of*
†apprendre (*pp* appris) *to learn*
l'apprenti *(m)* *apprentice*
l'apprentissage *(m)* *apprenticeship*
appuyer sur *to press*
après *after* d'après *according to*
après-demain *the day after tomorrow*
l'après-midi *(m or f)* *afternoon*
l'architecte *(m or f)* *architect*
l'architecture *(f)* *architecture*
l'argent *(m)* *money; silver*
arranger *to set right*
l'arrière-pays *(m)* *interior (of a country)*
l'arrivée *(f)* *arrival*
*arriver (à) *to arrive; to manage (to)*
l'artichaut *(m)* *artichoke*
l'artisan *(m)* *craftsman*
l'asperge *(f)* *asparagus*
asseyez-vous *sit down*
assez *enough; quite* en avoir assez *to have had enough*
l'assiette *(f)* *plate*
assister (à) *to be present (at)*
l'association *(f)* *association*
l'astronaute *(m/f)* *astronaut*
l'attaché culturel *(m)* *cultural attaché*
attaquer *to attack*
attendre *to wait (for)*
attiré *attracted*
l'attrait *(m)* *attraction*
aucun *no (adj)*
aujourd'hui *today*
aussi *also; therefore, so*
autant (que) *as much (as)*
automatique *automatic*
l'automne *(m)* *autumn*
autre *other* entre autres *among other things* autrement *otherwise; differently* autre chose *something else*
avance: à l'avance *in advance*
avant *before*
avantageux (*f* avantageuse) *advantageous*
avec *with*
l'avenue *(f)* *avenue*
l'avion *(m)* *aeroplane*
†avoir (*pp* eu) *to have*

B

bafouiller *to get tongue-tied*
les bagages *(m)* *luggage*
la baguette *loaf*
*se baigner *to swim, bathe (in the sea)*
le bain *bath* la salle de bains *bathroom*
le balbutiement *hesitation*
balnéaire: la station balnéaire *seaside resort*
la banane *banana*
la banlieue *suburb*
la banque *bank*
bas (*f* basse) *low*
le bar-tabac *bar with tobacconist's shop*
la batterie *battery*
le bateau (*pl* bateaux) *boat*
beau (*f* belle, *pl* beaux) *beautiful, fine*
beaucoup *much, many; a lot*
le beau-frère *brother-in-law*
beige *beige*
la belle-soeur *sister-in-law*
besoin: avoir besoin de *to need*
le beurre *butter*
la bicyclette *bicycle*
bien *well* merci bien *thank you very much* c'est bien *that's fine/good/nice*
bientôt *soon*
la bière *beer*
le bijou (*pl* bijoux) *jewel*
la bijouterie *jeweller's shop*
le billet *ticket; banknote*
la bise *kiss (on the cheek)*
le bisouilleur *someone fond of kissing (made-up word)*
blanc (*f* blanche) *white*
bleu *blue*
blond *blond, fair-haired*
†boire (*pp* bu) *to drink*
le bois *wood*
la boisson *drink*

la boîte *box; tin* la boîte à lettres *letter-box*
bolognais *from Bologna* à la bolognaise *bolognese*
bon (*f* bonne) *good*
bonjour *good morning/afternoon*
le bord *edge* au bord de la mer *at/to the seaside*
bordelais *from Bordeaux*
la botte *bunch*
la bouche *mouth*
la boucherie *butcher's shop*
le boulanger *baker*
la boulangère *baker (f); baker's wife*
la boulangerie *baker's shop*
les boules *(f)* *(game of) bowls*
le bout *end* au bout de *at the end of*
la bouteille *bottle*
le bras *arm*
brésilien (*f* brésilienne) *Brazilian*
breton (*f* bretonne) *from Brittany, Breton*
le briquet *cigarette lighter*
britannique *British*
la brochure *brochure*
le brouillard *fog*
brun *brown*
brut *dry (of cider, champagne)*
la bûche *log*
le buffet *buffet*
le bureau de tabac *tobacconist's*

C

ça (*short for* cela) *that* c'est ça *that's it* ça va *alright, OK*
le cabinet de toilette *screened-off washing facilities*
le cachemire *cashmere*
le café *café; coffee* le café-tabac *café and tobacconist's combined*
calme *quiet*
le camembert *camembert cheese*
le camion *lorry*
la campagne *countryside*
la capitale *capital city*
le canal (*pl* canaux) *canal*
le canard *duck*
le cantal *Cantal cheese*
le capot *bonnet (of car)*
la câpre *caper*
capturer *to capture*
car *for, since*
le car *coach*
la carafe *carafe*
la carotte *carrot*
carré *square*
la carte *map; card* la carte postale *postcard*
le cas *case* dans ce cas *in that case*
casser *to break*
le cassoulet *cassoulet*
ce (*f* cette, *pl* ces) *this; that*
ceci *this*
la ceinture de sécurité *safety belt*
cela *that*
célèbre *famous*
le cendrier *ashtray*
la cerise *cherry*
certain *certain*
la chambre *bedroom; hotel room*
le champignon *mushroom*
le championnat *championship*
la chance *luck*
changer *to change*
chanter *to sing*
chaque *each, every*
la charcuterie *delicatessen; pork butcher's*
le charcutier *man who works in charcuterie*
charger (de) *to load (with)*
le château (*pl* châteaux) *castle; country house*
chaud *hot, warm*
chauffer *to heat*
la chemise *shirt*
cher (*f* chère) *dear*
chercher *to look for*
le cheval (*pl* chevaux) *horse*
les cheveux *(m)* *hair*
la chèvre *goat*
chez Paul *at Paul's place/house/shop, etc*
le chien *dog*
chinois *Chinese*
la chipolata *chipolata*
le chocolat *chocolate*
choisir *to choose*
le choix *choice*
la chose *thing*
la choucroute *sauerkraut*
le cidre *cider*
le cinéma *cinema*
la circulation *traffic*
circuler *to move*
le citron *lemon*
la civilisation *civilisation*
clandestin *clandestine*
la clé (*or* la clef) *key*
la clientèle *customers*
le climat *climate*
le club *club*
le code *dipped headlight*
le coeur *heart*
le coin *corner* le coin du feu *fireside* du coin *local*
le col *mountain pass*
le collectionneur *collector*
le colon *settler (in colony)*
coloré *coloured*
combien (?) *how much/many (?)*
la commande *switch*
comme *as, like*
commencer (à) *to begin (to)*
comment *how*
le commerce *business, trade*
commercial (*pl* commerciaux) *commercial*
la compagnie *company*
compliqué *complicated*
composter *to date-stamp (a ticket)*
†comprendre (*pp* compris) *to understand*
service compris *service charge included*

compter *to count*
le comté *Comté cheese*
la conception *conception; idea*
le concombre *cucumber*
la condition *condition*
le conducteur *driver*
la confiture *jam*
confortable *comfortable*
le congé *holiday, time off*
†connaître (*pp* connu) *to know*
conseiller *to advise*
le conservateur *curator*
considérer *to consider*
construit *constructed, built*
le contact *ignition*
contemporain *contemporary*
content *happy*
le continent *mainland; continent*
continu *continuous*
continuer *to continue*
contre *against*
le copain (*f* copine) *friend*
le coq *cockerel*
la coque *cockle*
le cornet *cornet*
correct *correct*
la correspondance *connection*
la côte *coast; rib, chop*
le côté *side* à côté de *beside* du côté de *around, in the direction of*
le coton *cotton*
le cou *neck*
*se coucher *to go to bed*
la couleur *colour*
le couloir *corridor*
le coup de soleil *sunburn*
coupe: à la coupe *cut to your requirements*
couper *to cut*
couramment *fluently*
le courrier *post*
la courroie *fan-belt*
le cours *course* au cours de *in the course of, during*
le couscous *couscous*
coûter *to cost*
la coutume *custom*
couvert (de) *covered (in)*
créer *to create*
la crème *cream*
le crème *white coffee*
la crêpe *pancake*
la crêperie *pancake restaurant*
la crépine *sausage skin*
crevé *punctured*
la crevette *shrimp, prawn*
le crocodile *crocodile*
†croire (*pp* cru) *to believe, think*
le croissant *croissant*
la croissanterie *croissant shop*
le croque-madame (*pl* croque-madame) *same as* croque-monsieur *plus a fried egg*
le croque-monsieur (*pl* croque-monsieur) *toasted cheese and ham sandwich*
cru *raw*
les crudités (*f*) *raw vegetables*
cuire (*pp* cuit) *to cook*
la cuisine *kitchen; cooking*
la culture *culture*
culturel (*f* culturelle) *cultural*
curatif (*f* curative) *curative*
le cycle *cycle*

D

la dame *lady*
le danger *danger*
dans *in*
la danse *dance; dancing*
danser *to dance*
dauphinois *from the Dauphiné* le gratin dauphinois *potatoes in cream*
davantage *more*
de *of; from*
*se débrouiller *to manage, get by*
le début *beginning*
débuter *to begin*
décembre *December*
décider (de) *to decide (to)*
le déclin *decline*
décoré *decorated*
découvrir (*pp* découvert) *to discover*
dedans *inside*
défendre *to forbid* défense de . . . *. . . is forbidden*
défiler *to parade*
le dehors *outside, exterior* en dehors de *outside*
déjà *already*
déjeuner *to have lunch*
le déjeuner *lunch* le petit déjeuner *breakfast*
le délassement *relaxation*
délicieux (*f* délicieuse) *delicious*
demain *tomorrow*
demander *to ask (for)*
le démarrage *starting (of car)*
démarrer *to start (of car)*
la demeure *dwelling*
demi *half* demi-écrémé *semi-skimmed* demi-sel *slightly salted*
le départ *departure*
le département *administrative region (see p 23)*
dépasser *to overrun (time); to overtake*
dépendre (de) *to depend (on)*
depuis *since, for*
dernier (*f* dernière) *last*
derrière *behind*
dès que *as soon as*
désagréable *unpleasant*
*descendre *to go down*
désirer *to want*
le dessert *sweet, dessert*
le dessin *design, pattern*
dessus *on top*
détester *to hate*
devant *in front of*
développer *to develop*

†*devenir (*pp* devenu) *to become*
†devoir (*pp* dû) *to have to; to owe* je vous dois combien? *how much do I owe you?* vous devez changer *you must change* ils doivent connaître *they're bound to know*
le dialecte *dialect*
différent *different*
difficile *difficult*
dimanche *(m) Sunday*
dîner *to have dinner*
le dîner *dinner*
†dire (*pp* dit) *to say*
direct *direct*
la direction *direction*
diriger *to direct*
disposition: (mettre) à la disposition de *(to put) at the disposal of*
*se distraire (*pp* distrait) *to enjoy oneself*
le distributeur *machine (eg for coffee, tickets)*
divers *various*
la division *division*
donc *then, therefore*
donner *to give*
le dos *back*
double *double*
la douche *shower*
doux (*f* douce) *sweet (of wine); mild; soft*
la douzaine *dozen*
droit: tout droit *straight on*
la droite *right*
drôle *funny*
dur *hard*

E

l'eau *(f)* (*pl* eaux) *water*
échanger *to exchange*
l'écharpe *(f) scarf*
l'éclairage *(m) lighting, lights*
l'école *(f) school*
économique *economic*
écossais *Scottish*
écouter *to listen (to)*
écraser *to crush*
l'écureuil *(m) squirrel*
l'éditeur *(m) publisher*
effectivement *in fact*
l'effet *(m) effect* en effet *indeed; as a matter of fact*
également *also, as well*
l'église *(f) church*
l'éléphant *(m) elephant*
élevé: bien élevé *well-mannered*
l'élite *(f) elite*
embrasser *to embrace; to kiss*
emprunter *to borrow*
en *in; to; of it/them*
encore *still, yet; again*
l'enfant *(m/f) child*
enfin *in short; after all; at last*
enseigner *to teach*
ensemble *together*
ensoleillé *sunny*
l'ensoleillement *(m) sun (shine)*
ensuite *then, next*
entendre *to hear* entendu *understood* bien entendu *of course*
entier (*f* entière) *whole, entire*
entre *between*
l'entrée *(f) entrance; first course*
*entrer *to go in/come in*
enveloppé *wrapped*
envers *towards*
environ *about, roughly*
environnant *surrounding*
l'épagneul (*m*) *spaniel*
épais (*f* épaisse) *thick*
l'épaule *(f) shoulder*
l'épidémie *(f) epidemic*
les épinards *(m) spinach*
l'éponge *(f) sponge*
l'époque *(f) period, time*
l'équipe *(f) team*
l'esclavage *(m) slavery*
l'esclave *(m/f) slave*
l'Espagne *(f) Spain*
espagnol *Spanish*
l'espoir *(m) hope*
essayer *to try (on)*
essentiel (*f* essentielle) *essential*
l'essuie-glace *(m)* (*pl* essuie-glace) *windscreen wiper*
estimer *to consider*
l'estomac *(m) stomach*
et *and*
et cetera *et cetera*
l'été *(m) summer*
*s'étendre *to spread*
l'étoffe *cloth*
étranger (*f* étrangère) *foreign* à l'étranger *abroad*
†être (*pp* été) *to be*
étroit *narrow*
les études *(f) studies*
l'étudiant(e) *(m/f) student*
étudier *to study*
eux-mêmes *themselves*
exact *exact*
excessivement *too, excessively*
excuser *to excuse*
*s'excuser *to apologise*
l'exemple *(m) example* par exemple *for example*
exister *to exist*
expliquer *to explain*
exposé *exposed*
l'express *(m) black coffee*
exprimer *to express*
extrême *extreme* l'Extrême-Orient *(m) the Far East*

F

la fabrication *manufacture*
fabriqué *manufactured*
la façade *front*

face: en face de *opposite*
facile *easy*
faciliter *to facilitate*
la façon *way, manner*
la facture *bill*
faible *weak* avoir un faible (pour) *to have a weakness (for)*
†faire (*pp* fait) *to make, do* il fait beau *it (the weather) is fine*
le fait *fact* en fait *in fact* tout à fait *completely*
familier (*f* familière) *familiar; to do with the family*
la famille *family*
la fanfare *brass band*
fatalement *inevitably*
faut: il faut *I/you/we etc have to, need*
favorable *favourable*
favoriser *to favour*
la femme *wife; woman*
fermer *to close*
la fermeture *closing, closure*
férié: le jour férié *public holiday*
la fête *fête, festival* le jour de fête *public holiday*
la fiche *leaflet* la fiche horaire *timetable*
la figure *face*
le filet *fillet*
la fille *girl; daughter*
la fin *end*
fin *fine; small*
final *final*
la flûte *type of loaf*
le foie *liver*
la fois *time* à la fois *at the same time*
folklorique *traditional*
fond: au fond de *at the end/bottom of; on the far side of*
le foot(ball) *football*
les forces (*f*) *forces*
la forêt *forest, wood*
former *to form*
fort *strong; loud*
le four *oven*
frais (*f* fraîche) *fresh*
la fraise *strawberry*
franc (*f* franche) *frank*
le franc *franc*
français *French*
le frère *brother*
la friterie *chip shop/stall*
les frites (*f*) *chips*
froid *cold*
le fromage *cheese*
le fromager *cheese seller; cheese maker*
la fromagerie *place where cheese is made*
le fruit *fruit* les fruits de mer *sea-food*
fruité *tangy; fruity*

G

la galette *buckwheat pancake; cake*
la galettière *pan for* galette
gallois *Welsh*
le garçon *boy; son; waiter*
la gare *(railway) station*
garni *served with vegetables*
la gauche *left*
gazeux (*f* gazeuse) *fizzy*
le gemmologiste *gem expert*
général (*pl* généraux) *general*
la génération *generation*
les gens (*m*) *people*
gentil (*f* gentille) *nice; kind*
la glace *ice; ice cream; car window*
le glaçon *ice cube*
global (*pl* globaux) *global*
le golfe *gulf*
la gorge *throat*
gourmand *greedy; fond of food*
grand *big*
la grandeur *size; greatness*
gratin: au gratin *cooked till browned on top*
gratuit *free*
grave *serious* c'est pas grave *it doesn't matter*
grenoblois *from Grenoble*
grillé *grilled; toasted*
gris *grey*
gros (*f* grosse) *big; fat*
le groupe *group*
le gruyère *Gruyère*
guérir *to cure*
la guerre *war*
le guichet *ticket office*
la Guinée *Guinea*
la gymnastique *gymnastics*

H

l'habitant(e) *(m/f)* *inhabitant*
l'habitation *dwelling*
habiter *to live in*
l'habitude *(f)* *custom* d'habitude *generally*
le hamburger *hamburger*
le hameau (*pl* hameaux) *small village*
le hareng *herring*
le haricot *bean* les haricots blancs *haricot beans*
haut *high*
hebdomadaire *weekly*
hélas *alas*
l'herbe *(f)* *herb; grass*
hésiter *to hesitate*
l'heure *(f)* *hour; time* (à) quelle heure? *(at) what time?* (à) huit heures *(at) eight o'clock*
heureux (*f* heureuse) *happy*
l'histoire *(f)* *history; story*
historique *historic*
l'hiver *(m)* *winter*
hollandais *Dutch*
la Hollande *Holland*
l'homme *(m)* *man*
honnête *honest*
l'horaire *(m)* *timetable*

les hors d'oeuvre *(m)* *hors d'oeuvre, starter (of meal)*
l'hostilité *(f)* *hostility*
le hot dog *hotdog*
l'hôtel *(m)* *hotel*

I

ici *here* par ici *this way*
idéal (*pl* idéaux) *ideal*
l'idée *(f)* *idea*
identique *identical*
il y a *there is/are; ago*
illustré *made known*
impeccable *perfect*
l'importance *(f)* *importance*
important *important; big*
n'importe qui *anyone*
importé *imported*
l'impression *(f)* *impression*
inciter (à) *to encourage (to)*
inclus *included*
l'inconvénient *(m)* *drawback*
l'Inde *(f)* *India*
les Indes *(f)* *the Indies*
l'indicatif *(m)* *dialling code*
indiquer *to indicate* mal indiqué *badly signposted*
indispensable *indispensable*
individuel (*f* individuelle) *individual*
l'industrie *(f)* *industry*
initier *to start off, initiate*
l'insecte *(m)* *insect*
*s'installer *to settle down*
l'instant *(m)* *instant*
intellectuel (*f* intellectuelle) *intellectual*
intelligent *intelligent*
interdiction de ... *... is forbidden*
interdit de ... *... is forbidden*
*s'intéresser (à) *to be interested (in)*
l'intérêt *(m)* *interest*
l'intérieur *(m)* *inside*
intermittent *intermittent*
l'intime *(m/f)* *close friend, relative*
l'invité(e) *(m/f)* *guest*
l'Italie *(f)* *Italy*
italien (*f* italienne) *Italian*

J

jamais *ever; never* ne ... jamais *never*
la jambe *leg*
le jambon *ham*
le jardin *garden*
jaune *yellow*
jetable *disposable*
le jeu (*pl* jeux) *game*
jeudi *(m)* *Thursday*
jeune *young*
joli *pretty*
la jonction *junction*
jouer *to play*
le jouet *toy*
le jour *day*
la journée *day (long)*
juillet *July*
juin *June*
junior *junior*
la jupe *skirt*
le jus *juice*
jusqu'à *until, up to, as far as*
juste *right, correct; tight (of time)*
justement *that's so; exactly*

K

le kilo *kilo*
le kir *white wine with blackcurrant liqueur*
le klaxon *car horn*

L

là *there*
là-bas *over there; down there*
la laine *wool*
laisser *to let, allow*
le lait *milk*
la laiterie *dairy*
la langue *language; tongue*
le légume *vegetable*
lequel? (*f* laquelle?) *which one?*
la lettre *letter*
leur *their*
le lever du jour *sunrise*
la liberté *freedom*
le libraire *bookseller*
libre *free*
limiter *to limit*
la limonade *lemonade*
lire (*pp* lu) *to read*
la liste *list*
le lit *bed*
le litre *litre*
la littérature *literature*
la livre *pound; 500 grams*
le livre *book*
local (*pl* locaux) *local*
la location *hire*
loin (de) *distant, far (from)*
long (*f* longue) *long* le long de *along*
longer *to go along*
longtemps *a long time*
lorsque *when*
la luge *toboggan*
lundi *(m)* *Monday*
la lutte *struggle*
lyonnais *from Lyon*

M

macéré *marinated*
madame *(f)* (*pl* mesdames) *madam; Mrs*
mademoiselle *(f)* (*pl* mesdemoiselles) *Miss*
le magasin *shop* le grand magasin *department store*
le Maghreb *Arabic-speaking North Africa*

la main *hand*
maintenant *now*
maintenir (*pp* maintenu) *to maintain*
la mairie *town hall*
mais *but*
la maison *house*
mal *badly* pas mal *good-looking* pas mal de *quite a few* avoir du mal (à) *to have trouble (in)* j'ai mal au bras *my arm hurts*
malade *ill*
malgré *in spite of*
la maman *mum*
manger *to eat*
manifester *to show*
manuel (*f* manuelle) *manual*
maraîcher: le jardin maraîcher *market garden*
la marche *walking*
le marché *market*
marcher *to walk; to work (of mechanical things)*
la marée *tide*
mardi *(m)* *Tuesday*
le mari *husband*
le mariage *marriage*
*se marier *to get married*
le Maroc *Morocco*
marquer *to mark; to affect*
mars *March*
le matin *morning*
la matinée *morning; theatre matinee*
le maximum *maximum*
le mécanisation *mechanisation*
la Méditerranée *Mediterranean*
meilleur *better; best*
mélangé *mixed*
même *same; even; self* quand même/tout de même *nevertheless, all the same, even so*
la mer *sea* les fruits *(m)* de mer *sea-food*
merci *thank you*
mercredi *(m)* *Wednesday*
le message *message*
le métier *job*
le mètre *metre*
mettre (*pp* mis) *to put* mettre en route *to start up* mettre trois jours *to take three days*
le meuble *piece of furniture*
la miche *loaf of bread*
midi *midday*
le Midi *south of France*
le milieu *middle* au milieu de *in the middle of*
militaire *military*
le militaire *soldier*
le millier *thousand (approximately)*
minéral (*pl* minéraux) *mineral*
la minute *minute*
mis à part *except*
la mode *fashion* à la mode *fashionable*
le modèle *model*
moi *I; me*
le moine *monk*
moins *less, minus* du moins *at least*
le mois *month*
la moitié *half*
le moment *moment*
mon (*f* ma, *pl* mes) *my*
le monde *world; people* tout le monde *everybody*
la monnaie *money; change*
monsieur *(m)* (*pl* messieurs) *sir; Mr*
la montagne *mountain*
*monter *to go up/come up*
monter *to take up*
montrer *to show*
le monument *monument, historic building*
le morceau (*pl* morceaux) *piece*
le mot *word*
le moteur *motor, engine*
le motif *design*
la moule *mussel*
le moule *mould, shape*
*mourir (*pp* mort) *to die*
la mousse *mousse*
le moustique *mosquito*
le mouton *sheep; mutton*
le mouvement *movement*
moyen (*f* moyenne) *average*
municipal (*pl* municipaux) *municipal*
le Munster *Munster cheese*
le musée *museum*
la myrtille *bilberry*

N

nantais *from Nantes*
la natation *swimming*
national (*pl* nationaux) *national*
la nationalité *nationality*
nature *plain flavour*
naturel (*f* naturelle) *natural*
navigable *navigable*
le navire *ship*
ne . . . ni . . . ni *neither . . . nor . . . nor*
(ne . . .) pas *not*
né *born* je suis né(e) *I was born*
le négociant *trader*
négocier *to do business, negotiate*
le nerf *nerve* être sur les nerfs *to be on edge*
nettoyer *to clean*
neuf (*f* neuve) *brand new*
le nez *nose*
le niveau (*pl* niveaux) *level, standard*
noir *black*
le nom *name*
nombreux (*f* nombreuse) *numerous*
non *no; not*
le nord *north*
normal (*pl* normaux) *normal*
la note *bill; note*
notre (*pl* nos) *our*
nouveau (*f* nouvelle, *pl* nouveaux) *new* de/à nouveau *again*
novembre *November*
la nuit *night*
le numéro *number*

O

obligatoire *compulsory*
oc: la langue d'oc *language of Languedoc*
occitan *from* Occitanie *(see p 285)*
*s'occuper de *to look after, take care of*
octobre *October*
l'oeuf *(m)* *egg*
l'oeil *(m)* *(pl* yeux) *eye*
office: l'Office *(f)* du Tourisme *Tourist Office*
officiel *(f* officielle) *official*
offrir *(pp* offert) *to offer* c'est pour offrir? *is it a present for someone?*
l'oie *(f)* *goose*
l'oignon *(m)* *onion*
oïl: la langue d'oïl *language of Oïl (see p 294)*
l'olive *(f)* *olive*
l'omelette *(f)* *omelette*
l'opération *(f)* *operation*
l'opérette *(f)* *operetta*
l'orange *(f)* *orange*
ordinaire *ordinary*
l'oreille *(f)* *ear*
l'organisation *(f)* *organisation*
organiser *to organise*
l'Orient *(m)* *the East* l'Extrême-Orient *the Far East*
*s'orienter vers *to head for*
originaire de *originally from*
original *(pl* originaux) *original*
l'origine *(f)* *origin* à l'origine *originally*
osé *slightly naughty, daring*
ou *or*
où *where*
l'ouest *(m)* *west*
oui *yes*
ouvert *open*
l'ouverture *(f)* *opening*
l'ouvrier *(f* ouvrière) *worker*
ouvrir *(pp* ouvert) *to open*

P

la pacotille *trinkets*
le pain *bread*
le pamplemousse *grapefruit*
panaché *mixed*
le panaché *shandy*
le panneau *(pl* panneaux) *sign* le panneau des départs *departures board*
le pansement *bandage*
le pantalon *trousers*
le papier *paper*
le paquet *packet, parcel*
paquet-cadeau: faire un paquet-cadeau *to gift-wrap something*
par *by* par exemple *for example* par ici *this way* par là-bas *over that way*
le paradoxe *paradox*
parce que *because*
pardon *excuse me*
le parent *parent; relative*
parfait *perfect*
parfois *sometimes*
le parfum *perfume, flavour*
la parfumerie *perfumes (goods)*
le parking *car park*
parler *to speak*
parmi *among*
part: à part *except; separate*
la/le partenaire *partner*
particulier *(f* particulière) *particular*
le particulier *private person*
la partie *part; game* faire partie de *to be a member of*
*partir *to depart* à partir de *(starting) from*
partout *everywhere*
passage: de passage *passing through*
la/le passant(e) *passer-by*
le passé *past*
le passeport *passport*
passer *to pass; to spend (time)* passer un film *to put on a film*
*passer *to pass by, to call in*
*se passer *to happen*
le pastis *pastis (aniseed-based spirit)*
la pâte *pastry; dough*
le pâté *paté* le pâté de sable *sand-castle*
patient *patient*
patienter *to wait (a moment)*
la pâtisserie *cake shop*
le patron *owner*
la patronne *owner; owner's wife*
le pays *country; area, district*
la pêche *peach; fishing*
peine: cela vaut la peine *it's worth it*
la peinture *painting*
pendant *during, for*
penser *to think*
perdre *to lose*
la période *period*
le permis de conduire *driving licence*
la personne *person*
(ne ...) personne *nobody*
personnel *(f* personnelle) *personal*
la pétanque *game of bowls (see p 190)*
petit *small* petit à petit *little by little* le petit ami *boyfriend* le petit déjeuner *breakfast*
peu *little; few* un peu (de) *a little* à peu près *roughly, about*
le peuple *people*
peut-être *perhaps*
le phare *headlight*
la pharmacie *chemist's shop*
le physique *physical appearance*
le pichet *jug*
la pièce *room; coin* dix francs pièce *10F each*
le pied *foot* à pied *on foot*
la pierre *stone*
piéton *(f* piétonne) *pedestrian*
le pique-nique *picnic*
pique-niquer *to have a picnic*
la piqûre *injection; bite, sting*
piscénois *from Pézenas*
la pistache *pistachio nut*

la pizza *pizza*
la pizzéria *pizzeria*
la place *public square; job; space, vacancy*
placé *placed*
la plage *beach*
plaire (à) (*pp* plu) *to please* s'il vous plaît *please* ça me plaît *I like it*
la plaisance *pleasure*
le plan *street map; plan*
la planche à voile *windsurfing*
la plantation *plantation*
la plaquette de beurre *packet of butter*
le plat *dish* le plat du jour *dish of the day* le plat de résistance *main dish*
le plateau *tray* le plateau de fromages *cheese board*
plein *full* faire le plein *to fill up with petrol*
plier *to fold*
plus *more* de plus en plus *more and more* en plus de *as well as*
plusieurs *several*
plutôt *rather*
le pneu *tyre*
la pochette *small packet*
point: point de vue *point of view* à point *medium (of steak)*
la poire *pear*
le poireau (*pl* poireaux) *leek*
le poisson *fish*
la poissonnerie *fish shop/stall*
la poitrine *chest*
poivrer *to add pepper*
poli *polite*
la politesse *politeness*
la pomme *apple* la pomme (de terre) *potato*
le pont *bridge*
le porc *pig; pork*
le port *port*
porter *to carry; to wear*
poser *to put* poser une question *to ask a question*
la position *position* prendre position contre *to take a stand against*
posséder *to possess*
possible *possible*
postal: la carte postale *postcard*
la poste *post (office)*
le poste *mooring; telephone extension*
le pot *pot, jar*
le poulet *chicken*
pour *for; (in order) to*
pourquoi *why*
†pouvoir (*pp* pu) *to be able to*
pratique *practical*
pratiquer: pratiquer un sport *to take part in a sport*
précieux (*f* précieuse) *precious*
la préférence *preference*
préférer *to prefer; to like most*
premier (*f* première) *first*
†prendre (*pp* pris) *to take*
le prénom *first name*
préparer *to prepare*
près (de) *near*
présenter *to introduce; present*
préserver *to preserve*
pressé *in a hurry; squeezed* l'orange pressée *(f) squeezed orange*
le pressing *dry cleaner's*
la pression *draught (of beer)*
prêt *ready*
†prévenir (*pp* prévenu) *to inform*
†prévoir (*pp* prévu) *to plan ahead*
prier: je vous en prie *don't mention it*
prière de . . . *please . . .*
primaire *primary*
primordial (*pl* primordiaux) *vital*
principal (*pl* principaux) *principal*
le principe *principle*
le printemps *spring*
privé *private*
le prix *price*
le problème *problem*
prochain *next*
proche *near, close*
proclamer *to proclaim*
le produit *product*
professionnel (*f* professionnelle) *professional*
profiter de *to get the most out of, make use of*
profond *profound, deep*
le programme *programme*
programmer *to programme*
le progrès *progress*
le projet *plan*
*se promener *to walk, stroll*
la propriété *property*
protéger *to protect*
provençal (*pl* provençaux) *from Provence*
public (*f* publique) *public*
puis *then, next*
puisque *since, because*

Q

le quai *railway platform; quay*
la qualité *quality*
quand *when*
la quantité *quantity*
le quart *quarter*
que *than; that; which; what*
qu'est-ce que? *what?*
quel (*f* quelle) *what*
quelque chose *something*
quelquefois *sometimes*
quelques *a few, some*
la question *question*
qui *who; whom; which*
la quiche *quiche*
quitter *to leave*
quoi *what*

R

la raffinerie *refinery*
râpé *grated*

rapide *rapid*
rappeler *to recall*
rapport: par rapport à *compared with*
rapporter *to bring back*
la réalité *reality*
la récolte *harvest*
recommencer *to begin again*
la réduction *reduction*
†refaire (*pp* refait) *to do again, to re-do*
réfléchir *to think it over*
regagner *to get back to*
regarder *to look (at); to watch*
la région *region*
régional (*pl* régionaux) *regional*
le registre *register*
la règle *rule*
regroupé *grouped together*
régulier (*f* régulière) *regular*
remercier *to thank*
*remonter *to go up again*
rencontrer *to meet*
le rendez-vous *(m)* (*pl* rendez-vous) *appointment* prendre rendez-vous *to make an appointment*
le renouveau (*pl* renouveaux) *renewal*
*rentrer *to go/come home*
répandre *to spread out* répandu *widespread*
réparer *to repair*
*repartir *to leave again*
le repas *meal*
repasser *to iron*
*repasser *to come back*
*se reposer *to rest*
le représentant *representative*
la réservation *reservation*
réserve: la réserve du patron *the owner's special wine*
réserver *to reserve*
la résidence *residence*
résistance: le plat de résistance *main dish*
respecter *to respect*
le restaurant *restaurant*
le reste *remainder*
*rester *to stay, remain*
le retard *delay* être en retard *to be late*
*retourner *to return*
réussir (à) *to succeed (in)*
†*revenir (*pp* revenu) *to come back*
le revenu *income*
†revoir (*pp* revu) *to see again* au revoir *goodbye*
la révolution *revolution*
révolutionnaire *revolutionary*
le rez-de-chaussée (*pl* rez-de-chaussée) *ground floor*
riche *rich*
rien *nothing* (ne ...) rien *nothing* de rien *don't mention it; that's all right*
les rillettes *(f)* *kind of pâté*
rire (*pp* ri) *to laugh*
la rivière *river*
le riz *rice*
la robe *dress*
rochelais *from La Rochelle*
rosé *rosé (of wine)*
rouge *red*
la route *road; route*
routière: la gare routière *bus station*
rouvrir (*pp* rouvert) *to reopen*
la rue *street*
le rugby *rugby*

S

le sac *bag*
saignant *rare (of steak)*
sain *healthy*
la saison *season*
la salade *salad; lettuce*
la salle de bains *bathroom*
samedi *(m)* *Saturday*
le sandwich *sandwich*
sans *without*
le sapin *pine tree*
la saucisse *sausage*
le saucisson *salami*
sauf *except*
†savoir (*pp* su) *to know*
scandinave *Scandinavian*
scolaire: l'année *(f)* scolaire *school year*
la sculpture *sculpture*
second *second* en seconde (classe) *second (class)*
secondaire *secondary*
le séjour *stay*
séjourner *to stay*
le sel *salt*
selon *according to*
la semaine *week*
sembler *to seem*
senior *senior*
sensationnel (*f* sensationnelle) *splendid*
sensibilisé (à) *made aware (of)*
septembre *September*
sérieux (*f* sérieuse) *serious*
la serveuse *waitress*
le service *service*
servir *to serve* servir à *to be used for*
seul *single, one alone*
seulement *only*
si *if; so*
sicilien (*f* sicilienne) *Sicilian*
le siècle *century*
simple *simple* un aller simple *a single ticket* simple ou double *single or double*
sinon *if not*
le site *site*
situé *situated*
le ski *ski; skiing*
le slip *underpants; knickers*
la société *society*
la soeur *sister*
la soie *silk*
le soir *evening*
soit ... soit *either ... or*

le soleil *sun* le coup de soleil *sunburn*
son (*f* sa, *pl* ses) *his; her; its*
le sorbet *water ice*
la sorte *sort* en quelque sorte *in some way*
la sortie *way out; going out*
*sortir *to go/come out*
la soucoupe *saucer*
soufflant *blowing*
soulever *to raise*
la source *source*
le sourire *smile*
le souvenir *memory; souvenir*
souvent *often*
les spaghettis *(m)* *spaghetti*
la spatule *spatula*
spécialement *specially*
la spécialité *speciality*
le spectacle *play; film; concert; show*
le spectateur *spectator*
le sport *sport*
sportif (*f* sportive) *active/interested in sport*
le standing *reputation; status*
le starter *choke*
la station (de métro) *underground station* la station de taxis *taxi rank* la station balnéaire *seaside resort*
le steak *steak*
le sucre *sugar*
le sud *south*
suffisant *sufficient*
suffit: ça suffit *that's enough*
la Suisse *Switzerland*
suisse *Swiss*
suite: à la suite de *following* tout de suite *immediately*
suivant *following, next*
†suivre (*pp* suivi) *to follow*
le sujet *subject* à quel sujet? *what about?*
supérieur *better; higher*
supplanter *to replace, to take over (from)*
le supplément *supplement* en supplément *extra*
le supporter *supporter*
supposer *to suppose*
sur *on*
sûr *sure, certain* bien sûr *of course*
surtout *specially*
sympathique *nice*
le Syndicat d'Initiative *Tourist Information Office*
le système *system*

T

le tableau (*pl* tableaux) *picture, painting*
la tache *stain*
la taille *waist; measurement, size*
le tambourin *tambourin (a regional game related to tennis)*
tandis que *while*
la tapisserie *tapestry*
tard *late*
le tarif *price list, tariff*
la tarte *tart*
la tartelette *small tart*
le tas *heap*
la tasse *cup*
le taxi *taxi*
la teinturerie *dry cleaner's*
le teinturier *man who works in dry cleaner's*
le téléphérique *cable car*
le téléphone *telephone*
téléphoner (à) *to telephone*
la télé *telly, TV*
la télévision *television*
tellement *so* pas tellement *not very much*
le témoignage *evidence*
le temps *time; weather*
la tendance *tendency*
†tenir (*pp* tenu) *to hold; to keep (a shop)*
le tennis *tennis*
le terme *term, expression*
terminer *to finish*
la terre *earth* la pomme de terre *potato* la terre cuite *earthenware*
la tête *head*
le thé *tea*
le théâtre *theatre*
le ticket *ticket*
le timbre *stamp*
le tissu *cloth*
togolais *from Togo*
toi *you*
la toile *canvas*
la tomate *tomato*
*tomber *to fall*
la tomme de Savoie *type of cheese from Savoie*
ton (*f* ta, *pl* tes) *your*
la tonnellerie *barrel-maker's workshop*
total (*pl* totaux) *total*
toujours *always; still*
la tour *tower*
le tour *turn; walk*
le tourisme *tourism*
la/le touriste *tourist*
tourner *to turn*
tout *all* pas du tout *not at all* tout à fait *completely* tout de suite *straight away*
la trace *trace*
le tracteur *tractor*
le train *train*
la traite des Noirs *slave trade*
la tranche *slice*
le travail (*pl* travaux) *work*
travailler *to work*
travailleur (*f* travailleuse) *hard-working*
traverser *to cross*
très *very*
triangulaire *triangular*
trop (de) *too; too much/many*
le troubadour *troubadour*
la troupe *troupe (of actors)*
trouver *to find*
le truc *thingummyjig*
la truite *trout*
la Turquie *Turkey*

tutoyer *to call someone 'tu'*
le type *type, sort*

U

uniquement *only*
universitaire *university (adj)*
l'usage *(m)* *use*
utiliser *to use*

V

va: ça va *all right, OK*
les vacances *(f)* *holidays* les grandes vacances *summer holidays*
valable *valid*
valoir la peine *to be worthwhile*
la vanille *vanilla*
la vapeur *steam* les pommes vapeur *(f)* *boiled potatoes*
variable *variable*
le vase *vase*
le veau (*pl* veaux) *calf; veal*
le véhicule *vehicle*
la veilleuse *side-light*
le vélo *bike* en vélo *by bike*
la vendange *wine harvest*
vendre *to sell*
†*venir (*pp* venu) *to come*
le vent *wind*
le verre *glass*
vers *towards; about (of time)*
vert *green*
les vêtements *(m)* *clothes*
vétérinaire *veterinary*
la viande *meat*
la vie *life*
vieux (*f* vieille, *pl* vieux) *old*
la vigne *vine*
le village *village*
la ville *town, city*
le vin *wine*
violent *violent*
la virgule *comma; decimal point*
visiter *to visit*
vite *quickly*
la vitesse *speed*
la viticulture *vine-growing*
vivant *lively*
†vivre (*pp* vécu) *to live*
voici *here is/are*
la voie *way, track, path* le pays en voie de développement *developing country*
voilà *there is/are; there you are*
la voile *sailing*
†voir (*pp* vu) *to see*
voire *even*
voisin *neighbouring*
la/le voisin(e) *neighbour*
la voiture *car* en voiture *by car*
le vol *flight*
la volaille *poultry*
le volley(-ball) *volleyball*
les volontaires *(m)* *people who want to*
volontiers *willingly; that would be nice*
votre (*pl* vos) *your*
†vouloir (*pp* voulu) *to wish; to want to* veuillez ... *please ...* vouloir dire *to mean*
vouvoyer *to call someone 'vous'*
le voyage *journey*
voyant *striking*
vraiment *really*
la vue *view*

W

les WC *(m)* *lavatory*
le week-end *weekend*

Y

y *here; there; in it; on it*
le yaourt *yoghurt*
les yeux *(m)* *eyes*

Z

le zéro *zero*

Index: French language

Index: French life

Acknowledgements

FRANK ASH 212; BBC HULTON PICTURE LIBRARY 46, 263, 272 (bottom); CAMERA PRESS 225 (Thomas A. Wilkie); J. ALLAN CASH PHOTOLIBRARY 22 (top), 238, 249, 269; JANE COTTAVE 33, 34, 35, 112, 159, 178; VILLE DE DIJON 22 (bottom); F. DOERLER (FOR BBC) 10; FRENCH GOVERNMENT TOURIST OFFICE 32, 38, 253 (both), 292 (both); MICHEL GAILLAC 300; FRANCK PEDERSOL 134; AGENCE RAPHO 12 (St. Duroy), 75 (Carlos Freire), 88 (St. Duroy), 105 (Pierre Michaud), 138 (François Ducasse), 141 (Robert Doisneau), 161 (Monique Marceau), 176 (Georges Marry), 191 (Goursat), 245 (de Sazo), 288 (Lang Cipha); RESTAURANT PAUL BOCUSE 156; JEAN RIBIERE 79, 92; H. ROGER-VIOLLET 128, 150, 214, 226, 262, 271, 272 (top), 277; MARY SPRENT 95, 97, 100, 188 (both top pictures); SYGMA 301 (Andanson); SYNDICAT D'INITIATIVE, GRENOBLE 71, 205; SYNDICAT D'INITIATIVE, NANTES 217; SYNDICAT D'INITIATIVE, PEZENAS 230, 231; SARA TOMEI 268; TOPHAM PICTURE LIBRARY 13, 23, 57, 74, 278; DAVID WILSON 28, 29, 30, 50, 53, 55, 68, 72, 93, 116, 143, 188 (bottom), 194, 199, 266, 283.

Illustrations by Debbe Ryder.